THE FAR LEFT IN AUSTRALIA SINCE 1945

The far left in Australia had significant effects on post-war politics, culture and society. The Communist Party of Australia (CPA) ended World War II with some 20,000 members, and despite the harsh and vitriolic Cold War climate of the 1950s, seeded or provided impetus for the re-emergence of other movements. Radicals subscribing to ideologies beyond the Soviet orbit – Maoists, Trotskyists, anarchists and others – also created parties and organisations and led movements. All of these different far left parties and movements changed and shifted during time, responding to one political crisis or another, but they remained steadfastly devoted to a better world.

This collection, bringing together 14 chapters from leading and emerging figures in the Australian and international historical profession, for the first time charts some of these significant moments and interventions, revealing the Australian far left's often forgotten contribution to the nation's history.

Jon Piccini, University of Queensland, Australia.

Evan Smith, Flinders University, Australia.

Matthew Worley, University of Reading, UK.

ROUTLEDGE STUDIES IN RADICAL HISTORY AND POLITICS

Series editors: **Thomas Linehan**, *Brunel University*, and **John Roberts**, *Brunel University*.

The series *Routledge Studies in Radical History and Politics* has two areas of interest. Firstly, this series aims to publish books which focus on the history of movements of the radical left. 'Movement of the radical left' is here interpreted in its broadest sense as encompassing those past movements for radical change which operated in the mainstream political arena as with political parties, and past movements for change which operated more outside the mainstream as with millenarian movements, anarchist groups, utopian socialist communities, and trade unions. Secondly, this series aims to publish books which focus on more contemporary expressions of radical left-wing politics. Recent years have been witness to the emergence of a multitude of new radical movements adept at getting their voices in the public sphere. From those participating in the Arab Spring, the Occupy movement, community unionism, social media forums, independent media outlets, local voluntary organisations campaigning for progressive change, and so on, it seems to be the case that innovative networks of radicalism are being constructed in civil society that operate in different public forms.

The series very much welcomes titles with a British focus, but is not limited to any particular national context or region. The series will encourage scholars who contribute to this series to draw on perspectives and insights from other disciplines.

Titles include:

Migrant Britain
Histories and Historiographies. Essays in Honour of Colin Holmes
Edited by Jennifer Craig-Norton, Christhard Hoffmann and Tony Kushner

The Lesbian Revolution
Lesbian Feminism in the UK 1970-1990
Sheila Jeffreys

The Far Left in Australia since 1945
Jon Piccini, Evan Smith and Matthew Worley (eds.)

THE FAR LEFT IN AUSTRALIA SINCE 1945

Edited by Jon Piccini, Evan Smith and Matthew Worley

Routledge
Taylor & Francis Group

LONDON AND NEW YORK

First published 2019
by Routledge
2 Park Square, Milton Park, Abingdon, Oxon OX14 4RN

and by Routledge
711 Third Avenue, New York, NY 10017

Routledge is an imprint of the Taylor & Francis Group, an informa business

© 2019 selection and editorial matter, Jon Piccini, Evan Smith and Matthew Worley; individual chapters, the contributors

The right of Jon Piccini, Evan Smith and Matthew Worley to be identified as the authors of the editorial material, and of the authors for their individual chapters, has been asserted in accordance with sections 77 and 78 of the Copyright, Designs and Patents Act 1988.

All rights reserved. No part of this book may be reprinted or reproduced or utilised in any form or by any electronic, mechanical, or other means, now known or hereafter invented, including photocopying and recording, or in any information storage or retrieval system, without permission in writing from the publishers.

Trademark notice: Product or corporate names may be trademarks or registered trademarks, and are used only for identification and explanation without intent to infringe.

British Library Cataloguing-in-Publication Data
A catalogue record for this book is available from the British Library

Library of Congress Cataloging-in-Publication Data
Names: Piccini, Jon, editor. | Smith, Evan, 1981- editor. | Worley, Matthew, editor.
Title: The far left in Australia since 1945 / edited by Jon Piccini, Evan Smith & Matthew Worley.
Description: Abingdon, Oxon ; New York, NY : Routledge, 2018. | Series: Routledge studies in fascism and the far right | Includes bibliographical references and index.
Identifiers: LCCN 2018004351| ISBN 9781138043855 (hardback) | ISBN 9780429487347 (ebook)
Subjects: LCSH: Radicalism–Australia–History–20th century. | Right and left (Political science)–Australia. | Communist Party of Australia. | New Left–Australia. | Australia–Social conditions–20th century. | Australia–Politics and government–1945-
Classification: LCC HN850.Z9 R34 2018 | DDC 303.48/40994–dc23
LC record available at https://lccn.loc.gov/2018004351

ISBN: 978-1-138-04385-5 (hbk)
ISBN: 978-0-429-48734-7 (ebk)

Typeset in Bembo
by Taylor & Francis Books

CONTENTS

List of contributors	*vii*
Acknowledgments	*xi*
Abbreviations	*xii*

Introduction: The history of the far left in Australia since 1945	1
Jon Piccini, Evan Smith and Matthew Worley	

PART 1
Organisational histories   19

1	Australian Communism in crisis – 1956 *Phillip Deery*	21
2	The current of Maoism in the Australian Far Left *Drew Cottle and Angela Keys*	41
3	Breaking with Moscow: The Communist Party of Australia's new road to socialism *David McKnight*	59
4	'The "White Australia" policy must go': The Communist Party of Australia and immigration restriction *Jon Piccini and Evan Smith*	77

PART 2
The 1950s and 1960s: In and out of the Cold War   97

5	The far left and the fight for Aboriginal rights: The formation of the Council for Aboriginal Rights, 1951 *Jennifer Clark*	99

vi Contents

6 How far left?: Negotiating radicalism in Australian anti-nuclear
politics in the 1960s 118
Kyle Harvey

7 "1968" in Australia: The student movement and the New Left 134
Russell Marks

PART 3
The 1960s and 1970s: The valences of liberation **151**

8 Changing consciousness, changing lifestyles: Australian women's
liberation, the left and the politics of 'personal solutions' 153
Isobelle Barrett Meyering

9 Black Power and white solidarity: The Action Conference on
Racism and Education, Brisbane 1972 171
Lewis d'Avigdor

10 The Australian left and gay liberation: From 1945 to 2000s 191
Liz Ross

11 Beating BHP: The Wollongong Jobs for Women Campaign
1980–1991 210
Diana Covell

PART 4
Mainstreaming the far left **229**

12 Halcyon days?: The Amalgamated Metal Workers' Union and
the Accord 231
Elizabeth Humphrys

13 Reading and contesting Germaine Greer and Dennis Altman:
The 1970s and beyond 249
Jon Piccini and Ana Stevenson

14 The cultural front: Left cultural activism in the post-war era 267
Lisa Milner

Index *284*

CONTRIBUTORS

Isobelle Barrett Meyering is a Research Fellow at Macquarie University. She completed her PhD on children and the Australian women's liberation movement (1969–1979) at UNSW Sydney in March 2017. Isobelle has taught in a wide range of history and gender studies subjects at UNSW, and her work has featured in journals including *Australian Feminist Studies, Outskirts: Feminisms Along the Edge* and *History Australia*. Isobelle previously worked as a research assistant at the Australian Domestic and Family Violence Clearinghouse from 2009 to 2013.

Jennifer Clark is Head of the School of Humanities at the University of Adelaide. She is the author of *Aborigines and Activism: Race, Aborigines & the Coming of the Sixties to Australia* (UWA Press, 2008). She is currently researching the history of the Council for Aboriginal Rights.

Drew Cottle teaches history and politics at Western Sydney University. He maintains a deep interest in labour and capital history.

Diana Covell began a career in music but from 1975 became passionately involved in human rights, social justice and feminist politics. She launched and helped to organise the Wollongong Jobs for Women Campaign from 1980–1991, working for several of those years as a labourer and crane chaser and elected union delegate in the Port Kembla steelworks. She then attended university, gaining BA Honours Communications (UTS) in 1996. She has worked in advocacy, policy, dispute-resolution and community development mainly in the non-government community sector and was accepted into the PhD program in History at the University of Sydney, where she tutored for five years. She is now completing a book on the landmark anti-discrimination class action against BHP.

Lewis d'Avigdor is PhD candidate in the history department at Cornell University, where he is studying American and African-American history in a global context. He has written on the Australian New Left in the *Australian Journal of Politics and History*. He is currently researching the intellectual history of decolonisation.

Phillip Deery is Emeritus Professor of History at Victoria University, Melbourne. He has authored more than 100 scholarly publications in the fields of Cold War studies, labour movement history, and intelligence and security studies. He is the author, co-author or lead editor of six books, most recently *Red Apple: Communism and McCarthyism in Cold War New York* (New York, 2014, 2016), *The Age of McCarthyism: A Brief History with Documents, Third Edition* (Boston, 2016) and *Fighting Against War: Peace Activism in the Twentieth Century* (Melbourne, 2015). Phillip is a review editor of *Labour History*, was guest editor of *American Communist History*, is a research associate with LSE's Cold War Studies Program, and has been awarded research fellowships from the International Center for Advanced Studies and the Frederic Ewen Center at New York University.

Kyle Harvey is a research fellow at the University of Melbourne. He is the author of *American Anti-Nuclear Activism, 1975–1990: The Challenge of Peace* (Palgrave, 2014), and has published on Australian and US social movement history in *Labour History, History Australia*, and the *Journal for the Study of Radicalism*. Kyle was the 2013 C.H. Currey Memorial Fellow at the State Library of New South Wales, and has previously taught at Macquarie University and the Western Sydney University College.

Elizabeth Humphrys works at the University of Technology Sydney. Her latest research is on the phenomena of anti-politics, and the crisis of representation that leads people to increasingly see politics as detached from their lives. Her PhD examined the implementation of neoliberalism in Australia, and its relationship to the 1983–1996 social contract between the Australian Labor Party and the trade unions. A book based on this will be published with Brill's Studies in Critical Social Sciences series.

Angela Keys is a casual academic in the School of Humanities and Social Sciences, Charles Sturt University.

Russell Marks is a criminal defence lawyer at the North Australian Aboriginal Justice Agency, a policy consultant with the Victorian Greens and an Honorary Associate in La Trobe University's Department of Politics and Philosophy, where he completed his PhD in 2011 on the intellectual left's changing approaches to Australian nationalism during the 1960s and 1970s. He is the author of *Crime and*

Punishment: Offenders and Victims in a Broken Justice System (Black Inc., 2015) and writes occasionally for *The Monthly, Arena* and *Overland*.

David McKnight is an associate professor at the University of New South Wales, in Sydney, Australia. He is the author of a number of books in the fields of media, politics and history. They include *Rupert Murdoch: An Investigation of Political Power* (published in the UK as *Murdoch's Politics*), as well as *Beyond Right and Left: New Politics and the Culture War* which discusses renewal of the progressive political vision. He has also written on political surveillance during the cold war in *Australia's Spies and their Secrets* and on Soviet intelligence in *Espionage and the Roots of the Cold War*.

Lisa Milner is Senior Lecturer in the Media program at Southern Cross University, Coffs Harbour. She has been researching Australian left cultural activism for many years. Her published work includes *Fighting Films: A History of the Waterside Workers' Federation Film Unit* (Pluto Press, 2003). Her current research interests include a transnational study of left-wing theatre, representations of workers and trade unions on screen, and Australian labour history. Her latest book is *Swimming Against the Tide*, a biography of Australian feminist Freda Brown (Ginninderra Press, 2017).

Jon Piccini is a Teaching & Research Fellow at the University of Queensland, where he is working on a history of human rights in Australia. His first book, *Transnational Protest, Australia and the 1960s*, was published by Palgrave Macmillan in 2016.

Liz Ross has been active in Women's and Gay Liberation and socialist politics since the early 1970s. She is a founder and life member of the Australian Lesbian and Gay Archives (ALGA). As a union delegate in the 1980s and 1990s she was involved in and has written extensively about workers struggles. She is currently working on a book on workers and the Accord years. Author of "Dedication doesn't pay the rent! The 1986 Victorian Nurses Strike" in Sandra Bloodworth and Tom O'Lincoln (eds.), *Rebel Women in Australian Working Class History; Dare to Struggle, Dare to Win! Builders Labourers Fight Deregistration, 1981–94* (2004); "Building Unions and Government Reform: the Challenge for Unions" in the *Journal of Australian Political Economy* (2005) and "Defying the Stereotypes: Women Textile Workers in Bangladesh" in *Marxist Left Review* no. 8 (2014). Since the early 2000s she has contributed to the debate about climate change as author of *How Capitalism is Destroying the Planet* (Socialist Alternative, 2008), as well as conference presentations and articles. She is a regular contributor to *Red Flag* and *Marxist Left Review*. Her latest book is *Revolution is for us: The Left and Gay Liberation in Australia* (Interventions, 2013).

Evan Smith is a Research Fellow in the College of Humanities, Arts and Social Sciences at Flinders University, South Australia. He has written widely on the British and Australian left, anti-racism, immigration control and youth culture. He is the co-author of *Race, Gender and the Body in British Immigration Control* (Palgrave Macmillan 2014) and the co-editor of *Against the Grain: The British Far Left from 1956* (Manchester University Press 2014) and its companion volume, *Waiting for the Revolution* (Manchester University Press 2017). His first single authored monograph, *British Communism and the Politics of Race*, was published by Brill as part of its Historical Materialism series in 2017.

Ana Stevenson is a Postdoctoral Research Fellow in the International Studies Group at the University of the Free State. Her research about feminist rhetoric and transnational women's movements can be found in *Lilith: A Feminist History Journal, Humanity, Cultural & Social History* and *Camera Obscura*.

Matthew Worley is Professor of Modern History at the University of Reading. He has written widely on British labour and political history, including books on the Communist Party of Great Britain, Labour Party and Sir Oswald Mosley's New Party. His more recent work has concentrated on the relationship between youth culture and politics in Britain, primarily in the 1970s and 1980s. Articles have been published in such journals as *History Workshop, Twentieth Century British History, Contemporary British History, Journal for the Study of Radicalism, Journalism, Media and Cultural Studies, Punk & Post-Punk* and chapters in collections such as the Subcultures Network's *Fight Back: Punk, Politics and Resistance* (2015). A monograph, *No Future: Punk, Politics and British Youth Culture, 1976–84*, was published by Cambridge University Press in 2017.

ACKNOWLEDGMENTS

The editors would like to thank Stuart Macintyre, David Lockwood, Rowan Cahill and Graham Willet for their feedback on the introduction to this volume. Thanks also goes to Craig Fowlie for his enthusiastic support for the project since the beginning.

ABBREVIATIONS

ABS	Australasian Book Society
ABSCHOL	Aboriginal Scholarships
ACTU	Australian Council of Trade Unions
ACT-UP	AIDS Coalition to Unleash Power
ADB	Anti Discrimination Board (NSW)
AICD	Association for International Cooperation and Disarmament
AIM	Australian Independence Movement
AI&S	Australian Iron and Steel
ALP	Australian Labor Party
AMC	Australian Manufacturing Council
AMFSU	Amalgamated Metals Foundry and Shipwrights' Union
AMWSU	Amalgamated Metal Workers' and Shipwrights' Union
AMWU	Amalgamated Metal Workers' Union
ASIO	Australian Security Intelligence Organisation
ASLF	Australian Student Labor Federation
AUS	Australian Union of Students
BHP	Broken Hill Proprietary
BLF	Builder's Labourers' Federation
BWIU	Building Workers' Industrial Union
CAAH	Community Action Against Homophobia
CAMP	Campaign Against Moral Persecution
CAR	Council for Aboriginal Rights
CDNSA	Committee in Defiance of the National Service Act
CIA	Central Intelligence Agency
CICD	Committee for International Cooperation and Disarmament
CND	Campaign for Nuclear Disarmament
CPA	Communist Party of Australia

Abbreviations **xiii**

CPA (M-L)	Communist Party of Australia (Marxist-Leninist)
CPGB	Communist Party of Great Britain
CPSU	Communist Party of the Soviet Union
CPUSA	Communist Party of the United States of America
DLP	Democratic Labor Party
DRM	Draft Resistance Movement
DSP	Democratic Socialist Party
EOT	Equal Opportunity Tribunal (NSW)
FCAA	Federal Council of Aboriginal Advancement
FCAATSI	Federal Council for the Advancement of Aborigines and Torres Straight Islanders
FI	Fourth International
FIA	Federated Ironworkers' Association
GLM	Gay Liberation Movement
ILO	International Labour Organisation
IRG	Immigration Reform Group
IS	International Socialists
IWW	International Workers of the World
JFW	Jobs for Women
JFWAC	Jobs for Women Action Committee
JFWC	Jobs for Women Campaign
NAWU	North Australian Workers' Union
NLF	National Liberation Front (Vietnam)
NTC	National Tribal Council
PAI	People for Australian Independence
QuACE	Queers Against Corporate Exploitation
QUEER	Queers United to Eradicate Economic Rationalism
QPC	Queensland Peace Committee
RFA	Realist Film Association
RFU	Realist Film Unit
RWA	Realist Writers' Association
SAFA	Student Action for Aborigines
SAI	Students for Australian Independence
SCLC	South Coast Labour Council
SDA	Society for Democratic Action
SDS	Students for a Democratic Society
SLL	Socialist Labour League
SORA	Studio of Realist Art
SPA	Socialist Party of Australia
SWP	Socialist Workers Party
SYA	Socialist Youth Alliance
TDC	Trade Development Council
VAAL	Victorian Aborigines Advancement League
VAC	Vietnam Action Committee

VGS	Volunteer Graduate Scheme
VSP	Victorian Socialist Party
WAC	Workers' Arts Club
WAPC	West Australian Peace Council
WSA	Worker-Student Alliance
WWF	Waterside Workers Federation
WWFFU	Waterside Workers Federation Film Unit
YCAC	Youth Campaign Against Conscription

INTRODUCTION

The history of the far left in Australia since 1945

Jon Piccini, Evan Smith and Matthew Worley

The far left in Australia, as has been revealed by scholarship on its equivalents in the UK, USA and elsewhere,[1] had significant effects on post-war politics, culture and society. The Communist Party of Australia (CPA) ended World War II with some 20,000 members, and despite the harsh and vitriolic Cold War climate of the 1950s, seeded or provided impetus for the re-emergence of other movements. Radicals subscribing to ideologies beyond the Soviet orbit – Maoists, Trotskyists, anarchists and others – also created parties and organisations and led movements. All of these different far left parties and movements changed and shifted over time, responding to one political crisis or another, but they remained steadfastly devoted to a better world.

Equally, members and fellow travellers of the CPA and other far left groups instigated or became centrally involved in struggles for indigenous rights, gender equality, ending immigration restrictions, stopping the spread of nuclear weapons and fostering peace – alongside continuing work in trade unions. In starting these groups, providing personnel, funding and guidance, far left activists contributed in no small way to the reforms that have changed Australia from the racist, sexist and parochial society of 1945 to one which is now multicultural, champions gender equality and is open to the world. The far left's contribution to culture also cannot be ignored, with the CPA in particular providing a home for writers, poets, film makers and others who found their experimentation unwelcomed in an Australia in the grips of the cultural cringe.[2]

Lastly, the Australian far left has also had a fascinating – if troubled and convoluted – career of 'mainstreaming' itself, whether through aforementioned cultural organisations, or through working with the social democratic Australian Labor Party, forming their own electoral alliances, or reaching out with mass market books. As such, while the far left might have never led a revolution in Australia, it has inarguably played a central role in revolutionising it.

The study of protest movements is exploding around the world. Major research and publishing projects charting the far left – particularly set around that halcyon year of 1968 – have appeared in most western nations in recent years. Yet, no such comparable body of work exists for Australia's vibrant and exciting far left movements in the post-war era – from the Communist Party of Australia to smaller ideological groups, their intersections with broader movements for women's, indigenous and gay liberation, and broader effects on culture and society. By analysing far left movements in Australia from 1945 to the 1980s, these interconnections are explored in depth, and a light can be shone on the current state of Australia's left and progressive movements. This collection, bringing together 14 chapters from leading and emerging figures in the Australian and international historical profession, for the first time charts some of these significant moments and interventions, revealing the Australian far left's often forgotten contribution to the nation's history.

Outlining the history of the far left

The history of the far left in Australia is dominated by the Communist Party of Australia (CPA), which existed from 1920 to 1991, occupying the space to the left of the Australian Labor Party (ALP). Formed from several smaller groups of the socialist and anarchist left, the CPA became the dominant left-wing force in Australian politics during the inter-war period, only rivalled in the early 1920s by the Industrial Workers of the World (IWW). As a member of the Communist International (Comintern) the CPA promoted a pro-Soviet agenda throughout the 1920s and 1930s, despite significant internal resistance to 'Bolshevisation' in the late 1920s and early 1930s.[3] Despite its (mainly) uncritical support of Moscow throughout the inter-war period, the CPA was an influential force in the labour movement and at the forefront of the campaigns against fascism and war during the 1930s. Infamously refusing to support the war effort during the 'inter-imperialist war' phase of the Second World War, the CPA was banned by Robert Menzies as a wartime precaution in June 1940. By the time the ban was lifted, at the end of 1942, the USSR had joined the war effort and the CPA's fortunes rose. Membership reached an all-time high of over 20,000, influence in the labour and other progressive movements was pronounced and the party embraced a possible peaceful transition to socialism, a concept made possible by the Tehran agreement and popularised by Communist Party of the United States of America (CPUSA) leader Earl Browder and by Harry Pollitt, leader of the Communist Party of Great Britain (CPGB).[4]

The CPA's belief in this peaceful transition was shattered after the war, and the Party became much more militant than its counterparts in the UK and the USA, which had shifted towards an acceptance of the parliamentary road to socialism in the late 1940s. A number of factors contributed to this – most significantly the jailing of CPA leader L.L. Sharkey for seditious utterances and the influence of Asian Communist parties, in particular the Chinese Communist Party's October

1949 revolution.[5] The CPA enthusiastically supported decolonisation in Asia; members formed close bonds with fellow Communists in India, Malaya and Indonesia. With the Malayan Emergency, the CPA leader L.L. Sharkey was accused of liaising between Moscow and the Malayan Communist Party leadership,[6] while the CPA was also heavily involved in 'blacking' Dutch ships on their way to Indonesia.[7]

While the CPA had applied for entry into the ALP in 1945, only a few years later it had started to agitate against the Chifley government using its mass base in key trade unions. Inspired by the Chinese Communist Party, the CPA under Sharkey pushed this more militant agenda, which came to a head when the Chifley government sought to confront a strike by mineworkers across Australia in 1949, the culmination of several years of increasingly militant union demands. The miners' union, led by CPA members, refused to back down and Chifley sent in troops to break the strike, acting as a rudimentary workforce.[8] The severity of the strike worried many in government and while in Opposition, Robert Menzies announced that if it won power at the 1949 election, the Liberal government would seek to ban the Communist Party. At the height of the early Cold War, exacerbated by the outbreak of the Korean War and the Malayan Emergency, the Menzies government's victory saw it quickly attempt to outlaw the CPA. The Menzies government liaised with the Malan government in South Africa, which introduced similar legislation in the same month, as both settler colonies saw communism and the push for native rights to be twin 'threats' to their way of life.[9]

The Communist Party Dissolution Bill was first passed in 1950, but was challenged as unconstitutional by Communist unions in the High Court, supported by H.V. Evatt, the new leader of the ALP. The Act was withdrawn and in September 1951, a referendum was held to test the popular will for amending the constitution in order to ban the CPA as Menzies proposed.[10] In a very close contest, the 'no' vote won and Menzies shifted away from an outright ban to a sharper use of the Australian Security Intelligence Organisation (ASIO), founded under Chifley's government in the wake of the Venona cables scandal.

This shift towards a greater emphasis on ASIO in the Cold War arena paid off handsomely for Menzies when a senior figure with the Soviet Embassy in Canberra, Vladimir Petrov, defected weeks before the 1954 Federal Election. Petrov's defection was the catalyst for a Royal Commission into Soviet espionage in Australia, which was seen by many as Menzies replicating Joseph McCarthy's House of Unamerican Activities. A number of CPA members, as well as fellow travellers, were brought before the Royal Commission, which damaged their professional and personal lives. The eventual outcome of the Royal Commission proposed the charging of several CPA members, such as the journalist Rupert Lockwood, with a series of offences, but the main effect was to publicly shame people seen as Communist sympathisers in Australia.[11] Despite such pressure, CPA members during this time were able to make significant inroads into growing indigenous rights and peace movements while playing a leading role in cultural, literary and scientific production, as discussed in this volume.[12] CPA members were deeply involved in the 1965 Freedom Ride, and the Wave Hill walk off a year later, and significant peace congresses were held throughout the 1950s, culminating in the 1959 Australia New Zealand Peace Congress.[13]

After nearly a decade of intense pressure from without and significant decline in membership numbers due to the heightened anti-communism of the Cold War (estimates by Alastair Davidson and Tom O'Lincoln suggest that membership fell from over 16,000 in 1945 to between 6–8,000 in 1956),[14] the CPA faced its biggest battle in 1956 over new Soviet leader Nikita Khrushchev's 'Secret Speech' and the subsequent invasion of Hungary. The CPA leadership were reluctant to discuss the denunciation of the Stalin regime by Khrushchev and, like the British and American Communist Parties, the revelations caused a massive rift in the Australian party.[15] When the Soviets invaded Hungary in October of the same year, many who had reservations about the CPA's support for the Soviet Union chose to leave the Party, with around 2,000 people leaving or being expelled between 1956 and 1958.[16] A small group of these defectors went on to establish *Outlook* journal, consciously modelled on publications like *New Left Review* in the UK, constituting the first wave of Australia's New Left.

While a significant number left due to the events of 1956, a large portion of the CPA was pro-Soviet and against the 'revisionism' of Khrushchev. Its long association with Communist Parties in Asia, especially the Chinese Communist Party under whom many party leaders studied in the 1950s, also established a sizeable pro-Chinese section inside the CPA, with Sharkey being one of the Western leaders who was most sympathetic to Mao. As the Sino-Soviet split loomed larger in the late 1950s, Mark Aarons and others have suggested that the CPA was considering siding with the Chinese, alongside the smaller Communist Party of New Zealand.[17] It was for both practical and ideological reasons that the CPA eventually aligned itself with the Soviets, but after committing to the USSR in 1960, the anti-revisionists started to work for a new kind of organisation. Led by trade union lawyer Edward (Ted) Hill from the Victorian State Branch, several hundred anti-revisionists concentrated in Victoria and including significant union leaders formed the Communist Party of Australia (Marxist-Leninist) in 1964, denouncing the Khruschevite revisionism of the CPA.[18]

As well as seeing the first anti-revisionists split from the CPA, the early-to-mid-1960s opened up the left in other ways. The events of 1956, as in the UK and the USA, had seen a New Left emerge, tied to the emerging social movements, such as the peace movement, and the new Marxist-oriented journals, such as *Arena*. Much more so than in Britain, the CPA was heavily involved in the formative years of emerging social movements, such as peace, Aboriginal rights, anti-apartheid and women's liberation. For example, a number of those involved in the push for Aboriginal rights were members of the CPA,[19] while members of the Union of Australian Women, made up primarily of CPA members, played vital roles within the women's liberation movement.[20]

Around the Western world, the mid-to-late 1960s saw an explosion in industrial militancy and cultural radicalisation. The predominant catalyst for the upsurge in radicalisation in Australia was the Vietnam War, bringing into movement new forces, particularly students on ever-expanding university campuses. In April 1965, Prime Minister Menzies announced that Australia would be sending troops to support the USA and South Vietnam in the conflict. This led to the beginnings of a mass movement against the war and against conscription for overseas service, which was introduced in 1964. The CPA was quick to embed itself within the anti-war movement, but other Marxists and sections of the Labor left began to participate as well. While always in a minority within the anti-conscription and wider anti-war movement, which culminated in the 1970–72 Moratorium marches, far leftists played significant roles in leadership and organisation.

Trotskyism in Australia, bar a brief period of influence during the CPA's wartime popular front period, had been rather dormant since the 1930s.[21] However, the late 1960s saw a new dawn for Trotskyists, inspired by the groups in the USA and UK and a new youth politics sceptical of the USA and USSR in equal measure. By the mid-1960s, the Fourth International (FI) had split and both factions sought to form sister organisations across the globe.[22] In Australia, the Revolutionary Marxist Tendency (RMT) made some inroads through a journal called *International*. Nick Origlass, one of the original Trotskyists in Australia from the 1930s, was involved with this group alongside Denis Freney, who was also close to the IMG before going over to the increasingly pluralist CPA in the late 1960s.[23]

The first major Trotskyist group to emerge out of the student and anti-war movements was the Socialist Youth Alliance (SYA), established in 1968 as Resistance in Sydney by the Percy brothers, plus several others. Publishing the paper *Direct Action*, the SYA (changed from Resistance in 1970) was based in the Third World Bookshop in Sydney's CBD [central business district]. The group was inspired by the US Socialist Workers Party and from very early on, concentrated on anti-imperialism in the developing world, primarily looking to Vietnam and Cuba. By 1972, the SYA had led to the creation of the Socialist Workers League (SWL) at a Sydney conference attended by some 100 individuals. SWL was the 'parent' organisation with the SYA remaining as its youth wing.[24] The SWL's main competition was from the various groups inspired by the International Socialists (IS) in Britain.[25] Scattered across the Eastern States, several small groups influenced by the IS started to co-ordinate with each other and by 1972–73, groups in Melbourne, Hobart and Canberra had banded together to produce *The Battler* under the name of the Socialist Workers Action Group (SWAG), becoming the IS in December 1975.[26] Both were heavily involved in other radical and social movement groups in the 1970s, including the women's liberation, gay liberation, the anti-apartheid and anti-war movements, as well as the resistance to the Fraser government from 1975. While the SWL and SWAG/IS were the most prominent Trotskyist groups in Australia during the 1970s, a local version of the Healyite Socialist Labour League (SLL) was established in 1972. Although the SLL was able to briefly recruit figures such as Bob Gould in the mid-1970s, the League was unable to make much headway in Australia and was a pale imitation of its UK counterpart.[27]

At the same time as the proliferation in Trotskyist groups in Australia, Maoism in Australia was heavily inspired by the Chinese Party's Cultural Revolution and spread amongst radical elements of the student movement. The CPA (M-L) was the most prominent Maoist group in Australia but like the Communist Party of Britain (M-L), the fact that its existence pre-dated the Cultural Revolution meant that its make-up was less student recruits and more the established membership of industrial and white-collar workers (including trade union officials and lawyers). The other prominent group was the Worker Student Alliance (WSA), which was much more student-orientated, although still under the somewhat covert leadership of Hill's organisation.[28] Developing on the university campuses of Melbourne and Adelaide, the WSA was involved in the student radicalism that swept across Australia in the early-to-mid-1970s,[29] but was also heavily invested in sending students into factories to build the supposed alliance between the two groups, inspired by the Cultural Revolution.

The Maoist and Trotskyist groups offered radical alternatives to the CPA in the 1960s and 1970s, although the CPA itself was moving in different directions. Like the CPGB, the CPA of the mid-to-late 1960s presented a kind of proto-Euro-communism, embracing the rising new social movements seeking a parliamentary approach to socialism, closer ties with the ALP and a shift away from uncritical support of the Soviet Union. This came to a head at the 21st Party Conference in 1967, when a highly contentious 'Charter of Democratic Rights' was endorsed, and most significantly during the Soviet invasion of Czechoslovakia in 1968. Most Western Communist Parties (such as the British, French and Italian parties) criticised the USSR for this action, unlike the silence that followed similar events in 1953 and 1956. *Tribune* (the CPA's weekly newspaper) stated:

> We cannot agree to the pre-emptive occupation of a country by another, on the alleged threat from outside, particularly when such action is taken without prior notification to the government and CP of Czechoslovakia.... It is hard to believe that [the Soviet leaders] realise the damage they cause to their own standing and the image of socialism throughout the world by acting in this way.[30]

This response led to divisions inside the Party, with a sizeable section of the CPA's membership rallying against the leadership of Laurie Aarons, who had replaced Sharkey as General Secretary in 1965. More conservative members called for greater support of the Soviet Bloc and voiced suspicion about the new social movements, primarily women's liberation. Over the next few years, the National Congresses of the CPA were dominated by clashes between different sections of the Party and eventually in 1971, around 800 pro-Soviet members left the then-4,500 strong organisation to form the Socialist Party of Australia (SPA).[31]

By the early 1970s, the radicalism had spread from the anti-Vietnam War and student movements into many other areas, such as women's liberation, anti-apartheid, Aboriginal rights, gay rights and anti-imperialism, inspired by the global spread of the cultural militancy of '1968'. Many of those involved in these progressive social movements were involved in far left groups, primarily the CPA, the SYA/SWL and the SWAG/IS. The SPA, as well as the Maoists, were primarily anti-revisionist in their politics and were sceptical of many of these 'bourgeois' and 'reformist' social movements. Others involved in these movements were also sceptical of the role that these avowedly Marxist activists played within the movements. For example, Indigenous activist Paul Coe criticised the 'white left' for its lack of interest in Indigenous matters, particularly in places like Redfern.[32] Furthermore feminists organised around the *Mejane* editorial collective called out the 'destructive' tendencies of the Australian left in 1971.[33]

This radicalism eventually permeated the centre and popular momentum surged forward with the election of Gough Whitlam as Prime Minister in December 1972. While some embraced the promise of Whitlam's progressivism, such as the 'femocrats' who had been part of the women's liberation movement and later became involved in state-centred activism,[34] the radical left did not abate after the ALP victory. In some places, such as the university campuses, the struggle intensified and throughout 1973 and 1974, occupation of university buildings spread across Australia.[35] In Queensland, Joh Bjelke-Petersen's National Party clamped down on protest and the state became a focal point for the Australian left in a fight against creeping authoritarianism. Despite Whitlam's policy programme, there were many problems facing Australia that needed radical action, not merely the agenda put forward by the Labor government. But it is possible to argue that Whitlam's most significant reforms were accepted by the public because the left had already challenged many of the assumptions and prejudices that had previously stood in the way of reform. For example Whitlam's embrace of the women's liberation movement was only possible owing to its social weight.

Like the rest of Australia, the far left was shocked by 'The Dismissal' in November 1975, when the Governor-General Sir John Kerr dissolved the Whitlam government after the Opposition chose to block supply in the Senate.[36] There were fears of a coup by the right (in the wake of the overthrow of the Allende government in Chile two years earlier) and suspicion that the CIA and MI5, as well as ASIO, were involved in a plot to unseat Whitlam. Maintaining the rage that Whitlam encouraged against his Liberal replacement Malcolm Fraser's combative international relations (IR) and anti-communist agenda led many on the left to think that the Liberal government was Australia's answer to Augusto Pinochet,[37] and later in the 1970s (and early 1980s), as part of the wave of authoritarian populism that was represented by Margaret Thatcher and Ronald Reagan.[38] In hindsight Fraser was not the neoliberal warrior that the Australian far left feared he was, but his time in government was still characterised by oppositional trade union militancy and industrial confrontation.[39] The number of industrial disputes peaked sharply in 1981–82, although between 1968 and 1980, the number of disputes in

8 Jon Piccini, Evan Smith, Matthew Worley

Australia per year had never dropped below 2,000.[40] Both the CPA and the IS, as well as the SPA and the CPA(M-L), invested heavily in these strikes. As in Britain, the difference between the tactics of the Communists and the International Socialists centred on where these parties sought to influence the labour movement. The CPA, as had been established in the late 1940s, was particularly wedded to the trade union leadership, while the IS took inspiration from the British SWP and formed rank and file groups. These were especially noticeable in the various teachers', nurses' and public service unions, which also saw the IS grow from around 70 members in 1977 to 100 in 1980.[41] In certain areas, the SPA and the CPA(M-L) continued to have a trade union presence, but were outnumbered by the CPA and less prominent than the IS in most cases.

By the end of the 1970s, the radicalism that had exploded a decade earlier had all but dissipated, and many groups went into decline. A factor in this was the abolition of the Australian Union of Students (AUS), a sprawling organisation that had grown alongside a booming higher education system. Throughout the 1970s, the various groups of the left tussled for control of the AUS, its newspaper, and influence on each individual campus. The CPA, the Maoists and the Trotskyists jockeyed for positions with the AUS, but wildly disagreed on policy and outlook. Particularly heated debates took place between the Maoists and the Trotskyist Spartacist League. At the same time, the right, represented by both the Liberals and the National Civic Council, attempted to wrestle control of the AUS away from the left. An unholy alliance between the Maoists and sections of the right finally allowed for the AUS to be wound up in the early 1980s.[42]

While Fraser was seen at the time as the Australian version of Thatcherism and Reaganomics, the true onset of neoliberalism came with the Hawke government of 1983. One of Hawke's significant policies was to end the industrial relations strife of the 1970s. Like the 'Social Contract' agreed to by the Trades Union Congress and the Harold Wilson government in 1974 in Britain, Hawke and his former colleagues at the Australian Council of Trade Unions (ACTU) agreed to a series of Accords, which would end industrial action by the majority of trade unions in return for a restoration of the social wage and industrial restructuring. Unlike the CPGB's official opposition to the 'Social Contract', the CPA endorsed the Accord, with the CPA-controlled Australian Metal Workers' Union (AMWU) (one of the largest unions in Australia) supporting the reform as opening the way to a greater influence over industry. Although opposed to the Accord, the main Trotskyist groups were divided over how to deal with the shifting political and socio-economic landscape under Hawke. The SWL (by now the SWP) had its turn to industry and a number of its members went to work in blue-collar jobs, such as for BHP in Wollongong, with mixed results (as covered in this volume). The IS bitterly feuded over whether Tony Cliff's idea of the 'downturn'[43] applied to Australian conditions, leading to a split for most of the 1980s.

The 1970s and 1980s saw a new range of social movements concerning the environment, uranium mining and nuclear power emerge that had a distinct effect on the Australian left. Firstly, the Builders Labourers Federation (BLF), under

Introduction 9

leader Jack Mundey (also a member of the Communist Party), led the NSW section of the Federation into protest against unchecked urban development in the inner-city, colloquially known as 'green bans'.[44] While environmentalism, then as it is now, was often dismissed as petty-bourgeois politics, the BLF developed a movement against urban redevelopment that would have deprived working-class people of their housing and to protect the heritage and environment of Sydney's inner city. This position was adopted in other cities shortly thereafter. At the same time, several groups started campaigning against uranium mining in central and northern Australia, which combined sections of the radical left, Indigenous activists and the ALP. In 1977, the ALP, now in opposition, agreed to an indefinite moratorium on uranium mining (although this policy was overturned in 1982). This push against uranium mining combined with the concerns of the peace movement as the Cold War heated up in the early 1980s with Ronald Reagan's first term as President of the USA. The movement for nuclear disarmament grew exponentially in the first half of the 1980s, campaigning against the mining of nuclear materials and against nuclear weapons being stored in Australia. This led to protests, such as the Women's Peace Camp at Pine Gap in Northern Territory, which brought together different sections of the left and progressive movements in Australia.[45] Organisationally, it was arguably the SWP that was most receptive to these ideas about environmentalism and anti-nuclear politics, with the organisation becoming the Democratic Socialist Party (DSP) in 1990, and with *Direct Action* replaced by a new newspaper highlighting its environmental stance – *Green Left Weekly*.

By the end of the 1980s, the left across the western world was in flux, watching the Soviet Bloc in paroxysms over the policies of *perestroika* and *glasnost* under Mikhail Gorbachev, the long shift of China towards 'socialism with Chinese characteristics' under Deng Xiaoping, and the battering of the left in several countries due to the onset of neoliberalism, particularly in the USA, Britain and New Zealand. In Australia, many on the left were struggling to make sense of the changes in the international and domestic political and economic landscapes. The ALP, while embracing the neoliberal reforms that were developing worldwide during the 1980s, still had the loyalty of the majority of the trade union movement. The Communist Party was timid in its approach to the ALP, tied to the idea of the parliamentary road to socialism and closer links between the two parties. The other Trotskyist groups, as well as the SPA, were much more critical of the Hawke government and especially the SWP/DSP and the International Socialists were much more prepared to be involved in protest action against the government. For example, the ISO (renamed after the breakaway Socialist Action group rejoined in 1990) were heavily involved in actions such as the demonstrations at the AIDEX arms fair in Canberra in 1991 and anti-fascist protests against National Action in the early 1990s, with criticisms from other sections of the left for their 'violence' and 'adventurism'.[46]

The collapse of the Soviet Bloc between 1989 and 1991 had a massive effect on the Australian left, as it did across the globe. Similarly to the CPGB, the CPA, which had experienced a collapse in membership throughout the 1980s, decided at its last conference in 1991 to dissolve itself, forming the loosely organised New Left Party and establishing the SEARCH Foundation, which sought to act as a left-wing think tank in a post-Cold War world. The DSP and its reorganised youth wing, Resistance, argued that the Soviet Union had collapsed under its own contradictions, proposing that Third World revolutionary societies, such as Cuba, offered the way forward. The IS, having recently reunited, started to argue about the character of the former Soviet Bloc and whether the fall of Eastern Europe was a progression or regression. The IS long argued that the Soviet Bloc was 'state capitalist' and the line from the British SWP that the revolutions of 1989/91 were a move 'neither a step forward nor a step backwards, but a step sideways'.[47] This did not convince a number of Australian members, who argued that a much more critical eye needed to be cast over events in the former USSR and its satellite states – the Cliffites suggested that structurally little had changed, but some in the IS thought that something much more complex was underway. The SPA remained critically supportive of the Soviet Union until its demise and maintained its positive view of the Eastern Bloc, eventually taking over the moniker of the (now defunct) CPA in 1997.

The need for a history of the far left in Australia

The purpose of this collection is to explore the different contributions what we have defined as the far left has made over time, how organisations and individuals rose and fell, and what this all meant for Australia's broader political culture. Mark Aarons' uncharitable history of the CPA tells how its adherents championed "[m]any things that are taken for granted in Australian society [but] were not widely accepted in the recent past". From supporting aboriginal struggles to opposing apartheid, building the anti-Vietnam war movement and leading Australia's most militant unions, Aarons presents a CPA that 'popularise[d] ideas that have contributed to the quality of Australian society', while at the same time seeking to undermine its democratic foundations.[48] Aarons is amongst the latest of a long stream of scholars and activists who have turned their minds to Australia's largest far left grouping of the 20th century, joining a plethora of memoirs and reminiscences from members.[49] Wilton Brown, Robin Gollan, Tom O'Lincoln and Alastair Davidson have all explored the group's organisational and ideological politics, although few look seriously beyond the CPA's heyday in the 1940s.[50] Stuart Macintyre's authoritative *The Reds* takes readers up until the party's 1940 banning, and a promised second volume is yet to emerge.[51] This work's focus on the period after 1945, and particularly the 1960s to the 1980s, then fills a significant gap.

The CPA, while the biggest player in town, was on a more populated pitch in the post-war period. The party's splinter formations, Maoists in 1963 and Stalinists in 1971, have received only limited attention, while the plethora of Trotskyist groupings have fared better.[52] Before his death, John Percy had written two volumes of the history of his particularly Trotskyist formation (what was to become the Democratic Socialist Party but started life as youth group Resistance). The first

Introduction   11

volume, covering the period from 1965 to 1972, was published in 2005. A second volume covering the period from 1972 to 1992 has been published posthumously.[53] Hall Greenland has penned a biography of his mentor and leading Australian Trotskyist Nick Origlass, writings that have sparked backlash from factional rivals.[54] By far the largest body of work to explore the far left focuses on the 'social movements' these groups led or 'intervened' in, though they often only appear as peripheral players in these works. The CPA's leadership in the early women's movement has been catalogued by Joyce Stevens and Joy Damousi, while works by Jennifer Clark and Ravi De Costa cover well the CPA's politics on Indigenous Australians, Michael Saunders and Ralph Summy the CPA's dealings with the peace movement and Douglas Jordon the Party's work in the Trade Unions and related fields.[55] Verity and Meredith Burgmann have written on the 'Green Bans' of the CPA-led Builders Labourers Federation in the 1970s, while Diane Kirkby's work on the Seaman's Union of Australia chronicles this union's long history of militant activism on the global and local scene.[56] Contributions of those leftists outside of the CPA's orbit feature prominently in work by Graham Hastings and Mick Armstrong on the student movement of the 1960s and 1970s, in which different shades of far left were dominant, and Lani Russell, Kristy Yeats and Nick Irving have completed theses on Australia's intersecting New Left and anti-nuclear movements.[57] Women's liberation and gay rights – significant focuses of this collection – are less well documented, however Liz Ross' work on the left and gay liberation stands out.[58] Yet further work has examined the intersections of these different groups, including Verity Burgmann's case studies of different protest movements from the 1960s to the 1980s, Sean Scalmer on the 'political gimmick' and Jon Piccini on the transnational imagination of Australian far left activists in the 'long 1960s'.[59] The other side of the barricades – policing and government responses – has also been a focus of recent histories such as those by John Blaxland, Evan Smith and an edited collection by Meredith Burgmann.[60]

Yet, this scholarship is far from complete. Much of the work is dated or ideologically slanted, and big questions with significant bearing on Australia's history are left unanswered. This volume, while not pretending to be comprehensive, unearths the far left's centrality to some of Australia's most divisive and significant social movements, political debates and cultural events. The book's first section offers histories of Australian communism from the 1950s to the 1970s. Phillip Deery begins by exploring the politics of '1956', a cataclysmic year for Communist parties worldwide. Yet, contrary to the assumed narrative of a party leadership cracking down on dissent in the wake of Khrushchev's secret speech and the invasion of Hungary, there was no predictable, single trajectory for Australian party members. Some were bewildered by Khrushchev's revelations and accepted the assertion of Soviet authority in Hungary; a few hardliners were not touched by either event while others, and not only the 'intellectuals', were shocked by the first and affronted by the second, leaving in large numbers. Drew Cottle and Angela Keys' narrative begins only a few years after this, exploring the career of the Communist Party of Australia (Marxist-Leninist), formed after a 1963 split. Cottle and Keys have unearthed not an isolated, secretive sect, but a party which despite its seemingly alien ideas made significant inroads into the student, union and anti-war movements while leading a significant revitalisation of Australian political and cultural nationalism in the 1970s. The CPA's final, acrimonious split with Moscow occupies David McKnight's chapter, providing a long overdue scholarly account of this fractious moment. Matters of domestic concern – the inability of orthodox Marxism to explain Australian circumstances and the emergence of new, rebellious social movements outside of the CPA's orbit – were just as significant as international events such as the 1968 invasion of Czechoslovakia, McKnight argues, in motivating Party leaders in challenging the Soviets, moves which in turn saw the 1971 split of much of the Stalinist wing of the Party. Lastly, Evan Smith and Jon Piccini write of the CPA's troubled relationship with the politics of immigration in Australia. Never quite embracing the proletarian internationalism they espoused, or adopting the virulent racism of much of the mainstream labour movement, the CPA steered a middle course that condemned White Australia's racialism while advocating little or no net migration and demonising certain ethnic groups.

Such organisational histories, however, tell only part of the story. How the far left engaged with, led or critiqued social movements from the 1950s to the 1980s occupies the next two sections. These two sections each consider the far left's role in relation to the broader political context: firstly the Cold War of the 1950s and 60s, when Communist and other radical ideas were repressed or ignored, and this framework was finally challenged and broken. Jennifer Clark explores the relationship between those who professed or were sympathetic to the philosophies of the far left and were also involved with the Council for Aboriginal Rights during its early years in the 1950s, an organisation which has achieved limited scholarly attention to date. Clark presents this as a matter of negotiation, of ensuring that leading member's Communist allegiances did not cloud the group's goals, ensuring that their dutiful work in the organisation was alongside those of a diverse range of views and opinions. Kyle Harvey tackles another key, yet entirely under-explored, aspect of the Australian far left's social movement interventions – anti nuclear activism. Again, the Cold War posed barriers to far left involvement in wider campaigning organisations, as various peace organisations and campaigns conceptualised their image and approach in an era of anti-communist fervour. While many of the movement's key organisers, and a sizeable number of its rank and file owed much to the radical traditions and analyses that became taboo in the early Cold War, this had to be sublimated as anti-communists began to antagonise and marginalise those advocating for peace and nuclear disarmament. The Cold War broke in the mid-1960s, as protest around the Vietnam War, Indigenous rights and demands for greater student involvement in the running of universities overflowed its confines. Russell Marks traces how the New Left who led this rebellion moved from a liberal social democracy to embracing divergent forms of Marxism – from Trotskyism to structuralist Marxism (such as Althusser) or the 'humanist' Marxism proffered by the Prague Spring, new ideas that set the scene for the next decade's diverse movements for change.

Introduction   **13**

If the 1950s and 1960s were marked by conservatism, the 1970s and 1980s were decades of liberation movements – women's, queer and indigenous. Old movements adopted new demands while the previously marginal asserted their place in society, and the far left – contrary to conservative protestation – was caught as much off guard as the rest of society. Isobelle Barrett Meyering's chapter explores the challenges that women's liberation posed to socialist feminists, in particular the former's insistence on what was termed 'lifestylism'. Socialist feminists, who played a large role in the overall movement, persistently objected that a focus on lifestyle change promoted 'personal solutions' rather than collective action and created new 'norms' of feminist behaviour that were alienating to working-class women. On the other hand, they were concerned that neglecting lifestyle change would lead socialist feminists to lose touch with the wider women's movement, and many far leftists involved themselves deeply in such activism. Problems of new ideas and old certainties were equally present in the indigenous rights movement of the 1970s, which moved from the paternalism of the 1950s to embrace a new assertiveness. Lewis d'Avigdor's case study of the Action Conference on Racism and Education, held in Brisbane in January 1972, proves instructive here, with student radicals and black power militants coming to verbal conflict over Aboriginal leadership, the Marxian privileging of class over race and the role that Women's Liberation could play in the Black Power movement. While overshadowed by the emergence of the Tent Embassy at the same time, this conference provides a window into the conflictual, but at times supportive, relationship between white far leftists and black power activists.

The following two chapters continue this exploration of the far left's intersection with liberation movements, as well as focusing on the exploits of two of Australia's most prominent Trotskyist groupings: The Socialist Workers Party/Democratic Socialist Party and the International Socialists. Liz Ross explores another key movement of the 1970s – gay liberation – unearthing how fundamental far left activists were to its theoretical ideas and practical results. While openly hostile to queer rights in some quarters – particularly the pro-Chinese and Soviet splinter parties – the far left both in the mainline CPA and Trotskyist groups theorised gay liberation within Marxist frameworks, and engaged in what Ross calls a battle of ideas with those in the movement more committed to a civil rights or an apolitical community building approach. While at their strongest in the 1970s, Liberation movements continued well into the 1980s, as Diana Covell explains in her chapter on the Wollongong Jobs for Women Campaign: the struggle of 34 mainly eastern European women for jobs at BHP's Port Kembla Steelworks. Emerging from and largely led by activists within the Socialist Workers Party – though not uncontroversially – this campaign led to the first class action in Australia, Covell writes 'challenging longstanding labour traditions, practices and attitudes towards women, and traditional assumptions of the industrial worker in the Australian context as a mostly white, English-speaking and muscular male.'

Lastly, the collection tackles questions of mainstreaming. How have the far left sought to bring their ideas into the political mainstream through popular culture, or allowed their own ideas to be influenced by it? Elizabeth Humphrey's contribution explores such questions of mainstreaming in relation to the controversial decision of the CPA-led Australian Metal Workers Union, then the nation's largest and most powerful, to support the Prices and Incomes Accords of the Hawke/Keating governments, starting in 1983. This contribution considers the why and how the AMWU (and other CPA associated unions such as the Building Workers' Industrial Union) broke with their strategy of workplace militancy, to support a state-led economic project that ultimately resulted in the multi-layered disorganisation of labour – precipitating dramatic falls in membership throughout the 1990s and 2000s. The question of far left 'celebrity' is taken up by Jon Piccini and Ana Stevenson in their contribution on the remarkable, distinctive work of two significant Australian intellectuals of the 1970s – Germaine Greer and Dennis Altman – both of whom aligned themselves with and found influence in Australia's Marxist milieu. Greer's *The Female Eunuch* and Altman's *Homosexual: Oppression and Liberation* are now viewed as epoch-making texts. Yet, in many ways, these are actually very different books, written by very different people and received in very different ways, both by the mainstream press, public opinion and the radicals to whom both at least imaged to be writing. While becoming brief figures of interest to the media, they were attacked and sensationalised in the popular press, and had their radical credibility challenged within their respective movements. Finally, Lisa Milner explores how the CPA – far from merely doctrinaire political radicals – were centrally involved in Australia's cultural scene in the post-war period through groups like the New Theatre, the School of Realist Art, and the Waterside Workers Federation Film Unit. Whatever their genre – in literature, visual arts, drama, music, dance or cinema – their output was imbued with a sense of the collective strength of working-class solidarity. This chapter explores the rich diversity of Australian left cultural activist groups and analyses their motivations and legacy.

No one book can tell the entire history of the Australian far left, which has had as long a past, led as many campaigns and fragmented in as many different directions as that of many other nations. Yet, this volume brings together writers and thinkers from academia and activism, emerging scholars and leading experts, to begin the process of properly piecing together the far left's long term impact on Australia. As well as informing historical practice, we hope that this collection will also lead contemporary activists to look back to the past from the perspective of today's times. Walter Benjamin wrote that being an activist historian does not mean presenting the past 'as it really was', but rather 'appropriating a memory as it flashes up in a moment of danger'. Because moments of danger like ours, riven with conflict and political fragility, are also moments of possibility: possibilities that Benjamin saw as lying in the past, forgotten traditions of protest and resistance, and it is our job to 'wrest tradition away from the conformism that is working to overpower it".[61]

Notes

1 See John Callaghan, *The Far Left in British Politics* (Oxford: Blackwell, 1987); Alexander Trapeznik & Aaron Fox, *Lenin's Legacy Down Under: New Zealand's Cold War* (Dunedin,

NZ: University of Otago Press, 2004); Max Elbaum, *Revolution in the Air: Sixties Radicals Turn to Lenin, Mao and Che* (London: Verso 2006); Keith Laybourn, *Marxism in Britain: Dissent, Decline and Re-emergence, 1945–c.2000* (London: Routledge, 2006); Evan Smith & Matthew Worley (eds), *Against the Grain: The British Far Left from 1956* (Manchester: Manchester University Press, 2014); Howard Brick & Christopher Phelps, *Radicals in America: The US Left since the Second World War* (Cambridge: Cambridge University Press, 2015); Evan Smith & Matthew Worley (eds) *Waiting for the Revolution: The British Far Left from 1956* (Manchester: Manchester University Press, 2017).

2 Anthony Ashbolt & Rowan Cahill, '"And the Lives are Many": The Print Culture of Australian Communism', *Twentieth Century Communism*, 12 (2017): 37–61.

3 This was evident amongst most of the Western Communist Parties as the Communist International entered the 'Third Period' in 1928, which increased tensions between activists from the pre-1917 period and those who had joined the Communist Parties in the 1920s. See Matthew Worley, 'Courting Disaster? The Communist International in the Third Period', in Matthew Worley (ed.), *In Search of Revolution: International Communist Parties in the Third Period* (London/New York: IB Tauris, 2004): 1–17.

4 Stuart Macintyre, *The Reds: The Communist Party of Australia from Origins to Illegality* (St Leonards, NSW, Allen & Unwin, 1998): 412. On Browderist influence on the CPA see Phillip Deery, 'The Sickle and the Scythe: Jack Blake and Communist Party "Consolidation", 1949–56', *Labour History*, 80 (2001): 215–23.

5 On Sharkey's sedition see Laurence W Maher, 'Downunder McCarthyism: The Struggle Against Australian Communism 1945–1960', *Anglo-American Law Review* 27, 3–4 (1998): 438–71.

6 Phillip Deery, 'Malaya, 1948: Britain's Asian Cold War?', *Journal of Cold War Studies*, 9/1 (Winter 2007): 34–35.

7 CIA, *The Communist Influence in Australia* (11 April, 1949): 3, CIA-RDP78–01617A00300070002–5, CIA Online Library; Rupert Lockwood, *Black Armada* (Australasian Book Society, Sydney, 1975); Heather Goodall, 'Uneasy Comrades: Tuk Subianko, Eliot V. Elliot and the Cold War', *Indonesian and Malay World*, 40, 117 (July 2012).

8 Phillip Deery, 'The Chifley, the Army and the 1949 Coal Strike', *Labour History*, 68 (May 1995): 80–97.

9 Evan Smith, 'Policing Communism Across the "White Man's World": The Co-ordination of Anti-Communism within the British Commonwealth in the Early Cold War', *Britain and the World*, 10/2 (September 2017): 170–197.

10 Laurence W. Maher, 'Dealing with the King's Enemies: The Drafting of the Communist Party Dissolution Bill 1950', *Australian Historical Studies*, 44/1 (2013): 37–53.

11 Ibid., pp. 315–382.

12 See Clark, Harvey and Milner's contributions.

13 See Ann Curthoys, *Freedom Ride: A Freedom Rider Remembers* (Crows News, NSW: Allen & Unwin, 2002) and John McLaren, 'Peace Wars: The 1959 ANZ Peace Conference', *Labour History* 82 (May 2002): 97–108.

14 Alastair Davidson, *The Communist Party of Australia: A Short History* (Stanford: Stanford Hoover Institution Press, 1969): 120; Tom O'Lincoln, *Into the Mainstream: The Decline of Australian Communism* (Sydney: Stained Wattle Press, 1985): 62.

15 Phillip Deery & Rachel Calkin, '"We All Make Mistakes": The Communist Party of Australia and Khrushchev's Secret Speech, 1956', *Australian Journal of Politics and History*, 54/1 (2008): 69–84.

16 O'Lincoln, *Into the Mainstream: The Decline of Australian Communism*, p. 98.

17 Mark Aarons, *The Family File* (Melbourne: Black Inc., 2010): 192.

18 Nick Knight, 'The Theory and Tactics of the Communist Party of Australia (M-L)', *Journal of Contemporary Asia*, 28/2 (1998): 233–257.

19 See Deborah Wilson, *Different White People: Radical Activism for Aboriginal Rights 1946–1972* (Crawley, WA: University of Western Australia Publishing, 2015).

16 Jon Piccini, Evan Smith, Matthew Worley

20 Margaret Penson, *Breaking the Chains: Communist Party Women and the Women's Liberation Movement 1965–1975* (Broadway, NSW: Breaking the Chains Collective, 1999).
21 Hall Greenland, *Red Hot: The Life and Times of Nick Origlass* (Sydney: Wellington Lane Press, 1998).
22 For a brief outline of the split in the FI, see Callaghan, *The Far Left in British Politics*, pp. 65–68.
23 Denis Freney, *A Map of Days: Life on the Left* (William Heinemann Australia, Melbourne, 1991); John Percy, *A History of the Democratic Socialist Party and Resistance, vol. 1: 1965–72 – Resistance* (Chippendale, NSW, Resistance Books, 2005): 41–49.
24 Percy, *A History of the Democratic Socialist Party and Resistance*, p. 242.
25 For a history of the International Socialists, see Callaghan, *The Far Left in British Politics*, pp. 84–112; Ian Birchall, *Tony Cliff: A Marxist For His Time* (London: Bookmarks, 2011); Phil Burton-Cartledge, 'Marching Separately, Seldom Together: The Political History of Two Principal Trends in British Trotskyism, 1945–2009', in Smith & Worley (eds), *Against the Grain*, pp. 80–97.
26 See Phil Ilton, *The Origins of the International Socialists* (1984) http://users.comcen.com.au/~marcn/redflag/archive/ilton/SWAG.doc (accessed 8 July, 2017).
27 Percy, *A History of the DSP and Resistance*, pp. 204–207.
28 Daniel Robins, 'Melbourne's Maoists: The Rise of the Monash University Labor Club, 1965–1967', unpublished Honours thesis, Victoria University, 2005.
29 Kate Murphy, '"In the Backblocks of Capitalism": Australian Student Activism in the Global 1960s', *Australian Historical Studies*, 46/2 (2015): 252–268.
30 Cited in Andy Blunden, 'The International Break Up of Stalinism', www.marxists.org/subject/stalinism/origins-future/ch3-2.htm (accessed 8 July, 2017).
31 For membership figures see McKnight's contribution in this volume.
32 Gary Foley, 'Black Power in Redfern 1968–1972' (2001): 11–12. http://vuir.vu.edu.au/27009/1/Black%20power%20in%20Redfern%201968-1972.pdf (accessed 8 July, 2017).
33 Cited in the chapter by Barrett Meyering in this volume.
34 Hester Eisenstein, *Inside Agitators: Australian Femocrats and the State* (St Leonards, NSW: Allen & Unwin, 1986).
35 Graham Hastings, *It Can't Happen Here: A Political History of Australian Student Activism* (Adelaide, SA, Empire Times Press, 2003): 75–134.
36 See Jenny Hocking, *The Dismissal Dossier* (Melbourne: Melbourne University Press, 2015); Paul Kelly & Troy Bramston, *The Dismissal: In The Queen's Name* (Sydney: Penguin Books, 2015).
37 Tom O'Loughlin, "A Vicious Coup!', *The Battler* (29 November, 1975): 8.
38 Gavan Butler, 'The Rise of "The New Conservatism"', *Australian Left Review*, 76 (June 1981): 18–23.
39 Tom O'Lincoln, *Years of Rage: Social Conflict in the Fraser Era* (Sydney: Interventions Publishers, 2012): 53.
40 Jane Romeyn, 'Striking a Balance: The Need for Further Reform of the Law Relating to Industrial Action', Research Paper 33 (2007–08) Australian Parliamentary Library. www.aph.gov.au/About_Parliament/Parliamentary_Departments/Parliamentary_Libra ry/pubs/rp/RP0708/08rp33 (accessed 15 July, 2017).
41 Chris Gaffney, 'The Politics of the International Socialist Organisation and the Democratic Socialist Party' (1994). http://members.optushome.com.au/spainter/Gaffney.html (accessed 18 July, 2017).
42 Hastings, *It Can't Happen Here*, pp. 145–170.
43 Tony Cliff, 'Building in the Dowturn', *Socialist Review* (April 1983): 3–5; Ian Birchall, *Tony Cliff: A Marxist For Our Time* (London: Bookmarks, 2011): 441–454.
44 Meredith Burgmann & Verity Burgmann, *Green Bans, Red Union: The Saving of a City* (Sydney, New South Publishing, 2017).
45 Alison Bartlett, 'Feminist Protest in the Desert: Researching the 1983 Pine Gap Women's Peace Camp', *Gender, Place & Culture*, 20/7 (2013): 914–926.

46 See Iain McIntyre, *Always Look on the Bright Side of Life: The AIDEX '91 Story* (Parkville: Homebrew Cultural Association, 2008); Andy Fleming, 'Anti-Fascism in Melbourne: 1990s', *Slackbastard* (20 March, 2007). http://slackbastard.anarchobase.com/?p=623 (accessed 9 July, 2017).

47 Chris Harman, 'The Storm Breaks', *International Socialism*, 2/46 (Spring 1990): 82.

48 Aarons, *The Family File*, pp. xv–xvi.

49 The best include Eric Aarons, *What's Left: Memoirs of an Australian Communist* (Ringwood, Vic.: Penguin, 1993); Bernie Taft, *Crossing the Party Line: Memoirs of Bernie Taft* (Newham, Vic: Scribe, 1994); John Sendy, *Comrades Come Rally: Recollections of an Australian Communist* (Melbourne: Thomas Nelson Australia, 1978).

50 Wilton Brown, *The Communist Movement and Australia: An Historical Outline – 1890s– 1980s* (Sydney: Australian Labor Movement History Publications, 1986); Alastair Davidson, *The Communist Party of Australia: A Short History* (Stanford, CA: Hoover Institution Press, 1969); Tom O'Lincoln, *Into the Mainstream: The Decline of Australian Communism* (Carlton North, Vic.: Red Rag Publications, 2009); Robin Gollan, *Revolutionaries and Reformists: Communism and the Australian Labour Movement 1920–1955* (Canberra: ANU Press, 1975).

51 Macintyre, *The Reds*.

52 Liz Ross has written on the Maoist-led Federal branch of the Builders Labourer's Federation, *Dare to Struggle, Dare to Win!: Builders Labourers Fight Deregistration, 1981–94* (Carlton, Vic.: The Vulgar Press, 2004).

53 Percy, *A History of the Democratic Socialist Party and Resistance*; John Percy, *A History of the Democratic Socialist Party and Resistance vol. 2: 1972–1992 – Against the Stream* (Carlton, Vic.: Interventions, 2017).

54 Greenland, *Red Hot*.

55 Joyce Stevens, *Taking the Revolution Home: Work among Women in the Communist Party of Australia 1920–1945* (Fitzroy, Vic.: Sybylla Cooperative Press, 1987); Joy Damousi, *Women Come Rally: Socialism, Communism, and Gender in Australia, 1890–1955* (Melbourne: Oxford University Press, 1994); Jennifer Clark, *Aborigines and Activism: Race, Aborigines and the Coming of the Sixties to Australia* (Crawley, WA: UWA Press, 2008); Ravi de Costa, *A Higher Authority: Indigenous Transnationalism and Australia* (Sydney: University of New South Wales Press, 2006); Michael Saunders and Ralph Summy, *The Australian Peace Movement: A Short History* (Canberra: Peace Research Centre, Australian National University, 1986); Douglas Jordon, 'Conflict in the Unions: The Communist Party of Australia, Politics and the Trade Union Movement, 1945–1960' (PhD Thesis, Victoria University, 2011).

56 Meredith Burgmann & Verity Burgmann, *Green Bans, Red Union: Environmental Activism and the New South Wales Builders Labourers' Federation* (Sydney: UNSW Press, 1998); Diane Kirkby, *Voices from the Ships: Australian Seafarers and their Union* (Sydney: UNSW Press, 2008).

57 Graham Hastings, *It Can't Happen Here: A Political History of Australian Student Activism* (Adelaide: Student Association of Flinders University, 2003); Mick Armstrong, *1,2,3, What are we Fighting for? The Australian Student Movement from its Origins to the 1970s* (Melbourne: Socialist Alternative 2001); Lani Russell, 'Today the Students, Tomorrow the Workers! Radical Student Politics and the Australian Labour Movement, 1960– 1972' (PhD Thesis, The University of Technology Sydney, 1999); Kristy Yeats, "Australian New Left Politics, 1956–1972" (PhD Thesis, The University of Melbourne, 2009); Nick Irving, 'Global Thought, Local Action: A Transnational Reassessment of the Australian Anti-War Movement, 1959–1972' (PhD Thesis, The University of Sydney, 2017).

58 Liz Ross, *Revolution is for us: The Left and Gay Liberation in Australia* (Brunswick, Vic.: Interventions, 2013).

59 Verity Burgmann, *Power and Protest: Movements for Change in Australian Society* (St Leonards, NSW: Allen & Unwin, 1993); Sean Scalmer, *Dissent Events: Protest, the Media and*

the Political Gimmick in Australia (Sydney: UNSW Press, 2002); Jon Piccini, *Transnational Protest, Australia and the 1960s* (Basingstoke, UK: Palgrave, 2016).

60 John Blaxland, *The Protest Years: The Official History of ASIO, 1963–1975* (St. Leonards, NSW: Allen & Unwin, 2015); Evan Smith, 'Policing Protest in the Australian Capital Territory: The Introduction and Use of the Public Order Act 1971', *Journal of Australian Studies*, 40, 1 (2016): 92–108; Meredith Burgmann (ed.), *Dirty Secrets: Our ASIO files* (Sydney: New South, 2014).

61 Michael Lowy, *Fire Alarm: Reading Walter Benjamin's 'On The Concept of History'* (London: Verso Books, 2005): 42.

PART 1

Organisational histories

1

AUSTRALIAN COMMUNISM IN CRISIS – 1956

Phillip Deery

Russia

Just before midnight, on 24 February 1956, a political earthquake hit the Great Kremlin Palace in Moscow. Its shock waves radiated across the Soviet Union, the Eastern Bloc and the world communist movement. To an unscheduled closed session of the 20th Congress of the Communist Party of the Soviet Union (CPSU), the party's First Secretary, Nikita Khrushchev, revealed to a dumbstruck audience that, instead of the wise and beneficent object of their adulation, Stalin was a criminal tyrant responsible for systematic murder and psychological terror. This was the Secret Speech.[1] But, first, what was its context?

The death of Joseph Stalin in March 1953 created a power vacuum within the Soviet Union. The political manoeuvring within the USSR from then until February 1956, when Khrushchev denounced Stalin, was dominated by the struggle for power between four individuals: Beria, Malenkov, Molotov and Khrushchev. As with Stalin's rise to power in the 1920s, Khrushchev won by the others underestimating him. During this period, expressions of loyalty to Stalin's policies continued but significant changes in attitude were occurring. Articles appeared in *Pravda* that argued that Marxism-Leninism, which favoured collective leadership, was incongruent with the "cult of the individual". Khrushchev slowly began relaxing censorship and encouraged a measure of independent thinking.[2] Indicative was the publication of Ilya Ehrenburg's *The Thaw* in 1954, which referred to the Great Purge and negative aspects of Stalinism.[3] In June 1955, Khrushchev visited Belgrade and extended an olive branch to Tito, a step towards legitimising "national communism". In the aftermath of Lavrentiy Beria's execution in December 1955, the gates of the Gulag were opened to thousands of political prisoners. Although subtle rather than fundamental, gradual rather than sudden, such reforms were harbingers of what was to unfold on that fateful evening in February 1956.

22 Phillip Deery

Theoretically the ruling body of the CPSU, the party congress was normally a ceremonial and legitimising event. The 20th Party Congress, however, which convened in Moscow on 14 February 1956, was a momentous watershed in the history of international communism. Khrushchev's Secret Speech was delivered over four hours in the middle of the night of 24–25 February to a closed session of the congress – after the congress had formally ended – from which all "fraternal delegates" of foreign communist parties were excluded. The decision to make a dramatic denunciation of Stalin's reputation and puncture the dogma of Soviet infallibility was made primarily by Khrushchev himself, after some vacillation. It was strongly opposed by the majority of the Presidium, which prevented the incorporation of the speech into Khrushchev's formal, open report.[4] It was far more comfortable with the speech Vyacheslav Molotov had proposed for the Congress: "Stalin the Continuer of Lenin's work".[5] The closed session and the "secrecy" of the speech was a concession by Khrushchev to his Presidium opponents.[6]

Consequently, Khrushchev confined himself to Stalin's use of systematic terror against party members after 1934. Stalin's "violations of socialist legality" – the term "crimes" was avoided – was restricted to abuses against the loyal members of the party elite. Khrushchev also spoke approvingly of Stalin's struggle against Trotskyist and Bukharinist "oppositionists" in the 1920s and during the industrialisation drive of the 1930s. None of the party leaders purged between 1934 to 1938 was rehabilitated. Khrushchev did not question the one-party system, land collectivisation, or the command economy, since he remained committed to the structures of the Soviet state; only "distortions" needed to be identified and rectified. No mention was made of those other voiceless victims: the millions of Soviet citizens sent to the Gulag.

Despite these caveats, the Secret Speech was a bombshell. Khrushchev exposed the mechanism of terror and the system of arbitrary rule that had dominated the country for thirty years. He cited dozens of documents and a wealth of details to reveal the brutal character of Stalin's rule. Khrushchev revealed criminal acts including the "suicide" of Ordzhonikidze and the assassination of Kirov; lawless mass deportations of non-Russian peoples; political errors such as the breach with Tito's Yugoslavia; incompetent leadership, exemplified by the vulnerability of Russia to German attack in 1941; the methodical falsification of history written by Stalin himself or at his direction; and the replacement of the Leninist principle of collective leadership with the "cult of the personality".

In short, Khrushchev punctured the mystical aura that surrounded Stalin. Delegates were stunned: "Some wept, for they had sincerely worshipped Stalin. Some, relieved at the end of despotic terror, were alarmed: could the resultant shockwaves be controlled?"[7] The report of the speech is constantly punctuated with parenthetical asides – "Commotion in the hall", "Indignation in the hall" and "Movement in the hall". Apparently, some thirty delegates fainted or had seizures during the speech.[8] The words of a fictional character, Major Grachev, most likely echoed the thinking of many present: "[W]e have dealt ourselves a terrible blow.

How are we to continue the global revolution when we confess to such murderous acts against our own people? Who would want to join our cause? Who would want to become our comrades?"[9] Others in the audience were indignant. One interrupted the speech with the question what Khrushchev was doing while Stalin was committing these crimes against the Russian people; "Khrushchev snapped, 'Who said that?' Silence. 'Well', he replied, 'that is what I was doing too, keeping silent.'"[10]

On 1 March 1956 the text of the speech was distributed to senior members of the CPSU Central Committee and a week later several thousand copies of the summarised report, in the form of a red jacketed booklet with its "top secret" stamp removed, was distributed to all regional, city and district committees of the CPSU throughout the Soviet Union.[11] Even the abbreviated version was a shock; its impact was "like the explosion of a neutron bomb".[12] Khrushchev also sent copies to leaders of certain foreign communist parties.[13] The Secret Speech was not secret. Across the country, party members raised criticisms of the regime hitherto unheard of and thereby "unleashed the forces of public opinion beyond Khrushchev's wildest expectations."[14] There were several conduits through which the text may have reached the West. The customary explanation – which involves its passage from Moscow to Wladyslaw Gomulka's office in Warsaw to Wiktor Grajewski (a Polish-Jewish communist) to the Israeli embassy to Mossad to the CIA – has been disputed. However, in the most authoritative analysis yet of the dissemination of the Secret Speech, Mayzel argues that it was the CPSU leadership, including Khrushchev himself, and the KGB that were primarily responsible.[15] Another conduit to the West was Morris Childs, a high-ranking member of the Communist Party of the USA, who attended the Congress as a foreign delegate and who acquired a copy of the speech from Gomulka. Childs was also a double agent, working for the FBI and codenamed "Agent 58". Plausibly, it was he who passed his copy to the FBI, which forwarded it to the US State Department, which in turn "leaked" it to the *New York Times*.[16]

In Soviet bloc countries, the time seemed ripe to challenge the legitimacy of Soviet rule and Stalinist structures. Radical reform was now seen as both desirable as well as possible. In both Poland and Hungary defiance was expressed openly but resolved differently: the first, in June, through compromise; the second, in November, through Soviet tanks and brutal repression. Within communist parties throughout the West the Secret Speech wrought havoc.[17]

America

Of all the parties jolted by the Secret Speech, the Communist Party of the United States of America (CPUSA) underwent the greatest convulsions. The following discussion of the CPUSA will provide a litmus test, a comparative measuring stick, for analysing the Communist Party of Australia (CPA) and assessing whether the cataclysmic impact of 1956 in America was replicated in Australia. For CPUSA leaders, the Secret Speech presented an opportunity to review past approaches and

24 Phillip Deery

rethink future strategies. They missed this opportunity. For rank and file communists, 1956 forced a re-evaluation of their faith in and their loyalty to the communist party. They had to decide whether that faith and loyalty outweighed their sense of disillusionment and betrayal. This confusion, along with an uneasy mixture of shock, bewilderment and liberation, is evocatively captured by a steel mill worker in Pittsburgh:

> The 20th Party Congress struck me like lightning…I don't really know how to describe what happened to me, to a lot of us, then. My own immediate response to Khrushchev's report was: What the hell does it *mean*?…So we began meeting, a whole bunch of us, in a kind of regular irregular way – in Pittsburgh, in Boston, in Philly. And talking. Talking like we'd never talked before…People said things about themselves, their lives, the Party you'd never have dreamed were inside them waiting to get out. It was awful, simply awful. And yet, it was terrific, too. Exciting. Tremendously exciting to hear people rethinking their lives out loud.[18]

In the spring of 1956, vague rumours about a "special report" that referred to "errors" committed under Stalin, and a "cult of personality", had been circulating within the CPUSA but were believed to be baseless. Then, on the evening of 30 April, at the Jefferson School of Social Science where the National Committee was meeting, rumour became reality. The party's political secretary, Leon Wofsy, began to read from a document obtained from Sam Russell, the Moscow correspondent for the British *Daily Worker*. Notes were forbidden and confidentiality was sought. For the next three hours, dumbstruck delegates sat in a deathly, stunned silence as a résumé of Khrushchev's report on the Stalin era was read aloud. To the chairman of the meeting, the veteran organiser and proletarian hero, Steve Nelson, the words of Khrushchev's speech

> were like bullets, and each found its place in the hearts of the veteran Communists. Tears streamed down the faces of men and women who had spent forty or more years, their whole adult lives, in the movement…I felt betrayed. I said simply, 'This was not why I joined the Party'. The meeting ended in shock.[19]

Within half an hour Dorothy Healey was "convulsed with tears", and could not stop crying.[20] George Charney was "too shocked, too unstrung" to say anything. The mood was "eerie", he recalled. "Thus it was on that night each of us went home to die".[21] Indeed, on that night, Peggy Dennis, the wife of the general secretary, Eugene Dennis, recently released from jail, did experience a kind of spiritual death. In her West Harlem apartment, "I lay in the half darkness, and I wept…For Gene's years in prison…For the years of silence in which we had buried doubts and questions. For a thirty-year life's commitment that lay shattered. I lay sobbing low, hiccoughing whispers".[22] These traumatic private reactions were

Australian Communism in crisis – 1956 **25**

a foretaste of what soon happened generally within the party: "With the Khrushchev report, all the accumulated frustrations, discontents, doubts, grievances in and around the Communist party erupted with an elemental force".[23]

Howard Fast exemplified this "eruption". Fast, a celebrated writer and prominent communist, wrote in his regular column for the 12 June issue of the *Daily Worker* that, having read Khrushchev's speech, "something broke inside of me and finished".[24] His column was angry and anguished, remarkable for its candour, its bravery, its sense of moral outrage and betrayal and sorrow, and for its unparalleled sharp criticism of Soviet leaders. "There is little one can say", he began, "to take the deadly edge off the 'secret' Khrushchev speech". He continued:

> It is a strange and awful document, perhaps without parallel in history: and one must face the fact that it itemizes a record of barbarism and blood-lust that will be a lasting and shameful memory to civilized man...[M]y stomach turned over with the blood-letting, with the madness of vengeance and counter-vengeance, of suspicion and counter-suspicion.

He wrote that it was "some small comfort" that, until recently, he was ignorant of the facts in Khrushchev's report. He knew that Jewish culture was being systematically destroyed, that writers, artists and scientists were intimidated, that the "abomination" of capital punishment was enforced. But all these things, he rationalised, were "a necessity of socialism". Now, such blind faith was finished: "Never again can I accept as a just practice under socialism that which I know to be unjust".[25]

The editor of the *Daily Worker*, which published this column, was John Gates. In 1955 he had emerged from jail after a five-year sentence imposed under the Smith Act and was now jostling to displace William Z. Foster as general secretary.[26] As a "reformist" opposed to the rigidly orthodox Foster faction, Gates opened the pages of the *Daily Worker* to critical comment; it became a key vehicle for genuine debate within the CPUSA.[27] The staff was strongly aligned with the Gates faction. In comparable communist parties overseas there were debates and ideological fractures but not the agony of spirit or the overflow of despair and grief. There were several reasons for this intensity of reaction. One was that the party, by 1956 – in contrast to other Western communist parties – had been deprived of its mass industrial base, its connections with the Congress of Industrial Organization unions savaged by McCarthyism. This meant the capacity to immerse itself in day-to-day struggles was restricted and a greater inwardness resulted, characterised by taking more literally and seriously ideological issues.[28] Another reason was that the *Daily Worker* was the *only* communist paper in the world that printed Khrushchev's report. In the face of opposition from much of the CPUSA leadership, it appeared on the same day, 5 June 1956, that it was published by the *New York Times*. It was accompanied by a long, teeth-gnashing editorial. Thereafter, in the words of Gates – and here we can glimpse despair – "readers spoke out as never before, pouring out the anguish of many difficult years".[29]

26 Phillip Deery

By mid-1957, Foster and his hardliners were back in control. The reform movement was stymied. He had beaten his "revisionist" factional opponents by default: those who would have supported John Gates at the 16th National Convention in February 1957 (and initially Gates had "the numbers") had simply walked away from the party. One who later left, but was there, at the February convention, was a party organiser, Junius Scales. He painted a vivid picture of the party's convulsions and of his own sense of "utter futility and pain":

> By this time, the division and hatred inside the Party was just so thick you could cut it with a knife...Foster was vicious as a snake, and he was much more contained than the others. I wish I hadn't gone to the convention. Our differences of opinion were so great, and we had such contempt for the people who wanted to stay in this ingrown infected bubble, that there was just no possibility of working with these people anymore.[30]

Foster, now 77 and in poor health, failed to see that his victory was pyrrhic. When his indifference to the haemorrhaging of membership and the loss of valued comrades was challenged, he replied, "Let them go, who cares?".[31] These were people who had experienced the worst years of McCarthyism; many had experienced the abnormalities of life underground or in prison. They had once been animated by lofty ideals and burning desires to transform society. Now, they were dispirited, embittered or exhausted, their intimate bonds of camaraderie broken, their sense of loss palpable, their lives emptied of meaning. The *Daily Worker* ceased publication, the exodus of members continued and Gates, a veteran of the Comintern and political commissar in the International Brigades in Spain, was denounced as "an enemy of the working class". Cleansed of reformers, the enfeebled Party shrank further. By 1960, the CPUSA was moribund. The leadership, meanwhile, became more sectarian. As Peggy Dennis, a veteran of fifty years in the party, wrote in her strident six-page resignation letter:

> The lessons of the Stalin crimes revelations for our party here in the USA were never learned by the current leadership, instead since 1960 the leadership has rejected those lessons...For the past 15 years the current party leadership substituted declaratory denunciations of the new conceptual ideas being discussed in other Communist parties for serious analysis. Discussions within the party of these new theoretical and ideological questions were not allowed in our organization.[32]

Great Britain

Of all western communist parties, the British was the first to learn about the Secret Speech.[33] There is strong circumstantial evidence that the leading theoretician of the Communist Party of Great Britain (CPGB), Palme Dutt, was given a copy (by whom is unclear) almost immediately. He was one of three British delegates to the

CPSU Congress (along with Harry Pollitt and George Matthews), and apparently he concealed it from them.[34] He was Comintern-trained, read Russian, and was trusted by Moscow to echo the response of Maurice Thorez, the uncompromising leader of the French Communist Party (PCF, Parti Communiste Français). Thorez, who had acquired a copy of Khrushchev's speech in Russian, told a member of the PCF Central Committee: "There is no secret report…This report doesn't exist. Besides, soon it will never have existed. We must pay no attention to it."[35] If Dutt remained silent, Sam Russell, the *Daily Worker* correspondent in Moscow, did not. In early March 1956, he telephoned a six-page summary of the speech to the editor of the *Daily Worker*, Johnny Campbell. In the judgement of one party member, "If Campbell had printed Sam's six pages as they stood, the rest of 1956 would have turned out differently".[36]

But Campbell suppressed it. Instead he asked Russell to send a different story, acknowledging the speech but omitting details. It was this story that Campbell published on 19 March. His accompanying editorial referred to the "fiction" in the "capitalist press accounts of the speech".[37] It was not only *Daily Worker* staff, such as its features editor, Malcolm MacEwen, and TV critic, Alison Macleod – aware of Russell's original communiqué – that sought open discussion.[38] So too did the rank and file. Letters "flooded" into paper in the second week of March, which MacEwen had "the utmost difficulty" in getting published. After the 19 March issue, "the flood of letters became a torrent".[39] Throughout late March and into April, there were heated inner-party discussions within the Political Committee and the Executive Committee and at the closed session of the party's 24th Congress, which commenced on 30 March.[40] However, the hard line prevailed: Stalin had made "mistakes"; criticism of the Soviet system was "irresponsible", and the positive achievements of the Soviet Union must not be forgotten.

There is insufficient space to discuss the internal debates and their aftermath.[41] Suffice it to say that the consequences of 1956 were less profound than in the USA but they followed the same general trajectory – suppression, denial, limited debate, calls for inner-party democracy, expulsions of dissenters, an intransigent line on Hungary, and a small breakaway group of mostly intellectuals – that we shall see in the Australian Communist Party. Broadly, there were three groups that emerged within the CPGB in response to the Secret Speech. First, the majority, which, with some anguish, accepted that Stalin's cult of the individual was flawed, but the fundamental principles underpinning the political structures and historic attainments of the Soviet Union were intact. This was an episode to be regretted but the struggle for socialism above all else must continue. Second, a small group of hardliners, like Dutt, who regarded Khrushchev's revelations as grossly exaggerated and Stalin's actions wholly justified by historical exigencies: the threat of fascism and the consolidation of the Soviet state. Third, a dissident, indignant minority whose faith had been shattered, and who demanded open discussion of Stalin's crimes, reform from within, and an honest confronting of the past that was the only way forward for the party in the future. When the leadership, supported by the majority, refused to yield to such demands, these dissidents– including a third of all

Daily Worker journalists[42] – walked away from the party. One who walked away was the writer, Doris Lessing. In a private letter to E.P. Thompson (19 October 1956), she wrote that the CPGB had "degenerate[d] into a body of yes-men". After hoping in vain to "save 'King Street' from itself", she decided to escape "this straightjacket" and resign.[43]

Australia

Prior to 1956, the CPA, like the CPUSA under McCarthyism, was subjected to several blistering Cold War assaults. These included the prolonged general coal strike in the winter of 1949, interpreted by the Chifley Labor Government as a "communist conspiracy"; the prolonged publicity and Victorian Royal Commission following the defection and "revelations" of former communist leader, Cecil Sharpley, throughout the second half of 1949; the sustained attempts by the Menzies Government to ban the Communist Party through both legislation and referendum (1950–51); and the heated atmosphere in 1954 surrounding the Petrov defection and the subsequent Royal Commission into Espionage. It was not only the legal existence of the CPA under threat. Its strength in the trade unions was being eroded by the anti-communist Industrial Groups; its "front" organisations such as the Australian Peace Council, and the Party itself, were deeply penetrated by the security services (both Special Branch and ASIO), which bred intense but justified paranoia; and the CPA leadership was involved in a bitter inner-party struggle (or "consolidation"), which saw the elevation of E.F. Hill, the Victorian State Secretary, to the Central Committee Secretariat.[44] Diminished morale was echoed by falling commitment: by the end of 1955 party membership had dropped to fewer than six thousand. Like its American counterpart, the CPA was neither sufficiently strong nor free from internal conflict to confront the challenges posed by Khrushchev's speech. It was isolated and besieged. Moreover, by 1956, as Blake commented, there was a "defensive spirit among some Party members, linked with a turning inwards for the comfort of being among like-minded people".[45] This defensiveness was understandable, as it was with the CPUSA, but made the party less resilient when its shibboleths were shattered.[46]

The first report in the Australian communist press on the 20th Congress appeared in late February 1956. A *Tribune* article, "Press Lies 'Fantasies' Answered", written by the general secretary, L.L. Sharkey, sought to rebut claims in the "millionaire press" that Stalin was criticised – as indeed he was in the open sessions of the Congress by both Khrushchev and Anastas Mikoyan (First Deputy Premier and Presidium member). Sharkey acknowledged that the term "cult of the individual" was used by Khrushchev but it a "party mistake" and not attributable solely to Stalin. Instead, "the decisive thing" that emerged from the Congress was Khrushchev's outline of the Sixth Five-Year Plan of economic development.[47] This theme, of press lies about attacks on Stalin, was further articulated in a CPA talk on a Sydney radio station: "I have no hesitation in saying the daily press reports of this Congress were complete fantasies, wishful thinking and downright distortions of the truth".[48]

Readers of *Tribune* received no illumination about the "cult of the individual" from Sharkey's feature articles on the Congress on 21 March and 4 April[49] or the detailed report on 4 April provided by E.F. Hill, who attended the Congress.[50] But they learnt much about the "gigantic strides" and "colossal achievements" of the Soviet Union. According to a Central Committee member, Ralph Gibson, Sharkey's *Tribune* statements pouring ridicule on press reports "had me somewhat puzzled because I knew the CPSU tried to get the 'secret' report into the hands of fraternal delegates, of whom Ted Hill was one". He confirmed that Sharkey "knew the facts and insisted on their denial".[51]

Although rank and file communists were kept ignorant, a group of Melbourne CPA cadres was briefed by Sharkey on the "cult of the individual" on 26 March. There was no report of this internal meeting in the *Guardian* or *Tribune*, but an Australian Security Intelligence Organisation (ASIO) informant was present. While many ASIO reports, particularly dossiers compiled on individuals, must be read with circumspection, the overall veracity of this report seems indisputable.[52] Sharkey focused initially on the positive messages arising from the 20th Congress and then shifted his focus to the attacks being made against Stalin. "It was true that prior to the 19th Congress of the CPSU, there had arisen in the Soviet Union a cult of individualism. The cult...caused harm in the organisation of the party as it tended to stifle criticism and veered to hero worship".[53] This cult, he stated, led to a lack of collective leadership and to unilateral decision-making by Stalin. But he warned that questions being asked by some "waverers" within the party about how it had been permitted to develop in the CPSU were "dangerous". He compared these questions with those being asked by the capitalist press, and insisted that they would not be tolerated by the party. Sharkey refused to open up the meeting for discussion. This early clamp down contrasted with the relative greater openness displayed by the CPUSA.

Ted Hill, still in Moscow,[54] knew that the Secret Speech contained information that shattered the traditional views of Stalin. In early April 1956, Hill sent a letter to the Central Committee Secretariat that in turn was circulated to the Political Committee. The letter, which accompanied a copy of Khrushchev's Secret Speech, stated that "this version of the Khrushchev report was ninety-nine per cent correct but that there was no need to take much notice of the report because it was expected that the Molotov-Malenkov group would soon oust Khrushchev from the leadership".[55] Eric Aarons, the South Coast District secretary, was one who did not concur, for he *did* "take much notice" of Khrushchev's denunciation and sought a broader and more systematic analysis. In May 1956, in an article for the party's theoretical journal, *Communist Review*, Aarons argued that the 20th Congress had highlighted weaknesses in the ideological work of the Communist movement; this necessitated discussion of its significance for the CPA.[56] He identified a tendency within the party for dogmatic thinking and an over-zealous application of rules without consideration of some of the broader issues. He suggested that a critical appraisal of the cult meant that its impact must be recognised within an Australian context. This was inconsistent with the position of Hill and

30 Phillip Deery

Sharkey and other party leaders, such as Richard Dixon.[57] But it was consistent with the calls for open discussion emanating, in particular, from those associated with the *Daily Worker* and their editors in both Great Britain and the USA.

Aarons also gave a series of lectures on the 20th Congress, held in Sydney at the CPA headquarters. Assuming the detailed notes taken from these lectures by an ASIO informant are reliable, it would appear that Aarons explicitly referred to Stalin's abuses: "His terrible misuse of power is indicated by the treatment of the Polish Secretary of the Party." He explained how Gomulka had been framed – there being no proof of accusations – and jailed until after Stalin's death. He also referred to the "monstrous forms" of injustice that had been perpetrated against comrades within the party. In contrast to Sharkey's Melbourne meeting, after Aarons' lectures there were robust debates in which members were "reluctant to accept as gospel any propositions from the 20th Congress or from any of the current lecturers without searching, critical discussion and questioning." However, according to the ASIO report, he was unable to respond to many of the questions and, in some cases, accusations.[58] As another ASIO report noted, CPA leaders were "striving desperately to get clarity to the rank and file on the line they should present to the public."[59] But the floodgates were about to open. By now – mid May – the Political Committee had access to the Secret Speech, courtesy of Hill. Jack Blake recalled that "One copy of the speech was circulated to each member of the Political Committee in turn with instructions that it was to be read in the Party headquarters, initialised by each member and then handed in".[60] Soon, such precautions were rendered irrelevant.

On 5 June 1956 the *New York Times* printed the full text of Khrushchev's explosive Secret Speech.[61] *Tribune* responded with a tiny piece, "Still More Speculation About Stalin", which denied the authenticity of the report and disparaged the alleged source – the US State Department.[62] Rank and file communists and lower-ranking functionaries were less dismissive: Ian Turner bought a copy of the *New York Times*, which contained the report, "taking it to a café and reading and re-reading it with the sickening conviction, not only was this an authentic document, but that what Khrushchev had said was in essence true".[63] John Sendy and two comrades read it in an Adelaide public library and returned "ashen-faced".[64] Geoff McDonald read it "feverishly" and non-stop, oblivious to darkness descending.[65] Similar to the reaction of American communists described earlier, Roger Millis experienced "waves of shock" when he read it, "almost incredulously, gaping at the catalogue of horrors".[66] A "shaken" Bernie Taft knew the report was genuine and found it "devastating".[67] Amirah Inglis was "hit between the eyes" by the "full horror of Khrushchev's relentless inventory of Stalin's crimes".[68] For Len Fox, the Secret Speech was "shattering" and "a terrible shock",[69] and for a "shaken" Dorothy Hewett,

> the ramifications are unbelievable, the crimes monstrous, our beliefs and lives made ludicrous, naïve, even criminal, because we have lived this lie for years, and preached it everywhere – the lie of the perfection of Soviet society under

its great leader, Josef Stalin...Some ultimate innocence has been destroyed forever...Who now are the heroes and who the villains, after the Twentieth Congress?[70]

In the aftermath of the *New York Times* report, distinct cleavages developed within the CPA. First, the high-level leaders, who publicly denied its authenticity and argued that it should not be discussed; for them, belief in the inviolability of the Soviet Union was paramount. Of the Political Committee members, only Jack Blake confronted Stalin's crimes: in June he apologised to a stormy meeting of Jewish party members in Sydney for his earlier defence of the "Doctors' Plot".[71] Blake was labelled "the leader of the disrupters" and, soon after, relinquished all his official positions in the party.[72] Still, he did not resign from the CPA: "show me another party", he bleakly told one comrade.[73] Second, were the majority: those deeply disturbed by the revelations but who believed, for the sake of the party, that open conflict and robust open debate must be avoided. "I believed", recalled the previously ashen-faced John Sendy, "that if the contents of the secret report became widely known in the Party a wholesale exodus would result", and therefore acquiesced in the "official" party view that Khrushchev's speech was a CIA forgery. This was a time, after all, "to stand together to withstand the onslaught".[74] Similarly, Eric Aarons believed that "If we were to accept everything that was said and went completely on the defensive, we would open ourselves to attack from every quarter".[75] Ted Laurie agreed: despite his desire for greater internal democracy, when the leadership repressed discussion, he "willingly accepted the whip and toed the party line".[76] So, they kept silent, not wishing to be "cast out by the party...and isolated by bitterness and recrimination from a world movement in which we believed, and of which we wished to remain a part".[77] Third, were those who challenged that silence. The dissenters' position was well expressed by Ian Turner: "I insisted that there was no future for the party unless it confronted [the] truth."[78] There is also another group, of whom we know little: those who stopped attending branch meetings, or allowed their party dues to lapse and/or simply drifted away. Perhaps their experience was similar to that of John Steuben, a CPUSA rank and file activist. He told a reporter he wished to live out his life quietly "in agony and silence"; the reporter commented on his "acute spiritual pain".[79]

In Sydney a group of rank and file activists, exasperated by the party leadership's refusal to permit debate,[80] took matters into their own hands. Jim Staples, a young lawyer, Bob Walshe and Helen Palmer (both teachers) decided to circulate 500 roneoed copies of the *New York Times* report among party members.[81] This was not a time for toleration. Upon learning of this, Sharkey "and another heavy" went to Staples' flat and, finding nobody at home, "forced the door and seized the remaining copies".[82] But Staples remained unrepentant and, by August, was "in very bad odour with the Party" for refusing to comply with the party line.[83] Subsequently, he circulated what was then considered an incendiary document repudiating, in effect, the cardinal concept of democratic centralism.[84] Expulsion soon followed.[85] George Petersen, a public servant, obtained copies of the roneoed

32 Phillip Deery

document from Staples and Walshe and sought to distribute them, but "all hell broke loose. They didn't want to read it. That was the thing that amazed me. All these people whom I'd regarded as my friends, my comrades, the cream of the working class, just didn't want to read about a regime of murder."[86] But other comrades, in Sydney and elsewhere, did wish to read about Khrushchev's revelations.

Because of ASIO's penetration of the CPA, we know that heated discussions on the Secret Speech and its implications – reflecting sharp schisms between sections of the membership and leadership – were held throughout October during the Sydney District conference, within the Sydney University Branch, the West and East Sydney branches, the Melbourne University branch and at cadres' meetings in Sydney and Melbourne.[87] By November, ASIO informants reported feelings of general unrest and dissension and a readiness to criticise the party position "on all issues".[88] And by then, there were hundreds of resignations and numerous expulsions. It was these comrades who, according to Sharkey, "lost their balance" and their "faith in Marxism-Leninism and in the Party"; potentially they would "become irreconcilable enemies".[89] The door to democratisation was firmly closed.

It must be remembered that, in contrast to joining a social movement or political party today, being a member of the Communist Party then was an all-embracing, all-consuming commitment. It was akin to being a devout Catholic, complete with deification, quasi-religious training, a hierarchical structure, and pre-ordained, guiding principles. To be expelled, therefore, was to be excommunicated.

> Expulsion was dreaded. It was to be reviled as a renegade, a deserter, an opportunist. To be outside meant, in a sense, to lose one's 'family', the group who had shared your life for years…It was to enter the wilderness. It was to be shunned by old friends, have them cross the street to avoid you, or suffer their anger and abuse. And to be the subject of slander and malicious rumour.[90]

When Ian Turner, the secretary of the Australasian Book Society, was expelled in the aftermath of the events of 1956, it was falsely alleged he embezzled party funds and had been an ASIO informant. Ted Hill also spread the rumour that Turner and Stephen Murray-Smith, the editor of *Overland* and national secretary of the Australian Peace Council, were lovers.[91]

Hungary

As we shall see, Hungary was the trigger for Turner's expulsion and Murray-Smith's resignation. The party line on the uprising in Budapest and its suppression by Russian tanks was intransigent and dogmatic. There was none of the uncertainty and vacillation that characterised the response of some party leaders to the Khrushchev report. When the Hungarian students and workers repulsed the first Soviet invasion, they were depicted as a "frenzied counter-revolutionary mob" and "fascist bands" seeking to restore the capitalist-landlord regime.[92] Throughout

November, after the second, and successful, full-scale military invasion of the country and the savage repression of the revolt in Budapest, the party vilified the now-deposed Hungarian Premier, Imre Nagy, and his role in "the Fascist putsch"; emphasised the "unparalleled barbarity and brutality of the counter-revolution-aries" backed by foreign imperialists; and judged the "forcible action" by the Soviet Union as necessary to preserve a People's Democracy, counter a threat to the "whole Socialist world" and prevent a "fascist-military dictatorship" that would have initiated a "White Terror" and "surrendered [Hungary's] independence to the imperialist colonialists".[93] After the confusion earlier in 1956, with party leaders Eric Aarons, Jack Blake, Bill Brown and others holding a more flexible position than the intransigent Central Committee Secretariat, the party leadership reverted to its default position: unequivocal support for the actions of the Soviet Union. It clung with even greater determination to the familiar tradition of CPA authoritarian-ism. The fate of Peter Fryer, sent by the CPGB's *Daily Worker* to report on Hungary was imitated by an Australian correspondent for *Tribune*, the writer Eric Lambert. Both witnessed revolutionary workers' councils, not counter-revolutionary fascists; both believed the Hungarian uprising was "a true revolution" widely supported; both were expelled by their respective communist parties.[94]

According to one estimate, more than 7,000 British party members – over one fifth of the total membership – resigned after Hungary.[95] In Australia there was a similar exodus, although precise numbers or occupational backgrounds are difficult to determine.[96] What is certain is those whose faith was shaken by the 20th CPSU Congress had their doubts confirmed by the Soviet invasion of Hungary and its explicit endorsement by the CPA. After "two years of torment and bitterness",[97] Ian Turner, outraged by the execution of Imre Nagy, sent a letter of protest to the Russian journal *New Times* and the Victorian state executive. His party membership was terminated in early July 1958. The reason was "revisionism", which (like Staples' document two years earlier) questioned the theory and practice of the organisational principle and disciplinary framework enshrined as "democratic centralism".[98]

Another "revisionist" was Stephen Murray-Smith. His case provides us with a clear insight into the ramifications of 1956 on the far Left in Australia. It illumi-nates the disjuncture, if not duality, between public support of the party line and private doubts and misgivings. That the two co-existed so uneasily helps explain those two years of "torment and bitterness". On 8 July 1958, he sent the Victorian state committee his resignation letter. He wrote that the "immediate cause" of his resignation was the expulsion of his long-standing friend, Ian Turner.[99] Solidarity aside, his disillusionment predated 1956. "Hungary was bad enough, but [the execution of] Nagy was even viler", he wrote to the British writer and social critic, Claud Cockburn. "But, of course, the break wasn't because of Hungary or Nagy. The whole issue started earlier for us, even before the Twentieth Congress, and went deeper".[100] To Doris Lessing he referred to his "debilitating years of struggle" and how his battles "in and with the CP for many years" made it "impossible for me to continue any longer in the CP".[101] And to a close friend he commented, "My differences with the party go back a long long way".[102]

34 Phillip Deery

However, throughout all this period, Murray-Smith was a staunch public supporter of the communist project and a leading spokesman for Soviet foreign and domestic policies. As the Australian delegate to the World Peace Council, he travelled in 1957 to East Berlin and thereafter to Eastern Europe, Russia and China. His reports were unfailingly positive.[103] So too were his newsletters for the Russian language magazine, *Soviet Culture*, to which he contributed until July 1958.[104] As a "good" party member, Murray-Smith remained silent about issues that troubled his conscience. All this changed after July 1958, when he was frozen out of his work for the peace movement, battled with the party for the control of *Overland*, and was subjected to slander and vilification. Now, he spoke out:

> Owing I believe to certain narrow and mistaken policies we have the contradictory position that, in a period when the masses are starting to move in important way, the Communist Party is growing weaker and less able to lead them. The CP leaders are not prepared to make a real analysis of this, and by such actions as the folly of expelling Ian they weaken themselves and every cause they fight for. But they don't see it this way.[105]

Murray-Smith articulated what many defiant dissidents felt: the CPA was irreformable. Very few of the dissidents became apostates; most continued their involvement with progressive causes, whether through united action with (or membership of) the Labor Party or through an independent commitment to socialist humanism. Although the core CPA leadership – the hard men of the far Left – reasserted its control and remained in place, the party, as Murray-Smith predicted, became a less influential force, especially after Ted Hill and his many adherents in the trade union movement split from the party in 1963. After the Soviet invasion of Czechoslovakia in 1968, the CPA did what those cadres and rank and file members troubled or pained by the Secret Speech and Hungary wanted: it severed its ties to the CPSU and affirmed the principle of "independence" for national communist parties. But it was twenty-two years too late. The CPA, like the CPUSA, had missed the chance to confront its past, reform its structures and accommodate a plurality of opinion. The events of 1956 seriously damaged the party's legitimacy; the events of 1991 finally destroyed it.

Notes

1 It was first published in English in the *New York Times* in June 1956. Soon after the Russian Institute at Columbia University published it as *The Anti-Stalin Campaign and International Communism* (New York: Columbia University Press, 1956), 1–89, and an anti-Stalinist magazine published it as *The Crimes of the Stalin Era: Special Report to the 20th Congress of the Party of the Soviet Union* (New York: The New Leader, 1956, 1962), 7–65.
2 Alec Nove, *Stalinism and After* (London: Allen & Unwin, 1975), 129.
3 Its publication was not welcomed by the CPA, but for Amirah Inglis and Ian Turner, "the shock of his book was profound". Amirah Inglis, *The Hammer and the Sickle and the Washing Up* (Melbourne: Hyland House, 1995), 138.

Australian Communism in crisis – 1956   35

4   That report received the predictable "stormy, prolonged applause and cheers"; see N.S. Khrushchov [sic], *Report of the Central Committee of the Communist Party of the Soviet Union to the 20th Party Congress* (Moscow: Foreign Languages Publishing House, 1956), 144.

5   On the manoeuvrings within the Presidium prior to the Secret Speech being delivered, see William Taubman, *Khrushchev: The Man and his Era* (New York: W.W. Norton & Company, 2003), 273–82; Aleksandr Fursenko and Timothy Naftali, *Khrushchev's Cold War: The Inside Story of an American Adversary* (New York: W.W. Norton & Company, 2006), 86–7.

6   Taubman, *Khrushchev*, 283.

7   Nove, *Stalinism and After*, 131.

8   Carol Thornton and Willie Thompson, 'Scottish Communists, 1956–57', *Science and Society*, 6, 1 (1967), 77.

9   Tom Robb Smith, *The Secret Speech* (London: Simon & Schuster, 2009), 335.

10   Cited in Nove, *Stalinism and After*, 134. Like every other CPSU leader in 1956, Khrushchev was deeply implicated in the "crimes of Stalin". As Party boss in the Ukraine in the 1930s, he was responsible for signing lists that sent tens of thousands to their deaths. His faith in Stalin's infallibility only began to wane in World War 2.

11   See, for example, Igor Casu and Mark Sandle, "Discontent and Uncertainty in the Borderlands: Soviet Moldovia and the Secret Speech, 1956–1957", *Europe-Asia Studies* 66:4 (2014), 613–44.

12   Zhores A. Medvedev and Roy A. Medvedev, *The Unknown Stalin* (London: I.B. Tauris, 2006), 98.

13   Maxwell Adereth, *The French Communist Party: A Critical History (1920–1984) from Comintern to the "Colours of France"* (Manchester: Manchester University Press, 1984), 228.

14   Karl Loewenstein, "Re-emergence of Public Opinion in the Soviet Union: Khrushchev and Responses to the Secret Speech", *Europe-Asia Studies* 58:8 (2006), 1330.

15   Matitiahu Mayzel, "Israeli Intelligence and the Leakage of Khrushchev's 'Secret Speech'", *The Journal of Israeli History* 32:2 (2013), 257–83.

16   John Barron, *Operation Solo: The FBI's Man in the Kremlin* (Washington: Regnery, 1996), 54. Childs, then, was the "confidential source", to which the State Department referred in the prefatory statement to its release of the document; see *The Anti-Stalin Campaign*, p. 2.

17   The responses of European communist parties are outside the scope of this chapter. For the French and Italian parties, see *The Anti-Stalin Campaign and International Communism*, documents 3, 4, 6, 8, 9, 12, 16, 18. There is also a substantial literature on both parties' reactions. See especially François Fejtö, *The French Communist Party and the Crisis of International Communism* (Massachusetts: MIT Press, 1967); Joan Barth Urban, *Moscow and the Italian Communist Party: From Togliatti to Berlinguer* (London: IB Tauris, 1986).

18   Maurey Sachman, cited in Vivian Gornick, *The Romance of American Communism* (New York: Basic Books, 1977), 156–7 (emphasis in original). A great many rank and file communists "were lost trying to make sense of what had been their beliefs and their years of selfless work in the name of fighting for Communism". Maxine Louise Michel De Felice, *May the Spirit Be Unbroken* (Bloomington, IN: AuthorHouse, 2012), 215.

19   Steve Nelson, James R. Barrett and Rob Ruck, *Steve Nelson: American Radical* (Pittsburgh: University of Pittsburgh Press, 1981), 387.

20   Dorothy Healey and Maurice Isserman, *Dorothy Healey Remembers* (New York: Oxford University Press, 1990), 152, 154.

21   George Charney, *A Long Journey* (Chicago: Quadrangle, 1968), 270.

22   Peggy Dennis, *The Autobiography of an American Communist* (Westport CT: L. Hill, 1977), 225.

23   Al Richmond, *Long View from the Left: Memoirs of an American Revolutionary* (Boston: Houghton Mifflin, 1973), 369.

24 Howard Fast, "Man's Hope", *Daily Worker*, 12 June 1956; reprinted as "My Decision", *Mainstream* 10:3 (March 1957), 32.

25 Ibid.

26 The complexities of this power struggle are documented in David A. Shannon, *The Decline of American Communism: A History of the Communist Party of the United States since 1945* (New York: Harcourt, Brace & Company, 1959), 317–58; Joseph R. Starobin, *American Communism in Crisis, 1943–1975* (Berkeley: University of California Press, 1975), 224–30.

27 Malcolm MacEwan, "The Day the Party Had to Stop", in Ralph Miliband and John Saville (eds), *The Socialist Register 1976* (London: Merlin Press, 1976), 26.

28 See also Irving Howe and Lewis Coser, *The American Communist Party: A Critical History* (New York: Praeger, 1962), 491–2.

29 John Gates, *The Story of an American Communist* (New York: Nelson, 1958), 161.

30 Mickey Friedman, *A Red Family: Junius, Gladys, and Barbara Scales* (Urbana: University of Illinois Press, 2009), 86–7.

31 Healey and Isserman, *Dorothy Healey Remembers*, 164.

32 Letter, Peggy Dennis to Gus Hall, 7 June 1976, 1, copy in Morton Sobell papers, TAM 552, Box 7, Tamiment Library and Robert F. Wagner Labor Archives, New York University.

33 John Callaghan, *Cold War, Crisis and Conflict: The History of the Communist Party of Great Britain 1951–68* (London: Lawrence & Wishart, 2003), 62–4; John Saville, *Memoirs from the Left* (London: Merlin Press, 2003), 103–5.

34 Alison Macleod, *The Death of Uncle Joe* (London: Merlin Press, 1997), 52, 67, 76.

35 Ralph Miliband and John Saville (eds), *The Socialist Register 1976* (London: Merlin Press, 1976), 59. Thorez believed Khrushchev would soon be overthrown, as did (as we shall see) Australia's Ted Hill, who, like Dutt, learnt of the speech quickly.

36 Macleod, *Death of Uncle Joe*, 69.

37 *Daily Worker*, 19 March 1956, 1.

38 See Malcolm MacEwen, *The Greening of a Red* (London: Pluto Press, 1991).

39 Malcolm MacEwen, "The Day the Party Had to Stop", in Ralph Miliband and John Saville (eds), *The Socialist Register 1976* (London: Merlin Press, 1976), 26. Macleod estimates that more than 300 letters about Stalin were received; Macleod, *Death of Uncle Joe*, 75.

40 See CPGB Political Committee Minutes 1954–1991 (especially CP/CENT/PC/02/24–29) and CPGB Executive Committee Minutes and Papers 1943–1991 (especially CP/CENT/EC/03/24–26 and CP/CENT/EC/04/01–03), Archive of the Communist Party of Great Britain, Labour History Archive and Study Centre, Manchester, UK (henceforth CPGB Archive).

41 For evidence of the "sharp" inner-party debates within the CPGB occurring at this same time, see handwritten notes (by James Klugmann) attached to the Minutes of the Executive Committee Meeting of the CPGB on 12–13 May 1956; he referred to the "free and hard hitting discussion". Executive Committee Minutes and Papers, 1943–1991, CP/CENT/EC/03/24, CPGB Archive. See also *The Cult of the Individual. (The Controversy Within British Communism 1956–58)* (Belfast: British and Irish Communist Organisation, 1975); Socialist History Society, *The Communist Party and 1956* (London: SHS, 1993); Willie Thompson, *The Good Old Cause, British Communism 1920–1991* (London: Pluto Press, 1992); http://michaelrosenblog.blogspot.com.au/2014/02/how-did-british-communist-party-of-1957.html

42 Francis Beckett, *Enemy Within: The Rise and Fall of the British Communist Party* (London: Merlin Press, 1995), 135.

43 Doris Lessing, *Walking in the Shade: Volume 2 of My Autobiography, 1949 to 1962* (London: HarperCollins, 1998), 191, 192, 195. King Street, London, was the location of the CPGB headquarters.

44 See Phillip Deery, "The Sickle and the Scythe: Jack Blake and Communist Party 'Consolidation', 1949–56", *Labour History* 80 (2001), 215–23.

45 *Communist Review* 177 (September 1956), 302.
46 This section will focus only on the CPA, not the non-Stalinist far Left in Australia, whose adherents were miniscule in number, insignificant in influence, and dependant on overseas publications like *The Militant*. The small-circulation Trotskyist monthly newsletter, *The Socialist*, published in Sydney, delineated "between the Stalinist leadership of the Australian Communist Party and the communist rank and file...and working class militants". *The Socialist* 1:5 (December 1959), 5. However, it lasted only eight issues (July 1959 to April 1960). The largest group, in Melbourne, numbered only a dozen members. Hall Greenland, *Red Hot: The Life and Times of Nick Origlass* (Sydney: Wellington Lane Press, 1998), 208. However it should be noted that the events of 1956 propelled some young militants towards Trotskyism. Bob Gould was one; Denis Freney another. The latter began 1956 "a convinced Stalinist", and ended 1956 "a convert to Trotskyism". Denis Freney, *A Map of Days: Life on the Left* (Melbourne: William Heinemann, 1991), 92.
47 *Tribune*, 29 February 1956, 1–2.
48 "Soviet Union and Socialism", Talk No. 10, 13 March 1956, in "Voice of the Countryside" series, CPA Radio Broadcasts – 1953–1966, Mitchell Library, NSW [henceforth ML] MSS 5021 93 (155).
49 *Tribune*, 21 March 1956, 2. Sharkey continued to refer to the "Great Liars of the millionaire press", exclaiming "What a hell's brew from the sewers of the gutter press!" *Tribune*, 4 April 1956, 2.
50 In Hill's "Some impressions of the CPSU Congress" (*Tribune*, 4 April 1956, 6), Stalin's name was never mentioned.
51 Correspondence, Ralph Gibson to Jack Blake, 19 October 1986, ML MSS 5971/1/13. Gibson also commented, "What I didn't know till now was that the leadership had early knowledge of the authenticity of [Khrushchev's] report".
52 "Notes from meeting at New Theatre, Melbourne, 26 March 1956", National Archives of Australia, ACT [henceforth NAA]: A6119, 316.
53 Ibid.
54 Hill remained in the Soviet Union, where he underwent medical treatment for two months in a sanatorium thirty miles from Moscow, returned to Australia, via China, in September. See NAA: 6119/22, 344, folios 17 and 28 for ASIO phone intercepts concerning Russian doctors' reports of Hill's illnesses.
55 J.D. Blake papers, ML MSS 5971/1/10, Box 1/3, folder titled "Consolidation etc.". Amirah Inglis also confirmed that Hill wrote to the party leadership from Moscow, warning it of the allegations made about Stalin. Inglis, *Hammer and the Sickle*, p. 141.
56 E. Aarons, "The Congress and Ideological Work", *Communist Review* 173 (May 1956), 146–50.
57 See Dixon's report to the CPA City Section conference, 4–5 August 1956, NAA: A6119, 1715.
58 "Final lecture on 20th Congress of C.P.S.U.", 11 May 1956, NAA: A6119, 331.
59 "New South Wales Communist Party Twentieth Congress – Stalin", 14 April 1956, NAA: A6119, 344.
60 Undated typed document, J.D. Blake papers, ML MSS 5971/1/10 Box 1/3.
61 *New York Times*, 5 June 1956, 1, 6.
62 *Tribune*, 13 June 1956, 1. The article attempted to deflect discussion: the problem of Stalinism was limited to an analysis of the cult of the individual, which had been raised in the open sessions of the 20th Congress; see, for example, G.M. Malenkov, *Speech at the 20th Congress of the CPSU* (Moscow: Foreign Languages Publishing House, 1956), 9–10, in which he described the cult as a "distortion" and an "abnormality".
63 Ian Turner, "The Long Goodbye" in Leonie Sandercock and Stephen Murray-Smith (eds), *Room for Manoeuvre: Writings on History, Politics, Ideas and Play* (Melbourne: Drummond, 1982), 142.
64 John Sendy *Comrades Come Rally! Recollections of an Australian Communist* (Melbourne: Thomas Nelson, 1978), 100.

65 Geoff McDonald, *Australia at Stake* (Melbourne: Peelprint, 1977), 114.

66 Roger Millis, *Serpent's Tooth* (Ringwood: Penguin, 1984), 203.

67 Bernie Taft, *Crossing the Party Line: Memoirs of Bernie Taft,* (Melbourne: Scribe 1994), 92.

68 Inglis, *Hammer and the Sickle*, 139.

69 Len Fox, *Broad Left, Narrow Left* (Chippendale, APCOL, 1982), 145; Len Fox, *Australians on the Left* (Potts Point: Len Fox, 1996), 164.

70 Dorothy Hewett, *Wild Card: An Autobiography 1923–1958* (Ringwood: Penguin, 1990), 233.

71 *News and Views*, August 1956, in Stephen Murray-Smith Papers, Victorian State Library [henceforth VSL] MS 8272, Box 288/1–2. On the Doctors' Plot, see, *inter alia*, Jonathan Brent and Vladimir P. Naumov, *Stalin's Last Crime: The Plot Against the Jewish Doctors, 1948–1953* (New York: HarperCollins, 2003).

72 Audrey Blake, *A Proletarian Life* (Malmsbury: Kibble, 1984), 55. He had already been removed from the Central Committee Secretariat after the inner-party struggle in 1953–4. For Blake's important critique of Stalinism, first prompted by 1956, see J.D. Blake, *Revolution From Within* (Sydney: Outlook, 1971).

73 Peter S. Cook, *Red Barrister: A Biography of Ted Laurie QC* (Melbourne: La Trobe University Press, 1994), 126.

74 Sendy, *Comrades Come Rally!*, 101.

75 Eric Aarons, *What's Left* (Ringwood: Penguin, 1993), 116.

76 Cook, *Red Barrister*, 125.

77 Zoe O'Leary, *The Desolate Market: A Biography of Eric Lambert* (Sydney: Edwards & Shaw, 1974), 67.

78 Ian Turner, "The Long Goodbye", in Leonie Sandercock and Stephen Murray-Smith (eds), *Ian Turner: Room for Manoeuvre. Writings on History, Politics, Ideas and Play* (Melbourne: Drummond, 1982), 143.

79 *New York Times*, 19 January 1957, 10.

80 A party leader, W.J. Brown, did initially seek to encourage debate through a remarkable series of articles in the *Communist Review* (August, September and October) but was reprimanded by Hill and Sharkey and undertook self-criticism stating that his previous standpoint "was erroneous and I wish to repudiate this standpoint". *Tribune*, 24 October 1956, 2.

81 J. Staples, "Khrushchev on Stalin", ML MSS 2398 ADD-ON 813, Box KV7903.

82 Interview by John McLaren with Bill and Dorothy Irwin, 10 August 1985 (transcript in writer's possession).

83 Comment, ASIO field officer, 25 August 1956, NAA: A6119, 411.

84 "Statement on the Attitude of the Central Committee, Communist Party of Australia, to the Stalin Issue", Kenneth Gott Papers, VSL, MS 13047, Box 3768/7.

85 Similarly, Helen Palmer in Melbourne was expelled after announcing her intention to publish material designed to initiate discussion on democratic socialism. In June 1957, the first issue of *Outlook: An Australian Socialist Review*, which she edited, appeared. The British equivalent of *Outlook* was *The Reasoner*, produced by dissident party historians, especially E.P. Thompson and John Saville, from July to November 1956.

86 Interview by Ken Mansell with George Petersen, 28 April 1983, MLOH [Mitchell Library Oral History collection] 202/39. Petersen flirted with Trotskyism after 1956 before serving as a long-term Labor MLA in NSW.

87 NAA: A6119, 575; NAA: A6119, 2296 (see details of Sydney meetings in ASIO case files on John Malos, a dissenter); Bob Walshe, "1956 – Remembering and Reflecting", recording (2 cassettes), Sydney Branch, ASSLH, 18 May 2003 (in writer's possession); Bob Gould, "The Communist Party in Australian Life", *Labor Review* 34 (2001), 20–38 (for the Sydney cadres' meeting); Ralph Gibson, *The Fight Goes On* (Melbourne: Red Rooster Press, 1987), 213 (on the Melbourne meetings where "never did my exhortations have less effect").

Australian Communism in crisis – 1956 **39**

88 "Victoria. C.P. of A. Cadres Meeting", 19 November 1956, NAA: A6119, 344. It was at this cadres' meeting that Ted Hill said that party leaders deliberately encouraged rank and file members to believe the *New York Times* report to be a State Department forgery whilst knowing it to be authentic. Turner, "The Long Goodbye", 142–3.

89 L.L. Sharkey, "Report to the Central Committee", *Communist Review* 180 (December 1956), 395.

90 Cook, *Red Barrister*, 125.

91 Conversation with Bernie Taft, 2 March 2008. At the time, Taft, aware of Turner's philandering, rejected this, telling Hill: "I could show you a roomful of women to disprove that theory".

92 *Tribune*, 31 October 1956, 1.

93 *Tribune*, 7 November 1956, 1, 4; 14 November 1956, 2, 4; 21 November 1956, 3; 28 November 1956, 2, 3. As Eric Aarons noted, "The Party on the whole went along with these explanations, and so did I, despite my great discomfort". Aarons, *What's Left*, 120. E.W. Campbell was less equivocal: "Our Party leadership reacted correctly [in] supporting the Soviet Union's stand against counter-revolution". Handwritten notes [p. 55], CPA Records, ML MSS 5021 86 (155).

94 See *Tribune*, 21 November 1956, 8 ("Eric Lambert betrayed himself"); Zoe O'Leary, *The Desolate Market: A Biography of Eric Lambert* (Sydney: Edwards & Shaw, 1974), 71 and 70–5 for Lambert's letters from Budapest. Fryer joined Gerry Healy's Trotskyist group, the International Committee of the Fourth International (renamed the Socialist Labour League in 1959).

95 M. Adereth, *Line of March: Historical and Critical Analysis of British Communism and Its Revolutionary Strategy* (London: Praxis, 1994), 18. The overall membership loss in 1956 was approximately one third.

96 It was not, as customarily assumed, only the "intellectuals" who left; the West Como branch with predominately industrial workers in working-class Sydney was decimated, with only two members remaining. Alan Barcan, *The Socialist Left in Australia, 1949–1959* (Sydney: APSA, 1960), 15. Similarly, the CPGB lost leading trade unionists, such as John Horner and Laurence Daly.

97 Ian Turner, "My Long March", *Overland* 59 (Spring 1974), 40.

98 "On Revisionism: Statement by Communist Party Committee", *Guardian*, 17 July 1958, 8. For Turner's private response to this article, written by Ted Hill, see his letter to Bob [Gollan], 7 August 1958, copy in Stephen Murray-Smith Papers, VSL MS 8272, Box 291 (1–1); for Murray-Smith's response, in which he described Hill as dishonourable, despicable and spiteful, see letter to Mavis [Robertson] 22 July 1958, in ibid. Much to the chagrin of the CPA (*Guardian*, 17 July 1958, 8), on the same day the Melbourne *Herald* reported Turner's expulsion; see "Top Red Out of Party; Rift over Hungary", *Herald*, 17 July 1958, 2. Democratic centralism was a euphemism for top-down authoritarian decision-making. For an articulation of the concept, see E.F. Hill, "An Incorrect View of Party Democracy", *Communist Review* 180 (December 1956), 396–402.

99 Stephen Murray-Smith Papers, VSL MS 8272, Personal Papers: 1957–1958 [henceforth Murray- Smith Papers] Box 291 (1–1). He was also close to Eric Lambert and, arguably, was influenced by his interpretation of the Hungarian Uprising, conveyed in correspondence with Murray-Smith. O'Leary, *Desolate Market*, 77–8.

100 Letter, 23 October 1958, Murray-Smith Papers, Box 291 (1–1).

101 Letter, 26 October 1958, ibid.

102 Letter to Gwen [no surname], 22 July 1958, ibid.

103 See, for example, letter, 8 July 1957, Box 287.

104 See, for example, "Australian Newsletter", 17 October 1957, Box 288. That the party leadership did not "see it this way" was demonstrated by Sharkey's attack on revisionism at the April 1958 CPA Congress; see *Report of L.L. Sharkey, 18th Congress, April, 1958* (Sydney: Current Book Distributors, 1958), 38–44 (Part XII).

105 Letter to Bernie [no surname], 20 July 1958, Murray-Smith Papers, File 1, Box 6. Bernie was not persuaded; he replied (28 July): "Sometimes our right opinion is rejected, but in the end right prevails. Sometimes we hate to be criticised, but...we have to put up with it" [emphasis in original].

2

THE CURRENT OF MAOISM IN THE AUSTRALIAN FAR LEFT

Drew Cottle and Angela Keys

In the 1960s and 1970s, 'Australian Maoists' could be either members of the Communist Party of Australia (Marxist-Leninist) or non-members who shared a commitment to the struggle for an independent, socialist Australia. Maoists in Australia have been associated with militancy, and were arguably the most despised grouping within the Australian Far Left. They were most active in Victoria during the 1960s and 1970s. The Maoist social movement was a response to the existing order of life in Australia during that period. The Vietnam War and the existence of conscription for young Australian males influenced the heightened atmosphere and urgency for social change that characterised that era. Like others in the Far Left at the time, Australian Maoists began to question authority and the existing order. The revolution imagined by the Maoists took quite a different shape to that of other groupings of the Left. Maoists were influential among certain trade unions and on some university campuses. The Maoists were few in number but their impact was quite extraordinary in the 1960s and 1970s, and this caused some resentment and antagonism with other groups within the Australian Far Left. The Maoists were determined and dogmatic, and when it came to demonstrations and occupations they were not afraid to use violence, which they believed was ideologically justified. This chapter is about the trajectory of Maoism in Australia – how it came into being, the reasons for its establishment and growth, and its eventual decline.

The emergence of the Communist Party of Australia (Marxist-Leninist)

Australian communism, almost from the time of its foundation in 1920, had been aligned to the Communist Party of the Soviet Union. After Stalin's death in 1956 and Khrushchev's denunciation of the cult of Stalin's personality, the Soviet Union under Khrushchev sought a path of peaceful coexistence with the capitalist West and renounced revolutionary struggle throughout the world. The Chinese Communist Party saw this as a revisionist betrayal of Marxism-Leninism and socialist revolution internationally. China eventually split away from the Soviet camp to chart a new course devoted to socialist revolution. The Australian Communist Party (CPA) had, from the time of the liberation of China in 1949, sent over 100 of its members to People's China for extensive ideological training. From 1956 until the early 1960s, the leadership of the Australian Communist Party was confused and some began to question the Soviet Union's leadership of world communism.

Nikita Khrushchev's denunciation of Stalin, and his legacy, before the Soviet Communist Party Congress in February 1956 reverberated around the world. International communism was shaken to its foundations. In Australia, the Soviet leader's condemnation of Stalin's personality cult, led to resignations, expulsions, reassessments and new paths for Australian communism.[1] The Soviet military intervention into Hungary in October 1956 caused further ructions inside the Australian party. In the aftermath of Khrushchev's revelations, the leadership of the CPA was secretly divided, not only over the question of Stalin but also on Marxism-Leninism and Communist revolution. Communist China was openly critical of Khrushchev's vilification of Stalin and his policy of peaceful co-existence with Western imperialism instead of supporting revolutionary struggles in the Third World.[2]

By the early 1960s, CPA leaders remained divided over their loyalty to Soviet communism. Some sought greater ideological independence, increased internal democracy, a new, more open approach to the Australian Labor Party, and the parliamentary road to socialism. They never sought to break all ties with Moscow although there were moves to adopt a different course to Australian socialism free of the Soviet model, particularly after the Soviet intervention into Czechoslovakia in 1968.[3] Many of the CPA leaders who had received extensive training in Peoples' China during the 1950s were impressed by the methods of Chinese Communism.[4] However, the leaders of the CPA were not willing to renounce the achievements of the Soviet Union even though some questioned its future directions.

E.F. (Ted) Hill was the State Secretary of the Victorian Communist Party, and was also a member of the national Communist Party of Australia's Central Committee Secretariat. Hill, who had defended the Soviet position on Stalin in 1956, became increasingly critical of both the direction of the CPA and the Soviet Union. Within the CPA before and after the retirement of its long serving and ageing General Secretary, L.L. (Lance) Sharkey, there was a leadership struggle to be his successor. Ted Hill was a contender but ideologically isolated in Victoria whereas Laurie Aarons, from NSW, where the party was numerically strongest, was eventually elected General Secretary. During the acrimonious leadership struggle, Hill became a trenchant critic of the both the direction of the Soviet Union and the CPA.[5]

Although Hill had visited China several times on party matters, he had never been sent to China for extensive study and training, unlike many of his rivals for the leadership of the CPA. Due to China's fundamental criticisms of the Soviet Union's revisionism, Hill looked to China as the sole revolutionary beacon of international communism. Eventually, Hill, with several Communist trade union leaders and nearly sixty other comrades, almost all from Victoria, left the CPA and established their own communist party.

The emergence of the breakaway Communist Party of Australia (Marxist–Leninist) was not immediate but drawn out over three years from 1961 until 1964. Hill had first been removed from his position as Victorian State Secretary where he could and did exercise power and influence within the CPA.[6] The CPA's national leadership had initially kept Hill as a member of its expansive secretariat, where he remained isolated and outnumbered and was effectively politically neutralised. Members of Hill's 'Peking faction' had continued to attack and describe as 'revisionist' the leaders within the Victorian CPA and amongst its trade union followers. Two of Hill's closest associates, Flo(rence) Russell, the Victorian CPA's principal trade union supervisor and Duncan Clarke, the editor of the CPA's Victorian paper, *Guardian*, were expelled because of their open and continuing criticism of what they deemed the party's revisionist direction and ideology.[7]

The CPA national leadership of Sharkey, Dixon and Aarons believed they could contain the threat to party unity posed by the Hill faction. In their intra-party struggle against revisionism, Hill's group never won to their side even a minority of the Victorian CPA party members or affiliated trade union leaders. They virtually had no supporters from the CPA in the other states. An anti-Hill faction in the Victorian CPA led by its state executive members, Bernie Taft and H.K. Stanistreet and the academics Rex Mortimer and Alastair Davidson demanded the immediate expulsion of Hill and his associates. The Hill grouping's failure in the CPA's internal ideological and leadership struggle led to their departure, and their founding of the Communist Party of Australia (Marxist-Leninist).[8]

Hill argued that the founding of the miniscule Communist Party of Australia (Marxist-Leninist) in 1963–1964 was the re-constitution of Australian communism, not simply a split away from the existing CPA.[9] As a prominent Melbourne barrister specialising in compensation law, Hill had developed broad links with the organised labour movement in Victoria, unlike many of the paid functionaries of the CPA. Hill's CPA (M-L) was and remained partly open, but mostly secret. The secrecy of Hill's party, known as 'the Maoists', was entirely unlike the character and function of the CPA and the Trotskyist parties that also comprised the Australian Far Left in the 1960s and 1970s. The CPA (M-L) adopted this outlook and structure because it saw itself as an underground party of struggle, much like the Chinese Communist Party which operated clandestinely in the 'White Areas' under the control of the Kuomintang in China during the 1930s. Australia's Maoists also opposed the drug-taking culture that is often associated – rightly or wrongly – with the Australian Far Left during the 1960s and 1970s.[10]

Hill's understanding of the repressive power of the State was steeled in experience. He had been the legal representative of the CPA before the Victorian Royal Commission into Communism in 1947. He was the senior assisting counsel to the Opposition Labor leader, Dr H.V. (Bert) Evatt throughout the hearings of the Petrov Royal Commission in 1954, at the height of the Cold War in Australia. From the outset of his legal practice in the last years of the Great Depression in the 1930s, Hill had defended workers against the power of capital and the law in the courts. This service to the Party and the working class shaped Hill's outlook and also the structure of the CPA (M-L).[11] As a result of the political circumstances of its founding, the Party was secretive and conspiratorial. Unlike the CPA, which had paid full-time publically known officials and functionaries, public offices and bookshops in most states, party presses which published newspapers, journals and bulletins and maintained a network of branches in industries, suburbs and universities, the Hill group had few material resources, a tiny dedicated proletarian membership with virtually no base of popular support, who were concentrated in the industrial suburbs of Melbourne.[12]

Not until the 1970s did the CPA (M-L) have a visible and concrete public presence. Only then did they establish small bookshops in rented premises in central Melbourne, Sydney's Chinatown and later Adelaide. They sold English language books and magazines from revolutionary China, Chinese stamps, the party's weekly newspaper, *Vanguard*, and its theoretical journal, *Communist Review*. The bookshops were never seen nor used as 'revolutionary headquarters' where members would gather for party training or public meetings. For the first years of its existence, the party's survival in these conditions became the primary task, rather than its numerical increase or expanding its political influence.

In its earliest years, Hill was the public face of the CPA (M-L) and he remained its principal theoretician until his death in 1988. Later, the party's other 'public figures' became more publically prominent. There were militant labour leaders in Victoria: Paddy Malone and later Norm Gallagher of the Builders' Labourer's Federation; Clarrie O'Shea, the secretary of the Tramways Union, and Ted Bull of the Waterside Workers Federation.

By 1964, a functioning Maoist party in Australia existed. It looked East to China for revolutionary inspiration. This dawning of a new Communist party guided by Marxism-Leninism, and Mao-Tse Tung thought, was essentially the creation of Ted Hill whose inspiration was Communist China. Alone amongst the Australian Far Left, the Maoists, however crudely, did attempt to theorise an independent revolutionary road for Australia.[13] The CPA (M-L) defined themselves as true Marxist-Leninists and, as they understood it, only the East was Red.

The CPA (M-L), the Sino-Soviet split, and the wider Cold War context

Simplistically, the Hill grouping could be seen to be mechanically transferring their loyalties from their former bastion of Communism, the Soviet Union, to the new revolutionary beacon in the East, Mao's China. Their break from the CPA largely mirrored the Sino-Soviet split over the questions of revisionism and international revolution. These questions led to splits and schisms throughout the Communist world. The Albanian, Burmese, Ceylonese, Indonesian, Korean Laotian, Malayan, New Zealand and Japanese parties formally broke from the authority of Soviet Communism.[14] Other communist parties in Western Europe and Latin America endured divisions and separations. The split over the question of revisionism directly affected the communist international. Australian communism was never an isolated case of Antipodean exceptionalism. Nevertheless, in the Australian situation, there is a need to examine the context of the ideological struggle which drove Hill and other life-long communists out of the CPA and toward the example of revolutionary China.

The founding of Australian Maoism occurred at a crucial moment in the global Cold War. The Soviet Union and America had almost resulted in nuclear war when Castro's Cuba, threatened by American attempts at covert aggression, requested that Moscow install nuclear missiles on its soil for protection. In a divided Vietnam, the United States after President Kennedy's assassination had escalated its military commitment in an attempt to destroy the Vietnamese guerrilla forces fighting for national liberation. Throughout the Third World, liberation movements were emerging to struggle against imperialism. They looked to the Soviet Union or China for inspiration, support and assistance. People's China had been quarantined internationally by the American-led Free World after it finally 'stood up', as Mao put it, as an independent socialist country after 1949. An industrially under-developed China after the Korean War was militarily encircled and contained by American forces stationed in Japan, the Kuomintang-controlled Taiwan, and the Philippines, and through the ANZUS alliance with Australia and New Zealand. Maoist China had undergone a series of mass campaigns: the failed Great Leap Forward which attempted to diversify, intensify and localise industrial production and the relatively successful land collectivisation program through the commune system.[15]

As the split between the Soviet Union and China became wider and deeper, Soviet technical and scientific aid and assistance to its former fraternal ally was cancelled or withdrawn. Mao's leadership in the Chinese Communist Party was threatened and contested by rightist rivals who wanted to find either unity with the Soviet Union or to restore capitalism in China. An embattled Mao again turned to the masses, particularly the young, beyond the confines of party. He argued that there was a two line struggle between those who wanted both the restoration of capitalism and the preservation of the old China and the mass line of revolutionary struggle to build socialism. He declared that it was right to rebel against reactionaries. His appeals sparked the Great Proletarian Cultural Revolution. Spearheaded by the Red Guard youth, China was convulsed by a mass movement that sought to overthrow the Old Order.

When Hill's CPA (M-L) looked to China, it was at the beginnings of a revolutionary ferment led by the young. Everything was questioned. A new '*Fanshen*' was about to occur, where the revolutionary youth would turn the world upside down to follow the course of Mao. Hill believed that Maoist China was the revolutionary storm centre, the burning red banner of Marxism-Leninism.[16] Within this confluence of changing events in the global Cold War, Australia under the Prime Ministership of R.G. Menzies sent one thousand troops to Vietnam in April 1965. Washington never pressured Menzies or requested this military commitment to its Asian war. Menzies chose this course as one of his last acts as national leader.

Menzies' successor as Australian Prime Minister, Harold Holt, won the 1966 'Khaki Election' with a mandate to continue Australia's role in the Vietnam War. Holt had campaigned on the question of Australia's military commitment to the American War in Vietnam and a selective lottery-like form of military conscription. It was these events which had a direct bearing on both Hill's secretive Maoist sect and the radicalisation of a minority of a generation of young people, mainly university students, who sought revolutionary change. Organised student opposition to the American War in Vietnam and conscription began to stir at many of the university campuses.[17]

A case study of Maoist students: Monash University

Built by the federal government funding by the early 1960s, Monash University was a new, raw campus situated in Melbourne's eastern suburbs where its small student body grew increasingly rebellious. The members of Monash Labor Club which was formally aligned with the Labor Party and other Melbourne university student radicals were dismayed by the calamitous Labor Party defeat in the 1966 elections. Many had been attacked by the police during the peaceful protests against the visits of the president of South Vietnam, Marshall Ky, and later the US president, L.B. Johnson, which occurred weeks before the 1966 federal election. Increasingly they rejected the established Left methods of peaceful protest and working for change within the existing social and political system. They opposed Australia's military involvement in Vietnam and the imposition of selective military conscription. The Victorian government's decision to hang Ronald Ryan in 1967, despite a massive social protest against the death penalty, had an influence upon many students of that generation. Their radicalism was crystallised in the Monash Labor Club.[18]

When the Labor Party's Jim Cairns, militant unions, the CPA, church leaders and other university student organisations continued to hold peaceful demonstrations to end the Vietnam War, they were seen by many of the Monash Labor Club members as futile and merely symbolic. Within the Labor Club, Albert Langer, a Mathematics student, emerged as its leading radical activist. Langer and a growing number of other 'Monash radicals' at the time, including Michael Hyde, the then school teacher, Humphrey McQueen, and the ABC research officer and former Sydney University student pamphleteer, Darce Cassidy, began to look beyond the Labor Party, the straightjacket of parliamentary democracy and to the eventual removal of Australian military forces from the imperialist war in Vietnam.[19]

They wanted revolutionary solutions to the pressing problems of their time, not the bromide of reformist illusions. Langer was increasingly drawn to the example of the continuing revolutionary upsurge in China and the writings of Mao Tse Tung, particularly the concept of a guerrilla-protracted political warfare against the forces of imperialism. The Australian Maoists tried to apply this principle as a revolutionary method in all of their political struggles. Langer made contact with Hill, the leader of the CPA (M-L). Hill and the Maoist union militants, Clarrie O'Shea and Ted Bull, addressed student meetings convened by the Monash Labor Club about the Vietnam War and the class war in Australia. A collective decision was made to establish a 'revolutionary headquarters' of the Labor Club off-campus, at a rented dwelling at Jasmine Street, in South Caulfield. Later, other 'revolutionary centres' at the Bakery and Alice's Restaurant in Prahran replaced the 'Caulfield Cong'. At these places, social functions, planning sessions and political discussions occurred where young workers, high school students and radical Monash students fraternised.[20]

From these centres of radical activism was borne the Worker-Student Alliance (WSA) which would number nearly 500 members across metropolitan Melbourne by the late 1960s. WSA was a broad united front for the development of mass street action, student activism and factory organisation. The WSA was intended to unite workers and students in radical political activism. It sought to apply the CPA (M-L) strategies to immediate concrete situations. It was meant to develop 'revolutionary consciousness' through each of 'the people's struggles'. Many of the Monash radicals – increasingly influenced by Langer, the Vietnam War and the Cultural Revolution in China – began to identify themselves as Maoists. In contrast, radical students at other universities throughout Australia were influenced by Trotskyist, Guevarist and anarchist ideas. In the period from 1965 to 1970, Maoism at Monash was the dominant political tendency amongst students.[21]

Few of the Monash Maoists joined the CPA (M-L). Langer, after his student days at Monash, later became a Vice-President of the party. Three decades passed before Michael Hyde, another prominent Monash Maoist, claimed he had been an 'M-L'. The Monash Maoists were never the creation nor the instrument of the CPA (M-L). While Hill praised their rebellious spirit in their struggle against the Vietnam War, the student Maoists at Monash and later La Trobe and Flinders universities were not CPA (M-L) cadre, even though some later joined the Maoist party. Their Maoism was one manifestation of the revolutionary romanticism which was characteristic of the student New Left world-wide in the late 1960s and early 1970s. Their Maoism was inspired by the revolutionary struggle of the Vietnamese people against American imperialism. They idealised the Great Proletarian Cultural Revolution in People's China. Their opposition to Australia's military support for the Vietnam War, and military conscription, became increasingly militant. The student Maoists at Monash and later La Trobe and Flinders and the University of New South Wales, like other student radicals began to question and to rebel against the workings of Australian capitalism.[22]

Understanding the Maoist student movement

When Hill established the Party, it was miniscule, and it was primarily limited to expelled members of the Communist Party who followed Hill in creating the CPA (M-L). The members of the breakaway party were seasoned workers. A major change occurred when students became attracted to Maoism. Many students identified themselves as 'Maoists', but never became formal members of the secretive CPA (M-L). Maoism in the 1960s and 1970s became a broader social movement and extended beyond formal party membership. Students who identified as Maoists did not ask about the secretive party membership because they were likely to be viewed with suspicion and suspected of being police agents.

The Maoists were not Beijing's representatives in Australia, nor did they see themselves in that way. They wanted to bring about revolutionary change in Australia. They saw Australian capitalism as being dependent and dominated by foreign imperialism. They adopted a Third Worldist perspective to the Australian situation. One of the key arguments of the Maoists was that Australia had never achieved national independence. Australia had always been dependent on Imperial Britain and, in the post-Second World War period, Australia became dependent upon the United States. For the Maoists, the national question for Australia remained unresolved. By the 1960s, foreign ownership and control of Australia's economic sectors were dominated by multinational corporations, the majority of which were American. By the late 1960s, this question of foreign ownership and control of Australia was a critical one. Australia was the site of American war bases or 'joint facilities', which indicated another level of Australia's abject dependency.[23] This also led to the Maoists investigating Australia's past history, and what was highlighted was the resistance by Aboriginal Australians to colonial settlement and other forms of 'people's resistance' to foreign domination into the present. The flag of stars of the Eureka rebels of 1854, rather than the worker's red flag, became the Maoist symbol of the struggle for national independence. Other parties of the Left condemned the Maoists as nationalists and populists for considering these national issues and seizing the Eureka flag as a symbol of struggle. The other parties of the Far Left argued that there needed to be an international struggle for socialist revolution, and the Maoists were criticised for advocating a people's struggle for national independence.[24]

The Maoists and the penal powers struggle

By the early 1970s Australia was experiencing the end of the long post-war boom, as well as the difficulties of its involvement in the American War in Vietnam. A major problem for the organised working class was the industrial legislation known as the 'penal powers', which effectively outlawed any kind of strike action taken independently by workers or trade unions. The Menzies government had introduced the penal powers in the early 1950s to break the power of wharf-labourers. The penal clauses virtually ensured that every industrial dispute had to be settled through arbitration.

The Victorian Tramways Union had been penalised for taking industrial action and not agreeing to the arbitration of its disputes. The secretary of the Victorian Tramways Union and member of the CPA (M-L), Clarrie O'Shea, resolved that the union would not pay the fines imposed upon it through the penal powers. He was imprisoned for his refusal. A number of 'rebel unions' in the Victorian labour movement supported the refusal by O'Shea, and when he was imprisoned, these unions called for a widespread strike by all workers to support the campaign to free O'Shea and break the penal powers. Tens of thousands of workers across Australia responded to the call by striking in support of O'Shea's defiance of the penal powers. Although the gaoled representative of a small union, O'Shea's stand as a leading Maoist militant represented a challenge to trade union officialdom, which had tended to abide by the rulings of the arbitration system and accepted the penal power provisions. The gaoling of O'Shea in May 1969 provoked a massive strike wave across Australia. Few of those on strike waited for trade union approval for their action. The Worker-Student Alliance organised mass rallies and protests against the penal powers and the gaoling of Clarrie O'Shea. Eventually, after this spontaneous mobilisation of striking workers supported by students, O'Shea was freed and his fines were paid anonymously.

The period from 1969 to 1972 in Australia saw the occurrence of numerous strikes in all industries in defiance of the penal powers and the arbitration system. These mass struggles by workers resulted in significant wage increases and other gains. They demonstrated the power of the working class in the struggle against capital. While the arbitration system had been adhered to from 1952 to 1969, there had effectively been a brake on industrial action, and minimal wage rises. The occurrence of strikes during 1969 to 1972 caused many workers to recognise their own power, and the fear of the penal powers dissipated.[25]

The Maoists and the Builders' Labourers Federation: Black Bans, Green Bans and Norm Gallagher

The 'Green Bans' struggle in Sydney is remembered as one of the most significant achievements of the Australian Far Left, and was a campaign which united communities with union members. Jack Mundey, the NSW State Secretary of the Builders' Labourers Federation (BLF) and a member of the CPA Central Committee, imposed 'Green Bans' to stop work by property developers and saved working-class housing in Sydney's inner suburbs of The Rocks, Glebe and Woolloomooloo, as well as bushland in Sydney. BLF members in NSW banned all work on these sites after Mundey responded to resident action group's pleas to save their suburbs.[26]

However, it is often forgotten that while the Green Bans movement was occurring in Sydney, the BLF in Victoria was imposing 'Black Bans' on vacant and historical sites and working-class housing. The actions of the BLF in Melbourne saved the Victoria Market, the Melbourne City Baths, the Regent Theatre, Mac's Hotel and the Windsor Hotel.[27] The Black Bans in Victoria were smaller in number and significance, but they have been overshadowed by the more prominent Green Bans campaign in Sydney.

Where the Victorian BLF was influenced by the CPA (M-L), the NSW BLF was aligned to the CPA, and a significant rivalry existed between the two union branches. After Paddy Malone's death in 1970, the BLF in Victoria under the new leadership of Norm Gallagher was effectively the only industrial bastion of radical Maoism in Australia. The deep ideological hatreds between Jack Mundey and Norm Gallagher were a part of the intra-union struggle in the 1970s. In 1974, Gallagher, who was the National and Victorian Secretary of the BLF, controversially intervened in the CPA-controlled branch of the NSW BLF.

Gallagher and a group of Maoist building workers seized control of NSW BLF office and expelled the CPA-affiliated officials of the union. The Green Bans of the BLF had won immense popular support amongst many inner city residents of Sydney and Gallagher's takeover of the NSW BLF was damned as Maoist thuggery. Physical fights between builder's labourers from either the Maoist or CPA factions occurred on many large city construction sites in Sydney. While the Maoist intervention by Gallagher is often dismissed as an unjustified demonstration of power, it also represented the depth of the ideological enmity between the CPA and the Maoists whose power base in the unions was threatened by the popularity of Mundey's Green Bans.[28]

At BLF mass meetings in Sydney during the Green Bans campaign, Sydney residents, who were not members of the BLF, addressed the workers and often voted on the imposition of the Green Bans. Traditionally, it had been the case that only trade union members were permitted to vote in trade union meetings and on matters relating to the union. It was an extraordinary departure from trade union protocols to have non-union members voting and influencing the decisions of the union. This issue is often overlooked in accounts of the BLF's intra-union power struggle.

The Maoists and the era of the Whitlam government

In 1974, there had been a 'Long March' organised by the Maoists from Sydney, Melbourne and Adelaide to the American military base located at North-West Cape in remote Western Australia. This act of protest sought to highlight Australia's lack of independence and to challenge the American military presence within Australia.[29]

Once the Whitlam Labor government came to power, there was a growing demand for Australian culture to be promoted and government policies aimed to achieve this. Whitlam established the Australian Film and Television School as part of the zeitgeist of this emerging new nationalism. The Maoists sought to promote a form of progressive and radical nationalism that was based upon the notion of the people's struggle. To this end, the Maoists produced books and magazines which explored Aboriginal resistance to colonial settlement, examined the stories of bushrangers and other Australian outlaws, and explained the Eureka rebellion and other workers' struggles.[30] Other parties of the Australian Left criticised the Maoists for their nationalist focus, and emphasised that nationalism was regressive, reactionary and backward. Members of the Left who opposed the Maoists reminded them that 'the workers have no country', as 'the workers must win their country'. The Maoists, however, viewed themselves as internationalists who followed Mao's dictum to 'keep the country in heart and the world in mind'.

Victorian-based organisations such as the Worker-Student Alliance (WSA), the Australian Independence Movement (AIM), Students for Australian Independence (SAI), and People for Australian Independence (PAI), were influenced by the Maoists, but were not orchestrated or overseen by the CPA-ML. Some groups within the Australian Left denounced these organisations as Maoist fronts or flunkies. However, WSA, AIM, SAI and PAI were broadly united with the CPA-ML because they espoused arguments for Australian independence and socialism.[31]

These organisations emerged and mobilised in response to the 1975 Constitutional Coup which saw the Whitlam government ousted by the Governor-General, John Kerr, who used reserve powers to legitimise the sacking of Whitlam.[32] For some Australians, the Coup represented a pivotal moment in their political awakening. The extraordinary action taken by Kerr to dismiss a democratically elected national government prompted mass protests and outrage on the part of many Australians.

Even after the Coup and the subsequent election of the Fraser government, protests against Kerr continued until his unusually early retirement from office. The actions of the Australian Left generally and others among the population who protested the Coup were focused on a call to 'Sack Kerr' and reinstate the Whitlam government. The Maoists, in contrast, waved banners bearing the slogans: 'Away With All Colonial Relics' and 'Independence for Australia'. The Maoists never argued for the reinstatement of Whitlam, but viewed the Coup as exposing the problems of the Australian political system.

The Maoists viewed the Coup as the final act in the destabilisation of the Whitlam government, which had sought to develop a more independent foreign policy and was seeking ways to assume greater Australian ownership and control of energy sources. Whitlam had threatened to name the CIA operatives working in Australia, and was contemplating whether to renew the lease agreements for the American military bases or 'joint facilities' on Australian soil.[33]

The Coup was viewed by the Maoists as a direct American intervention to destabilise and oust the Whitlam government. Key to this interpretation of the events of the Coup was the role of Marshall Green, who was appointed the US Ambassador to Australia in early 1973. Green had a reputation as a CIA 'Coup Master', and had been involved in destabilisation which had resulted in coups in South Korea, Indonesia, Greece, and Chile. In the context of the Cold War, the independent path taken by the Whitlam government was troubling for Washington. It has been suggested that a destabilisation campaign against the Whitlam government was orchestrated by the CIA's secretive Task Force 157, and that a cable from CIA agent, William Shackley, delivered the day before the Coup, had

52 Drew Cottle and Angela Keys

urged ASIO to act against the Whitlam government.[34] The Coup was an important incident in the Maoists' understanding of Australia as a nation dependent upon and servile to American interests.

The Maoists and campaigns on the cultural front

The principal demand of the Maoists was for Australian independence, and one of the channels through which this was pursued was culture. Post-1975 there was an effort by the Maoists to wage campaigns on the cultural front. Australia's Maoists sought to follow the credo of Mao by 'listening to the masses', and 'being at one with the people'. Mao had argued in China that it was essential to have the support of the masses. Australian Maoists were similarly inspired, and sought to wage campaigns to build connections and links with Australians who were members of the working class. Australian workers, small business people and small farmers were viewed as important by the Maoists in their attempts to build a social movement. The Maoists sought to 'narrow the target and broaden the base', by which they aimed to create a mass movement focused on achieving Australian independence from foreign domination.[35]

As part of their campaigns on the cultural front, the Maoists organised a cultural festival on the 100th anniversary of the death of the Australian bushranger, Ned Kelly. The Maoists saw Ned Kelly as a folk hero, a rebel who defied authority. The Maoists were also involved in organising the Carcoar Ben Hall Festival to commemorate the bushranger, Ben Hall, in the town where he had been killed by the police. During the post-1975 era, the Maoists published a monthly magazine called *The Independent Australian*, and various free weekly newspapers including *The People's Voice*, and *Independent Voice*. From their involvement in Maoist-influenced United Front organisations, some former students in this period became the authors of works which together formed a growing radical intellectual scholarship. These works investigated aspects of Australian politics, history and culture that challenged the prevailing academic orthodoxy, which had largely adhered to the official colonial discourses on these matters.[36]

Maoist students at Flinders University formed the folk-rock band, Redgum, whose music gave expression to the struggles of the Australian people, and workers in particular. Redgum musicians performed at building construction sites as well as rented community halls and other venues in Adelaide, Melbourne and Sydney, and released two albums. Maoist slogans used in the music of the Redgum group included 'If You Don't Fight, You Lose', and 'Dare to Struggle, Dare to Win'. Another Australian folk band with Maoist links was The Bushwhackers. They performed at folk concerts throughout Australia, and had greater commercial success than Red Gum. The Bushwhackers performed songs about bushrangers and the struggles of the poor in rural, colonial Australia.[37]

The Maoists were instrumental in the establishment of the community radio station, 3CR, which continues to broadcast from Melbourne today. This was the first community radio station to be established in Australia. At the height of Maoist involvement with the radio station during the 1970s, the station provided a voice for sections of the population marginalised or unheard of on commercial broadcasters: women, prisoners, migrants, environmentalists, Palestinians, building construction workers, local musicians and members of Australia's Indigenous peoples. The community radio station was run by volunteers, many of whom had been radicalised during their time as university students in the 1960s and 1970s.[38]

Maoist and Trotskyist rivalries within the Australian Far Left

Trotskyism barely had a political presence in Australia until the late 1930s, when a small number of former CPA members, repelled by the Hitler–Stalin pact and the Moscow show-trials, joined Nick Origlass, a Balmain ironworker, to form the Communist League of Australia, the Australian section of the Fourth International, Leon Trotsky's international organisation of anti-Stalinist Marxist revolutionaries.

Trotskyism only emerged as a significant force of the Australian Far Left from the early 1960s, after the CPA was shaken by Khrushchev's denunciation of Stalin and the events in Hungary in 1956. The instigators of the Trotskyist parties were mainly university students radicalised by the war in Vietnam who linked with existing Trotskyist parties in Europe, Britain or the United States. By the late 1960s, the Trotskyists were a major presence within the Far Left, primarily in Sydney, who competed with the CPA and the Maoists for members and support among university students.

The mutual hatred of the Trotskyists and Maoists for each other was not simply over ideological differences.[39] The Maoists were seen by Trotskyists as ignorant, dogmatic Stalinist thugs, prone to violence and lost to the quest of reactionary nationalism. Maoists denounced Trotskyists as police agents, full of talk about the need to build the international socialist revolution, wreckers or cowards. In a 1970 *Vanguard* article, Trotskyism was condemned as an apolitical diversion in its promotion of drug-taking, sex-obsession, homosexuality and pop culture.[40]

Maoist students were known to resort to physical violence against 'Trotskyites' in demonstrations and on campus. At Flinders University in 1972 Maoists bashed Trotskyist paper-sellers. Maoist activists at the gates of car plants in Adelaide and Melbourne jostled and punched Trotskyist speakers and paper-sellers. A Trotskyist activist was beaten unconscious by a student Maoist after a rowdy meeting at La Trobe University in 1977. In 1978, Maoist students threw another Trotskyist student through a plate glass window at La Trobe University. Maoists often attacked Trotskyist activists at union rallies. Maoist demonstrations often involved violent confrontations with the police. Maoists destroyed the Nazi Party headquarters in Carlton after a mass rally at the Yarra River in Melbourne was called to protest their activities. Trotskyists condemned this act of 'people's violence against fascism'.[41] The Maoists were arguably the most divisive grouping of the Australian Far Left in the 1960s and 1970s.

The CPA (M-L) and China

Hill and the CPA (M-L) looked to China for revolutionary inspiration. China was seen as the beacon of Marxism-Leninism. The party that Hill founded was devoted to People's China, whatever its change of political line. The Australian Maoists did not have any close ties to communist parties overseas except for their relations with China. Hill made innumerable trips to China to meet leading officials in a virtually ongoing pilgrimage. Hill demonstrated a devotion to China that was reflected in all of his theoretical writings, and this would prove to be a major obstacle and failing of the party. Mao's China was largely underdeveloped, unindustrialised and peasant-based in contrast to industrialised Australia. The problem of following China as one of the few examples of communism in practice was particularly evident after 1966, when China was subject to radical political changes. The Australian Maoists idealised and romanticised the Chinese example.

From the late 1970s, the various struggles for Australian independence from foreign domination had either faltered or were petering out. The revolutionary elan of Mao's China virtually disappeared in Australia after Mao's death. With the ousting of the Gang of Four in 1978, all vestiges of Mao's China, as was imagined of Australian Maoists, rapidly disappeared. With the coming of Deng Xiao-Peng, capitalism was almost restored overnight in China. China was opened to foreign investment in a form of 'Market-Leninism', where the Party dominated the state.

The Australian Maoists were ideologically linked to the trajectory of China. There was an idealisation of the revolutionary achievements of China amongst the Party, which ultimately became problematic, particularly with the radical redirection of China's foreign policy. This redirection left Maoists in Australia dismayed, disenchanted, divided and in decline.

Conclusion

One of the crucial aspects of the Australian Maoists was that they had broken away from an existing party. Most other Maoist formations in, for example, Latin America, the United States, India and Europe, were overwhelmingly comprised of radicalised students who, inspired by Mao, established their own party. The Australian Maoists were exceptional because they were formed by a group of disillusioned Communist Party members.

In a book published posthumously, Ted Hill, almost as a self-criticism, explained that party he had founded had, in its early period, too often acted as a propaganda group mechanically following Chinese Communist Party decisions and statements. This 'worship of the foreign' by Australian communists had been encouraged by the Soviet Party through the Comintern, whereas Mao Tse Tung insisted that it was the responsibility of communists in their country to work out the correct revolutionary theory for that country.[42] Only later, from the mid-1970s, did Hill's writings begin to develop an independent revolutionary theory for Australia. Hill died in 1988.

The Maoists' influence among the Builders' Labourers Federation in the 1970s was well recognised. When the prices and incomes 'Accord' was introduced in 1983, the union movement was restructured and the BLF, as a dissident union, was 'disciplined and at times excluded from the benefits the system delivered'.[43] The Accord signalled the end of the renegade, guerrilla actions of the BLF to stop work and take radical protest activities. The BLF was deregistered in the mid-1980s and members of the union were effectively blacklisted from the construction industry.[44] The destruction of the BLF was a significant blow for the CPA (M-L).

The Maoists represented a radical moment in the history of the Australian Far Left. They arose at a time of radical social change, and, in some ways, they were representative of that social change. They represented the rebellion of the young against the existing social order, the parliamentary system and the War in Vietnam. They were committed to changing Australia into a more independent country based on social equality. They were a rebellious fraction of the Australian Far Left.

There are a number of factors which explain the appeal that Mao's China held for this small group of Australian Maoists, and it was not simply a case of China's proximity to Australia. The Great Proletarian Revolution in China was an inspiring example for these Australian radicals – whether they were members of the CPA (M-L) or students associated with the party – and it occurred at a time when the Soviet Union's policy of peaceful coexistence with world capitalism was creating disillusionment for some among the Australian Far Left. China appeared to be achieving an idealised people's revolution at a time when the Soviet Union was seemingly abandoning a revolutionary road. After the Hungarian Uprising in particular, it was increasingly difficult for those on the Left to ignore criticisms of the Soviet Union, and, in contrast, China was viewed by some as a beacon of revolution. For Maoist students in Australia, China's revolution was an inspiration during a time when they opposed military conscription and the war in Vietnam, but found they could do little to alter Australia's involvement in that war. Like many nations that experienced a radical student movement in the 1960s and 1970s, Australia also experienced the decline of that radicalism by the late 1970s. Australia's Maoist student movement dissipated, and the CPA (M-L) remains a secretive party today.

Notes

1 W.J. Brown (1986) *The Communist Movement and Australia: An Historical Outline – 1890s to 1980s*, Haymarket, New South Wales: Australian Labor Movement Publications, p. 261; E.F. Hill (1989) *Communism and Australia: Reflections and Reminiscences*, Fitzroy, Victoria: Communist Party of Australia (Marxist-Leninist), pp. 118–124.
2 A.B. Davidson (1964) 'The Effects of the Sino-Soviet Dispute on the Australian Communist Party', *The Australian Quarterly*, 26(3), p. 67.
3 Alastair Davidson (1969) *The Communist Party of Australia: A Short History*, Stanford, California: Stanford Hoover Institution Press.
4 Jon Piccini (2013) '"Light from the East": Travel to China and Australian Activism in the "Long Sixties"', *The Sixties: A Journal of History, Politics and Culture*, 6(1), pp. 25–44;

Angus Macintyre (1978) 'The Training of Australian Communist Cadres in China, 1951–1961', *Studies in Comparative Communism*, 11(4), pp. 410–23.

5 Justus M. Van Der Kroef (1970) 'Australia's Maoists', *Journal of Commonwealth Political Studies*, 8(2), pp. 87–116; E.F. Hill (1989) *Communism and Australia: Reflections and Reminiscences*, pp. 118–124.

6 Justus M. Van Der Kroef (1970) 'Australia's Maoists', pp. 87–116; Justus M. Van Der Kroef (1974) 'Australian Communism: The Splintering Prism', *Journal of International Affairs*, 28(2), January 1, pp. 207–208.

7 Justus M. Van Der Kroef (1970) 'Australia's Maoists', p. 94.

8 Justus M. Van Der Kroef (1970) 'Australia's Maoists', pp. 87–116. On this matter, Humphrey McQueen has argued that the CPA (M-L) split from the CPA in 1963–64 because it saw itself as the mirror image of the old party not over the question of revisionism versus revolution. It was a fight between essentially two revisionist positions. This overlooks the kind of party Hill formed in its fraught political context. Never was the old CPA as closed, secretive or as doctrinaire as the CPA (M-L) would be and remained. See Humphrey McQueen (1970) 'Some Comments on "Australia's Maoists"', *Journal of Commonwealth Political Studies*, 17(1), July, p. 68.

9 Justus M. Van Der Kroef (1970) 'Australia's Maoists', pp. 87–116.

10 See for example: Anonymous (1972) '"Goddam the Pusherman!"': Oppose the "Drug Culture"!', pamphlet produced by Communist Party of Australia (Marxist-Leninist), Melbourne. A copy of the pamphlet is held by the National Library of Australia.

11 E.F. Hill (1989) *Communism and Australia: Reflections and Reminiscences*, pp. 1–29.

12 E.F. Hill (1989) *Communism and Australia: Reflections and Reminiscences*, pp. 105–117; Justus M. Van Der Kroef (1970) 'Australia's Maoists', pp. 87–116; Nick Knight (1998) 'The Theory and Tactics of the Communist Party of Australia (M-L)', *Journal of Contemporary Asia*, 28(2), pp. 239–241.

13 E.F. Hill (1989) *Communism and Australia: Reflections and Reminiscences*, pp. 166–175.

14 Justus M. Van Der Kroef (1970) 'Australia's Maoists', pp. 87–116; Nick Knight (1998) 'The Theory and Tactics of the Communist Party of Australia (M-L)', pp. 236–239.

15 Malcolm H. Murfett (2012) *Cold War Southeast Asia*, Singapore: Marshall Cavendish International.

16 Nick Knight (1998) 'The Theory and Tactics of the Communist Party of Australia (M-L)', pp. 235–240.

17 Mick Armstrong, 'The Radicalisation of the Campuses, 1967–74', *Marxist Interventions* (archive website of the online journal, Marxist Interventions) <www.anu.edu.au/pols ci/marx/interventions/students.htm>

18 Daniel Robins (2005) 'Melbourne's Maoists: The Rise of the Monash University Labor Club, 1965–1967', unpublished Honours thesis, School of Social Sciences, Faculty of Arts, Victoria University, pp. 20–35. <www.lastsuperpower.net/Members/dmelberg/m elbmaoists>; Mick Armstrong, 'The Radicalisation of the Campuses, 1967–74'.

19 Daniel Robins (2005) 'Melbourne's Maoists: The Rise of the Monash University Labor Club, 1965–1967', pp. 30–35.

20 Daniel Robins (2005) 'Melbourne's Maoists: The Rise of the Monash University Labor Club, 1965–1967', pp. 35–49.

21 Ken Mansell (1994) 'The Yeast Is Red', unpublished Master of Arts thesis, Department of History, University of Melbourne, pp. 85–90; Ken Mansell (2011) 'A Critical Review', [Review of the book *All Along the Watchtower – Memoir of a Sixties Revolutionary* by Michael Hyde], Reason in Revolt: Source Documents of Australian Radicalism. <www.reasoninrevolt.net.au/objects/pdf/d0891.pdf>

22 Mick Armstrong, 'The Radicalisation of the Campuses, 1967–74'.

23 Anonymous (2016) 'US Military Bases in Australia – Pine Gap – The Campaign Continues', pamphlet produced by Spirit of Eureka, September, pp. 7–19; Anonymous (1975) *Builders' Labourers' Song Book*, Camberwell, Victoria: Widescope International Publishers in association with the Australian Building Construction Employees' and Builders' Labourers' Federation, pp. 188–194.

24 See the discussion on 'Nationalism: A Road to the Right' in 'Chapter 10: Issue on the left' in Tom O'Lincoln (1993) *Years of Rage: Social Conflicts in the Fraser Era*, Melbourne, Victoria: Bookmarks Australia. <www.anu.edu.au/polsci/marx/interventions/years/10issues.htm>

25 Katie Wood (2013) 'Fighting Anti-union Laws: The Clarrie O'Shea Strikes', *Marxist Left Review*, No. 5, Summer. <http://marxistleftreview.org/index.php/no5-summer-2013/87-fighting-anti-union-laws-the-clarrie-oshea-strikes>

26 Meredith Burgmann and Verity Burgmann (2011) 'Green Bans Movement', *Dictionary of Sydney*. <http://dictionaryofsydney.org/entry/green_bans_movement>

27 Norm Wallace (2013) 'Revisiting the Past, Renewing the Present', *The Builders Labourers Federation 'Never Powerless': Lessons for the 21st Century*, 14 September. <www.spirito feureka.org/index.php/resources/the-builders-labourer-federation-qnever-p owerlessq-lessons-for-the-21st-century>

28 Meredith Burgmann and Verity Burgmann (2011) 'Green Bans Movement'; Anonymous (2011) 'The Green Bans that Saved Sydney', *New Matilda*, 19 July. <https://newmatilda.com/2011/07/19/green-bans-saved-sydney/>

29 Anonymous (2016) 'US Military Bases in Australia – Pine Gap – The Campaign Continues', pamphlet produced by Spirit of Eureka, September, pp. 7–19.

30 See, for example: Anonymous (1975) *Builders' Labourers' Song Book*; Tom O'Lincoln (1993) *Years of Rage: Social Conflicts in the Fraser Era*.

31 See 'Nationalism: A Road to the Right' in 'Chapter 10: Issue on the Left' in Tom O'Lincoln (1993) *Years of Rage: Social Conflicts in the Fraser Era*.

32 Nick Beams, Greg Adler, Lynn Grey, Derek Moore and Allan Harris (1976) *The Canberra Coup! A Documentary on the Sacking of the Labor Government*, November 11, 1975, Waterloo, New South Wales: Maxwell Printing.

33 Nick Beams, Greg Adler, Lynn Grey, Derek Moore and Allan Harris (1976) *The Canberra Coup! A Documentary on the Sacking of the Labor Government*, November 11, 1975.

34 'The CIA in Australia: Part 2', Watching Brief, Public Radio News Services (October–November 1986) transcript of radio documentary. <www.serendipity.li/cia/cia_oz/cia_oz2.htm>; Nick Beams, Greg Adler, Lynn Grey, Derek Moore and Allan Harris (1976) *The Canberra Coup! A Documentary on the Sacking of the Labor Government*, November 11, 1975, pp. 76–79; Phillip Frazer (1984) 'Dirty Tricks Down Under: Did the CIA Topple the Australian Government?', *Mother Jones*, February–March, pp. 13–20; 44–72.

35 See for example: 'Chapter Eight: Aspects of Australia's Independence and Dependence' in E.F. Hill (1977) *The Great Cause of Australian Independence*. <www.marxists.org/his tory/erol/australia/hill-great-cause/index.htm>

36 Some of these former Maoist students who became radical authors included Humphrey McQueen, Michael Dunn, Barry York and Fergus Robinson.

37 See 'Chapter 2: Oz Rock and the Ballad Tradition in Australian Popular Music', in Jon Stratton (2007) *Australian Rock: Essays on Popular Music*, Perth, Western Australia: Network Books.

38 Anonymous (2016) *Radical Radio: Celebrating 40 Years of 3CR*, Fitzroy, Victoria: McPherson's Printing Group and 3CR Community Radio.

39 See for example: Anonymous (1972) 'Trotskyism and Revisionism: Teachers by Negative Example', pamphlet produced by Communist Party of Australia (Marxist-Leninist), Melbourne. A copy of the pamphlet is held by the National Library of Australia.

40 Anonymous (1970) 'Youth Are The Most Vigorous Force In The Revolutionary Movement', *Vanguard*, June 24, p. 4.

41 Anonymous (1972) 'Action Against Nazis Is Correct', *Vanguard*, June 22, p. 5.

42 E.F. Hill (1989) *Communism and Australia: Reflections and Reminiscences*, pp. 137–138.

43 Liz Ross (2004) *Dare to Struggle, Dare to Win! Builders Labourers Fight Deregistration, 1981–1984*, Melbourne: Vulgar Press, cited in David Peetz and Janis Bailey (2011) 'Neoliberal Evolution and Union Responses in Australia', in Gregor Gall, Adrian Wilkinson and Richard Hurd (eds) *International Handbook on Labour Unions: Responses to Neo-liberalism*,

Cheltenham: Edward Elgar, pp. 62–81. A pre-publication copy of the Peetz and Bailey chapter is available online: <http://www98.griffith.edu.au/dspace/bitstream/handle/10072/42399/75405_1.pdf?sequence=1>

44 David Renton (2004) 'A Review of the Book *Dare to Struggle, Dare to Win! Builders Labourers Fight Deregistration, 1981–1984*', *Labour History*, 87, November, pp. 281–282. A copy of the review is reproduced on the book publishers' website: <www.vulgar.com.au/dareToStruggleReview.html>

3

BREAKING WITH MOSCOW

The Communist Party of Australia's new road to socialism

David McKnight

For many years after its formation in 1920 the Communist Party of Australia (CPA) was loyal to the Soviet Union and the brand of Marxism practised by the Communist Party of the Soviet Union (CPSU). But in the mid-1960s the CPA began to evolve toward an independent stance which became increasingly critical of the Soviet Union, especially after its invasion of Czechoslovakia in August 1968. This stance was linked to a new kind of theory and practice which later saw the CPA begin to embrace an emerging radical politics which included support for feminism, environmentalism and gay liberation. During this period the CPA split and a pro-Moscow group formed the Socialist Party of Australia (SPA) in 1971. After a period of renewal in the 1970s, the CPA declined through the 1980s and in 1989 decided to wind down its activities and support the formation of a New Left Party, a position reaffirmed at its last congress in 1991 when the party began a short process of dissolution.[1] This chapter will examine the CPA's evolution from 1966 to 1971 during which it made its decisive break with the Soviet Union's orthodox brand of Marxism. It will be argued that the break with Moscow arose within a wider internal debate about the achievement of socialism in Australia and the relevance or otherwise of orthodox Marxism. That is, it will argue that the CPA's domestic political practice was at least as central as issues of international affairs.

The literature covering the CPA in the late 1960s and early 1970s is not extensive and is sometimes polemical. All accounts agree that until the early 1960s the CPA was a devoted follower of the Soviet model but they often disagree in their interpretation of what followed. Davidson's history of the CPA concludes at the time these changes began.[2] He argues that the CPA always had a dual nature, having been "formed by Australian socialists as a response to the Russian revolution".[3] Although under the tutelage of the Soviet Union for most of its life, under its then new leader, Laurie Aarons, the CPA "is following a stumbling march back to the Australian socialist traditions and party autonomy", he concluded.[4] This dual

60 David McKnight

nature was part of the underlying context for the divisions of the late 1960s and 1970s. In his history of communism and the labour movement, Gollan notes that by the early 1930s:

> the Australian party, in organisation and style of work, was a replica, on a minute scale, of the CPSU [Communist Party of the Soviet Union]. Thenceforward, until some re-thinking began in the 1960s, it responded directly to all trends within Russia. As the CPSU became steadily more authoritarian in organisation and dogmatic in ideology, so did the Australian party.[5]

A subsequent history of the CPA, O'Lincoln's *Into The Mainstream*, is flawed by its insistence that the CPA should have recognised that the Soviet Union was a "capitalist imperialist" society.[6] O'Lincoln argues that in this period the CPA rejected Stalinism but that it replaced it with "liberal and reformist ideas that were no real improvement".[7] Another CPA history is Brown's *The Communist Movement and Australia* which recounts the history of the CPA as a narrative of unblemished achievements until "the problem years" of the late 1960s.[8] Brown's interpretation amounts to dogged justification of the actions of CPA members who split and formed the Socialist Party of Australia party in 1971. An article by Mallory provides a scholarly account of the internal debates and the ideas behind them, particularly related to the trade union movement and the formation of the Socialist Party of Australia.[9] Some memoir literature exists that deals directly with this chapter's theme. Eric Aarons' autobiography, *What's Left?* and Bernie Taft's *Crossing the Party Line* contain detailed accounts by participants about the internal CPA divisions and relations with the Soviet Union.[10] As well, Mark Aarons, a member of the family central to the life of the CPA, but not a leading participant himself, gives an account in *The Family File* of aspects of the CPA's break with Moscow.[11]

The secret speech

The roots of the CPA's rejection of Soviet-style communism lie in the 1956 "secret speech" of CPSU secretary Nikita Khrushchev to the 20th Congress of the CPSU which acknowledged the crimes of Stalin. The CPA, after a period of indecisiveness and worried reflection, accepted the explanation offered by the Soviets that the cause was the "cult of the personality" of Stalin. It speedily shut down further debate and expelled dissidents who wanted to discuss the implications of Khrushchev's revelations.[12] Shortly afterwards, the CPA acquiesced in the Soviet suppression of the 1956 Hungarian revolution.

Khrushchev's speech also promoted strategic propositions that ran counter to previous orthodoxy. These included the possibility of peaceful co-existence between capitalist and socialist countries; that world war was not inevitable; and that a peaceful transition to socialism was possible.[13] These views, along with the denunciation of Stalin, were not accepted by the leadership of the Chinese Communist Party and a division deepened which resulted in what became known as the Sino-Soviet split.

Initially, the CPA was supportive of the Chinese stance. Its new, younger leaders had spent significant amounts of time at party schools in China and had been impressed. Although the CPA formally accepted the outcomes of the 20th Congress out of a sense of discipline, the CPA general secretary, Lance Sharkey, privately agreed with Chou En-lai's criticism of Khrushchev's attack on Stalin.[14] Publicly, Sharkey attacked the Yugoslav communists and their views on national roads to socialism. What then happened within the CPA leadership in 1960–61 is 'obscure', according to Davidson but it resulted in a shift of position by Sharkey but not by fellow member of the Political Committee (and secretary of the CPA in Victoria) Ted Hill. By the middle of 1961, the majority of the CPA leadership had shifted to favour the Soviet position and in 1963 it expelled Ted Hill who had become the leader of its pro-Chinese wing.[15] Hill then formed a new party, the Communist Party of Australia (Marxist-Leninist). One wholly unexpected result of this split, noted the Victorian CPA leader, Rex Mortimer, was a robust, internal debate in the CPA.

> [F]or the first time the organisation as a whole debated at great length and in detail all the vexed issues dividing the communist movement … a climate was generated favouring extensive changes in the party's policies and methods. Criticism erupted on all sides and in the prevailing conditions was tolerated and examined with extraordinary scrupulousness. The party leadership, in revulsion against the extremism of its departed colleagues, moved to meet the demands for reform by moderating the party's rigid and intolerant political attitudes and relaxing its bureaucratic discipline.[16]

Another CPA leader, Eric Aarons described the Sino-Soviet split as "a major catalyst in the development of the process of fundamentally re-thinking the principles on which we based our movement".[17] The CPA's exaggerated respect for both these parties meant that when the Russians and Chinese disagreed, it began to realise there might be a third option of developing an independent stance. This had been reinforced earlier by another theme in Khrushchev's speech that signalled a favourable attitude toward different "national roads to socialism" and this encouraged the CPA to begin a process of distancing itself from the Soviet Union.[18]

When Khrushchev was suddenly deposed as leader and consigned to obscurity in October 1964, the CPA took the unusual step of issuing a mildly critical statement in *Tribune*. [19] The same point was argued by Laurie Aarons at a meeting with Soviet leader, Mikhail Suslov who gave him a "frosty reception".[20] The CPA began to look elsewhere for models. At its congress in 1964 the CPA set a strategic perspective of building a "mass party", looking to the Italian, French and British parties for guidance.[21]

The following year, a number of CPA leaders co-wrote a pamphlet that was guardedly critical of the publication in the Soviet Union of an anti-Semitic pamphlet and they called for "a vigorous campaign" in the Soviet Union to eliminate all surviving remnants of "virulent anti-Semitism".[22] The CPA leader Eric

Aarons discussed anti-Semitism on a visit to Moscow in 1965 but the officials to whom he spoke protested that they could not control everything in such a vast country. He later recalled wondering "whether criticism of the CPSU or the Soviet system would have brought the same laid-back response".[23] Later that year the Soviets urged Aarons to put the CPA's name to an attack on the Chinese Communist Party but he declined. It was not just that the CPA had decided to discontinue the anti-Chinese polemics but also that "we were no longer going to be a stooge for anyone".[24] The other crucial factor in this process was generational change symbolised by the resignation of Lance Sharkey in May 1965 and his replacement as general secretary by Laurie Aarons who represented a younger and reform-minded trend.

In February 1966 the CPA made its first significant public criticism of the actions of the Soviet leadership. In a letter to the Soviet leadership it criticised the arrest and jailing of two Soviet writers, Andrei Sinyavsky and Yuli Daniel for "anti-Soviet propaganda". While disagreeing strongly with some of the writers' actions, the general secretary, Laurie Aarons argued that:

> What seems questionable is the necessity for state action against such insignificant figures. After more than 48 years of Soviet power ... their anti-Soviet writings certainly will find no response among the Soviet people ... From this point of view would it not be sufficient to expose them publicly, answer their 'arguments' in public debate (if necessary) and allow public opinion to deal with such people?[25]

In his column in the party newspaper, *Tribune*, the artist Noel Counihan argued that the "persistence of a censorship mentality in official Soviet circles is of deep concern to all friends of the Soviet Union ... who have responded warmly to the great liberalisation of Soviet cultural life since the Stalin era".[26] The criticism led to a spate of letters in *Tribune*, supporting or opposing the party's public stance, including one from the writer Frank Hardy who supported the CPA's stance, presciently remarking "there is more at stake than the fate of Sinyavsky and Daniel".[27] Another correspondent attacked the CPA stance, arguing that the writers were "punished in accordance with Soviet law after an open and fair trial". He concluded: "I can see no reason why these traitors should be set free to continue their double-faced treachery."[28] The debate closed after several weeks with letters variously professing to be "amazed and disgusted" at the dissidents or describing the CPA protest as "a breath of fresh air".[29]

The CPA was not alone in these early criticisms of Soviet actions. Many European parties also criticised the undemocratic way in which Khrushchev was ousted in 1964. The trial of Sinyavsky and Daniel which symbolised the end of the Khrushchev reform era "evoked a storm of criticism from Western parties".[30] Among others, the French communist writer Louis Aragon attacked the writers' trial in the Communist Party's newspaper, *L'Humanité*.[31] As well, at this time, and partly as a result of the Sino-Soviet split, the Italian Communist Party leader

Togliatti developed his notion of "polycentrism" in the communist movement as an alternative to the centralised, Soviet-led notion of internationalism.

The CPA's newfound openness took a further step at its 21st National Congress in June 1967. The congress was preceded by an unusually vigorous internal debate on the new approaches to the local struggle rather than attitudes to the Soviet Union. However, in an article in the internal pre-Congress journal, Alf Watt, later a leader of the breakaway group, criticised the central committee and warned that "a fashion has developed among some communists to look for opportunities of denigrating the Soviet Union". He justified the jailing of Sinyavsky and Daniel on the basis that the "Soviet people" supported it.[32] In the subsequent journal two CPA members disagreed. B. Rosen (Sydney) praised the CPA's handling of the writers Daniel and Sinyavsky as a "more mature approach" and D.G of Perth urged the congress to demand the release of the two writers.[33]

The congress largely focussed on the CPA's new approach to Australian domestic politics and discussion of the Soviet Union was avoided. A resolution calling for the release of "imprisoned Soviet writers, Daniel and Sinyavsky" was put aside and not dealt with and the Congress recorded its "special pleasure at receiving fraternal greetings from the Central Committee of the CPSU" and also noted "the great inspiration the Soviet people are providing to the world socialist movement."[34] In his report to the congress, the new national secretary, Laurie Aarons, noted "a new quality evident" in the pre-Congress discussion "with old ideas and rigid positions questioned and new ideas emerging".[35] The congress itself proposed a new orientation for the CPA expressed by the formula "a Coalition of the Left". This reflected, a member of the national committee later recalled, not only a new willingness to seek out immediate allies in struggle, but a different vision for a socialist society which would include more than one political party.[36] "This differs from the old concept, expressed in the CPA program of an alliance led by one Marxist party", explained Laurie Aarons who affirmed the "concept of a multi-party socialist society and its guarantees of freedom of speech, thought and organisations", alluding to "bureaucratic deformations" that had arisen in existing socialist societies. As part of this move, the congress decided to draw up a Charter of Democratic Rights in Australia, linking it to plans for electoral reform. Aarons' report also argued that "The labor [sic] movement needs co-operation of radical intellectuals and must overcome narrowness towards ideas and suspicion of intellectuals [who also] need co-operation with the labor movement".[37]

Another report to the congress, by national executive member Eric Aarons, urged the party to engage in the "battle of ideas" and noted the rising number of books being published about Marx and Marxism. His report suggested that many Marxists had previously made assumptions about parties, classes, the state, democracy and forms of revolution "that now require ... deeper consideration. Many things thought to be universal, have turned out to be particular to a given set of conditions, and sometimes plain wrong."[38] Among many communist parties around the world, he later said, "dogmatism and stagnation of thought are gradually being swept away and this will prepare the ground for a new advance".[39]

64 David McKnight

Symbolically, the congress changed the title of its foremost leader from General Secretary to National Secretary and of its leading body from Central Committee to the National Committee which was then elected with a significantly lower average age than the previous committee. It also changed the name of its theoretical organ, *Communist Review,* to *Australian Left Review* which now described itself modestly as "a Marxist journal of information, analysis and discussion". The journal became a major forum for the reform-minded CPA forces to discuss new interpretations of both capitalism and socialism. In an optimistic and outgoing mood after the congress, the leaders of the CPA looked forward to a growth in the CPA and proposed a series of party building activities, including revitalised fund raising, promotional leaflets on the CPA's ideas, a book of Marxist essays on the Australian way to socialism, a fund for research scholarships, a boosting of the *Australian Left Review* through visiting overseas lecturers and the opening of a Marxist research library.[40]

The year 1967 also saw the last reasonably friendly contact between the CPA and CPSU when Laurie Aarons spoke at a seminar on the 50th anniversary of the 1917 revolution in Moscow on the theme of socialism and democracy. He received a "frigid" reception to the talk whose main theme was that "ideas require free contest, not confined in a framework of established dogmas that can become a rigid or even ossified edifice".[41] This was also the last occasion when the Soviet party gave money to the CPA, in this case to buy a new printing machine for its weekly newspaper *Tribune.*[42] Another sign of the CPA's break with Soviet-style practice was its preparedness to open the pages of its weekly newspaper to critical commentary from non-CPA members. In early 1968 the CPA published its Draft Charter of Democratic Rights. Much of the Charter was an unexceptional affirmation of democratic rights and processes, with a reframing of socialist struggle as one in which democracy extended into all institutions and enterprises. As innocuous as an affirmation of democratic rights may seem it became a catalyst for vigorous debate between those who disregarded the rights of dissidents under democratic centralist forms of organisation versus those who advocated that a more universalistic notion of rights was compatible with Marxism, as Piccini notes.[43] The subsequent call for commentary produced a mixed reaction. Philosophy lecturer, Max Charlesworth, regarded it as "a collection of generalities and truisms" but welcomed its "modest and non-doctrinaire tone … [and] its refreshing freedom from the tired and bombastic jargon and clichés of older Communist statements".[44] The Maoist student leader, Mike Hyde, was highly critical, arguing that "the ruling capitalist class in this country should have nothing to fear" and that the charter's authors had ceased to be communists.[45] Within the CPA itself, a significant number of members opposed it, because they believed "you shouldn't allow the class enemy the freedom to write against the regime".[46] Criticism from the wider left that the CPA's renewal process was a cover for increasing ideological softness were to intensify in the years leading to the split with the pro-Moscow wing in 1971.

Czechoslovakia

In early 1968, the CPA's criticisms of the Soviet model of socialism and its groping toward an independent stance received a significant impetus when the Czechoslovak Communist Party initiated its Action Program which began a wave of changes, including the liberalisation of censorship, the acknowledgment of democratic rights and limitations on the party's monopoly of power. CPA leaders seized on the Czech example with fascination and hope. A CPA leader, Bernie Taft, who visited Czechoslovakia at the time, later recalled it as a time "full of hope and great expectations. There was electricity in the air."[47] In April, Laurie Aarons wrote an article titled "The Czech renaissance lights a way for us" which hailed the Action Program as a "new stage of socialist development". It had not always been recognised, he said, that a socialist revolution "does not automatically bring complete political democracy". The reforms, he added, "are showing in practice that the ideas for Socialist Australia we advanced at our 21st Congress and developed in the draft Charter of Democratic Rights ... are neither a dream nor a manoeuvre".[48] A week later the CPA national executive hailed the "inspiring" Czech example which "began correction of the Stalinist distortion of socialism".[49] At a meeting in Melbourne Town Hall, Bernie Taft said that socialism was "coming of age" and that centralized planning was now "inadequate" and further economic development needed socialist democracy.[50]

An article in *Tribune,* written from Prague, described the atmosphere in the following terms: "No censorship anymore ... no false optimism ... no closed subjects ... no doctored public opinions ... no ponderous announcements of leaders which have to be repeated ad nauseam".[51] In July 1968, *Tribune* published a series of articles by its Moscow correspondent, Eric Thornton, arguing that the liberalisation of Czech society was widely supported within the country. Czechoslovakia was "certainly not sliding into chaos, capitalism, neutralism or anything else", he argued, a rebuff to such accusations from the enemies of the "Prague Spring".[52] Other communist parties were also examining the new developments in Czechoslovakia and also felt hopeful. The French and Italian parties had committed themselves to the success of the Czech Action Plan.[53] The secretary of the Italian Communist Party, Luigi Longo, visiting Czechoslovakia in May 1968, said the Czech experiment assisted those communist parties in capitalist countries to portray a new kind of socialist society, "young, open and modern".[54]

However, the clock was counting down for this experiment in a democratic kind of socialism. In late July *Tribune* published an accusatory letter to the Czech leadership from eastern European and Soviet communist parties which warned that "the offensive of reactionary forces ... threatens to push your country off the road to socialism and that consequently it jeopardises the interests of the entire socialist system".[55] The same edition of *Tribune* published a reply to this letter from the Czech Communist Party alongside a CPA statement titled "Czechs must decide own destiny".[56] The latter also added that the success of the Czech program for renewal "would greatly assist the struggle for socialism in the capitalist world". At a

350-strong meeting of CPA members on the eve of the invasion, an ASIO agent commented: "Aarons gave the best report I have ever heard him give. He was emotionally upset and flushed in the face he spoke as though the future of humanity depended on what was under discussion."[57] When the invasion of Czechoslovakia finally came on 21 August a CPA national executive meeting unanimously called for "the withdrawal of the occupation troops".[58] In Sydney the CPA urgently convened a 1,000-strong meeting in Sydney Town Hall to condemn the occupation. National Secretary Laurie Aarons said that the CPA protested the invasion "because we support socialist democracy and national independence for all countries in the world."[59] He attacked Prime Minister Gorton for his hypocritical opposition to the invasion: "if you support national self-determination, why are you in Vietnam?" He framed his criticism in terms of the local struggle for socialism, saying that the Soviet action had "harmed the cause of socialism [but that despite] this massive departure from principles, not only will socialism triumph but there will emerge a better understanding of principles and ways to fight for socialism". A resolution endorsing the stand was passed with 70 dissenting. Similar meetings were held in Melbourne and Brisbane. In the days following the occupation the West Australian CPA branch distributed copies of the full Action Program of the Czech CP.[60] Similar reactions occurred world-wide with condemnation from many communist parties including the Spanish, Italian, French, British Belgian, Greek, Romanian and Japanese.[61]

The occupation gave impetus to the CPA's critique of Soviet-style socialism. In September the CPA national executive member, Eric Aarons, outlined four reasons for the "wrong and unjustified" intervention.[62] These were that the interests of the Soviet Union had "become identical with the interests of socialism as a whole"; a powerful bureaucracy had emerged in the USSR; pressure for democracy was regarded as a departure from socialism; and a theory which emerged in particular conditions had become rigid and was given state sanction.

In the wake of its stance on Czechoslovakia, the CPA leadership opened up a formal debate in the pages of *Tribune* about "attitudes to the Soviet Union seen in relation to the struggle for socialism in Australia".[63] The debate which lasted seven weeks saw sharp criticism of the CPA leadership for its "obsession" with the Czech issue from figures such as the writer, Judah Waten.[64] Others such as trade unionist, Jack Mundey, disagreed. Communists did their own cause damage "if we gloss over serious errors and make excuses," he said.[65] At the same time a pro-Soviet opposition began to emerge openly within the CPA. Just three weeks after the invasion, an ASIO report quoted a leader of this opposition, Alf Watt, claiming that 35 per cent of CPA members opposed the party's position on Czechoslovakia.[66] An assessment by the CPA leadership described it as the "biggest division for forty years" with states such as South Australia "evenly balanced".[67] At a meeting in Newcastle, some CPA members heckled during a speech by Laurie Aarons.[68] It was clearly going to be a damaging split.

Almost from the start, the emerging pro-Soviet opposition was in direct contact with the Soviet embassy. This contact was noted by ASIO which commented that

"It is doubtful if Laurence Aarons is aware of [opposition leader, Bill] Brown's meeting with the Soviets in Sydney on 30 August, 1968."[69] Five months after the invasion, it was clear that a powerful minority was organising against the leadership. In January 1969 the CPA national executive warned that some members, opposed to the decision on Czechoslovakia were "circulating documents and organising against party decisions".[70]

At this stage the CPA's new thinking took shape on the domestic front. In early 1969 it sponsored the Left Action Conference, the embodiment of its new views on the coalition of the left. The invitation to the conference was expansive, welcoming all "left and anti-Establishment forces" to debate a range of issues and "to propose concepts of how to effect radical social change".[71] The conference was rated an "outstanding success" by *Tribune*, drawing the "leading representatives of all radical student groups and nearly every university in Australia, as well as over 300 blue and white collar workers".[72] In his conference paper, CPA leader Laurie Aarons emphasised the CPA's analysis of new developments in capitalism, especially the "scientific and technological revolution" which meant that the strategic forces for social change now included students and the intellectuals.[73] Linked to this revolution was the "demand for popular control – in factory, school, university and suburb".

In parallel with its willingness to work with the New Left, the CPA leadership's criticism of the CPSU developed. In June 1969, at an international meeting of communist parties in Moscow, Laurie Aarons reaffirmed the CPA's condemnation of the military intervention in Czechoslovakia which he said "harmed our cause".[74] He agreed with a proposal by the Italian Communist Party that the meeting express its support for "national independence, sovereignty and non-interference". He described the Soviet-inspired main document as uninspiring and superficial in its analysis of the new revolutionary forces at work in the world. At a ceremonial endorsement of a joint statement, he signed but added the words: "This signature ratifies only section 3 of this document" (which contained a statement of unity against imperialism).[75] A more thoroughgoing repudiation of the Soviet position by a communist party is hard to imagine.

In the wake of the Moscow meeting the CPA's National Committee in July 1969 passed a resolution which affirmed the party's independent course and argued that "there is no leading party or centre to which any other party, either directly or by implication, owes allegiance as a test of internationalism or adherence to Marxism-Leninism".[76] It warned against any party interfering in the affairs of another party and added that each party must develop its own strategy within "national conditions, traditions and level of development". Significantly, a minority of ten voted against this resolution with 27 supporting it. By this time, the pro-Soviet opposition was out in the open, was significant in size and formally challenging the CPA leadership's direction with the support of the CPSU. In late 1969, a leading figure in the pro-Soviet minority, Bill Brown, was invited to the Soviet Union and Czechoslovakia to "study the mass media" in those countries. The CPA leadership noted that such an invitation was "a most unusual and

68 David McKnight

incorrect procedure". Such an invitation should go to mass organisation or to the party but not to an individual, it said. When phoned by Laurie Aarons in late December Brown refused to defer his travel and hung up.[77]

The position of the opposition

Over the succeeding seven months before the CPA's 22nd Congress in March 1970, the pro-Soviet minority consolidated. Its ideas were expressed in *A Programme for a Socialist Australia*, written by Edgar Ross as an alternative to the official draft resolution. Ross, who had been a leading figure in the Miners' Federation, became a leader of the CPA pro-Soviet minority.[78]

The programme claimed that "the socialist states have come up against many problems, made many mistakes but they are being solved while those facing capitalism are insoluble".[79] It was the duty of communist parties "to popularise the achievements of the Soviet Union and systematically combat its traducers". The document echoed previous CPA programmes from the 1950s and 1960s. It was critical about "the infiltration of capitalist ideas" into the CPA "under the guise of 'bringing Marxism-Leninism up to date'". Such ideas denigrated the role of the working class, it said, and replaced the class struggle with "moral maxims" which meant "not the working class but intellectuals are leaders of the socialist cause".[80]

A month before the 1970 National Congress, the national secretary, Laurie Aarons, characterised the internal CPA differences on several issues including "the concept of socialism". On this he argued that "Older ideas, particularly after their distortion under Stalinism, no longer fully meet the possibilities within human society nor express the ways these are felt by potentially revolutionary forces, particularly the youth."[81] Another issue, he said, concerned internationalism. This majority's draft Congress document expressed "the support of all socialist countries against imperialism while retaining the right of independent judgement and action". The view of the opposition, he said, confined the meaning of internationalism to the "support of every policy and action of a single socialist country, the USSR".

On the eve of the Congress 100 young radicals, some CPA members, others not, but all under 30 years of age, addressed an appeal to the CPA.[82] The appeal suggested several future alternatives, in one of which the CPA "can develop into a revolutionary party, relevant to Australian conditions" which would appeal to young radicals. The alternative was one in which the party could take "the road to political suicide, more interested in defending existing socialist countries than fighting for the revolution in Australia". The appeal went on to attack the document circulated by the pro-Soviet opposition for its patronising tone and misunderstanding of the worldwide youth revolt.

The CPA reformers won a majority at the 1970 Congress which described countries such as the Soviet Union as "socialist based", rather than simply socialist. The main congress document described the flaws and weaknesses of "socialist-based countries" as "over centralised control of the economy"; the "existence of a bureaucracy"; "the tendency of the communist party to substitute its leadership for that of the working class".[83] It also criticised "curtailments of political democracy and intellectual freedom". All of this, it said, created "dogmatic ideologies ... which express a distorted concept of socialism".

This angered the pro-Soviet minority which escalated its organising, and decided to produce its own newspaper for which they appealed for funds. It also held a series of separate meetings, effectively establishing a parallel organisation. A meeting of the National Committee following the congress invited minority leader Edgar Ross to attend and justify the opposition's appeal for funds to establish a "Socialist Publications" organisation, after which the Committee reprimanded him and his colleague, Alf Watt.[84] This had no effect on the minority who began to publish their own newspaper, *The Australian Socialist*, in mid-1970 and continued to hold closed meetings while remaining nominal CPA members. At this stage the dissidents' strategy was to "stay in and fight" and force the leadership to expel them. The next National Committee meeting in October did just that and expelled Watt and Ross from CPA membership.[85] According to Edgar Ross the Victorian CPA leader, John Sendy, had "sought a more tolerant attitude" foreshadowing later differences between the Victorians and the Aarons leadership group.[86] An ASIO analysis of the situation at this point noted that the dissidents had seriously hampered CPA fund raising, had taken over several branches including the large Sydney Maritime Branch and had established a national body of their own. Contact between the Soviet embassy and the dissidents was "cordial and increasingly frequent" although no direct evidence existed of Soviet material assistance.[87]

In early 1971, the Soviet weekly, *New Times*, published an attack on the CPA. It catalogued errors beginning with its condemnation of the invasion of Czechoslovakia, its stance at the 1969 meeting of the world communist movement and its 1970 Congress description of non-capitalist countries as "socialist based" countries. The article was reprinted in *Tribune* which noted the article was probably the first open attack on another communist party since the Sino-Soviet split.[88] A rebuttal by the CPA leadership reaffirmed its position on Czechoslovakia and the need to analyse Stalinism. It defended its expulsion of the pro-Soviet minority leaders arguing that this was not for their dissenting ideas but for setting up "an exclusive separate group within the party, with its own platform, loyalty and discipline".[89] A meeting of the National Committee shortly after this expressed its concern at the repression of a group led by the Soviet dissident Andrei Sakharov and directed its delegation to the impending CPSU congress "to inquire into this and other problems of socialist democracy".[90]

The following meeting of the National Committee in May 1971 saw the first division between the "Aarons group" and the Victorian leadership of Bernie Taft. As a way of bringing issues to a head, the former group proposed that the annual card reissue be used to refuse party cards to any member who would not dissociate themselves from the actions of the pro-Soviet minority. The Taft group took a softer approach proposing an appeal to dissidents, a suspension of existing disciplinary actions and a further review by the National Committee at an unspecified

70 David McKnight

time.[91] At the subsequent card re-issue, a number of members were refused cards and in December 1971 the pro-Soviet group founded the Socialist Party of Australia. The split weakened the CPA with probably 800 members leaving or being excluded from an overall membership of 4,500, many of them in the trade union movement. The number of weekly *Tribune* sales dropped from 10,437 in August 1969 to 8,286 in October 1970, with a cut in the order from the Soviet Union of 550 copies and a drop in Australian sales of 1,601.[92]

Untangling the CPA's evolution

So far this chapter has focussed on the CPA's evolving attitudes toward the Soviet Union. These attitudes defined the debate and demarcated its different participants from the earliest tentative criticisms to a highly critical overall CPA position which guaranteed a damaging split in the party. But were the fundamental differences mainly about attitudes to the Soviet Union?

The CPA's early criticisms of Soviet style socialism were not merely reactive nor isolated. They arose within a wider internal CPA debate over domestic political practice and the weaknesses of orthodox Marxism that guided that struggle. For example, in 1966 in the first issue of the CPA's new look theoretical magazine, *Australian Left Review*, Bernie Taft acknowledged that "post-war economic developments have posed a challenge to Marxist thinking".[93] The long post war boom of the 1950s and 1960s, he said, "is contrary to what Marxists generally expected". Taft identified "a certain stagnation of Marxist thinking in the forties and fifties" as well as "a slowness to examine new phenomena, free from dogma and preconceived ideas". This was echoed by another Victorian CPA leader, John Sendy, in an article about the CPA itself, who urged that "The dust should be shaken off the textbooks. Lubrication must be provided for minds clogged with the formulae of yesteryear".[94] While classical Marxism should be studied, his main point was that "there is the necessity also to develop and apply Marxism to the modern, changing Australian circumstances".

The need to localise and update Marxism took shape in the reformers' desire for a coalition of the left to unite potential allies in the struggle within Australia. The obstacle to this was the orthodox notion of the vanguard party as the repository of wisdom and sole leader of struggle. Eric Aarons criticised this notion at its weakest point: the apparent need for future socialist societies to be one-party states, like the Soviet Union. There was a tendency "to take the Russian experience as identical with Marxism, as a universal truth applicable everywhere" which, he said, sometimes led to "inadequate attention to Australian traditions in political democracy".[95] The need to rethink Marxism in local conditions also led the CPA reformers to study the work of Italian communist Antonio Gramsci who criticised the economic determinism of orthodox Marxism and emphasised the "battle of ideas" in advanced capitalist countries.[96]

All of this preceded the August 1968 invasion of Czechoslovakia. It would therefore be one dimensional to see the split within the CPA as being entirely based on different attitudes to the Soviet Union. An equally strong case could be mounted that the CPA reformers believed the struggle within Australia was the primary issue and was being damaged by the dogmatic version of Marxism associated with the Soviet Union and the undemocratic abuses associated with it. Certainly, as demonstrated in many of the quotations above, the CPA leaders (and others, such as the statement by 100 young people) frequently linked their criticism of the Soviet Union to the struggle for socialism in Australia. In this way the cult of Moscow symbolised what was failing in the local struggle. All of these issues came to a head at the invasion of Czechoslovakia: it was not only a violation of independence but also a blow to a new concept of socialism more relevant to countries like Australia quite apart from damaging the public reputation of communists. As Warren Osmond and Kelvin Rowley observed, commenting on the 1970 Congress: "This is not a debate about whether the Soviet Union's actions were right or wrong ... this is a debate about the very *meaning* of the word 'socialism' " [original emphasis].[97] A similar point was made by veteran party leader Jack Blake who argued that the Czechoslovakia events had the "catalytic effect" of precipitating debate about the authoritarian Stalinist version of socialism previously widely accepted.[98]

Such an interpretation makes sense of a statement in January 1970 by National Secretary, Laurie Aarons, as the CPA moved towards its watershed congress. He noted a "misconception that these differences are only or mainly about international issues" such as Czechoslovakia.[99] The real differences, he said, were over "an Australian socialist strategy ... the new potential challenges to capitalist domination" as well as "what kind of socialist society" and the "socialist concept of human liberation". Symbolically, the same National Committee meeting that expelled the leaders of the pro-Soviet minority also passed resolutions signalling the arrival of a new kind of politics. One resolution condemned "the rapid growth of environmental pollution and destruction" and another called for a new policy on "women and social liberation".[100] The CPA's embrace of the new social movements continued to deepen after the 1970 Congress and the split.

The related question to which this period gives rise is more difficult to answer: What were the key forces which impelled the CPA to reject Stalinism? On this question the literature is sketchy and sometimes questionable. Most accounts agree that the new leadership of the CPA played a key role. Mallory suggests that the changes occurred because the new leadership, especially Laurie and Eric Aarons, were motivated by a desire to advance socialist strategy and were thus determined to "break down the orthodoxy" and to "analyse Marxism in humanistic terms" which led them to influence and be influenced by New Left activists.[101] While Brown agrees that the changes initiated by leaders like Laurie and Eric Aarons were central to the events, this forms part of an accusation that the CPA was "penetrated and seriously divided" by "anti-communist ideological trends" such as Eurocommunism, Maoism and Trotskyism from the 1960s to the 1980s.[102] At another point Brown argues that academics such as Davidson who was sympathetic to the CPA reformers and whose book on the history of the CPA appeared in 1969, were

72 David McKnight

sponsored by major corporations and possibly even intelligence agencies.[103] O'Lincoln's account also acknowledges the role of Laurie and Eric Aarons but also tends to invoke an economic determinist explanation for the CPA's course. He suggests the main reason for the CPA's rejection of Stalinism was the post war economic boom which also saw a decline in class struggle. This gave rise to a belief in the CPA (false in O'Lincoln's view) that stability would persist and that a political strategy based on struggle around moral and cultural issues, as well as class struggle, was needed.[104] The other main reason, he argues, was the "growth of the class struggle and the student radicalisation in the late sixties" which, he says, forced the communists to rethink because of the danger of being "outflanked by radical new forces".[105]

This latter comment suggests that breaking with Stalinism constituted some kind of instrumental manoeuvre as well as attributing bad faith. The evidence tends to show that the CPA leadership's initial dissent from and ultimately rejection of Soviet-style Marxism began with local efforts to find a new path. This was followed by shock at events like Czechoslovakia, although presumably the fear of being outflanked and a desire to rejuvenate the party may have also been motives. Moreover, this concern was framed by new ideas about a more democratic socialism and the strategy to achieve it in Australia. Certainly, a strong case can be made that the CPA leaders, rather than any other factor, played the formative role in changing their party's orientation and that their actions displayed intellectual courage of a high order, given that this involved renewing and rejecting much of their previously held views.

Notes

1   Details of this process and final resolutions are contained in *Praxis: Communist Party of Australia National Newsletter* (Ultimo: Communist Party of Australia, 1991).
2   Alastair Davidson, *The Communist Party of Australia: A Short History* (Stanford: Hoover Institution Press, 1969).
3   Davidson, 175.
4   Davidson, 181.
5   Robin Gollan, *Revolutionaries and Reformists: Communism and the Australian Labour Movement 1920–1955* (Canberra: ANU Press, 1975), 287.
6   Tom O'Lincoln, *Into the Mainstream: The Decline of Australian Communism* (North Carlton: Red Rag Publications, 2009), 135.
7   O'Lincoln, 7.
8   W. J. Brown, *The Communist Movement and Australia: an historical outline, 1890s to 1980s* (Haymarket: Australian Labor Movement History Publications, 1986).
9   Greg Mallory, "The Communist Party of Australia, 1967–1975 and the circumstances surrounding the formation of the Socialist Party of Australia", *The Hummer*, Vol. 3 No. 7 (Summer 2001–02), 16, 17.
10 Eric Aarons, *What's Left? Memoirs of an Australian Communist* (Ringwood: Penguin Books, 1993). Bernie Taft, *Crossing the Party Line: the memoirs of Bernie Taft* (Newham, Vic: Scribe, 1994).
11 Mark Aarons, *The Family File* (Melbourne: Black Inc., 2010).
12 Phillip Deery and Rachael Calkin, "'We all make mistakes': the Communist Party of Australia and Khrushchev's secret speech, 1956", *Australian Journal of Politics and History*, Vol. 54, No. 1 (2008), 69–84. See also Davidson, 119.

13 Davidson, 119, 158.
14 Davidson, 148–149.
15 Davidson, 152–155.
16 Rex Mortimer, "Dilemmas of Australian Communism" in *Australian Politics. A Second Reader* (Melbourne: F. W. Cheshire, 1969), 386.
17 Eric Aarons, *What's Left?*, 129.
18 Davidson, 180.
19 Statement of the Political Committee of the CPA, "Changes in the Soviet", *Tribune*, 21 October 1964, 1.
20 Mark Aarons, *Family File*, 206.
21 "Party building and the path to a mass party: report to the February 1965 meeting of the Central Committee", MLMSS 5021, Box 16, Communist Party of Australia records, 1920–1987, Mitchell Library.
22 Philip Mendes, "A convergence of political interests: Isi Leibler, the Communist Party of Australia and Soviet Anti-Semitism, 1964–66," *Australian Journal of Politics and History*, 55, No. 2 (2009), 165.
23 Eric Aarons, *What's Left?*, 142.
24 Eric Aarons, *What's Left?*, 151.
25 Copy of letter from Communist Party of Australia to Communist Party of the Soviet Union, dated 28th February 1966. "Documents of the State Committee, 1958–1980", Box 6, MLMSS 6381, J. R. Hughes Papers (1929–1993), 2. A public statement was also made. "Arrests, jailings were unnecessary and wrong", *Tribune*, 23 February, 1966, 4.
26 Noel Counihan, "The two Soviet writers", in *Tribune*, 2 March 1966, 6.
27 "More discussion about Soviet writers' case", *Tribune*, 9 March 1966,4.
28 Ted Jones, "More letters on the case of the 2 Soviet writers", *Tribune*, 16 March 1966, 4.
29 "For and against: the case of the two Soviet writers", *Tribune*, 30 March 1966, 4.
30 Leonard Shapiro, "Soviet attitudes to national communism in Western Europe," in *National Communism in Western Europe: a third way to socialism?* ed. Howard Machin (London: Methuen & Co, 1983), 49.
31 Vincent Wright, "The French Communist Party during the Fifth Republic: the troubled path", in *National Communism in Western Europe: a third way to socialism?* ed. Howard Machin (London: Methuen & Co, 1983), 94.
32 Alf Watt, "Australia and international aspects" *Discussion Journal: on the documents for the 21st National Congress of the Communist Party of Australia*, No. 1. March 1967, 19.
33 B. Rosen (Sydney) "Step forward in correct direction", *Discussion Journal*, No. 2, April 1967, 30. D. G. (Perth), "The CPA and the CPSU" *Discussion Journal*, No. 2, April 1967, 49.
34 Minutes of the 21st National Congress – Communist Party of Australia, MLMSS 5021 Box 1, item 5, 1967, 9, 10, CPA records, Mitchell Library.
35 Untitled and anonymous article summarising the report to congress by Laurie Aarons, *Tribune*, 21 June 1967, 11–12.
36 Rex Mortimer, "Dilemmas of Australian Communism", *Australian Politics. A Second Reader*, ed. Henry Mayer (Melbourne: F. W. Cheshire, 1969), 390.
37 Untitled article summarising the report to congress by Laurie Aarons, *Tribune*, 21 June 1967, 11–12.
38 "Communists and the Battle of Ideas", Delivered by Eric Aarons, 9–12 June 1967, MLMSS 5021 Box 1, item 5, 21st Congress, 1967, 3, CPA records, Mitchell Library.
39 Eric Aarons, "The Communist Congress: Two Perspectives", *Arena*, No. 13 (1967), 38.
40 Letter from the National Office to State Committees, NSW Bureau, District Committees and National Committee Members, 26 July 1967. MLMSS 5021, Box 15, CPA records, Mitchell Library.
41 Mark Aarons, *The Family File*, 213.

42 Mark Aarons, *The Family File*, 214.
43 Jon Piccini, "'More than an abstract principle': reimagining rights in the Communist Party of Australia, 1956–1971", *Journal of Australian Studies*, 39, 2 (2015), 208–210.
44 Max Charlesworth, "Major change in Australian communist ideas", *Tribune*, 3 July 1968, 6.
45 Mike Hyde, "Do we have a 'democratic' tradition?" *Tribune*, 3 July 1968, 6–7.
46 Eric Aarons, letter to author, 10 July 2013.
47 Taft, *Crossing*, p.154.
48 Laurie Aarons, "The Czech renaissance lights a way for us", *Tribune*, 10 April, 1968, 3.
49 Statement by the National Executive of the CPA, "Czech changes an 'inspiring contribution'", *Tribune*, 17 April, 1968, 10.
50 Victorian correspondent, "Socialism now coming of age, says Taft", *Tribune*, 24 April 1968, 12.
51 Prague correspondent, "The Czech uplift: it's absolutely terrific", *Tribune*, 1 May 1968, 5.
52 Eric Thornton, "Czechoslovakia's 'new style' socialism", *Tribune*, 3 July 1968, 5.
53 Peter Morris, "West European communist parties and international communism" in *National Communism in Western Europe: a third way to socialism?* ed. Howard Machin (London: Methuen & Co, 1983), 40.
54 Jiri Valenta, "Eurocommunism and Czechoslovakia" in *Eurocommunism between East and West*, ed. Vernon V. Aspaturian, Jiri Valenta and David P. Burke (Bloomington: Indiana University Press, 1980), 170.
55 On behalf of the Bulgarian Communist Party, Hungarian Socialist Workers Party, Socialist Unity Party of Germany, Polish United Workers Party and Communist Party of the Soviet Union, "'Your social system is being threatened", *Tribune*, 24 July 1968, 4.
56 Special Tribune Supplement. *Tribune*, 24 July 1968.
57 Communist Party Interest in Czechoslovakia, Laurence Aarons, Vol. 28, A6119 item 4234, 30, National Archives of Australia (NAA) ACT.
58 Unanimous resolution of a special meeting of the National Executive of the CPA, "Clear violation of socialist principle", *Tribune*, 28 August 1968, 9.
59 No author, "Why communists condemn Czechoslovak occupation", *Tribune*, 28 August 1968, 1.
60 The pamphlet is titled: *This Caused Czech invasion* in "Documents and Leaflets, ACP, Nov 38-September 1968" in Box 6, MLMSS 6381, J. R. Hughes Papers.
61 Jan F. Triska, "Eurocommunism and the decline of proletarian internationalism," in *Eurocommunism between East and West*, ed. Vernon V. Aspaturian, Jiri Valenta and David P. Burke (Bloomington: Indiana University Press, 1980), 79.
62 Eric Aarons, "Czechoslovakia and the USSR: Why?", *Tribune*, 4 September 1968, 1.
63 No author, "Soviet Union and you", *Tribune*, 29 January 1969, 2.
64 Judah Waten, "Leading anti-imperialist force", *Tribune*, 19 February 1969, 8.
65 Jack Mundey, "Greater socialist democracy essential", *Tribune*, 26 March 1969, 8.
66 Alfred Deakin Watt, in Laurence Aarons, Vol. 29, A6119 item 4236, 51, NAA.
67 CPA Reaction to Soviet-Czech crisis, in Laurence Aarons, Vol. 28, A6119 item 4234, 98, NAA.
68 CPA Czech/Soviet Dispute, Laurence Aarons, Vol. 29, A6119 item 4236, 41–42, NAA.
69 Contact Report – Wilton John Brown, in Laurence Aarons, Vol. 27, A6119, Item 4233, 226, NAA, ACT.
70 Letter from National Executive to all party organisations, 6 January 1969, in folder "1969 and before. National Committee, State and District correspondence", MLMSS 5021, Box 15, CPA records, Mitchell Library.
71 Anonymous, "'Forces of left' conference for 1969", *Tribune*, 27 November, 1968, 12.
72 Staff Correspondent, "Left links up in Easter meet", *Tribune*, 9 April, 1969, 1.
73 Laurie Aarons, "Prelude to basic change", *Tribune*, 16 April, 1969, 7.

74 International meeting of Communist and workers' parties, Moscow, June 1969, Speech of Laurie Aarons, in Laurence Aarons, Vol. 36, A6119, item 4264, 117, NAA.

75 Anonymous, "Aarons places CPA's position 'on record'", *Tribune*, 25 June 1969, 3.

76 CPA National Committee, "Looking at the World Communist Movement", *Tribune*, 6 August 1969, 5

77 Letter to National Executive from National Officers, 19 December 1969, in folder "1969 and before. National Committee, State and District correspondence", MLMSS 5021, Box 15, CPA records, Mitchell Library.

78 While Ross's background reflected the base among blue collar unionists of the opposition minority, Ross's co-leader, Alf Watt, had been a long term party functionary. This included being the Tribune correspondent in Moscow (1963–1965) immediately before the divisions began on the Soviet Union in the CPA.

79 *A Programme for a Socialist Australia*, "written by Edgar Ross, NC member", filed loosely in Box 1, MLMSS 5021, CPA records, Mitchell Library, 1.

80 *A Programme for a Socialist Australia*, 5.

81 Laurie Aarons, "Big issues in congress clash of ideas," in *Tribune*, 25 February 1970, 3.

82 No author, "1000 Words: an appeal to members of the Communist Party of Australia", *Tribune*, 4 March 1970, 8.

83 "Statement of aims, methods and organisation", 22nd CPA Congress, March 1970. In *CPA Documents of the Seventies* (Sydney: Red Pen Publications 1977), 6.

84 Minutes of National Committee meeting, held 29, 30 and 31 May 1970, in MLMSS 5021, Box 25, CPA records, Mitchell Library.

85 Minutes of National Committee meeting, held 9, 10, 11 October 1970, in MLMSS 5021, Box 25, CPA Papers, Mitchell Library.

86 Edgar Ross, *Of Storm and Struggle* (Sydney: Alternative Publishing Co-operative, 1981), 140.

87 Dissension within the CPA since 22nd National Congress, 20 October 1970, Formation of the Socialist Party of Australia, Vol. 2, A6122 item 2387, 98–100, NAA.

88 "*New Times* attacks CPA policies", *Tribune*, 27 January 1971, 8.

89 "An Open Letter to *New Times*", *Tribune*, 3 February 1971, 8.

90 "Minutes of National Committee meeting, 12th – 14th March, 1971", MLMSS 5021, Box 25, CPA records, Mitchell Library.

91 "Minutes of National Committee meeting, 21st – 23rd May, 1971". National Committee correspondence 1971–1974, MLMSS 5021, Box 18, item 4 CPA records.

92 The overall membership figure comes from a statement by Laurie Aarons in a television interview in 1969 sourced to an ASIO document, "Transcript of portion of the ABC TV program 'Today Tonight' shown on 9 July, 1969", in Laurence Aarons, Vol. 36, A6119, 4264, 87, NAA. The figure of 800 comes from W. J. Brown, *The Communist Movement and Australia*, 277. The details of Tribune sales come from a letter from the National Executive, 11 December 1970, MLMSS 5021, Box 17, CPA records, Mitchell Library.

93 B. Taft, "Changes in modern capitalism", *Australian Left Review*, No. 1 (June–July 1966), 1–2.

94 John Sendy, "Democracy and the Communist Party", *Australian Left Review*, No. 1 (June-July, 1966), 35.

95 Eric Aarons, "Socialism: Only one party?", *Australian Left Review*, No. 4 (December 1966–January 1967), 39.

96 Apart from publishing a series of articles on Gramsci in *Australian Left Review* (ALR Nos 11,12,13,15) the journal also published a book based on those articles: Alistair Davidson, *Antonio Gramsci: the man, his ideas* (Sydney: Australian Left Review Publications, 1968).

97 Warren Osmond and Kelvin Rowley, "Whither the Communist Party?", *Arena*, No. 22, 1970, 44.

98 J. D. Blake, *Revolution from Within: a contemporary theory of social change* (Sydney: Outlook, 1971), 67–68.

76 David McKnight

99 Laurie Aarons, "What CPA's congress is going to be about", *Tribune*, 14 January 1970, 3.
100 Minutes of National Committee meeting, held 9, 10, 11 October 1970 in MLMSS 5021, Box 25, CPA records, Mitchell Library.
101 Mallory, 15, 16, 17.
102 Brown, 262.
103 Brown, 269–271.
104 O'Lincoln, 143–145.
105 O'Lincoln, 141.

4

'THE "WHITE AUSTRALIA" POLICY MUST GO'

The Communist Party of Australia and immigration restriction

Jon Piccini and Evan Smith

The Australian far left has a long and conflicted history of engagement with the politics of whiteness. The Immigration Restriction Act, colloquially known as the 'White Australia Policy', was amongst the first acts of the newly created Australian commonwealth in 1901. It was strongly argued for by the left of politics, particularly the Australian Labor Party, who saw it as a means of securing the union movement's gains from cheap foreign labour. Against such a backdrop, this chapter examines the Australian far left's opposition to immigration controls, asking to what degree was its intervention significant in the eventual ending of the policy in 1973. Early, frustrated opposition to the policy by the Communist Party of Australia (CPA) was given energy by the end of World War II, which saw both the first cracks in the policy – as southern and eastern European migration was encouraged for the first time – and the emergence of a stronger line of far left critique. The CPA published a pamphlet interrogating White Australia in 1945 and opposed the deportation of Chinese refugees as well as a host of others in the immediate post-war era. At the same time, however, the CPA was calling for immigration quotas owing to housing shortages and opposed the immigration of particular nationalities, derided as 'Balts', who were seen as anti-communist.

The CPA's equivocal position was rejected in the early 1960s by the early actions of Australian New Left, who formed a group called Student Action to oppose White Australia, using strategies borrowed from the American civil rights movement. Yet, this and movements such as the Immigration Reform Group were more closely aligned with modernising currents in the ALP than the far left, which instead supported the struggles of Indigenous Australians and opposing the Vietnam War. This chapter concludes by considering this contradiction: that while protesting in solidarity with an Asian people seen as subjugated by imperialism, the Communist Party often remained on the side-lines practically, leaving the task of abolishing Australia's racialist immigration policy to centrists in the ALP.

Labourism and 'White Australia'

Australia, a British colony since 1788, became a federated nation-state under a parliamentary democracy offering universal suffrage for both men and women over 21 (at federal level) in 1901. An eight-hour work day and minimum wage were legislated, and legalised trade unions were represented in parliament through the social democratic Australian Labor Party. Australian workers seemed to enjoy the same political and economic benefits enjoyed by the most advanced sections of the European working class.[1]

However these benefits were only offered to those who were considered 'white', with Aboriginal and non-European (and in some cases, non-British) migrants being excluded from this 'worker's paradise'.[2] The legislative framework established at Federation explicitly excluded these groups of people, with the Constitution and the Commonwealth Franchise Act 1902 removing citizenship status for the Aboriginal population and the Immigration Restriction Act 1901 effectively barring entry to non-European migrants, colloquially known as the 'White Australia Policy'.[3]

One of the important aspects of the 'White Australia Policy' was its protection of the rights of 'white workers'. In the late 1800s, various ethnic groups were recruited to perform certain jobs, such as Pacific Islanders in the sugar cane trade, Japanese pearl divers and Afghan cameleers, particularly in the tropics of northern Western Australia and Queensland. Kay Saunders has argued that Queensland created two segregated labour zones, incorporating a tropical zone with 'unfree, largely non-European labour force' and a more traditional urban/rural zone with 'an urban bourgeoisie, a skilled British workforce and small white farmers'.[4]

But this segregated colonial economy, promoted by the British and multinational companies, was not favoured by many Australian politicians or the trade union movement.[5] Before 1901, these ethnic minorities had specific places within a colonial economy, but after Federation, the majority of employment was reserved for white workers, with several pieces of legislation severely restricting the access of non-white people to jobs. Until the 1960s, the organised labour movement in Australia worked to ensure that white (British and northern European) workers remained at the top of this hierarchy and were firmly attached to the concept of the 'White Australia Policy'.[6]

The industrial workers of the world

Neville Meaney has written:

> There are no heroes who from the beginning of 'white Australia' fought against great odds… unless possibly they [were] members of the International Workers of the World (IWW) or the Australian Communist Party, and it would be a brave soul indeed who argued that case.[7]

And this was indeed the case. Prior to the formation of the Communist Party of Australia in 1920, the most prominent opponents to the White Australia Policy were the Industrial Workers of the World (also known as the Wobblies). As part of an internationalist movement, the IWW opposed the racism and nationalism that was central to the mainstream labour movement in Australia at the time, taking aim at both the Australian Workers' Union (AWU) – the nation's largest – and various craft unions. In its paper *Direct Action*, the Wobblies stated:

> The I.W.W. is a class organisation of the working class. It is organised upon the basis of the class struggle. Therefore it welcomes all members of the working class, irrespective of their varying creeds, colours, religious beliefs, languages, etc.[8]

The same article further outlined the programme of the IWW, stating that the organisation stood for 'Revolutionary Economic International working-class unity', which meant that 'coloured workers of the North have to be organised' and could not be ignored.[9] 'They are an economic factor, either for or against the working class', the paper argued, 'They MUST be organised FOR their own class against the employers.'[10]

In an article criticising the craft unions for supporting the White Australia Policy, the IWW pointed out that 'craft unionists do not object to being robbed... of four-fifths of what they produce by a white purchaser of labour-commodity, but strongly object to being exploited by a gentlemen of colour'.[11] For the Wobblies, the real enemy were the bosses, not fellow workers from the colonial sphere. As A. E. Brown wrote in 1916:

> Contrast the narrow parochial outlook evidenced by the "White Australia" policy with the world-outlook of Karl Marx, when he sent his famous cry down the ages: "Workers of all countries, Unite!"[12]

In his study of the Australian labour movement, Frank Farrell called the anti-racist and internationalist stance of the IWW 'crude, emotional, irresponsible, and escapist', as well as 'impractical'.[13] The reason for this, Farrell argued, was that the IWW did not comprehend the central nature of racism and exclusionism to the protectionism of the Australian labour movement. Verity Burgmann has criticised Farrell's depiction of the IWW as stunted by their 'dogmatic internationalist purity', writing that if the IWW had abandoned its anti-racism, it would've lost much of its identity – 'anti-racism was a fundamental tenet of its ideology'.[14] Burgmann has celebrated the Wobblies for issuing 'the first effective challenge ever to working-class racism in Australia',[15] but the IWW was subsumed over the course of the 1920s by the Communist Party of Australia, who, by the end of the decade, were the foremost anti-racist and internationalist political party in Australia.

The Communist Party of Australia and the Comintern in the 1920s

The Communist Party of Australia was formed in 1920 and immediately applied for membership to the Communist International (Comintern). From the inception of the Comintern in 1919, the international communist movement was imbued with an anti-colonial agenda and agitated against the 'colour bar' that operated in the colonial sphere and in the former settler colonies, including Australia – what Marilyn Lake and Henry Reynolds have described as 'white men's countries'.[16] For example, the 1922 theses on the Eastern Question drafted at the Fourth Comintern Congress stated that 'the international proletariat does not harbour any racial prejudice' and any antagonisms between coloured and white workers served to fragment and weaken the unity of the workers' movement.[17] In an issue of *The Proletarian*, one of the pre-existing journals that became an outlet of the newly formed CPA, Pearl Hanks criticised the Australian worker for 'ignor[ing] the existence of the colored man while they can, and when that is no longer possible, to meet him with open hostility'.[18] Quoting the Indian member of the Communist Party of Great Britain, Shapurji Saklatvala, Hanks reminded readers: 'A dream of Communism for white races only is the height of folly, because... the industries in England cannot be taken over by the workers while the sources of raw material remain in the hands of the capitalists'.[19]

This realisation, Hanks argued, forced the conclusion 'that we must give up either our color prejudice or our hopes of Communism', further stating, 'there is no justification for the color bar, because a civilisation which excluded the colored races would benefit only a comparative handful of the world's inhabitants'.[20]

Although anti-racist rhetoric was quickly incorporated into the Communist Party's literature and the party platform, this did not necessarily transform into practical political activism, with the CPA continuing to campaign against 'mass immigration' and others in the party arguing that 'race' was not a significant issue for the CPA. For example, in 1922, Fred Wilkinson, in a report to the Comintern's Anglo-American-Colonial Section, wrote that 'employers want cheap coloured labour imported', but wrote approvingly that the 'trade unions are, of course, opposed to this'.[21] In December 1924, *The Workers' Weekly* claimed that 'the boss class finds in immigration a powerful weapon for the degradation of the condition of the Australian workers' conditions'.[22] The paper seemed to lament the Australian labour movement was not strong enough 'to control such dangers as immigration' and argued that the strategy, for the time being, was to ensure that 'immigrants were met at once and enrolled in unions', with 'an embargo imposed on all who refused'.[23] Another article from 1925 titled 'Immigration Menace' proclaimed that the Communist Party recognised 'this present immigration campaign [by the Australian government and employers] is the biggest immediate problem before the Australian working class'.[24] To counter this, the CPA announced preparing material in Italian to appeal to migrant workers 'to stand firm alongside Australian trade unionists in the fight for the preservation of the conditions which have been won only by the hard fighting of Australia's workers'.[25] To help build links with these Italian workers, the CPA called for 'an abandonment of all irritation tactics against the fellow workers who have been shanghaied across from Europe'.[26] A few weeks later, the CPA conceded: 'It is not immigration as such that troubles the working class in Australia. It is unemployment, and the cause of that is found in the anarchic character of the capitalist system.'[27]

At the Fifth Congress of the Comintern in June 1924, Dora Montefiore, a veteran socialist and suffragist representing the CPA, admitted that the trade unions were opposed to non-white workers and acknowledged that 'it would be pointless to ignore the question of coloured workers'.[28] Montefiore argued that the CPA were not calling for 'bringing in cheap coolie coloured labour', but, influenced by Marx's 'Proletarian of all lands unite!', the position of the CPA was 'we cannot accept any exploitation of coloured workers, because any such exploitation is bound to be followed by reduction of the wages of white workers'.[29]

Throughout the mid-1920s, the CPA continued to campaign against 'mass immigration', particularly government sponsored immigration from the British Isles (seen as a way of British imperialism transferring its poor to another part of the empire)[30] and from southern Europe. The Party argued that 'the wholesale importation of immigrant workers into Australia', was 'a deliberate attempt on the part of the capitalists to flood the country with cheap labour' and thus called upon Australian workers to 'take every possible step to combat the dangers of large scale immigration'.[31] Labourers from Italy were specifically targeted by the Communist Party, with the party press identifying a particular 'problem' in Queensland where:

> colonies of Italian workers have developed and their lack of knowledge of the English language and the hostility of certain unions… have forced these workers to become easy prey of the capitalist class and a menace to the conditions of the Australian workers.[32]

But an edition of *The Workers' Weekly* from August 1927 warned against its readers being hostile towards Italian workers, reminding them:

> The Italian workers did not drop from heaven, but, to the contrary, come from a country that experienced a working class revolution, with the Labor movement developed to a higher degree than in Australia. The Italian workers have been members of the Communist Party, Italian Labor Party and the trade union movement before their arrival out here and if given the opportunity they will demonstrate their trade union traditions equally with other workers that have done so here.[33]

This highlighted a contradiction in the CPA's outlook towards immigration and the 'White Australia Policy'. While stressing that the unions still needed to 'protest against the State aided mass immigration of Labor',[34] the Party also emphasised that they were internationalists and 'welcome[d] workers from any land'.[35] The programme of the CPA during this period consisted of the following:

1. To agitate for the discontinuance of state aided immigration schemes and international post war agreements.
2. To impress upon their trades unions the necessity of recruiting into their ranks all immigrants on arrival.
3. To advise their trade union and labor councils to affiliate to the Red International of Labor Unions... with the definite object of securing the unity of the rival organisations into an all inclusive trade union international organisation.[36]

John Pepper, a Hungarian-American member of the Comintern's Anglo-American Secretariat harshly criticised the Communist Party of Australia's contradictory stance in 1926, in response to a report by the CPA's Edgar Ross on the 'Australian question'. Pepper called the white working class in Australia 'a proletariat with many privileges', which was reinforced by the White Australia Policy.[37] For Pepper, the Party 'did not fight energetically enough against the White Australia ideology of the workers' and warned that if the CPA 'does not want to become something similar to the official Labour [sic] Party, it had to combat the White Australia Policy'.[38] The following year, the CPA resolution declared:

> In opposition to the chauvinistic and racial policy of the A.L.P. as manifested in its White Australia Policy, the C.P. must put forward a policy of opposition to State aided immigration whilst insisting on the elimination of all racial barriers in the Immigration Laws; at the same time formulating a programme for receiving and organising immigrant workers into the working class movement of Australia.[39]

The conflicted agenda was agreed to by the Comintern as its own resolution on the 'Australian Question' put forward something similar, proposing that the Communist Party 'must conduct an ideological fight against [the] social chauvinism' of the Australian labour movement, by 'championing an internationalist policy', as well as 'insisting upon... free admittance for the workers of all countries'.[40] But at the same time, the Comintern called for the CPA to criticise and condemn the 'plans of the British and Australian governments for mass migration'.[41] Robert Bozinovski has described this approach as the Party's 'commendable opposition to White Australia in the face of virulent racism', but also noted that the Comintern continued to complain that the CPA 'was not sufficiently vocal in its opposition'.[42] Stuart Macintyre has suggested that this contradictory position was because of the social and political origins of the Communist Party and its attachment to the international communist movement. 'The concern for the purity of the race was a persistent theme of the Australian labour movement', Macintyre explained, and because the CPA was 'a by-product of that movement', as well as a 'member of an internationalist organisation committed to the unity of the workers of the world', the Party 'found itself torn between old habits and new loyalties'.[43]

From the Third Period to World War II

Despite the sharpening of anti-colonial and anti-racist politics of the international communist movement during the 'Third Period' (between 1928 and 1934) and the greater focus on the Aboriginal struggle and Australian colonialism in New Guinea by the CPA, its position on the White Australia Policy largely stayed intact throughout the 1930s. As more southern European workers came to Australia fleeing the Great Depression and political upheaval in Europe, the Communist Party attempted to appeal to these workers. In an open letter in *The Workers' Weekly*, the CPA announced:

> The Communist Party of Australia, as the only internationalist party in this country, presents itself to you, the emigrant workers, Maltese, Italians, Greeks, Yugo-Slavs, and toilers of all other nationalities, as the only political party defending your interests and consistently carrying out a programme and policy leading to emancipation, to bread and work and freedom for all members of our class.[44]

But the Party still campaigned against state aided migration programmes, arguing that while the CPA 'want[ed] to see Australia populated' and 'want[ed] to see [a] great, growing and economically secure working-class population', they insisted that 'the State mass migration schemes must be resisted'.[45]

The rise of fascism in Europe also shifted the Communist Party's thinking about immigration and anti-racism. Since the 1920s, Italians had come to Australia to escape the Fascist regime under Benito Mussolini and after the Nazi's ascension to power in 1933, a small number of Germans fled to Australia, followed by a small number of Jewish refugees in the late 1930s (who were initially refused permission by the Australian government).[46] These refugees from fascism ignited sympathy amongst many Australian workers, with the Communist Party, trading on its anti-fascist credentials, pushing for a greater intake of refugees and criticising the Australian government for its racialism. In August 1937, the Party castigated the Lyons government and the mainstream press for using 'the language of Hitler' in referring to incoming migrants as 'undesirable' and 'physically and mentally inferior'.[47] 'This question of "superiority" and "inferiority" in races', the Party editorialised, 'is one of the vilest features of fascism and its ideology', and was also, according to the CPA, 'one of the most effective weapons in the hands of capitalism for splitting their ranks'.[48]

Until the outbreak of the Second World War, the CPA campaigned for a greater intake of refugees from Europe. For example, an editorial from February 1939 stated:

> The great Australian labor movement must fight for the rescue of these [refugees], our brave fellow-workers. The working class must see that these destitute people of our own class are not allowed to starve or be returned to the fascist terror merely because they have no money...

> The Lyons government must be compelled to assist financially working-class refugees from fascist barbarism.[49]

Although the Communist Party continued to argue against 'mass immigration', it characterised the arrival of these refugees as a 'special problem' that had been 'created with the rise of fascism'.[50] The Party thus claimed that the Australian working class 'can be nothing but sympathetic to the victims of fascist terror and anxious to assist in securing sanctuary for them'.[51]

The Party built a small cadre of migrant members amongst the Italian, Greek and Jewish communities, especially in Melbourne and Sydney, and became increasingly involved in mobilising the Jewish community towards anti-fascism and support for the war effort. Unlike the British and American Communist Parties,[52] which had built significant Jewish membership in the 1930s due to their militant anti-fascism, the Australian party had to make significant concrete efforts to welcome Jewish members into the Party and combat anti-semitism amongst its members (and the wider labour movement). A 1943 document, intercepted by the security services, outlined the important responsibility of the Australian Communist Party in this field:

1. To mobilise the labour movement and people generally to understand the nature of anti-semitism, to stamp it out and expose the fascist plans of its purveyors.
2. To win the Jewish people for the National Front for active participation in the fight against fascism for all progressive activities of the Australian people and for active steps to combat anti-semetism [sic].
3. To support every step which has as its aim the saving of as many Jewish people as possible from Nazi controlled Europe, to fight for the reconstruction of Jewish life after the war with full rights for all Jews. To participate in carrying out these tasks is the special duty of all Jewish Communists irrespective of what their particular Party activity or responsibility may be, where they may work or amongst whom they may mix.[53]

'Australia's Monroe Doctrine': critiquing White Australia

By the war's end, the Australian far left was in a buoyant mood – the Soviet Union was held in high esteem, European colonies around the world were declaring independence, and with some 23,000 members in 1944 and an ability to exert control over at least 40 per cent of Australia's unions, the previously marginal CPA had become a force to be reckoned with.[54] At the height of this momentary euphoria, the Party's Assistant Secretary Richard 'Dick' Dixon wrote a short pamphlet entitled *Immigration and the White Australia Policy,* which captured the Party's partial awakening to the issues of race and migration – openly attacking the White Australia policy for the first time. Yet, Dixon's pamphlet straddled a difficult course – challenging the labour movement's long history of opposing coloured immigration, while arguing to retain the wages and conditions that 'white Australia' maintained.

The pamphlet proposed a new position on migration for the Australian labour movement: one based on the recognition of Asia as a vital location for Australian diplomacy – as well as proud people struggling for independence – all while advocating a very low, non-discriminatory, level of immigration to Australia. The pamphlet sought to achieve this first by underplaying the level of racism present in the historic Australian labour movement, arguing that 'The extent to which the working class movement has embraced "White Australia" is nothing more than an indication of the degree of employer class influence in the labor movement'.[55] Such apologism should not be surprising, as it was in line with the language of the Popular Front period, officially promulgated in 1934 by the Comintern, which saw the CPA reimagine itself as the inheritor of all of Australia's radical tradition and mellowed its language towards the ALP. Dixon remarked of the 1938 sequicentenary anniversary of Australian nationhood that 'We are the real Australians... the inheritors of everything that is good and decent in the history of Australia.'[56] An article popularising the Party's new stance, appearing in its national organ *Tribune*, sought to recast Australian history as one with immigration at its centre, with mention made of the Polish explorer Strzlecki and the multicultural Eureka Stockade, while the role of Asian workers in Australia in the struggle against Japan was highlighted.[57]

In keeping with this new fondness for inclusive nationalism, Dixon also cast White Australia as an imperialist policy 'of building Australia as a "British race" so that this country might stand as "trustees" for British, as well as Australian, interests in the Pacific'. In this way, it stood as 'Australia's "Monroe Doctrine" – its object the preservation of the British Australian nationality'. The White Australia policy was then constructed, not as a pact between labour and capital to each protect their respective gains, but as a conspiracy of bourgeois ideology and imperialist interest, with the CPA standing as defender of the working class and inheritor of Australian egalitarianism. White Australia, in Dixon's approximation, was not a progressive leitmotif, but 'an outrageous insult to our great allies in the people's war against fascism – China, India and Indonesia – because it proclaims "white" superiority' – and as such constituted a stymie to better regional relations.[58] Australian communists were furthering their connections with foreign parties in the 1930s and 1940s, and many members had Asian postings during the war. The Army newspaper, *Salt*, was a conduit for the opinions of many CPA members in the army, who having met with independence forces in Malaysia, India and elsewhere, felt that 'In the interest of justice we owe [them] every assistance in their struggle', as one recruit put it, concluding that 'No lasting peace can be established so long as one subject people remains in the world'.[59] Another writer condemned the White Australia policy as a 'closed door policy to particular races that fans the embers of war [and] fosters mistrust and widens the gap between countries'.[60]

Such solidarity with Asian peoples, and opposition to discriminatory immigration policies, did not however mean that the party opposed the use of the Immigration

Act to limit migration. If anything, quite the opposite was true, as the party was a vocal opponent of the federal government's rhetoric of 'populate or perish'. The party's 1945 constitution makes no mention of its opposition to White Australia, instead only articulating a desire for 'an immigration policy adjusted to industrial conditions so that the living standard established by the long struggle of the labor movement will not be undermined'. The wording of this was even harsher than that adopted at the 1938 congress, which spoke of Australia's need to 'bear... a share in giving asylum to the refugees from fascist brutality', posing questions as to just how much of a shift had taken place.[61] Dixon went to some effort in the pamphlet to argue that the 'White Australia' policy was not an economic policy designed to protect living standards – as the mainstream argument went – but a racist policy detrimental to Australia's interests. Rather than a racial system premised on British superiority, Dixon stated, 'the number of immigrants each year should be determined by the economic situation in Australia'. What this meant concretely was elucidated at the 1948 Party Conference, which supported 'a quota system of immigration, based on the country's capacity to absorb new migrants, a system that would not discriminate against potential migrants on grounds of colour, race or creed'.[62] As such, the Party was able to express a somewhat contradictory position of solidarity with Asian peoples, while enforcing a policy that would ensure Australia was not 'overrun by Asiatics', as it was put. The Party's incongruous position was soon to be tested.

Good and bad refugees: opposing mass migration and contesting deportations

During World War II, Australia accepted some 6,000 wartime refugees from the Asia–Pacific region, 'who normally would have been refused admission', on what Immigration Minister Arthur Calwell termed 'compassionate grounds".[63] These refugees, including many seamen moored in Australia harbours during the Japanese advance, were given refuge on the understanding, as Calwell put it, that 'these people would return to their own countries at the conclusion of hostilities'.[64] Drew Cottle has explained well the formation in the late 1930s of an alliance between left-wing Chinese-Australians and white Australians around the Sydney waterfront, particularly members of the Communist-dominated Seaman's Union of Australia (SUA). This alliance, allowed by the formation of a 'popular front' in China between Communist and Nationalist forces, saw children of leading Chinese-Australian merchants form a branch of the Koumintang's (KMT) Chinese Seaman's Union (CSU) in Sydney in 1942, despite none of them actually working on the waterfront. The CSU claimed membership of all the Chinese wartime refugees in Australia, and organised successful campaigns for improved hours and working conditions amongst stranded wartime seamen, particularly owing to a walk off by 500 sailors in Western Australia in 1942. CSU members also played significant roles in the struggle for Indonesian independence, helping to enforce a ban on Dutch shipping leaving Australian harbours instigated by Indonesian seamen in 1947.[65] The Party's close relationship with Chinese, as well as Malaysian and Indonesians working in Australia, saw them vocally defend these 'enslaved peoples' when the White Australia policy was utilised against them. In March 1945, the instance of eight mistreated Indian seamen who absconded from a Dutch vessel being turned away from Australia using 'the notorious dictation test' – a written examination employed against immigrants that could be undertaken in any European language – served as an early point of protest. While intended 'as a protection for Australia against low living standards... The "White Australia" policy [is] being used to enforce the very slavery it was intended to prevent!'[66]

The Party used similar language to attack the Immigration Minister, whom they dubbed '"Concentration Camp" Calwell', over his determination 'to consolidate his position as the most unpopular statesman of the Eastern Hemisphere' by deporting those recalcitrant wartime refugees who refused to follow his directives.[67] The party campaigned widely on the issue, offering the pages of *Tribune* to both leading figures in the CSU and the Australian wives of the proposed deportees, who set up their own group. Samuel Wong, a leading CSU member and former head of the Australian Kuomintang, wrote approvingly in a letter to the paper of the CPA's quota policy, and warned that discrimination against these refugees, who had 'rendered great service to Australia during the war', would 'cause... much resentment in Asia'.[68] The deportee's Australian wives prepared a petition accusing Calwell of 'having infringed the whole preamble of the United Nations universal declaration of human rights, and so many articles of that great world document as to make us wonder whether he had become a law unto himself', concluding that 'we fear Mr. Calwell as millions of the world's people feared Hitler and Togo during the last decade'.[69] The CPA's wide network – from trade unions to church and student groups – was utilised to pass motions and agitate on the deportees' behalf.[70]

The CPA's propaganda in defence of Asian workers as proud trade unionists with war records on the allied side sat perhaps incongruously alongside their 'prolonged and bitter campaign' against migrants from areas of Eastern Europe under Soviet control, who presented as deserters and fascists.[71] Commenting on the imminent deportation of a Malaysian serviceperson, *Tribune* lamented: 'The British subject with the RSL badge on his coat lapel and the wound scars on his arm has to get out so that a Balt fascist can take his place.'[72] This scolding of 'Balts' – racist shorthand for Displaced Persons of Eastern European descent – was a constant feature of the CPA's reportage in the late 1940s, a sentiment seemingly in contradiction with the Party's stated policy of non-discrimination that became a locus for the organisation's anxiety of mass overseas migration driving down hard won living standards for white Australians. Stories in *Tribune* attacked 'Balts' as scabs and anti-union saboteurs willing to 'work 48 hrs for 40 hrs pay' who were 'better cared for than Australians'.[73] The Labor government was accused of favouring these migrants owing to their strong anti-communism, a claim borne out by subsequent research.[74] At a time of great housing shortage, where many Australians were living in 'humpies and tents...labour and materials needed to build homes for Australians have been diverted to build Balt camps', *Tribune* protested.[75] Communist controlled unions black-banned work on so called 'Balt hostels', and championed industrial action to stop persons from Eastern Europe working in communist-dominated industries such as mining.[76] The Party went so far as to accuse 'Pro-Nazi Balts with cameras' of surveilling Australian defence bases, and the recently constructed Woomera rocket range.[77]

Such fears of being swamped by anti-communist migrants ensured that, by late 1949, the Party had reversed its previous position of quotas, instead favouring a 'halt to immigration... until housing is available for those persons already in Australia'.[78] Such a stance is a logical outcome of the CPA's policy, that while highly advocating a non-discriminatory border policy, placed an individual's right to a better life well behind the collective rights of Australians to decent wages and conditions. During the 1950s, the CPA continued to highlight the impropriety of government deportations, including against Chinese workers it claimed were smuggled into the country as 'slave labour'. Exceptions under the Immigration Act allowed Chinese-Australian merchants to sponsor labourers from Hong Kong or Taiwan, whereupon 'slavery conditions are being imposed' and 'Chinese workers who revolt or merely complain are threatened with the sack and ultimate deportation'. Such scams, which saw Chinese workers paid 'only $2 a week', were not only an affront to these workers' rights to be paid and join trade unions, but 'a threat to Australian working and living standards'.[79] The far left's focus on ensuring a non-discriminatory, if highly regulated, migration system aimed to align with the economic needs of Australia was soon challenged by a new crop of young activists.

An 'immoral policy'?: Communism and White Australia in the 1960s

As the 1960s dawned, the Immigration Reform Group (IRG) published a pamphlet entitled *Immigration: Control or Colour Bar?* Selling out its initial print run of 8,190 in a matter of weeks, the pamphlet's authors – academics and students from universities in Melbourne and Sydney – adopted a very different tone to previous leftist critics of White Australia.[80] It was an 'immoral' policy, they wrote, that 'lump[s] together diverse individuals because of a single common quality', one which 'in the modern world, is becoming less and less indicative of the possession of any other quality'.[81] They, however, went beyond the Communist Party's argument that such a policy merely damaged Australia's diplomatic relations in Asia, or as an insult to proud nationalist peoples who the Party sympathised with. As the IRG put it, 'it is not enough to hear about misery in Asia and the efforts to end it', instead it was 'important to know Asians at first hand and to help them at first hand by including them, as far as practicable, amongst the beneficiaries of our migration program'.[82] Such conceptions of the importance of contact – of experience – both presaged the global New Left's emerging discourse of authenticity, and harkened back to many of the author's involvement in groups like the Volunteer Graduate Scheme (VGS). As Kate Darian-Smith and James Waghorne have recently written, IRG's positions 'owed less to politics and more to... personal

'The "White Australia" policy must go' **89**

contact between Australians with Asian students' who often lived in 'suspicion of [the] racial prejudice which our immigration policy evokes'.[83] Equally, many had served in Indonesia under the VGS programme, a Colombo Plan initiative where Australian students would work alongside Indonesians on development projects, refusing wages above those of a local worker.[84] The IRG saw reform to immigration laws as part of a broader suite of changes Australia needed to undergo to become a part of the Asian region, as 'to drop the White Australia Policy merely because of the effect on Asian and African opinion is to take too narrow a view of what is at stake'.[85] And while personal contacts had been important for members of the Australian far left, the IRG's mode of activism strayed far from the CPA's line of the early 1960s.

The CPA continued to oppose White Australia in the 1960s in much the same language as it had in the past. While the Party's newspaper makes no mention of the IRG's activities, it covered significant conflicts at Menzies' yearly Australian Citizenship Convention and various protests by Asian and African nations at international forums. At the 1959 Convention, academics, scientists and religious leaders were reported as condemning what was viewed as the continued prevalence of false genetic readings of race, and supporting an admission system of Asians 'by quota', which was both IRG and CPA policy. The article concluded that it was 'regrettable' that the head of the Australian Council of Trade Unions was quoted at the same time 'as supporting White Australia'.[86] After the Sharpeville Massacre, as Jennifer Clark has argued, Menzies stood out as South Africa's only friend in the Commonwealth, and the Party relished in reporting the 'highly embarrassing' questioning and attacks from newly decolonised states.[87] Against this backdrop of growing criticism, the Party continued to campaign for an end to the mass migration programme until housing and jobs could be guaranteed for all, while taking up the cause of Italian and Greek migrants who protested in the Bonegilla migrant camp, and opposed the deportation of unwanted migrants from Portugal and Malaysia. Protests in 1961 by migrants and Bonegilla about poor camp conditions and lack of work opportunities were presented as a 'blow... against the dishonest and callous "mass migration" policy'.[88] ASIO were particularly concerned about the relationship between the CPA and the migrant communities from southern Europe, especially those from Italy, Greece and Cyprus, where there was a tradition of large Communist Party and militant trade union membership.[89] Douglas Jordan wrote that while 'a positive approach towards these migrants was not always uniform or consistent..., it was in general a continuation of the internationalist outlook' of the CPA.[90]

Cases of racially motivated deportations proved equally powerful ammunition. Two particular cases, of Malayan pearl divers in Darwin who had been residents of Australia for over a decade, and of a British-Ceylonese seaman who absconded from his ship in Perth, claiming abuse by his captain, were presented as evidence that White Australia was a notion foreign to Australians. Darwin's citizens were reported as signing a petition 'almost unanimously' and some 500 attended a protest meeting to ensure the Malayans, who had 'many friendships' and were 'thoroughly integrated into local life', be allowed to stay.[91] The case of Thomas Palmer, a 25-year-old shipping engineer threated with deportation because he 'doesn't look European', proved another example of a discredited, unpopular policy. The CPA used its party, trade union and women's section to send letters to the Department of Immigration, with the Union of Australian Women pointing this case out as an example of the 'sinister side to the supposedly innocent "White Australia Policy"'.[92] Again, public sympathy for the deportee was central to the Party's reportage, with *Tribune* reporting that 'Public opinion in WA has shown itself overwhelmingly against the White Australia policy'. It was reported that the 12 letters Perth's *Daily Mail* received regarding the matter 'unanimously condemned the Palmer decision', demonstrating that 'Returned Servicemen's League leaders and many Labor and Liberal politicians, who are so vocal in their support for the "White Australia" policy, are out of step with democratic opinion in Australia'.[93] An excerpt from a new book by leftist historian Russel Ward, published in 1962, made this point even clearer, labelling the policy 'an un-Australian import'. On the point of the policy's unpopularity the IRG and the CPA were in accordance: this was a policy whose time had passed.[94] It would not be, however, until 1965 that 'White Australia' would be removed from the ALP programme, 'undermining over 60 years of bipartisanship' on the issue, and presaging the policy's dilution in 1966 by the Holt Government, and final removal in 1973.[95] Yet, the policy's effects lingered.

'So-called refugees': Vietnamese boat people and the left in the 1970s

'White Australia', John Lack and Jacqueline Templeton argue, 'fell with Saigon and the end of the Vietnam War in 1975'.[96] Large numbers of Asian immigrants only began arriving in the late 1970s, with thousands fleeing the new regime in Saigon for what they hoped to be friendly shores. This fall was, initially at least, met with hostility from the political left. The far left had turned to Asia significantly in the late 1960s and early 1970s, motivated largely by the Vietnam War and the Chinese Cultural Revolution – two examples of a proud, revolutionary, and distant struggle. Students, claiming to be 'fight[ing] behind the lines' for Vietnamese revolutionaries, and many activists undertook revolutionary pilgrimages to Asian revolutionary hotspots, returning with stories of self-sacrificing youth so different to their apathetic Australian counterparts. Yet, solidarity activism could often in fact marginalise Asian voices, many of whom were present on the campuses that members of the growing far left attended. Intellectual and women's activist Anne Summers remembers watching an anti-war rally march past her university office, thinking that 'the fate of the Third World was being determined, or so it seemed, on the streets outside', while an Asian student interviewed many years later recalled his distance from anti-war students: 'I [didn't] go out to the pub with them that often'.[97] And, while Australians students protested alongside their Malaysian counterparts – who made up some 60 per cent of Asians students in Australia – to challenge repression in their homelands, the arrival of Vietnamese refugees from the Communist takeover received a very different reception.[98]

The imminent fall of Saigon was welcomed in *Tribune* with the banner headline reading 'Peace Near' – and a warning – that a 'cynical propaganda campaign' was being used in Australia to tarnish this victory by reporting on 'refugees fleeing the communists'. 'Refugees', *Tribune* warned, who were 'the wealthy, the corrupt and the collaborators' – not genuine people in need, like those fleeing fascist Chile or Spain.[99] The far left consciously politicised the arrival of so-called 'boat people' from Vietnam, relying on rhetorical tools of White Australia to draw distinctions between 'deserving' and 'undeserving' arrivals. Some of this was reminiscent of the 1940s discourse around 'Balts' as favoured immigrants, with one article entitled 'The Great Humanitarian Refugee Con: Only Reactionaries Need Apply' leaving little to the imagination. Chilean refugees, suffering under a 'bloody right-wing coup', were only allowed into Australia in small numbers, and 'after extensive delays and an undertaking not to engage in political activity'. On the other hand, refugees from South Vietnam were said to receive 'a warm welcome' amid 'paroxysms of anti-communist hysteria' from the press. *Tribune* warned that these refugees were already being used as indentured labour at a time of high unemployment, and could even be 'expatriate terrorists determined to sabotage' the new government.[100] Another article resorted to similarly ugly language, describing Vietnamese refugee arrivals as 'amongst the wealthiest this country has seen', bringing 'not only large quantities of gold, but servants as well'. One family was said to have bought a comfortable Perth home within a week of arriving, while others were 'making handsome profits from the sale of their supposedly unseaworthy boats' – all of which was 'a far cry from descriptions in the press of poor and hapless Vietnamese washing up on the north-west coast'.[101] Whether intentional of not, *Tribune* was employing a language of racial exclusion with a long history in the Australian labour movement.

Such racially charged language was also evident in the Australian Labor Party – with minister Clyde Cameron reporting that Whitlam responded to the fall of Saigon that he did not want 'hundreds of f—ing Vietnamese Balts coming into this country'.[102] Whitlam spoke along similar – if more restrained – lines at a gathering of the Australia-Vietnam Society, a CPA sponsored solidarity group charged with raising funds for reconstruction and spreading reports of the struggling nation's successes, in late 1978. 'So-called' refugees, who Whitlam remarked were offering handsome bribes to local officials in order to leave, were 'creating social tensions among the Australian people'.[103] 'Most of Australia is uninhabitable', Whitlam later added, 'and the refugees from Vietnam will be coming to Australia to live overwhelmingly in Sydney and Melbourne, which are also quite crowded', casting the perceived threat of over-population in highly racial terms.[104] The return of such rhetoric – even from avowed opponents of racialized restrictions – demonstrates the left's continuing ambiguity.

Conclusion

In the first half of the twentieth century Australia's labour movement was arguably amongst the world's most privileged, owing to its support for a regime of immigration restriction targeting coloured peoples. As this chapter has shown, the Australian far left was not immune from such racism, and indeed in its desire to provide leadership to the labour movement, justified policies far from the spirit of proletarian internationalism. While the IWW provided noble opposition in the 1910s, the CPA was throughout its existence torn between a professed global solidarity and the realities of the Australia's position as a bastion of white skin privilege. The Comintern criticised the CPA for this, and an uneasy compromise was made whereby the party extended a 'friendly hand' to migrant workers in Australia, but campaigned against 'mass immigration' from Europe at the same time.

After World War II, the party began calling out the White Australia Policy as un-Australian, imperialistic and racialist – an insult to struggling peoples in Asia – all the while singling out groups of migrants for vilification and maintaining a policy of either no or very little immigration in order to maintain Australian worker's high standards of living. In the end, it was neither the CPA's ambiguousness nor the IRG's morality but instead geopolitical expediency which drove the policy's 'long, slow death'.[105] Today, it is easy to question whether rumours of the policy's death were indeed overstated. Much as Vietnamese refugees were targets of far left campaigns in the 1970s, the contemporary left is prone to bouts of nationalistic bordering – with the ALP a continuing proponent of offshore detention of asylum seekers, and trade unions opposing the use of temporary visas to employ foreign workers on an 'Australians first' basis. The continuation of such rhetoric, even from a party which officially abandoned the policy over 50 years ago and trade unions who hold strong to their supposedly internationalist traditions, illustrates White Australia's long, lingering shadow over this nation's progressive politics.

Notes

1   Neville Kirk, *Labour and the Politics of Empire: Britain and Australia 1900 to the Present* (Manchester: Manchester University Press, 2011), p. 23.
2   Neville Kirk, *Comrades and Cousins: Globalization, Workers and Labour Movements in Britain, the USA and Australia from the 1880s to 1914* (London: Merlin Press, 2003), pp. 70–71.
3   Marilyn Lake & Henry Reynolds *Drawing the Global Colour Line: White Men's Countries and the Question of Racial Equality* (Melbourne: Melbourne University Press, 2008), pp. 150–157.
4   Kay Saunders, '"A New Race, Bred of the Soil and Sun": Conceptualising Race and Labour, 1890–1914', in Mark Hearn & Greg Patmore (eds) *Working the Nation: Working Life and Federation 1880–1914* (Annandale, NSW: Pluto Press, 2001), p. 80.
5   Raymond Evans, 'Keeping Australia Clean White', in Verity Burgmann & Jenny Lee, *A Most Valuable Acquisition: A People's History of Australia since 1788* (Fitzroy, Vic.: McPhee Gribble Publishers, 1988), p. 173.
6   Neville Kirk, 'Traditionalists and Progressives: Labor Race, and Immigration in Post-World War II Australia and Britain', *Australian Historical Studies*, 39/1 (2008), pp. 53–71.

'The "White Australia" policy must go' **93**

7 Neville Meaney, 'The End of "White Australia" and Australia's Changing Perceptions of Asia, 1945–1990', *Australian Journal of International Affairs*, 49/2 (1995), p. 171.

8 Tom Barker, 'The AWU in the Northern Territory', *Direct Action*, 1 April 1915, p. 2.

9 Barker, 'The AWU in the Northern Territory', p. 2.

10 Barker, 'The AWU in the Northern Territory', p. 2.

11 A.E. Brown, 'Craft Union Delusions', *Direct Action*, 1 July 1916, p. 1.

12 Brown, 'Craft Union Delusions', p. 1.

13 Frank Farrell, *International Socialism & Australian Labour: The Left in Australia* (Sydney: Hale & Iremonger, 1981), p. 84.

14 Verity Burgmann, *Revolutionary Industrial Unionism: The Industrial Workers of the World in Australia* (Cambridge: Cambridge University Press, 1995), p. 91.

15 Burgmann, *Revolutionary Industrial Unionism*, p. 91.

16 Marilyn Lake & Henry Reynolds, *Drawing the Global Colour Line: White Men's Countries and the Question of Racial Equality* (Carlton, Vic.: Melbourne University Press, 2008), pp. 6–7.

17 'Theses on the Eastern Question', in John Riddell (ed.), *Toward the United Front: Proceedings of the Fourth Congress of the Communist International, 1922* (Chicago: Haymarket Books, 2011), p. 1181.

18 Pearl Hanks, 'The Color Problem', *The Proletarian*, 7 December 1920, pp. 11–12.

19 Hanks, 'The Color Problem', p. 13.

20 Hanks, 'The Color Problem', p. 13.

21 Minutes of meeting of the Anglo-American-Colonial Section of the Executive of the Comintern, 6 April 1922, p. 5, 495/72/2 RGASPI, Moscow.

22 'How to Deal with Immigrants', *The Workers' Weekly*, 12 December 1924, p. 1.

23 'How to Deal with Immigrants', p. 1.

24 'Immigration Menace', *The Workers' Weekly*, 5 June 1925, p. 4.

25 'Immigration Menace', p. 4.

26 'Immigration Menace', p. 4.

27 'The Immigration Menace', *The Workers' Weekly*, 17 July 1925, p. 2.

28 Dora Montefiore, 'Speech at the 5th Congress of the Comintern Moscow, 25th June 1924', www.marxists.org/archive/montefiore/1924/labour.htm (accessed 4 April 2017).

29 Montefiore, 'Speech at the 5th Congress of the Comintern Moscow, 25th June 1924'.

30 The Empire Settlement Act 1922 saw the introduction of a programme by the British government to send a large number of people, especially returned soldiers and their families, to the settler colonies, including Australia, New Zealand, Canada and southern Africa. See John A. Schultz, 'Finding Homes Fit for Heroes: The Great War and Empire Settlement', *Canadian Journal of History*, 18/1 (1983), pp. 99–111.

31 'Immigration Policy', *The Workers' Weekly*, 15 January 1926, p. 2.

32 'Immigration Policy', p. 2.

33 Chas Nelson, 'Miners and Italians', *The Workers' Weekly*, 12 August 1927, p. 2.

34 Nelson, 'Miners and Italians', p. 2.

35 W.E.P., 'Foreign Workers in Australia', *The Workers' Weekly*, 19 August 1927, p. 4.

36 'Immigration Policy', p. 2.

37 John Pepper, 'Meeting of the Secretariat (British)', 22 April 1926, p. 2, RGASPI, 495/72/14.

38 Pepper, 'Meeting of the Secretariat (British)', p. 5.

39 'Australia in the Scheme of Empire', *The Communist*, 1 March 1928, p. 9.

40 'Resolution on the Australian Question', 31 October 1927, p. 12, RGASPI, 495/3/30.

41 'Resolution on the Australian Question', p. 12.

42 Robert Bozinvoski, 'The Communist Party of Australia and Proletarian Internationalism, 1928–1945' (Victoria University: Unpublished PhD thesis, 2008), p. 70.

43 Stuart Macintyre, *The Reds: The Communist Party of Australia from Origins to Illegality* (St Leonards, NSW: Allen & Unwin, 1998), p. 126.

44 'Communist Party's Appeal to All Foreign-Born Workers', *The Workers' Weekly*, 10 August 1934, p. 3.

45 'Against State-Aided Migration', *The Workers' Weekly*, 24 January 1936, p. 3.

46 Gianfranco Cresciani, *Fascism, Anti-Fascism and Italians in Australia, 1922–1945* (Canberra: ANU Press, 1980); Klaus Neumann, *Across the Seas: Australia's Response to Refugees – A History* (Collingwood, VIC: Black Inc., 2015); Andrew Markus, 'Jewish Migration to Australia, 1938–49', *Journal of Australian Studies*, 7/13 (1983), pp. 18–31.

47 '"Undesirable" Aliens and Desirable Parasites', *The Workers' Weekly*, 24 August 1937, p. 2.

48 '"Undesirable" Aliens and Desirable Parasites', p. 2.

49 'No Worker Need Apply – Lyons and the Refugees', *The Workers' Weekly*, 28 February 1939, p. 2.

50 Tom Wright, 'Trade Unions and Migration: Aid Political Refugees', *The Workers' Weekly*, 26 August 1938, p. 2.

51 Wright, 'Trade Unions and Migration', p. 2.

52 Henry Srebrnik, *London Jews and British Communism, 1935–1945* (London: Valentine Mitchell, 1995); Jason Heppell, 'A Rebel, Not A Rabbi: Jewish Membership of the Communist Party of Great Britain', *Twentieth Century British History*, 15/1 (2004), pp. 28–50; Bat-Ami Zucker, 'American Jewish Communists and Jewish Culture in the 1930s', *Modern Judaism*, 14/2 (May 1994), pp. 175–185; Jacob A. Zumoff, *The Communist International and US Communism 1919–1929* (Chicago: Haymarket, 2015), pp. 172–186.

53 'The Tasks of Jewish Communists in the Struggle against Anti-Semitism and for the Rights of the Jewish People', 1943, A6122 444, National Archives of Australia.

54 While the Communist Party of Australia changed its name to 'Australian Communist Party' in 1942 in response to a government ban, herein the party is referred to by the acronym, 'CPA'.

55 R. Dixon, *Immigration and the 'White Australia Policy'* (Sydney: Current Book Distributors, 1945), www.marxists.org/history/australia/comintern/sections/australia/1945/white-australia.htm (accessed 4 April 2017).

56 Macintyre, *The Reds*, p. 317.

57 *Tribune*, 14 July, 1945, p. 7.

58 Dixon, *Immigration*.

59 B. Harwood, letter published in *Salt*, Vol. 10, 7 (4 June 1945) p. 54. Quoted in Lachlan Grant, 'The Second AIF and the End of Empires: Soldiers' Attitudes Toward a "Free Asia"', *Australian Journal of Politics & History*, 57, no. 4 (December 2011), p. 489.

60 M.D. McGrath, letter published in *Salt*, Vol. 9, 7 (4 December 1944), pp.45–46. Quoted in Grant, 'The Second AIF', p. 485.

61 On 1945, see 'Constitution of the Australian Communist Party, adopted by the 14th National Congress of the Australian Communist Party, held in Sydney August 10th, 11th, 12th, 1945', http://handle.slv.vic.gov.au/10381/155033 (accessed 4 April 2017); on 1938 see 'THE WAY FORWARD ORGANISE A PEOPLE'S FRONT FOR A FREE AND HAPPY AUSTRALIA: Decisions of the 12th National Congress, Communist Party of Australia, 1938', http://handle.slv.vic.gov.au/10381/155134 (accessed 4 April 2017).

62 'The Way Forward: Draft Resolution for 15th National Congress Australian Communist Party May 7, 8, 9 and 10, 1948', http://handle.slv.vic.gov.au/10381/127317 (accessed 4 April 2017).

63 *CPD*, 30 August 1945, p. 5030.

64 Ibid.

65 Drew Cottle, 'Forgotten Foreign Militants: The Chinese Seaman's Union in Australia, 1942–46', in Hal Alexander and Phil Griffiths (eds), *A Few Rough Reds: Stories of Rank & File Organising* (Canberra, ACT: Australian Society for the Study of Labour History, Canberra Branch, 2003), pp. 135–151; Drew Cottle, 'Unbroken Commitment: Fred

Wong, China, Australia and a World to Win', *The Hummer: Publication of the Sydney Branch, Australian Society for the Study of Labour History* 3, No. 4 (2000), http://asslh.org.au/hummer/vol-3-no-4/unbroken-commitment/ (accessed 4 April 2017).

66 *Tribune*, 20 March 1945, p. 5.
67 *Tribune*, 24 August 1949, p. 6; *Tribune*, 19 February 1949, p. 1.
68 *Tribune*, 7 September 1949, p. 3.
69 *Barrier Daily Truth*, 5 September 1949, p. 4.
70 For example, see *Tribune*, 12 November 1949, p. 3 and *Tribune*, 12 October 1949, p. 8.
71 Douglas Jordan, 'Conflict in the Unions: The Communist Party of Australia, Politics and the Trade Union Movement, 1945–1960' (PhD Thesis, Victoria University, 2011), p. 162.
72 *Tribune*, 4 June 1949, p. 4.
73 *Tribune*, 14 August 1948, p. 3. For '48 hrs"; *Tribune*, 3 November 1948, p. 6 for 'better cared for'.
74 Mark Aarons, *War Criminals Welcome: Australia, a Sanctuary for Fugitive War Criminals since 1945* (Melbourne: Black Inc., 2001).
75 *Tribune*, 10 September 1949, p. 6.
76 *Tribune*, 9 July 1949, p. 6 for 'black-banned'; *Tribune*, 4 September 1948, p. 6 for 'industrial action'.
77 *Tribune*, 8 September 1948, p. 8.
78 *Tribune*, 7 September 1949, p. 5.
79 *Tribune*, 25 March 1953, p. 10.
80 Kate Darian-Smith and James Waghorne, 'Australian-Asian Sociability, Student Activism, and the University Challenge to White Australia in the 1950s', *Australian Journal of Politics and History* 62, no. 2 (2016), pp. 203–204.
81 Kenneth Rivett (ed.), *Immigration: Control of Colour Bar? The Background to 'White Australia' and a Proposal for Change* (Melbourne: Melbourne University Press, 1964 [1960]), p. 87.
82 Ibid., p. 88.
83 Darian-Smith and Waghorne, 'Australian-Asian Sociability", p. 208; Rivett, *Immigration*, p. 96.
84 Agnieszka Sobocinska, 'A New Kind of Mission: The Volunteer Graduate Scheme and the Cultural History of International Development', *Australian Journal of Politics and History* 61, no. 3 (2016), pp. 369–387.
85 Rivett, *Immigration*, p. 88.
86 *Tribune*, 28 January 1959, p. 3.
87 Jennifer Clark, *Aborigines & Activism: Race, Aborigines and the Coming of the Sixties to Australia* (Crawley, WA: University of Western Australia Press, 2008), Chap. 1. *Tribune*, 22 February 1961, p. 4.
88 *Tribune*, 19 July 1961, p. 12.
89 Phillip Deery, '"Dear Mr. Brown"; Migrants, Security and the Cold War', *History Australia*, 2/2 (2005), pp. 40.1–40.12.
90 Douglas Jordan, *Conflict in the Unions: The Communist Party of Australia, Politics & the Trade Union Movement, 1945–60* (Sydney: Resistance Books, 2013), p. 163.
91 *Tribune*, 20 September 1961, p. 10; *Tribune*, 4 October 1961, p. 9.
92 *Tribune*, 3 May 1961, p. 9
93 *Tribune*, 17 May 1961, p. 9.
94 *Tribune*, 14 February 1962, p. 7.
95 Gwenda Tavan, *The Long, Slow Death of White Australia* (Carlton North, Vic: Scribe Publications, 2005), p. 155.
96 John Lack and Jacqueline Templeton, *Bold Experiment: A Documentary History of Australian Immigration since 1945* (South Melbourne: Oxford University Press, 1995), p. 150.
97 Jon Piccini, *Transnational Protest, Australia and the 1960s: Global Radicals* (Basingstoke, UK: Palgrave Macmillan, 2016), pp. 185, 188.

98 Ibid., Chapter 7.
99 *Tribune*, 1 April 1975, p. 1.
100 *Tribune*, 6 July 1977, p. 6.
101 *Tribune*, 10 August 1977, p. 11.
102 Clyde Cameron, *The Cameron Diaries* (Sydney: Allen & Unwin, 1990), p. 801.
103 *The Canberra Times*, 23 March 1979, p. 6.
104 *The Canberra Times*, 1 August 1979, p. 9.
105 Tavan, *Long, Slow Death*.

PART 2

The 1950s and 1960s: In and out of the Cold War

5

THE FAR LEFT AND THE FIGHT FOR ABORIGINAL RIGHTS

The formation of the Council for Aboriginal Rights, 1951

Jennifer Clark

Although the relationship between far left politics and Aboriginal rights is complex, those who had sympathies for one were often found to have sympathies for the other. This chapter explores how supporters of the far left realised an opportunity to advocate for Aborigines in the establishment of the Council for Aboriginal Rights (CAR) in Melbourne in 1951. In so doing they moved concern for Aborigines outside of the party or union meeting and the work place to a broad-based nationally- focused public organisation. They developed useful networks and built a knowledge base about Aboriginal issues that could then be used to change public opinion, influence government policy and ultimately support the growth of a national indigenous voice. When CAR began in 1951 what did far left involvement look like?

The story, in short

In 1951 Fred Nadpur, better known as Fred Waters, gained national attention. Waters was a Larrakia man who, on the face of it, appeared to be a secondary participant in Darwin's Aboriginal strike of 27 November 1950. The impetus for action was a demand for better food and conditions within the Berrimah Aboriginal Reserve and a weekly wage of £7.[1] The *Northern Standard*, the newspaper of the North Australian Workers' Union (NAWU), reported that Aborigines complained of receiving only tea and bread for breakfast without any butter or jam. Lunch was no different and dinner was mostly a thin stew 'sometimes little bit meat, sometimes little bit potato, little bit onion'.[2] Wages were also poor ranging from £1 to £3 for men, with most receiving the lowest rate – in 1949 the minimum rate was £1 per week for Aboriginal male pastoral workers. Women mostly received £1 or less and no more than 30/-. One housemaid reportedly received only 4/- per week.[3] Aborigines doing street cleaning and grass cutting in Darwin received £2 per week while white workers doing the same jobs received £11/0/9.[4] Aborigines were paid approximately one-fifth of the basic wage.[5]

After a 16 January march on Darwin by thirty-two Aborigines, the leaders, Lawrence Urban and Billy Palata, were arrested and gaoled for four months and one month respectively, leaving Fred Waters as the new leader of the action. He was described in the *Barrier Miner* as 'grey-haired, intelligent, well spoken and literate'.[6] It may have been the case that the Darwin strike would have had limited coverage and impact had it not been for what happened next.

On 11 February 1951 Waters led a protest on the Aboriginal Reserve. Afterwards, the Director of Native Affairs for the Northern Territory, acting under sections 6 and 16 of the *Aboriginals ordinance 1918–1947* ordered that Waters be removed from Darwin and transported to a reserve at Haasts Bluff, some 2,000 kilometres south for 'creating a nuisance and organizing protest action'.[7] Section 6 permitted the Director to take control of any Aborigine for his own best interest. Section 16 allowed the Director to keep an Aborigine within any reserve as long as that Aborigine was not 'lawfully employed' as described under the terms of the ordinance. It was this action, the apparent 'shanghaiing of Waters', that really drew attention to the strike.[8] Murray Norris, who led the NAWU between 1947 and 1951, took Waters' case to the High Court by filing a writ of habeas corpus. Norris' involvement was not a spontaneous response. Fred Waters had been in discussion with the NAWU for at least four years before the February action.[9] Norris described him as a 'hidden leader'.[10] 'We had found', explained Norris, 'that when a Aboriginal became a leader or spokesman for his people he didn't last long afterwards. He was either sent back bush or framed up on some charge and sent over to Delissaville … Sometimes they died in questionable brawls.'[11] Norris related how 'Fred Waters became this hidden leader and he was a good one.'[12] Being hidden did not save him as Norris believed that Waters was subsequently 'framed' on an alcohol charge in September 1951, was sent to Delissaville, and was 'killed in a "brawl"'.[13]

Mr Justice Fullagar heard the case and determined that Fred Waters was not employed under the terms of the ordinance. George Gibbs, an organiser for the North Australian Workers' Union had applied to employ two Aborigines. The union employed Fred Waters as caretaker of the union-owned Darwin Stadium. The issue was that Aborigines had to be employed by an individual. Under the terms of the ordinance, Fred Waters was not 'lawfully employed' in February: 'George Gibbs had a licence to employ, but he never employed the plaintiff. If the union employed the plaintiff, it had no licence.'[14] Mr Justice Fullagar also did not find evidence of abuse of power and this was largely because the Director's powers were very wide.[15] However, he did comment upon the reasons for Waters' removal. He thought it probable that Waters' protest activities led to the Director's action to send him to Haasts Bluff and that Waters had been 'incited thereto by officers of the union, into whose motives I see no need to inquire'.[16] But Justice Fullagar did go on to expose the actions of the union leader Norris as contriving to bring the case before him. 'Only one conclusion seems possible', explained Fullagar in connection with Waters' supposed employment at the Darwin Stadium, 'and that is that an attempt has been made to set up a fictitious contract of employment with a view to bringing the case within the exception of s. 16 of the Ordinance.... [T]he matters which I have mentioned do tend to make the whole case ring false, and give the impression that there is a degree of hypocrisy about it.'[17] The judgement ended by Justice Fullagar declaring that he had no jurisdiction.

Communism in Australia

Murray Norris was a Communist from 1932 until his death in 1986. His leadership of the NAWU was indicative of the way in which Communists saw the union movement as a working-class vehicle of change. Historians have demonstrated that Communist influence within Australian unions was strong even though numbers within the party itself were small.[18] Party membership rose to 23,000 at its peak in 1944 and dropped sharply to 13,000 in 1949 and 6,000 by 1952, largely as a result of the political climate of distrust and fear of Stalinism (made clearer after 1956 as a result of Krushchev's secret speech), the impact of Cold War rhetoric, the defeat of major coal strikes, the Korean War and the rise of anti-communist organisations such as the Catholic Social Studies Movement led by B. A. Santamaria.[19] The Darwin strike action of late 1950 and early 1951 also coincided with Prime Minister Robert Menzies' determination to ban the Communist Party, presented as a bill to parliament in April 1950. Menzies argued that the Communist Party of Australia (CPA) was a threat to national defence. The case for injunction began in November 1950 where the judgement was delivered against the government's position ruling that the bill to ban the Communist Party was unconstitutional. But Justice Fullagar argued that each state could act on its own to ban the CPA. Menzies pursued his cause and proposed to change the constitution through Referendum in September 1951 to allow the Federal Government to ban the CPA constitutionally. Although the referendum was defeated, the agitation around Communist influence in the unions resulted in the 1955 split within the Australian Labor Party (ALP) resulting in the formation of the Democratic Labor Party (DLP) in 1957.

The Union campaign to the Minister

Even before Waters' case was heard both the union paper and the mainstream press began to explore the wider implications of the Aboriginal action including its connection with Communism. The philosophical charge came from members of labour organisations and representatives of the Communist Party. The issue that grabbed attention was Waters' forced removal to Haasts Bluff after he led a protest. The relationship between those two actions led to a raft of statements in the press that described Waters' treatment as 'shocking', 'brutal', a 'sentence without trial', and an episode that should 'make Australians blush'.[20] Unions around the country were called on to take action. Murray Norris made personal pleas across the eastern states and literally left one meeting to go to the next.[21] By the end for February, 30 separate unions had written protest letters to the Acting Minister for the Interior, Hubert Lawrence 'Larry' Anthony.[22] The issue had now become more broadly human rights and freedom from exploitation rather than simply better food and £7 per week.

The letters to Larry Anthony universally addressed the 'forcible removal of Fred Waters' and evoked the 1948 Universal Declaration of Human Rights of the United Nations General Assembly that had provisions against detention and exile.[23] Waters' removal was referred to as 'deportation'.[24] But the letters also explored the political context of the action against Waters, describing it as one that 'savours of facisim [sic]' and an 'attack on democratic rights' that would ultimately cause Australia international embarrassment.[25] The fear of international judgement on Aboriginal policy was a genuine concern for the federal government and a known point of vulnerability for activists.[26]

Aboriginal rights, as human rights, and in connection with the right to strike and the right to protest inevitably shone through as a moral argument in the letters addressed to Larry Anthony. There was genuine concern emerging that beneath the rhetoric was evidence that 'our aboriginal brothers' were not being treated properly and the 'real owners of Australia' were being treated 'worse than animals'.[27] Not all letters came from unions. 'We are a few house-wives lunching together', said one letter, 'and discussing the dreadful treatment of our aborigines generally, and the treatment of Fred Waters in particular.'[28]

When Larry Anthony replied to his correspondents about the episode in Darwin he condemned the strike as inspired by Communists. He replied to one letter in March 1951 by explaining: 'My information is that Waters foolishly allowed himself to be the instrument of outside interests who were endeavouring to provoke agitation amongst the natives'.[29] For Anthony, the implication was clear. He argued that the action was politically motivated, and was not fundamentally concerned with the welfare of Aborigines who were being used and exploited to destabilise the country. 'There was little doubt', *The Age* reported Anthony as saying, 'that strikes by aborigines in the northern Territory were part of a Communist-inspired plan for general industrial disturbance.'[30] In the 1950s and 1960s, disturbance was feared as much as any outcome from it. Anthony's easy separation of the two ideals – far left principles and Aboriginal rights – is telling. He did not see a legitimate role for the left ideology within the Aboriginal rights environment, but neither did he acknowledge genuine Aboriginal need for social and civil reform. Rather he defended the action taken by police and the Director of Native Affairs as intended to preserve law and order. He read the public interest as something created by biased newspaper reports.[31]

Not surprisingly, Anthony's perspective was refuted in the letters addressed to him and in the press by dismissing the outside agitator position in favour of arguments that Aborigines had genuine need, their exploited situation was sanctioned by an uncaring government, and that all workers had the right to strike for better conditions. The Federated Ironworkers' Association of Australia wrote to Anthony that: 'We disagree with the clarion call of the government, that every action by workers to demand a just share in the present prosperity of this country, is a "red plot"'.[32] This argument raised the confusion between progressive politics and Communism in a Cold War climate. Moreover, were it found that Aborigines were being indoctrinated by Communists, explained the Federated Clerks' Union, then they should not be punished for that in recognition of their vulnerable state.[33] The early 1950s were years of ideological struggle, claim and counter claim, but in the middle of it all were people of good will wanting to help Aborigines. Many of them identified with the political far left.

The formation of the Council for Aboriginal Rights

Of all the actions Norris was involved with during his career he claimed the Fred Waters case as the one of which he was most proud.[34] Norris believed that Fred Waters' leadership was instrumental in initiating change for Aborigines in the Northern Territory. That leadership was supported by the North Australian Workers' Union both initially and in the aftermath of Waters' domestic deportation; it was also supported by a mixed group of Melbourne intellectuals, humanitarians and Communists who responded to Norris' pleas for help and who formed the Council for Aboriginal Rights (CAR) in March 1951.[35]

When one of the foundation members of CAR, Shirley Andrews, related how the organisation came into being she specifically referred to the connection between CAR and the North Australian Workers' Union and Norris' drive for support saying 'they set up this organisation in Melbourne'.[36] Murray Norris was one of the speakers at the public meeting that resulted in the formation of CAR.[37] Socialist labour historian Douglas Jordan has also described this connection as conscious, explicit and pivotal in the way it represented a new avenue for Communist influence:

> The defeat of the 'Communist-led' leadership in the NAWU, combined with the punitive measures against Aboriginal strike leaders by a hostile and unyielding Federal government, meant that the traditional working class strike weapon was no longer viable. It had led to the persecution and isolation of Aboriginal leaders who had emerged to lead the struggle. What was needed now was an organisation with a national focus that would campaign consistently and strongly for Aboriginal civil rights and place pressure on the Federal government to hang their policies. This became the next step forward for Communist union activists committed to the issue of Aboriginal rights.[38]

That organisation was the Council for Aboriginal Rights, the first organisation dedicated to pursuing Aboriginal rights nationally. By July 1951 CAR had moved well beyond being a simple response to the Waters case to an organisation with a much bigger purpose. The Honorary Secretary, Henry Wardlaw, wrote to the Secretary of the North Australian Workers' Union suggesting that they needed to

104 Jennifer Clark

know the facts of the Waters case so that they could act appropriately in the future. CAR was ready for the long haul. 'Should there be further cases of injustice in which you feel the need for assistance', wrote Wardlaw, 'please let me know of them, for I feel sure that you can count on the support of my council.' CAR now sat outside the Waters case and was ready to pursue a broader agenda yet to be determined.[39]

The far left and CAR in action

By looking at the relationship between the demands of Aborigines in Darwin, the support they received from the North Australian Workers' Union under the leadership of Murray Norris, and the establishment of CAR, we have the opportunity to tease out some of the complex links between the far left and the push for Aboriginal rights in the early 1950s at the height of the anti-communist political climate. CAR became an enormously important organisation that was in turn instrumental in the establishment of the national association for indigenous people, the Federal Council for Aboriginal Advancement (FCAA) which ultimately became the Federal Council for the Advancement of Aborigines and Torres Straight Islanders (FCAATSI).

Historians have already acknowledged links between Communists and the pursuit of Aboriginal rights but any explicit expression of that relationship is far less clear. Ann Curthoys is unequivocal that 'The Communist Party of Australia (CPA) was especially active on Aboriginal rights'.[40] Marilyn Lake talks about an easy move into Aboriginal affairs from those on the left of politics.[41] John Chesterman says the CPA 'had certainly taken a keen interest in Aboriginal affairs' but to say it 'orchestrated' events 'was overstating the position'.[42] Jon Piccini also identifies the importance of the CPA platform on indigenous issues as establishing an agenda around workers' rights from the late 1920s giving rise to his view that 'the Communist Party of Australia had been involved in indigenous rights struggles in various guises'.[43] Sue Taffe believed that some of the ideas of the CPA were influential, largely because the CPA 'was the only political party in Australia which had policy concerning Indigenous Australians' but this did not mean activists were 'uncritical of CPA policy'.[44] Pat Ranald says that if Communists were 'not directly involved, the work could be accused of being "communist-inspired" and hence suspect'.[45] More specifically Richard Broom has labelled the executive of the Council for Aboriginal Rights members of the Communist Party and Jennifer Hibben refers to individual involvement being 'underpinned by communist ideals' describing CAR as one of a number of 'communist-inspired activities'.[46] Elsewhere I have argued that a pragmatic approach to Aboriginal issues existed from those who saw a benefit to left-wing support but ultimately saw Aboriginal politics as different from the pursuit of any political dogma.[47] Aboriginal writer Kevin Gilbert was paradoxically clear: 'Thank Christ for Commos!' he wrote in 1973. 'They know that Aborigines don't give a damn for their dogma, any more than they do for the dogmas of the bible bashers, but they are nevertheless willing to give

The fight for Aboriginal rights   **105**

practical aid to blacks more often, more reliably and unconditionally than other groups'.[48] So how did this relationship play out in practice? If we look closely at the establishment and early days of the Council for Aboriginal Rights, an unusually complex relationship emerges between Communists, Socialists, progressives, humanists, unionists, Christians, anthropologists and those who, for whatever reason, recognised a wrong in the way Aborigines were treated in 1951. The far left was enormously important in promoting Aboriginal rights, but is it possible to tease out the finer detail of the story?

CAR principles

When CPA member Shirley Andrews issued a public invitation on 27 February 1951 for interested people to attend a meeting scheduled for a little over two weeks' later, in response to the 'intolerable position of Darwin aborigines', it was within the language not of party politics or class but human rights.[49] The invitation clearly referenced the United Nations Universal Declaration of Human Rights, proclaimed 10 December 1948 and in so doing immediately lifted CAR away from its founding impetus, the Fred Waters case, to position it within an international and generalised movement. By making this intellectual shift, the issue became much more than advocating for striking workers, but rather, the support of Aborigines for full rights and liberties.

The CPA always had an international focus. In 1922 Australian Communists affiliated with Comintern, an international organisation that promoted the spread of Communism across the world. In 1928 they published a statement supporting African-Americans as an oppressed people separate from the working class.[50] In 1931 the CPA wrote its own *Draft Program of Struggle Against Slavery*, published in the *Workers' Weekly* in September 1931.[51] But after 1948 the United Nations was a far more acceptable and mainstream point of reference. The initial CAR meeting's resolution made the shift from union action to international obligation seamless and clear:

> This meeting records a strong protest against the treatment meted out to aboriginal leaders in the Northern Territory as a result of their endeavours to obtain improved living conditions and brings before the Government the position of the aborigines as it is related to Australia's obligations under the United Nations Charter.[52]

When E. J. Walker, as the Acting Honorary Secretary, wrote to Prime Minister Menzies to inform him that CAR had been constituted on 13 April 1951, he announced its purpose as 'winning better rights and conditions for Australian aborigines'.[53] He sent the same letter to the Leader of the Opposition, Ben Chifley, but this time with the additional information that the meeting was also attended by representatives from 'important trade unions affiliated to the A.L.P.' – it was better not to tell Menzies that. Chifley replied very narrowly and, reflecting the industrial and class interests of the Labor Party of the 1950s, said that 'One of the first duties of Labor's Minister for the Interior will be to institute a thorough review of aboriginal industrial conditions.'[54] But the issue was much broader than merely working conditions and it required a far bolder vision. In the political climate of 1950, it was much easier to reference the United Nations Declaration of Human Rights than the Communist Party's Draft program of Struggle against Slavery and any outcomes were probably more achievable as a result as well.

Jon Piccini has explored the way in which members of the Communist Party worked with the idea of Human Rights especially in the years after Krushchev's 1956 speech shattered Stalin's hold on the imagination and as part of a shift in leadership that occurred in 1965.[55] Before that, the issue of human rights was somewhat at odds with the idea of a worker's utopia. In 1951 Communists were clearly at the forefront of the justification for intervention on behalf of Aborigines not only as workers but as human beings with broader rights than those identified by the North Australian Workers' Union. Wendy Lowenstein, herself a Communist, related to Shirley Andrews that Barrie Christophers, who eventually joined CAR, viewed the CPA's action on Aborigines as being quite different from that of individual members. Lowenstein and Andrews agreed that the party was more interested in 'political problems' rather than people. They saw themselves as 'humanitarians more than revolutionaries'. As a result their concerns were about fairness, justice and a simple desire to correct a situation where Aborigines 'weren't getting a good deal'.[56]

The CAR constituency – leadership

Although the impetus for CAR's establishment was Murray Norris' visit to Melbourne to promote Fred Waters' case, the task of building the committee fell to what superficially appeared to be a very mixed group including an Anglican vicar, a popular writer and an Aboriginal Church of Christ minister originally from Cumeragunja supported by an engineer and, unusual for 1951, a female bio-chemist. However, those driving the action were members of the Communist Party; those with figurehead roles were not. In 1951 that was an important strategic decision. To what extent it was a conscious one is open to debate. Sir Charles Lowe, in reporting the findings of the 1950 Royal Commission into the Communist Party in Victoria, certainly made clear his understanding of how clergymen were approached to 'give added respectability' to the activities of Communist fractions.[57] As for Norris, he became an occasional correspondent and, with his wife, Communist Bertha Laidler, a small donor as well.

The primary figurehead at the first public meeting was Canon Maynard. Farnham Edward Maynard was an English Anglican clergyman who was posted to the Diocese of Rockhampton in 1910. It was in Queensland that he became interested in the lives of the miners, even working as a goldminer for a short period of time where he became a member of the Australian Workers' Union. In 1925 he supported the Seamen's strike and the next year he moved to Melbourne to take up

The fight for Aboriginal rights **107**

the position of Vicar at St Peter's Eastern Hill, afterwards becoming Canon of St Paul's Cathedral from 1942 until his retirement from the priesthood in 1964. Maynard's predisposition to support the far left was confirmed when he delivered a lecture at Melbourne's St Paul's Cathedral on 'Christianity and Socialism'. Along with two other lectures, one given by the Marx scholar Kurt Merz on 'Marxian Socialism', and the other by Ralph Gibson on 'What Socialism would mean to Australia', Maynard's lecture was published in 1944 under the title *A Fair Hearing for Socialism*. Although Maynard never joined a political party, Ralph Gibson was a member of the CPA from 1932.

Maynard's lecture was both an apology for Socialism which he described as a philosophy that 'aspires to be the expression of the essential brotherhood of the whole human race', and an advocacy for Christian cooperation to bring about a Socialist order which he likened to 'the incoming tide'.[58] Maynard's position was unequivocal. He saw Socialism as the means to bring about a just redistribution of wealth, an outcome aligned to the Christian desire for human justice. He acknowledged the Russian success as Socialism's vindication and visited the USSR in 1952. Colin Holden is right in his assessment of the mix of Maynard's political views when he explained how 'Christian conviction did not totally account for his socialism' but it resulted in its 'particular direction and temper'. Maynard feared that Communism would leave men soulless unless it was 'reanimated by Christianity'.[59]

Co-convenor of the public meeting was Doug Nicholls, a Yorta Yorta man from Cummeragunja who became a Church of Christ minister in 1945. Nicholls took over from William Cooper as secretary of the Australian Aborigines League in 1940 and by 1951 was a pastor in Fitzroy. He became well known as an Aboriginal leader and public figure but he never joined the Communist Party. He represented a small but growing group of Aborigines who began to emerge as leaders of the movement to bring about changes in Aboriginal policy. Their interest was clearly personal, not doctrinal. The third co-convenor of the CAR meeting was Alan Marshall. Best known as the author of *I can Jump Puddles*, Marshall began his writing career submitting articles to the *Workers' Voice* published by the Communist Party's Victorian branch and the *Communist Review*.[60] He never became a member of the party.

When CAR was established and the first non-provisional committee constituted, Henry Wardlaw became Honorary Secretary under Canon Maynard as President. Methodist theologian and Minister of the Prahran Methodist Mission, Colin Williams was elected as Vice-President in absentia. Serving on the committee was Shirley Andrews, bio-chemist and Communist who left the party in the mid-1950s in response to Stalinism; Doug Nicholls, Mollie Bayne who was a member of the Women's International League for Peace and Freedom; the Secretary of the Sheet Metal Working, Agricultural Implement & Stove-Making Industrial Union – Victorian Branch; and E. J. Walker who was co-opted. Walker was involved with the Asian Pacific Peace Committee and was a convenor of fractional CPA meetings in Melbourne. Walker had also served as Acting Honorary Secretary from the commencement of CAR to the election of the first committee.

108 Jennifer Clark

The first secretary of the Council for Aboriginal Rights was Henry Wardlaw. He was an Engineer and Town Planner who moved to Melbourne from Wollongong in NSW in 1950 to take up a position as Planning Officer for the Melbourne and Metropolitan Board of Works. In that same year he was described by ASIO operatives as 'well worth watching'.[61] He was also a part-time lecturer in Town and Regional Planning at the University of Melbourne. In May 1952 he applied to his employer for seven months' leave without pay to organise the Conference for Peace in the Pacific that was to be held in Peking. He was refused and consequently resigned from his job in June 1952.[62] In November of the same year he tried to book the Supper Room at the Melbourne Town Hall to hold a meeting for the Victorian Sponsoring Committee for Delegates to the Asian and Pacific Regions Peace Conference but was refused. The Town Clerk, A. J. Steele, replied that he would 'not under any circumstances permit any portion ... to be used for such a purpose'.[63] On the panel of potential speakers was Canon Maynard. By 1953 Wardlaw had left Melbourne and was working as a Town Planner in Gosford.

There is no doubt that the power base of the Council for Aboriginal Rights belonged to the political far left, but at the same time the public face of CAR was far more diverse but perhaps no less committed to the general principles of human rights and social justice. It may well be that what Sir Charles Lowe called a 'non-communist fascade' had a ring of truth to it in this case.[64] While Canon Maynard was President the outward position of CAR was respectable, connected with the Anglican Church and not directly linked to a political party, or in 1951, to a significant Cold War player. There is some evidence to suggest that this might have been a conscious decision.

When Canon Maynard resigned his position as President to take an extended overseas trip, he was replaced by Reverend Colin Williams. Williams had just returned from Drew University after taking a degree in Divinity. He left to prepare for the Methodist Mission for the Nation that began in April 1953 and ran for six months at which point Shirley Andrews tried to fill his vacated position. She wrote first to Reverend Stuart Babbage who was newly appointed as the Principal of Ridley College, a theological training college in Melbourne, and who had publicly endorsed Aboriginal rights. She followed this unsuccessful approach with one to R. Douglas Wright, Professor of Physiology at the University of Melbourne.[65] Andrews explained to Professor Wright that the duties were light and he was only expected to attend meetings occasionally in order to become generally acquainted with the work of CAR. Moreover, she added, 'the main requirement is to have a chairman known to people so that they have confidence in the type of organisation it is, which is naturally a reflection of its office bearers'.[66] When Professor Wright declined, she approached Reverend Percy Parnaby saying that the committee would be very pleased if they had another clergyman as their President. Again she made it clear to him that 'we have never expected our president to do anything except preside at meetings'.[67] In 1951 and 1952 it was important to have an acceptable face heading a committee that tried to break down entrenched social barriers and which drew on support from known Communists and Communist sympathisers. That collective face represented secular humanitarianism, Christian principles, as well as left wing politics of every shade. All were men and women of social conscience. Indicatively, the speakers list for the 19 June public meeting in the Melbourne Town Hall included Canon Maynard as the Chair, Scottish-born Presbyterian doctor from Adelaide Charles Duguid, Aboriginal pastor Doug Nicholls, Joe 'Yorky' Walker, onetime Secretary of the North Australian Workers' Union and communist sympathiser; and Methodist theologian Colin Williams.

It is clear that the Council for Aboriginal Rights in its founding and initial operations was heavily influenced by men and women of the organised far left, but it was not wholly so. The social justice focus within CAR was tuned by a range of influences both spiritual and secular, international and domestic. There was a genuine concern for the conditions of Aborigines in general and Aboriginal workers in particular. Because there was very little accurate information about Aboriginal life, the conditions of working Aborigines was easiest to access through the filter of unionism. The supporting structures of the CPA and the United Nations through its Declaration of Human Rights provided a framework through which those men and women of conscience could act and justify their demands for change. Those driving CAR, that is, those most responsible for its activities, outreach and direction were those also most closely linked to the CPA, notably, Shirley Andrews, who initiated the first call for the establishment of CAR but who did not assume the secretary's position until some twelve months after establishment. In the interim Shirley Andrews travelled with Margaret Walker's Unity Dance Group to the World Youth Festival in Berlin followed by travels into several Communist countries in Europe. Margaret's husband, John Walker was a member of CAR. Shirley Andrews' influence over the first ten years of CAR was unrivalled. Her interest in Aboriginal workers, her scientific background which emphasised data acquisition followed by objective analysis, and her appreciation of organisation informed by her experience as a Communist Party member, shaped the way CAR operated while she was Honorary Secretary and then afterwards while she worked as a research officer.

The CAR constituency – mailing list

When CAR finally began to build its networks and develop a sense of direction, the influence of the far left was strong. In its initial phase, CAR was mostly concerned with making connections among those who had some knowledge of Aboriginal conditions and gathering as much information as possible about the living and working lives of Aborigines, especially in the Northern Territory. The reason for the focus on the Northern Territory was obvious. Not only was this the site of the Waters case, which provided the initial impetus for the formation of CAR, but the Northern Territory employed large numbers of Aboriginal people on cattle stations as well as within Darwin. Moreover, the Northern Territory was governed from Canberra, so a concentration of activity there meant that CAR

110 Jennifer Clark

could legitimately claim to be an organisation with a national focus. Furthermore, public perception followed the lead of anthropologists who differentiated between Aborigines not by self-identification but by a crude percentage measure of Aboriginal blood. As a result it was easier to talk about Aborigines in the Northern Territory rather than the Eastern states where the numbers were far fewer and less visible. For all of these reasons CAR focused on the Northern Territory. But men and women of conscience living in Melbourne who were the stalwarts of CAR were very far removed from the Northern Territory, had little if any first-hand experience and realised that their main task must be information gathering and distribution before anything substantial could be achieved.

The mailing list in the first year of establishment represents an attempt to gather and disseminate information about Aborigines and to build a network of people interested in either giving or receiving information. As a consequence, the list of correspondents is quite diverse but such diversity suggests that those who expressed everything from commitment to CAR to a mere passing interest were not necessarily strong defenders of the far left but fell across a broadly left leaning political spectrum influenced by a range of doctrines with social justice at their core. The list contained recognised unionists, known political radicals, members of the CPA, Christians, Socialists, humanitarians and those who did not fit any political label but who were concerned with what they saw as simple fairness. Anna Vroland, for example, was a staunch campaigner for the Women's International League for Peace and Freedom and an executive member of the Communist led Victorian Council Against War. She was dismissed from her position as Headmistress of Woodstock Girls' School in Albury because of her leftist views although she never joined the CPA.[68] She credited her interest in Aboriginal welfare as stemming from the impact of personal association rather than from any political groups that she claimed 'have proved arrant humbugs in this matter'.[69] Helen Palmer, the daughter of socialist writer Vance Palmer, was a teacher, writer and historian who was active in the NSW Teachers' Federation and established the independent socialist magazine *Outlook*. She was a member of the Communist Party for twenty years before being expelled. She attended the Peace Conference of the Asian and Pacific Regions in Peking in 1952, the same conference that cost Henry Wardlaw his job. Palmer also lost her job with the Department of Education because of her political views, expressed in her 1953 book *Australian Teacher in China*.[70] Alfred Jacobs was a Melbourne doctor who spent most of his career in Western Australia. He served as the Honorary Secretary of the Narrogin Native Welfare Committee during the 1950s and was strongly opposed to Menzies' attempts to ban the Communist Party but he was never a member. He was interested in Aboriginal rights from the libertarian perspective.[71] Mary Bennett was a humanitarian who corresponded regularly with CAR in its first year because she had long been involved with teaching Aboriginal children and advocating on their behalf.[72] R. Douglas Wright, Professor of Physiology and Chancellor of the University of Melbourne was a civil libertarian but not a Communist. Edith Hedger was Honorary Secretary of the League of Women Voters.

The fight for Aboriginal rights **111**

Apart from individuals, there were representatives of various affiliating organisations such as J.C. Chandler of the Building Workers' Industrial Union of Australia, P. W. Hill, Secretary of the Sheet Metal Working, Agricultural Implement and Stove-Making Industrial Union of Australia, B. Flanagan from the Federated Ironworkers' Association of Australia, and Gordon Lewis representing the Operative Painters' and Decorators' Union of Australia and of course the North Australian Workers' Union. Unions were well represented in the correspondence list; sometimes invited to meetings, and on other occasions giving donations to CAR in the form of membership fees of £2.20. In the first year of operation, February to December 1951, of the 244 pieces of inward and outward correspondence at least 34 were with unions, branches of the Labor Party or individual unionists, but 21 were with people who identified with religious organisations including churches and church schools, 16 were with anthropologists, 43 with government departments and government funded organisations, 14 with members of the University of Melbourne community and 25 with Aboriginal organisations or individual Aborigines.

It is certainly true that a solid percentage of the correspondence was with clearly identifiable far left groups, and if we add the 15 pieces of correspondence to non-labour organisations and individuals such as Anna Vroland from the Women's International League for Peace and Freedom, then the percentage would rise, but it is also true to say that significant correspondence was between government departments and anthropologists seeking information, together totalling 59 pieces of correspondence. In the day-to-day affairs of CAR the far left was only part of the story of network building and information gathering. Moreover, some of the individuals with whom CAR corresponded fell into politically complex categories, such as socialist but not Communist, Christian and socialist, humanitarian but not Communist, and the non-committed curious. However, when a sub committee was formed to generate policy around economic conditions, of the seven people nominated, at least six can be identified as unionists or Communists.[73] By 1956 when Shirley Andrews described the members of the committee to a potential new president, only one of the twelve mentioned by name and a distinguishing feature was described as a member of the Communist Party.[74]

CAR policy

Those who were part of CAR were keen to see a policy document produced that outlined the CAR position on Aboriginal affairs. As perhaps the primary statement of CAR to what extent can it be read as a far left manifesto? When the Communist Party of Australia advocated for Aborigines it set out a list of fourteen demands published in The *Workers' Weekly* in September 1931. The list covered full and equal rights for Aborigines, political freedom, freedom of movement, the elimination of decisions based on colour, the end of forced labour, the provision of full wages to Aborigines, the prohibition of slave labour, the release from gaol of all Aboriginal prisoners until Aborigines sat on juries, the prohibition of taking

112 Jennifer Clark

children from their families, maintenance of the sanctity of the family, the end of missions and the establishment of an independent Aboriginal state. The manifesto ended with the cry: 'Struggle with the aborigines against Australian Imperialism! Workers and oppressed peoples of all lands, unite!'[75]

CAR began to work on its policy document almost immediately and by July 1951 Henry Wardlaw wrote to anthropologist Professor A .P. Elkin that the draft was nearly complete and he would be asked to provide comment on it.[76] By 18 August Wardlaw was sending out copies for comment to a range of correspondents with the note that sub-committees had been established to work on various aspects of the policy.[77] By the end of that month detailed responses came back to CAR for consideration and revision of the policy document.[78] The resulting policy, which was further revised and amended over the coming years, was divided into eight sections: citizenship, rights and government responsibility; economic conditions; education; housing; reservations, missions and settlements; health; preservation of Aboriginal traditional artefacts; and co-operation.[79] In some respects the CAR policy reflected the concerns of the CPA manifesto of 1931 around full citizenship rights, the removal of colour discrimination, equal pay provisions, full access to government services, better education and Aboriginal management of reserves. The main difference between the two documents was in political and ideological language and the inclusion or omission of significant detail.

The CAR policy made no mention of imperialism, slave labour, forced labour, capitalism, kidnapping, extermination, or aboriginal republics. In other words, the strongly ideological language was removed, while the sentiments around work, family and sustainable communities were rephrased in terms of opposition to discrimination, support for equal wages, welfare support, and the inviolability of reserves. The language was far milder, far more dispassionate and consequently far less easily identifiable as Communist but the outcomes were the same – equality of experience under the law through the recognition of citizenship and workplace entitlements.

Significantly, perhaps because of a less doctrinal position, the CAR document made no mention of forced removal of children, something that was to become a source of national reproach after the disclosure of the 1997 *Bringing them Home* Report, whereas this was a prominent part of the CPA document. Clause 8 was unequivocal and unambiguous: 'Absolute prohibition of the kidnapping of aboriginal children by the A.P.B., whether to hire them out as slaves, place them in "missions", gaols or "correction" homes'.[80] Even though the forced taking of Aboriginal children was not part of the policy document, it was a topic of correspondence. Members of CAR were aware of the practice and disapproving of it.

Also significant, although not reflected in the Communist document, the CAR policy did not differentiate, classify or identify Aborigines most notably making no mention of tribalised or detribalised Aborigines, half-castes or part-Aborigines, all of which was common anthropological language in parlance throughout the 1950s strongly impacting policy formulation and implementation. Although CAR relied heavily on anthropological research for information about Aborigines, the classification system was not reproduced in the policy.

The CAR policy reflected the far left concern with working conditions and the humanitarians' concern with civil rights. It did not reflect the CPA concern with class war, revolutionary change or race empowerment. Perhaps this was a reflection of the times. The CAR document was written in 1951 but refined over the next ten years. Point 1f advocated for the ratification of the International Labour Organization convention, 1957 (No.107) which covered the 'protection and integration' of Indigenous peoples.[81] Point 1d was in response to the momentum around revision to the constitution which would become the campaign for the Yes vote in the 1967 Referendum. The Economic Conditions section reflects the interests of the unions around wage parity and entitlement but did not address economic racism more broadly. In that sense the policy document did not suggest the lifestyle idealism of the New Left. In terms of education there was no mention of equality of opportunity which was to feature strongly in the New Left manifesto but rather it reflected a desire for the government to provide education to all Aboriginal children and at the same standard as that received by white children. One significant difference was the support for education to be delivered in Aboriginal languages where appropriate.

Conclusion

Historians have long recognised that there is a relationship between advocacy for Aboriginal rights and the far left. But when we look more closely at an example of how that plays out, we see complexity that can be hidden by a general statement. The case of CAR reveals a clear connection between members of the Communist Party in the first instance through the Communist-run North Australian Workers' Union of the late 1940s and very early 1950s and the support of Aborigines wishing to gain better working conditions. However, as a result of the crackdown on the Communist Party from the conservative Menzies Government and the disengagement with Communism within the labour movement throughout the early 1950s, a new broad-based nationally focussed public organisation was well suited to help Aborigines not just seek wage parity but also better conditions across a range of social indicators. CAR filled that need. Driven by individual Communists rather than the party itself, CAR also provided a vehicle for humanists, socialists, Christians and unaligned men and women of conscience to reach out to Aborigines and to each other.

Acknowledgement

I wish to acknowledge funded support for this research from the State Library of Victoria and the University of Melbourne.

Notes

1 *Barrier Miner*, 24 January 1951, p. 2.
2 *Northern Standard*, 26 January 1951, p. 12.

114 Jennifer Clark

3 *Northern Standard*, 26 January 1951, p. 12.
4 Address by Murray Norris, 12 February 1951, Council for Aboriginal Rights Papers (CAR), MS 12913, Box 8, File 1, State Library of Victoria, Melbourne.
5 'National Petition towards Equal Wages for Aborigines', Barry Christophers Papers, 1951–1981, MS7992/8, National Library of Australia, Canberra.
6 *Barrier Miner*, 12 February 1951, p. 2.
7 'No Justice for Fred Waters and No Appeal', *The Maritime Worker*, 24 February 1951, p. 2.
8 *Northern Standard*, 23 February 1951, p. 1.
9 Judith Elton, 'Comrades or Competition? Union Relations with Aboriginal Workers in the South Australian and Northern Territory Pastoral Industries, 1878–1957', PhD thesis, University of South Australia, 2007, p. 341.
10 Murray Norris, 'Rebuilding the North Australian Workers' Union, 1942–1951', in Hal Alexander and Phil Griffiths eds, *A Few Rough Reds: Stories of the Rank and File Organising* (Canberra: Australian Society for the Study of Labour, 2013), p. 106.
11 Norris, 'Rebuilding the North Australian Workers' Union', p. 106.
12 Norris, 'Rebuilding the North Australian Workers' Union', p. 106.
13 *Courier Mail*, 7 September 1951, p. 1; Norris, 'Rebuilding the North Australian Workers' Union', p. 109. The death register for Fred Waters indicates death in 1958 from a fractured skull aged 58. Northern Territory Aboriginal Deaths 1953–1962, Centre for Indigenous Family History Studies, www.cifhs.com (accessed 22 November 2016).
14 Waters v Commonwealth (1951) 82 CLR 188, 194.
15 Waters v Commonwealth (1951) 82 CLR 188, 194.
16 Waters v Commonwealth (1951) 82 CLR 188, 195.
17 Waters v Commonwealth (1951) 82 CLR 188, 196.
18 Zora Simic, 'Butter not Bombs: A Short History of the Union of Australian Women', *History Australia* 4.1 (2007), 7.1; Deborah Wilson, *Different White People: Radical Activism for Aboriginal Rights 1946–1972* (Crowley, WA: UWA Press, 2015), pp. 3, 17; Elton, 'Comrades or Competition?'
19 Sean Scalmer, 'Marxist Ideology inside the Communist Party of Australia 1942–1956', *Journal of Political Ideologies*, 3:1 (1998), pp. 45–61; John McLaren, 'The End of an Affair: Intellectuals and the Communist Party, 1956–1959', *Journal of Australian Studies*, 27 (2003), pp. 71–82. Wilson, *Different White People*, pp. 26–27; Pat Ranald, 'Women's Organisations and the Issue of Communism', in Ann Curthoys and John Merritt eds, *Better Dead than Red: Australia's First Cold War: 1945–1959*, Vol. 2 (Sydney: Allen & Unwin, 1986), p. 53; Victoria, Royal Commission into *The Origins, Aims, Objects and Funds of the Communist Party in Victoria and Other Related Matters*, Final Report (1950), p. 43.
20 *Northern Standard*, 23 February 1951, p. 1; *The Cessnock Eagle and South Maitland Recorder*, 6 April 1951, p. 3; *Northern Standard*, 2 March 1951, p. 9.
21 Elton, 'Comrades or Competition?', p. 361; Norris, 'Rebuilding the North Australian Workers' Union', pp. 108–019.
22 '30 Unions Demand Release of Waters: Protest this Crime', *Northern Standard*, 23 February 1951, p. 1.
23 Mrs E. Carroll, Hawthorn Branch Union of Australian to H. L Anthony, 5 March 1951. Representations on behalf of. NAA: A431 1950/3697 Part A, Canberra.
24 Helen Cornish, Honorary Secretary Aborigines Advancement League of SA to H.L Anthony, 21 February 1951. Fred Waters and Lawrence. Representations on behalf of. NAA: A431 1950/3697 Part A, Canberra.
25 James W. Lambert, NSW Fire Brigade Employees' Union, 26 February 1951; Murray Branch Secretary, WA Eureka Youth League, 7 March 1951. Fred Waters and Lawrence. Representations on behalf of. NAA: A431 1950/3697 Part A, Canberra.
26 On the significance of Aboriginal rights to Australia's international profile see Jennifer Clark '"Something to Hide": Aborigines and the Department of External Affairs, January 1961–62', *Journal of the Royal Australian Historical Society*, 83 (1997), pp. 71–84; John

The fight for Aboriginal rights **115**

Chesterman, 'Defending Australia's Reputation: How Indigenous Australians Won Civil Rights, Part One', *Australian Historical Studies*, 32 (2001), pp. 20–39; 'Defending Australia's Reputation: How Indigenous Australians Won Civil Rights, Part Two', *Australian Historical Studies*, 32 (2001), pp. 201–221; Sue Taffe, 'Australian Diplomacy in a Policy Vacuum: Government and Aboriginal Affairs, 1961–62', *Aboriginal History*, 19 (1995), pp. 154–172.

27 B.F. Flanagan, Branch Secretary – Victoria, Federated Ironworkers' Association of Australia, 21 February 1951; Lambert, 26 February 1951 Fred Waters and Lawrence. Representations on behalf of. NAA: A431 1950/3697 Part A, Canberra.

28 Nellie Quinlan, Irene McGowan, Iris Wright, Mary Wright to H.L Anthony 19 February 1951. Fred Waters and Lawrence. Representations on behalf of. NAA: A431 1950/3697 Part A, Canberra.

29 H.L Anthony to Mrs Parker, 12 March 1951. Fred Waters and Lawrence. Representations on behalf of. NAA: A431 1950/3697 Part A, Canberra.

30 'Reds Blamed for Native Strikes Action against N.T. Leaders Defended', *The Age*, 20 February 1951, p. 5.

31 H.L Anthony to T. Peel, Acting Secretary, North Australian Workers' Union, 1 February 1951; H.L Anthony to E.H.D. Russell, M.P. Port Pirie, 10 March 1951, Fred Waters and Lawrence. Representations on behalf of. NAA: A431 1950/3697 Part A, Canberra.

32 K. McKeon, Federated Ironworkers' Association of Australia to H.L Anthony, 5 March 1951. Fred Waters and Lawrence. Representations on behalf of. NAA: A431 1950/3697 Part A, Canberra.

33 State Secretary of the Federated Clerks' Union of Australia (Victoria Branch) to H.L Anthony, 23 February 1951, Fred Waters and Lawrence. Representations on behalf of. NAA: A431 1950/3697 Part A, Canberra.

34 Norris, 'Rebuilding the North Australian Workers' Union', p. 109.

35 *Northern Standard*, 23 February 1951, p. 1; 6 July 1951, p. 7.

36 Shirley Andrews interviewed by Peter Read, Oral TRC 2303/33, 2 March, 1989. National Library of Australia, Canberra.

37 Victorian Aboriginal Group, Twenty-Second Annual Report, 1951, CAR Papers, MS 12913, Box 5.

38 Douglas Jordan, 'Conflict in the Unions: The Communist Party of Australia, Politics and the Trade Union Movement, 1945–1960', PhD thesis, Victoria University 2011, pp. 302–303.

39 Henry Wardlaw to The Secretary, North Australian Workers' Union, 3 July 1951, CAR Papers, MS 12913, Box 1, File 1, State Library of Victoria, Melbourne.

40 Ann Curthoys, *Freedom Ride: A Freedom Rider Remembers* (Crows Nest: Allen & Unwin, 2002), p. 11.

41 Marilyn Lake, *Faith: Faith Bandler, Gentle Activist* (Crows Nest, NSW: Allen & Unwin, 2002), p. 31.

42 John Chesterman, *Civil Rights: How Indigenous Australians won Formal Equality* (St Lucia: UQP, 2005), p. 58.

43 Jon Piccini, *Transnational Protest, Australia and the 1960s: Global Radicals* (London: Palgrave Macmillan, 2016), p. 169.

44 Sue Taffe, 'The Federal Council for the Advancement of Aborigines and Torres Straight Islanders: The Politics of Inter-racial Coalition in Australia, 1958–1973', PhD thesis, Monash University, 2001, p. 7; Sue Taffe, 'The Cairns Aborigines and Torres Strait Islander Advancement League and the Community of the Left', *Labour History*, 97 (2009), p. 150. See also, Bob Boughton, 'The Communist Party of Australia's Involvement in the Struggle for Aboriginal and Torres Strait Islander Peoples' Rights, 1920–1970', in Raymond Markey, *Labour and Community: Historical Essays* (Wollongong: University of Wollongong Press, 2001), pp. 263–294.

45 Ranald, 'Women's Organisations and the Issue of Communism', p. 53.

46 Richard Broom, Nicholls, Sir Douglas Ralph (Doug) (1906–1988), *Australian Dictionary of Biography*. adb.anu.edu.au/biography/nicholls-sir-douglas-ralph-doug-14920 (accessed 6 December 2016); Jennifer A. Hibben, 'Shirley Andrews: A Prismatic Life', PhD thesis, University of Melbourne, 2011, pp. 19, 198.

47 Jennifer Clark, *Aborigines & Activism Race, Aborigines & the Coming of the Sixties to Australia* (Crawley, WA: UWA Press, 2008), pp. 58–59.

48 Kevin Gilbert, *Because a White Man'll Never Do It* (Sydney: Angus & Robertson, 1973), p. 28.

49 Shirley Andrews, Correspondence Secretary, 27 February 1951, Circular, CAR Papers, MS 12913, Box 1, File 1, State Library of Victoria, Melbourne.

50 The 1928 Comintern Resolution on the Negro Question in the United States. www.marx2mao.com/Other/CR75.html#1 (accessed 11 February 2017).

51 Boughton, 'The Communist Party of Australia's Involvement in the Struggle for Aboriginal and Torres Strait Islander Peoples' Rights, 1920–1970', p. 267; 'Communist Party's Fight for Aborigines Draft Program of Struggle against Slavery', *The Workers' Weekly*, 25 September 1931, p. 2.

52 E.J. Walker to Menzies, 29 March 1951, CAR Papers, MS 12913, Box 1, File 1, State Library of Victoria, Melbourne.

53 E.J. Walker to Menzies, 29 March 1951, CAR Papers, MS 12913, Box 1, File 1, State Library of Victoria, Melbourne.

54 Chifley to Walker, 6 April 1951, CAR, MS 12913, Box 1, File 1, State Library of Victoria, Melbourne.

55 Jon Piccini, '"More than an Abstract Principle": Reimagining Rights in the Communist Party of Australia, 1956–1971', *Journal of Australian Studies*, 39.2 (2015), p. 206.

56 Shirley Andrews, Interviewed by Wendy Lowenstein, Oral TRC 3111/1, 4 April, 1994, National Library of Australia, Canberra.

57 Victoria, Royal Commission into *The Origins, Aims, Objects and Funds of the Communist Party in Victoria and Other Related Matters*, Final Report (1950), p. 53.

58 Farnham E. Maynard, 'Christianity and Socialism', in *A Fair Hearing for Socialism* (Melbourne: n.p.; 1944), pp. 39, 46.

59 Colin Holden, *From Tories at Prayer to Socialists at Mass: St Peter's, Eastern Hill* (Melbourne: Melbourne University Press, 1996), pp. 200, 225.

60 Alan Marshall, *I Can Jump Puddles* (Melbourne: F W Cheshire, 1955).

61 SECRET – New Series No 4, 23 November 1950, Henry Wardlaw, NAA, A6119 3302, Canberra.

62 Henry Wardlaw to Secretary, Town Planning Branch, 9 May 1952; Wardlaw to Secretary Town Planning Branch, 14 May 1952, Henry Wardlaw, NAA A6119 3302, Canberra.

63 A.J. Steele, Town Clerk, to Henry Wardlaw, 17 November 1952, Henry Wardlaw, NAA A6119, 3302, Canberra.

64 Victoria, Royal Commission into *The Origins, Aims, Objects and Funds of the Communist Party in Victoria and Other Related Matters*, Final Report (1950), p. 53.

65 Stuart Barton Babbage, *Memoirs of a Loose Canon* (Brunswick East, Vic.: Acorn Press, 2004).

66 Shirley Andrews to Professor Wright, 16 August 1953, CAR Papers, MS 12913, Box 1 File 7, State Library of Victoria, Melbourne.

67 Shirley Andrews to Rev. Parnaby, 27 August 1953, CAR Papers, MS 12913, Box 1 File 7, State Library of Victoria, Melbourne.

68 www.womenaustralia.info/leaders/biogs/WLE0707b.htm (accessed 11 February 2017); Sitarani Kerin, '*An Attitude of Respect': Anna Vroland and Aboriginal Rights 1947–1957* (Clayton, Vic: Monash publications in History, 1999), pp. xii, xiv.

69 Anna Vroland to Mrs Hadow, 28 November 1952, Anna Vroland Papers, MS10301, Box 4339, State Library of Victoria, Melbourne.

70 Robin Gollan, *Australian Dictionary of Biography*, adb.anu.edu.an/biography/palmer-helen-gyneth-11333 (accessed 11 February 2017).

The fight for Aboriginal rights 117

71 Jan Wilson, 'Jacobs, Alfred Nailer (1897–1976)' *Australian Dictionary of Biography*, adb. anu.edu.au/biography/jacobs-alfred-nailer-10603 (accessed 11 February 2017).
72 Alison Holland, *Just Relations: The Story of Mary Bennett's Crusade for Aboriginal Rights* (Crowley, WA: University of Western Australia Press, 2015), p. 291.
73 Henry Wardlaw to M. Bayne, 19 August 1951, CAR Papers, MS 12913, Box 1, File 2, State Library of Victoria, Melbourne.
74 Shirley Andrews to Mr Derrick, 10 May 1956, CAR Papers, MS 12913, Box 2, File 4, State Library of Victoria, Melbourne.
75 'Communist Party's Fight for Aborigines. Draft Program of Struggle against Slavery. Full Economic, Political and Social Rights', *The Workers' Weekly*, 24 September 1931, p. 2.
76 Henry Wardlaw to A.P. Elkin, 30 July 1951, CAR Papers, MS 12913, Box 1, File 2, State Library of Victoria, Melbourne.
77 Henry Wardlaw to Ross Hornshaw, 18 August 1951, CAR Papers, MS 12913, Box 1, File 2, State Library of Victoria, Melbourne; Henry Wardlaw to Mary Bennett, 21 August 1951, CAR Papers, MS 12913, Box 1, File 2, State Library of Victoria, Melbourne.
78 A. Jacobs to Henry Wardlaw 27 August 1951, CAR Papers, MS 12913, Box 1, File 2, State Library of Victoria, Melbourne.
79 Council for Aboriginal Rights, Policy, CAR Papers, MS 12913, Box 4, File 4, State Library of Victoria., Melbourne
80 *The Workers' Weekly*, 24 September 1931, p. 2.
81 International Labour Organization, C107 – Indigenous and Tribal Populations Convention, 1957 (No. 107). www.ilo.org/dyn/normlex/en/f?p=NORMLEXPUB:12100: 0::NO::P12100_ILO_CODE:C107 (accessed 28 March 2018).

6

HOW FAR LEFT?

Negotiating radicalism in Australian anti-nuclear politics in the 1960s

Kyle Harvey

From its origins in 1945, anti-nuclear sentiment in Australia underwent an evolution that was based on international developments in nuclear weapons proliferation and occurred in response to the domestic and international trajectory of communism. What scholars call the Australian "peace movement" in these years was built on networks of communists, left wing trade unions, factions of the Australian Labor Party (ALP), and various religious figures.[1] Within this movement, opposition to nuclear weapons was a relatively consistent feature. This opposition brewed in response to Cold War developments, such as the onset of nuclear weapons tests by the Soviet Union (1949), Britain (1952), France (1960), and China (1964). Affected by domestic anti-communism, and simultaneously influenced by the international communist-aligned peace movement, Australians engaged in anti-nuclear campaigning, developed a style of opposition which gradually evolved from public meeting, congresses, and petitions to a more radical style of performative dissent.[2] This evolution stuttered throughout the 1950s, as anti-nuclear action was so closely tied to the fortunes of the Communist Party of Australia (CPA), which suffered through a decade of anti-communism, scandal, and internal strife.[3] From the ashes of this internal division, largely prompted by dissatisfaction with CPA's commitment to the Soviet model of communism, a non-aligned socialism emerged, devoted less to the ideological trappings of a rigid communism and more to an Australian expression of socialist humanism that was broad, pluralist, and committed to national democracy.[4] It also refused to view nuclear weapons as a symptom of a bipolar Cold War world, and instead campaigned for unilateral nuclear disarmament, taking cue from the Campaign for Nuclear Disarmament (CND) and its radical offshoot the Committee of 100 in Britain.

This chapter follows the evolution of this type of socialist thinking in Australian anti-nuclear activism in the 1960s, as it experimented with radicalism and more performative and disruptive expressions of dissent. Opposition to nuclear testing in these years intensified, matching the global movement for a ban on atmospheric nuclear testing which succeeded, in part, with the signing of the Partial Test Ban Treaty between the United States, Britain, and the Soviet Union in 1963. Australian anti-nuclear campaigning continued into the late 1960s due to the French government's aboveground nuclear testing program that took place from 1966 in the South Pacific. From 1960 in Australia's capital cities – chiefly Brisbane, Sydney, and Melbourne – small groups of students, white collar professionals, and other middle class activists initiated campaigns that were *exclusively* anti-nuclear, not simply dedicated to a broader desire for "peace" in a polarised Cold War region and world. During the 1950s, the very notion of "peace" carried communist connotations, and affected the ability of non-aligned peace campaigns to attract official or public support.[5] In the 1960s, however, these connections were less clear-cut, and a cadre of Australians less attached to the CPA forged new paths in their activism, encouraged in part by a more receptive ALP. A key component of this new direction were the Australian iterations of the British Campaign for Nuclear Disarmament, the largest and most influential peace group in Britain. CND groups in Australia were founded independently of each other, in Melbourne in 1960, and in Brisbane, Sydney, and Perth in 1962. Whilst small and relatively ineffective, their activities highlight the evolution of an Australian experimentation with dissent that would be expanded later in the decade as the movement against the Vietnam War and conscription intensified.

It is this trajectory that this chapter explores. In doing so, it demonstrates how a younger generation of activists – what many call the New Left – was integral to the development throughout the 1960s of an experimentation with dissent that influenced the radical tone of the anti-war movement later in the decade.[6] The anti-nuclear protest that flourished in this era was distinct in some ways from the institutional boundaries of the labour and communist movements.[7] Of course, "old left" figures were important in this newer kind of socialist-inspired action in the 1960s, especially those who had broken away from the CPA in the mid-1950s. However, the most significant factors in the evolution of anti-nuclear activism in the 1960s were younger activists, migrants, and ideas about protest imported and translated from peace movements in Britain and the United States.[8] Each of these factors injected an element of risk, an embrace of radical ideas, and a willingness to experiment with the public expression of dissent into Australian anti-nuclear protest. That many individuals involved went on to play key roles in anti-war organisations in the second half of the 1960s is also testament to the pivotal role of CND groups in the evolution of Australian radicalism.

Their influence, though, was limited. The number of individuals involved with CND was small, and CND groups were beset by a revolving membership, a perennial lack of funds, and internal division. More significantly, the announcement in late 1964 of a National Service Scheme, introducing military conscription for eligible males, led to the rapid development of an anti-war movement that sapped energy and attention from anti-nuclear campaigning. This chapter details the hesitant, stuttering momentum of these small groups of activists and their engagement

120 Kyle Harvey

with a politics of radicalism that was central to the evolving left in Australia in the 1960s.

A new radicalism?

From its beginnings, opposition to nuclear weapons, nuclear testing, and associated issues, as Tom O'Lincoln argues in his partisan history of Australian communism, was "remarkably insipid".[9] Fitting with the pattern of respectable middle class protest developed in Britain and the United States, and frequently following the mould of the communist-aligned World Peace Council, Australian peace organisations engaged in familiar activities. The Stockholm appeal – a worldwide anti-nuclear petition – was a primary focus in the early 1950s.[10] Large peace congresses took place in Sydney in 1950 and 1956, and in Melbourne in 1953 and 1959, and were augmented by a plethora of smaller activities, such as public marches and rallies, art exhibitions, youth carnivals, fairs, discussion groups, lectures, gala balls, film screenings, and so on.[11] From the mid-1950s, however, small numbers of activists began to engage in more visible, risky displays of dissent. Neil Glover, a Melbourne-based Church of England minister, was arrested in 1957 for demonstrating in public with a sandwich board displaying a variety of anti-nuclear slogans, and served a prison sentence for his refusal to pay court costs.[12] The same year, Melbourne activists vandalised a Navy frigate with a "Ban The Bomb" slogan, whilst activists in Adelaide painted the same slogan on the wall of Government House.[13] In 1958 a similar protest took place in Brisbane, where a visiting American warship was painted with the familiar "Ban The Bomb" slogan – this time augmented with "CCCP", the Russian abbreviation for the Union of Soviet Socialist Republics – and was later bombarded with flour bombs from the Storey Bridge above.[14]

These incidents, however, were relatively rare, and did not reflect the character of the organised peace movement, especially as it attempted to capture a "broad front" of public support.[15] It was not until the early 1960s that a newer form of public demonstration began to gain traction, distinct from the annual Labour Day or May Day marches that served as regular outlets for trade union demonstration for peace. Hiroshima Day marches were organised from 1961, as were marches at Easter, in the tradition of the British CND marches to – and later from – the Aldermaston Atomic Weapons Research Establishment in Berkshire.[16] Although the composition of these Australian marches relied on the foundations of the established peace organisations – chiefly the Committee for International Cooperation and Disarmament (CICD) in Melbourne, the Association for International Cooperation and Disarmament (AICD) in Sydney, the Queensland Peace Committee (QPC) in Brisbane, and the West Australian Peace Council (WAPC) in Perth – it was the influx of younger participants that was significant. Noticing how vibrant these new demonstrators were, the WAPC despaired at its traditional protests of public meetings and petitions. "We are very disappointed with the form and presentation of the petition", its secretary complained to his counterparts in

Sydney in 1962. "It is dull, dreary and old fashioned. Just the opposite to what the trend is in other directions (brighter marches etc.)."[17]

News from Sydney demonstrated to the Perth organisers just how much the protest scene was changing. The WAPC recognised the need to change, and urgently. In a 1962 circular to its members, its secretary wrote:

> There is no doubt that our own Council will fit into the new picture but we must be wary of precipitate action. The emergence of the CND here as a numerically strong body (about 100 people meet once each month) is the brightest sign and we are doing all we can to encourage it to become something of a mass movement.[18]

CND represented the anti-nuclear face of what John Murphy calls "a small, non-aligned New Left", which emerged in the wake of the 1956 exodus from the CPA over the Soviet invasion of Hungary and the Party's dogmatic adherence to Russian communism.[19] In Sydney, the socialist magazine *Outlook* was also a part of this new guard, launched in 1957 after its editor, Helen Palmer, was expelled from the CPA over her attitude towards Khrushchev's Secret Speech of 1956. *Outlook* appreciated CND groups' commitment to an intellectual socialist dissent expressed with mass direct action. CND marches, *Outlook* commented, were "flexible, informal, sociable" and were remarkable for the combination of younger and older attendees. *Outlook* surmised that this form of activity was inherently a more satisfying way of expressing opposition to nuclear weapons than meetings or petitions, as "hundreds of people ... feel they've done something much more significant than merely attending a public meeting".[20]

Australian protests of this variety, however, lacked the drama of arrests by police, nor the sheer numbers present in British or American demonstrations. Australian anti-nuclear groups such as CND, hoping to follow their British counterparts' example, were "small fry" by comparison. As *Outlook* argued, Australian CND demonstrators were "pretty much the 'hard core' of peace activists, their relatives and friends". Yet this was a new phenomenon, representative of a new style of protest, "informal yet disciplined" and increasingly acceptable to Australian sensibilities of airing political grievances in public. As *Outlook* surmised, "onlookers are obviously coming to accept that protest marching is not such an un-Australian way of behaving after all".[21] Indeed, as Catriona Elder has suggested, the "Australianness" of public protest has a lengthy history, intimately tied to the labour movement and its changing role in public life.[22] In the 1960s, though, anti-nuclear campaigns such as CND sought to rejuvenate the public spectacle of protest, inspired by the extensive popularity of British CND marches, and invoking Australia's own tradition of labour mobilisation.

Just how radical was all this polite public demonstration of opposition to nuclear weapons? These early years of CND activity in the capital cities represents a critical moment in the development of modern modes of political dissent in Australia. Largely free from the public reputation and internal political strife of the CPA,

CND groups practiced a non-aligned, issue-specific activism directly aimed at the nuclear testing programs of all nuclear powers, and were notable for their "belligerent neutralism".[23] CND groups, whilst small, were remarkable for their diversity, from personnel allied with the ALP left, to religious figures, Trotskyists, pacifists, and others interested in socialist humanism, rationalism, and Fabianism. CND groups in Sydney, Brisbane, and Melbourne were also notable for the presence of migrants, who brought with them the radical heritage of British and European socialism. Along with ideas and inspiration from CND and the Committee of 100 in Britain, and the radical peace activism of groups such as the Committee for Non-Violent Action in the United States, it was this mix of personnel, youth, and experimentation that was critical in the development of a new radicalism.

Radical personalities and the practice of dissent

The evolution of Australian CND groups in the early 1960s owed much to the unique groupings of personnel involved. In particular, the 1956 exodus from the CPA, the subsequent founding of *Outlook*, and the diversity of socialist thinking on the Australian left influenced the direction and composition of CND groups. The Fourth International, the global movement based on Leon Trotsky's philosophy of workers' internationalism, had a small number of adherents in Sydney, Melbourne, and Brisbane, many of whom were also involved in CND.[24] Trotskyists in Australia denounced the class-oriented repression and violence found in both the United States and the Soviet Union, and advocated a politics based on support for national liberation movements, for the Cuban revolution, and opposed to imperialism and nuclear proliferation. Hence, Australian followers of Trotskyism supported unilateral disarmament and found an ideal home in the non-aligned CND movement, which was willing to denounce Soviet and Chinese nuclear weapons testing, unlike the CPA. Migrants also added a vitality and international experience to this mix, offering Australians ideas and inspiration from their political lives in Italy, Britain, and China. Although CND groups "stood out as a fringe group [and] always remained outside the mainstream of the peace movement", their composition of personalities and political interests ensured that ideas about radical dissent evolved from discussion and debate to reality.[25]

The 'fringe' nature of CND's membership requires closer examination, as do the personal histories of its key members. The co-founder of Sydney CND, Brian Maltby, had been peripherally involved with the CPA and the left-wing cultural group the Fellowship of Australian Writers in the early 1950s whilst a student at Sydney University.[26] Maltby had served in the Royal Australian Air Force during the Second World War, and by the mid-1950s was living in Sydney with his wife Phyllis and two sons, working as a clerk in the Department of Works.[27] By the late 1950s Brian and Phyllis were separated.[28] It was around this time that Brian met Veronica Radom, who was born in China in 1930 to Russian Jewish parents, and arrived in Australia in 1947.[29] Veronica's marriage to another European émigré was dissolving about the same time, and it appears that Brian and Veronica travelled to Britain in 1959 where they were married.[30] In London, the couple became involved with the Committee of 100 – the radical splinter group from British CND – and were inspired to form a CND group of their own back in Australia, failing to draw sufficient interest in an Australian Committee of 100 chapter.[31]

The Maltbys formed Sydney CND in March 1962, along with a discussion group called the Disarmament Research and Action Group, a body they hoped would

> help mature our movement-for-peace, from protest to a way of life ... we would like to see the activities of our movement woven into the fabric of life. This makes evident our deep belief in the unity of all peace movements, no matter how different their methods of working toward disarmament and the resolving of conflict through United Nations Organisation. We hope therefore that our Research and Action Group will not be seen as a splinter or, even worse, as competing with other groups.[32]

The couple also began self-publishing a small periodical called *Scrap* – Studies, Comment, Reviews, Art, Poetry – which was mostly concerned with peace, disarmament, and radical thought.[33] In *Scrap*, the Maltbys advocated a mass movement of revolutionary dissent, based on a rejection of the failures of democracy to safeguard nations from the threat of nuclear war.[34] Of course, they did not discount the value of protest groups in igniting this mass movement, and their CND group grew to about 200 members by 1963, comprising a mixture of academics, students, and professionals, Many of these CND members were drawn to the non-aligned socialism of *Outlook* and a broader network of socialists and progressives involved in *Outlook* discussion groups in Sydney, Melbourne and Brisbane, Labour Clubs at Melbourne and Sydney universities, and in Fabian, Rationalist, and humanist societies.

This network of individuals, as Murphy has written, "represented a form of politics struggling, in different ways, to shake off the effects of the Cold War".[35] Geoffrey Edwards, for example, was a solicitor who had been involved with the Sydney University Labour Club, a communist affiliated group which suffered an exodus of members in 1956 following a quashed "socialist revolt" the previous year.[36] Like other socialists disenchanted with the CPA's position on Hungary and the Secret Speech, Edwards left the Club, forming a rival ALP club and later joining Sydney CND.[37] Judith Radom was Veronica Maltby's sister, also born in China and migrating to Sydney with the Radom family in 1947. By the early 1960s Judith worked as a bio-chemist at Sydney University alongside another Jewish CND member, and fellow bio-chemist, Hyam Hoffman. The key figure in Sydney CND, though, was Bob Gould, a young Sydney radical who had been a CPA member during the 1950s. Like many communists disenchanted with the Party after the revelations of the excesses of Stalinism in 1956, Gould was expelled from the CPA, re-oriented his politics, and in 1962 became involved with the

Maltbys and their new Sydney CND group. His embrace of the principles of the Fourth International led him to join Nick Origlass' Trotskyist group, although Gould soon rejected Origlass' unblinking dedication to Greek Trotskyist leader Michel Pablo. With other young Trotskyists, Gould supported the Fourth International leadership of Livio Maitan, Ernest Mandel and Pierre Frank, elected after the 1963 Congress in Rome. Despite the significant and often intractable differences between the two Sydney Trotskyist factions, both remained dedicated to achieving the radicalisation of a mass movement from within the ALP, rather than separately, as the CPA preferred.[38] With other CPA exiles – including Gould's then wife Mairi, Roger Barnes, Sylvia Hale, Alan Roberts, and June Macdougall – Gould brought a distinct edge to the direction and philosophy of Sydney CND and its role as a protest group allied to the ALP left.[39]

By 1963, the Maltbys were no longer involved with the group they founded; according to Bob Gould, Brian Maltby was "too militant for us".[40] Margaret Devoo, a Trotskyist friend of Gould, described the Maltbys as "anarchists" and "very interesting people", although she felt "some of their ideas are a bit wrong", especially their attitudes towards communism in the Soviet Union.[41] The Maltbys seemed to lack the inclination to cooperate with Gould and the other CND Trotskyists in the development of a radical movement for political dissent from within the political establishment. In addition, they worried that in Australia, the splintering within peace groups – of which they had first-hand knowledge – could be attributed to an unwillingness to engage in what they termed "real dissent". As they argued in an issue of *Scrap*, Australian peace groups

> are lost and distracted. Is this because we dare not recognize the awakening of a real revolutionary spirit elsewhere? In spite of genuine protest from countries we dare not treat as brother-nations, their zeal fails even to infect our own peace work which degenerates into grudge and gripe about the side-effects of nuclear testing. Following this path, we will have entirely fizzled out in another few years.[42]

The Maltbys drew inspiration from "a core of real revolutionaries" in Britain, the United States and Europe whose examples they hoped to emulate in Australia.

> Many of us, working in the light of these major dissenters, feel our ideals to be hypocritical unless we can be involved completely in the change we advocate. How many who protest really want to change only for others and where it will not divest them of security and comfort. What they are in fact saying is: "Let's revolutionise ideas without revolution – and gradually, very gradually." ... And this is why some peace movements are coming to a dead end.[43]

Of course, Sydney CND continued on without the couple for several more years, yet despite its own members' growing interest in disruptive protest, which they would use to dramatic effect in anti-war demonstrations from 1965,

Sydney CND failed to realise the radical potential of direct action so desired by its founders.

Victorian CND – based in Melbourne – was similarly comprised of academics, students, and other white-collar professionals. Like in Sydney, a combination of migrants and radicals exiled from the CPA, including several Trotskyists, were involved. Robert Magit, another Russian Jew born in China, played "a leading role" in CND. Magit had arrived in Australia in 1951 at age nine and grew up in Melbourne, studying Arts and Science degrees at the University of Melbourne, and afterwards working as a computer programmer.[44] His father Israel, later known as Isador Magid and a leader in the United Israel Appeal, was described by an ASIO source as a "typical shady businessman" due to his various black market business dealings in Shanghai, including his collaboration with the occupying Japanese forces during the Second World War. The family fled Shanghai in 1949 after Israel was arrested by the Kuomintang, for which he had to pay a substantial bribe for his release.[45] The Magit family, like the Radom family, were among tens of thousands of Russians living in Manchuria and the port cities of Quingdao and Shanghai since the early twentieth century, many of whom had fled Russia amidst the turmoil of the Bolshevik Revolution and the civil war. Among these stateless Russians was a sizeable Jewish community, bolstered by many more Jews fleeing anti-Semitism in Europe in the 1930s and 1940s. Following the Second World War, Russian Jews like the Magit and Radom families managed to migrate to Australia, despite strict Australian barriers to the intake of Jews, especially those from Russia and other Soviet states.[46] As a student, Robert Magit dove enthusiastically into anti-nuclear and later anti-war activism, before embarking on a varied business career in the Philippines, Israel, and Britain, and before returning to Australia in the 1990s where he has since become a wealthy property investor.[47]

Italian migrants whose experiences with the European left, including the communist resistance during and after the Second World War, also influenced the radical direction of Victorian CND. Giuseppe 'Renzo' Abiuso, who arrived in Australia in 1956, had been involved with the Fourth International and its leader Livio Maitan in Rome, and had flirted with other varieties of Italian socialism in the late 1940s and early 1950s. Abiuso worked around Queensland on cane fields before settling in Brisbane and studying a Bachelor of Arts at the University of Queensland. It was here he developed a friendship with fellow Italian migrant Salvatore 'Ted' D'Urso of Brisbane CND, but shortly thereafter moved to Melbourne where he undertook further study.[48] Along with a fellow Italian migrant Marcello D'Amico, and several Australian-born students, Abiuso was part of a younger guard in CND who were hoping to reform the Melbourne group "out of the debating society tone given to it by the old committee", which had founded CND in 1960 based on several members' experiences with CND in Britain.[49] Like in Sydney, the direction of Victorian CND at this time seemed to be largely aligned to the ALP left: the group counted Jim Cairns amongst its supporters, and attempted to gain influence in ALP youth organisations and student groups, such as the Melbourne University Labour Club with which David Hudson, another CND member, was involved.[50] Despite this radical potential and political heritage, the Melbourne group's activities remained relatively lacklustre. Members undertook vigils, marches, and cavalcades as was common for other peace groups around the country.

The Brisbane group, however, demonstrated a greater propensity toward the sort of risky, disruptive action envisaged by Brian and Veronica Maltby. The group was founded by Janet D'Urso, whose husband Ted was a Sicilian-born school-teacher, the organiser of the Brisbane *Outlook* discussion group, and, following his resignation from the CPA in the mid-1950s, a Trotskyist.[51] Ted had substantial input into the operation of Brisbane CND due to his relationship with Janet, yet maintained a distance from formal involvement due to fears it could affect his employment.[52] His friend Ken Kemshead – the "key Brisbane Trotskyist" and a British migrant – was also involved, as was another Trotskyist migrant, Lajos 'Lou' Gugenberger, an Italian-born Hungarian who had arrived in Australia in 1949.[53] Not formally involved with the group, but friendly with its members and attending many protests was Humphrey McQueen, a university student who was instrumental in Queensland Young Labor and active with a host of student politics, including with CND's co-founder and fellow student Liz Tarnawski. McQueen was also associated with the Humanist Society with CND President Frank Fyfe, and founded a Free Thought Society, whose publication *The Freethinker*, a leaflet printed by Fyfe in July 1962, resulted in McQueen's suspension from the University of Queensland. Merely in his early twenties, McQueen maintained a keen awareness of Trotskyist thought, despite never allying himself with the faction spearheaded by Bob Gould in Sydney.[54]

Through the east coast network of Trotskyists and its journal *International*, Ted D'Urso and Ken Kemshead knew Bob Gould. Since CND groups formed independently of each other, communication between them was initially infrequent. Janet D'Urso communicated frequently with British CND secretary Peggy Duff, who encouraged her to collaborate with the three other CND groups in view of forming a national organisation.[55] At Janet D'Urso's initiative, contact was made with Gould proposing an initial conference that would bring together representatives of all four CND groups. However, Gould's slow progress frustrated Janet, who complained that correspondence from London was significantly more prompt than from Gould in Sydney.[56] The one meeting of an Australian CND eventually took place in Sydney in December 1963, producing a constitution and list of aims that emphasised each group's commitment to unilateral nuclear disarmament.[57] The Brisbane group appeared to be the only attendees advocating the new organisation affirm a commitment to direct action campaigning, along with a strong commitment to ongoing communication and coordinated campaigning, a national CND newspaper, and a refusal to affiliate with any political party.[58]

This was a complicated relationship that Australian CND groups had developed with the broader far left. On one hand, many CND members maintained their membership in other organisations, from the ALP to university Labour clubs, to the CPA and its splinter groups. In Melbourne, CND maintained a "candid distance from the old peace movement", and whilst cooperating with organisations such as CICD, remained critical of its adherence to the bipolar view of the Cold War world.[59] Likewise, in Brisbane, CND maintained friendly relations with the QPC but continued to affirm its position on unilateral disarmament. Collaboration with the QPC's Norma Chalmers in Hiroshima Day marches proved useful, but the stigma of CND's association with communists proved too much for an early CND member Roy Forward, who resigned in February 1964 due to CND and QPC cooperation on a peace march from Ipswich to Brisbane that was to take place that April.[60] Brisbane CND attempted to draw a broad net in its relationships, yet was often unsuccessful. The Australian Labour Day Celebration Committee, for example, refused to grant CND's request to join its 1963 Labour Day march, as the QPC had already been granted permission to march, and its presence alone would "adequately represent the wishes and desires of the trade union movement for peace".[61] This lack of cooperation was typical of the fraught relationship between the 'old' and 'new' left, largely based on ideological rifts that had developed since the schisms of the mid-1950s. It is also significant that younger radicals and migrants were a part of the peace movement driving this gradual move towards radical action, despite its slow progress. It would be several years before activists would engage in a more dramatic style of dissent against the Vietnam War and conscription, utilising inspiration from American protests and building on the foundations laid by CND groups from 1962 to 1964.[62]

Tentative experiments with dissent

If CND's anti-nuclear activism was indicative, as Ralph Summy argues, of an "unconventionality" or "new militancy" in Australian peace protest, what exactly did this entail? The Perth, Sydney, and Melbourne campaigns were marked by an inclination towards a less genteel, more colourful and more youthful expression of public demonstration, yet these were most frequently expressed by leafleting, public marches, and pickets, often attracting very few participants.[63] CND groups' commitment to unilateral disarmament was consistent, yet their numbers prohibited the sorts of vibrant demonstration that CND enjoyed in Britain, and the spectacle of civil disobedience of British CND's radical splinter group the Committee of 100. Perhaps surprisingly, the Brisbane CND group appeared more willing to take up the challenge posed by the Committee of 100 and its plea for "mass nonviolent action in every country which possesses nuclear weapons or where bases are situated".[64] Despite significantly harsher restrictions on public assembly than other states, under the Queensland Traffic Act, the state criminal code, the Vagrants, Gaming and Other Offences Act, the Crimes Act, and city council ordinances relating to parks, the Brisbane group proceeded to experiment with the limits of legal dissent.[65]

Like most other peace groups, Brisbane CND organised vigils, pickets, and public marches, despite limitations imposed by police restrictions on the march route, the signage displayed, leaflets distributed, and other issues left to the discretion of the police.[66] Frustrated with the legal limitations imposed on its public activity, the group also engaged in riskier behaviour, defacing the toilets at the French Vice-Consulate offices with "Ban French Tests" graffiti, and throwing bundles of leaflets off taller buildings in the city centre to avoid restrictions on leafleting in public places.[67] Along with Janet and Ted D'Urso, Liz Tarnawski, and Frank Fyfe was a Sydney couple, George James and Wendy Holloway. Wendy had recently separated from her husband Frank Moorhouse, and moved to Brisbane for a journalism job at the Australian Broadcasting Commission in 1962. By chance, the new couple rented a house next door to Frank Fyfe, and threw themselves into CND activity. Mary Fyfe, then a girlfriend of Frank's and a Young Labor and CND member, recalled that the small group "found their planning of possible action exciting – almost a spy versus spy sort of game".[68]

In June 1963, Brisbane CND received a package from a Committee of 100 offshoot called "Spies for Peace", which contained the complete text of *Danger! Official Secret*. This was a document that revealed the secret location of Regional Seat of Government 6 (RSG6), one part of a network of nuclear bunkers to be used to house an elite cadre of wealthy Britons in the event of a nuclear war. The publication of this document had caused a major scandal in Britain some months prior, and despite extensive investigations by security police, no charges were ever laid.[69] Sydney CND published excerpts from the document in its newsletter, as did the CPA's *Guardian* newspaper in Melbourne, yet in Brisbane, the document was published in its entirety with a byline of "Spies For Peace (Australia, Inc.)".[70] The decision to publish the document in Brisbane, despite the likely risks, was undertaken by Frank Fyfe, who worked as a typewriter mechanic with Olivetti.[71] Fyfe had learned to alter typewriters by mixing keys from various machines in order to conceal the origin of a particular publication, and also printed CND literature and other publications for various groups. Wendy Holloway recalled that Fyfe had an "anarchic streak [which] was ignited by the Spies for Peace activity, where he came into his own".[72] Despite several interviews with Fyfe, knowledge of his occupation as a typewriter mechanic, and tests of his typewriters, Queensland security police never succeeded in determining his culpability.[73]

The following year, Frank and Mary Fyfe and two other CND members used a screen-printing machine to produce some thirty mock *Courier-Mail* headline posters reading "French H-Test Death Cloud Warning". One night, the four "borrowed" wire frames left outside newsagents and shops, and replaced the existing *Courier-Mail* headline posters with their own, placing the frames throughout Brisbane in strategic locations.[74] Mary Fyfe recalled that "it seemed quite a dangerous thing to do at the time", considering the Queensland police's approach to political activity.[75] Like the "Spies for Peace" scandal, this activity might seem relatively innocuous, but each demonstrates the propensity of Australian CND groups towards the sort of risky political activity that their counterparts in Britain were engaging in more frequently, and on a much larger scale. In Brisbane, a combination of personalities surrounding the *Outlook* discussion group, and sympathetic to Trotskyism, succeeded in radicalising the practice of anti-nuclear activism, whilst "putting into practice", as Brisbane CND argued, "the theoretical principles of democracy".[76]

Conclusion

By 1965, the four CND groups in Australia had begun to turn their attention elsewhere. The national organisation had come to naught and, like the broader peace movement, the war in Vietnam demanded activists' attention. Although France was still developing its nuclear testing site in French Polynesia, at which it would begin testing atmospherically from mid-1966, the conscription of young Australian men to fight in Vietnam emerged the more pressing and immediate issue for the peace movement. The majority of Sydney CND became involved in Gould's new venture, the Vietnam Action Committee.[77] In Melbourne, CND continued until at least mid-1966, when the Vietnam Day Committee began to dominate the attention of Roger Holdsworth, as it did with many other CND members, including Holdsworth's then wife Carol Siansky, David Pope, and Michael Jorgensen.[78] The movement against conscription and the war in Vietnam owed much to this earlier experimentation with anti-nuclear and peace protest, and key organisers "had been trained through apprenticeships" in CND, as Chris Guyatt argued in 1968.[79] The drama and radical promise of overseas ideas and tactics, too, influenced these anti-war organisers just as it had influenced anti-nuclear organisers several years prior, although inspiration from the anti-war movement and draft resistance campaign in the United States had a much more pronounced impact.[80]

Anti-nuclear protest remained an infrequent issue for the peace movement for the remainder of Australia's military involvement in the Vietnam War. From 1972, a much broader coalition of opposition to French nuclear testing developed, which for the first time counted on the involvement of non-communist trade unions and the Australian Council for Trade Unions. Although CND groups were not revived, a more long-standing series of organisations were founded, such as Friends of the Earth and Greenpeace, which continued to oppose French nuclear testing until its conclusion in 1996.[81] Yet there was little in this renewed protest movement to indicate the pioneering activism of the CND campaigns a decade prior. The inner workings of the four CND groups, their small numbers, their relationships with more established peace organisations, and the political thought of their diverse membership each contributed to their status on the fringes of the Australian left. Yet the radical presence of migrants in their ranks, many with experiences of socialism and direct action in Britain, America and Europe, demonstrates a more lasting contribution to the evolution of radical peace protest in Australia. The overlap with the burgeoning movement against conscription and Australian involvement in Vietnam points to anti-nuclear protest from the fringes of Australian politics as a key influence in the development of a politics of expression, of disruption, and of performance that would occupy a central and controversial place in the anti-war movement for the remainder of the long 1960s.

Notes

1 On this history, see Malcolm Saunders and Ralph Summy, *The Australian Peace Movement: A Short History* (Canberra: Peace Research Centre, Australian National University, 1986).

2 For an overview of these developments, see Barbara Carter, "Opposition to Nuclear Weapons in Australia, 1945–1965" (M.A. thesis, University of Melbourne, 1982).

3 On this history as it related to the CPA and trade union interest in peace, see Douglas Jordan, *Conflict in the Unions: The Communist Party of Australia, Politics and the Trade Union Movement, 1945–1960* (Ultimo, NSW: Resistance Books, 2013), Chapter 3.

4 See John Murphy, *Harvest of Fear: A History of Australia's Vietnam War* (Sydney: Allen & Unwin, 1993), 123.

5 See Ralph Summy, "The Australian Peace Council and the Anticommunist Milieu, 1949–1965", in *Peace Movements and Political Cultures*, ed. Charles Chatfield and Peter van den Dungen (Knoxville: University of Tennessee Press, 1988), esp. 240–49. On connections between communism and "peace" in Britain during this era, see Nicholas Barnett and Evan Smith, "'Peace with a Capital P': The Spectre of Communism and Competing Notions of 'Peace' in Britain, 1949–1960", *Labour History Review* 82, no. 1 (2017).

6 On the New Left in Australia, see Russell Marks, "Towards an Intellectual History of the Australian New Left: Some Definitional Problems", *Melbourne Journal of Politics* 34 (2009–10); Alan Barcan, *From New Left to Factional Left: Fifty Years of Student Activism at Sydney University* (North Melbourne: Australian Scholarly Publishing, 2011); and Kristy Yeats, "Australian New Left Politics, 1956–1972" (Ph.D. thesis, University of Melbourne, 2010).

7 On this point, see Jon Piccini, *Transnational Protest, Australia and the 1960s: Global Radicals* (Basingstoke: Palgrave Macmillan, 2016), 11.

8 See Nick Irving, "Answering the 'International Call': Contextualising Sydney Anti-Nuclear and Anti-War Activism in the 1960s", *Journal of Australian Studies* 40, no. 3 (2016); and Kyle Harvey, "Nuclear Migrants, Radical Protest, and the Transnational Movement against French Nuclear Testing in the 1960s: The 1967 Voyage of the *Trident*", *Labour History*, no. 111 (2016).

9 Tom O'Lincoln, *Into the Mainstream: The Decline of Australian Communism* (Sydney: Stained Wattle Press, 1985), 91.

10 Barbara Carter, "The Peace Movement in the 1950s", in *Better Dead Than Red: Australia's First Cold War, 1945–1959*, ed. Ann Curthoys and John Merritt (Sydney: Allen and Unwin, 1986), 61.

11 See Phillip Deery, "War on Peace: Menzies, the Cold War and the 1953 Convention on Peace and War", *Australian Historical Studies* 34, no. 122 (2003): 251–2.

12 See Neil Glover, *Why I Went to Gaol*, booklet, 1957, Box 55, Series 3/115, Campaign for International Co-Operation and Disarmament Collection, University of Melbourne Archives (hereafter CICD Collection).

13 Steven Murray-Smith, "Slogan on Warship Marks Australian Will for Peace" [October 1957], Box 55, Series 3/113, CICD Collection; "Frigate Gets Slogan", *Tribune*, 13 November 1957, 1; "Anti-Bomb Slogan on Govt. House Wall", *Tribune*, 31 July 1957, 1.

14 "Bomb Slogan on U.S. Warship", *Sydney Morning Herald*, 1 May 1958, 1.

15 Deery, "War on Peace", 252.

16 On the translation of these marches from Britain to Australia, see Irving, "Answering the 'International Call'", 294–97.

17 H.G. Clements to Australian Assembly for Peace, 16 June 1962, Box 74, Folder "West Australian Peace Council", People for Nuclear Disarmament Records, MLMSS 5522, Mitchell Library, Sydney (hereafter PND Records).

18 H.G. Clements, circular, 13 October 1962, Box 74, Folder "West Australian Peace Council", PND Records.

19 Murphy, *Harvest of Fear*, 123.
20 "Walk Not Run", *Outlook* 6, no. 3 (May–June 1962), 16.
21 "Nuclear Protest: A Turning Point", editorial, *Outlook* 6, no. 3 (May–June 1962), 2.
22 Catriona Elder, *Being Australian: Narratives of National Identity* (Sydney: Allen & Unwin, 2007), 264.
23 Ralph Summy, "A Reply to Fred Wells", in *Conscription in Australia*, ed. Roy Forward and Bob Reece (St Lucia: University of Queensland Press, 1968), 208.
24 On the trajectory of Trotskyism in Australia in these years, see Rick Kuhn, "The Australian Left, Nationalism and the Vietnam War", *Labour History*, no. 72 (1997), 174–76; and John Percy, *A History of the Democratic Socialist Party and Resistance, Volume 1: 1965–72* (Chippendale, NSW: Resistance Books, 2005), esp. 41–84.
25 Summy, "The Australian Peace Council", 252.
26 ASIO report cards, 1950, A6119, 6579, National Archives of Australia, Canberra (hereafter NAA); ASIO assessment form [1954], A6119, 6579, NAA.
27 Brian Maltby service record, A9301, 71540, NAA; ASIO assessment form, [1954], A6119, 6579, NAA.
28 ASIO field officer report, 28 March 1962, A6119, 6579, NAA.
29 See Boris Radom [Radomishelsky], application for registration, 1947, SP11/2, RUSSIAN/RADOM B, NAA.
30 ASIO field officer report, 19 June 1962, A6119, 6579, NAA.
31 P.V. West, "Spies for Peace Pamphlet", report, 12 July 1963, M1505, 1219, NAA; Lawrence Wittner, *Resisting the Bomb: A History of the World Nuclear Disarmament Movement, 1954–1970* (Stanford: Stanford University Press, 1997), 203.
32 "Disarmament R.A.G., Programme for June-July 1962", Box 65, Folder "Campaign for Nuclear Disarmament", PND Records.
33 ASIO report, 10 July 1963, A6119, 6579, NAA.
34 See, for example, "The Abracadabra of Law", *Scrap*, no. 3 (1962), 5–14.
35 Murphy, *Harvest of Fear*, 125.
36 Alan Barcan, *Radical Students: The Old Left at Sydney University* (Carlton, VIC: Melbourne University Press, 2002), 298–300.
37 ASIO annotated list of Sydney CND executive, [1963], M1505, 1219, NAA; Barcan, *Radical Students*, 302–303.
38 On the factionalism of the Sydney Trotskyist group in the early 1960s, see Percy, *A History of the Democratic Socialist Party*, 44–48.
39 ASIO annotated list of Sydney CND executive, [1963], M1505, 1219, NAA.
40 Notes of an interview between Sgt. Stevens and Bob Gould, 25 June 1963, 7, M1505, 1219, NAA.
41 ASIO phone intercept report, 20 June 1969, A6119, 6579, NAA.
42 "Pale Peace Groups and Real Dissent", *Scrap*, no. 9 (1963), 8.
43 Ibid., 8–9.
44 ASIO summary of Magit family, [1974], A6119, 4660, NAA.
45 Ibid.
46 See Suzanne Rutland, *Edge of the Diaspora: Two Centuries of Jewish Settlement in Australia*, 2nd ed. (Sydney: Brandl & Schlesinger, 1997), 233–244.
47 Rogert Magid. interview with *Mideast Dig*, 31 May 2017, www.mideastdig.com/ten-questions-australias-robert-magid-eyeless-gaza-documentary-skewers-western-media-coverage-last-israel-hamas-war (accessed 10 July 2017).
48 Percy, *A History of the Democratic Socialist Party*, 43; Gaetano Rando, "Literature and the Migration Experience: Twenty-One Years of Italo-Australian Narrative (1965–1986)" (Ph.D. thesis, University of Wollongong, 1988), 83–87, 97n12; Humphrey McQueen, "Labour History – Radical Brisbane: A Chance to Stray", www.surplusvalue.org.au/McQueen/lab_history/lab_hist_brisb.htm (accessed 4 March 2014).
49 Roger Holdsworth, email to the author, 17 June 2017; Renzo Abiuso to Janet D'Urso, 7 August 1963, Box 1, Folder 2, Salvatore D'Urso Papers, UQFL 72, Fryer Library,

University of Queensland, Brisbane (hereafter D'Urso Papers); Roger Holdsworth, informal conversation with the author, 21 June 2017, Melbourne.

50 Renzo Abiuso, VCND circular, 7 August 1963, Box 1, Folder 2, D'Urso Papers; Percy, *A History of the Democratic Socialist Party*, 160, 314; VCND *Monthly Newsletter* 1, no. 3, 29 October 1962, 5.

51 ASIO annotated list of persons interviewed in Brisbane in connection with "Spies for Peace", [1963], M1505, 1219, NAA.

52 The couple went so far as to change Janet's surname from D'Urso to Lewis for the purposes of CND organising and promotion. Ted D'Urso, telephone conversation with the author, 25 May 2017.

53 Hall Greenland, *Red Hot: The Life and Times of Nick Origlass, 1908–96* (Sydney: Wellington Lane Press, 1998), 303; Kenneth Kemshead immigration file, 1949, BP23/1, 6564, NAA; Percy, *A History of the Democratic Socialist Party*, 42; Photo of Liz Tarnawski, Ted D'Urso, and Lou Gugenberger, Easter 1963, Box 1, Folder 4, D'Urso Papers; Lajos Gugenberger, incoming passenger card, 1949, BP25/1, GUGENBERGER L HUNGARIAN, NAA.

54 ASIO annotated list of persons interviewed in Brisbane in connection with "Spies for Peace", [1963], M1505, 1219, NAA; McQueen, "Labour History"; Jon Piccini, "'Up the New Channels': Student Activism in Brisbane During Australia's Sixties", *Crossroads* 5, no. 2 (2011): 78; Free Thought Society ephemera, FVF 188, Fryer Library; and Bob Gould, "The Life and Work of the Self-employed Socialist Intellectual, Humphrey McQueen", *Ozleft*, January 2004, http://members.optushome.com.au/spainter/HMcQueen.html (accessed 17 June 2017).

55 Janet Lewis, CND circular, 12 February 1963, Box 1, Folder 2, D'Urso Papers; and Peggy Duff to Janet D'Urso, 17 January 1963, Box 1, Folder 1, D'Urso Papers.

56 Janet Lewis to Bob Gould, 23 January 1963, Box 1, Folder 2, D'Urso Papers.

57 "Constitution and Aims of ACND [Australian CND]", Box 1, Folder 4, D'Urso Papers.

58 Brisbane CND, draft submissions to national CND conference, presented at 1st regional CND conference, 1 December 1963, Box 1, Folder 4, D'Urso Papers.

59 Murphy, *Harvest of Fear*, 125.

60 Roy Forward to Janet Lewis, 12 February 1964, Box 1, Folder 1, D'Urso Papers.

61 B.M. Smith to Janet Lewis, 19 April 1963, Box 1, Folder 1, D'Urso Papers.

62 Summy, "The Australian Peace Council", 252; Sean Scalmer, *Dissent Events: Protest, the Media, and the Political Gimmick in Australia* (Sydney: UNSW Press, 2002), 13; and Holdsworth conversation.

63 Holdsworth conversation; ASIO report on VCND demonstration, 2 November 1964, A6119, 6037, NAA.

64 Michael Randle to Bill Morrow, 13 July 1961, Box 2, Folder "Committee of 100", PND Records.

65 Brisbane CND, "Report of Direct Action Subcommittee", December 1963, 15–21, Box 1, Folder 4, D'Urso Papers.

66 Ibid., 2–14.

67 Janet Lewis to Renzo Abiuso, 27 September 1963; and Janet Lewis to Bob Gould, 3 October 1963, both in Box 1, Folder 2, D'Urso Papers.

68 Mary Fyfe, emails to the author, 6 and 18 July 2017.

69 Nicolas Walter, *Damned Fools in Utopia: And Other Writings on Anarchism and War Resistance*, ed. David Goodway (Oakland: PM Press, 2011), Chapter 7.

70 See "Spies for Peace" supplement to *CND Newsletter* [Sydney], no. 5 (July 1963); "Spies for Peace – This Document Rocked U.K.", *Guardian*, 23 May 1963, 7; copy of Brisbane "Spies for Peace" publication in M1505, 1219, NAA.

71 D'Urso telephone conversation.

72 Quoted in Mary Fyfe, email to the author, 18 July 2017.

73 ASIO Spies for Peace memo, 2 July 1963, A6717, A79, NAA; J.C. Woodmansey, police report, 10 July 1963, M1505, 1219, NAA.

74 Accompanying material to MSI-Papers-12052, Mary Fyfe Collection, Alexander Turnbull Library, Wellington, New Zealand.
75 Email to the author, 20 June 2017.
76 Brisbane CND, "Report of Direct Action Subcommittee", 2.
77 See Summy, "The Australian Peace Movement", 106n39, 174.
78 See Roger Holdsworth, letter to the editor, *Australian*, 2 June 1966, copy in A6119, 6037, NAA; ASIO report on the Australian Congress for International Cooperation and Disarmament, 7 June 1966, A6119, 6037, NAA; Holdsworth, email to the author, 17 June 2017.
79 Chris Guyatt, "The Anti-Conscription Movement, 1964–1966", in *Conscription in Australia*, ed. Roy Forward and Bob Reece (St Lucia: University of Queensland Press, 1968), 187.
80 See Scalmer, *Dissent Events*, esp. 13–15, 42–50; and Nick Irving, "Anti-Conscription Protest, Liberal Individualism and the Limits of National Myths in the Global 1960s", *History Australia* 14, no. 2 (2017), esp. 190–91.
81 See Lorraine Elliott, "French Nuclear Testing in the Pacific: A Retrospective", *Environmental Politics* 6, no. 2 (1997), 144–49.

7

"1968" IN AUSTRALIA

The student movement and the New Left

Russell Marks

The year 1968 looms large in the global history of protest and radicalism. Across Europe, the United States, Latin America and the Caribbean, authorities – many of them authoritarian – were challenged by marches and demonstrations involving thousands of young people. Against the backdrop of the war in Vietnam, young people marched in the streets demanding greater democracy from institutions, whether they be university administrations or governments. Often, students provided the moral, intellectual and administrative leadership for these waves of protest which became known as the "student movement" and the New Left (to distinguish it from an older left, associated with the labour movement and communist parties). Sometimes the authorities reacted with terrible force, as in Mexico City where police and paramilitary units opened fire on protesters in the Plaza de las Tres Culturas ten days before the opening of the summer Olympics, killing at least dozens and perhaps hundreds. Events in that year took on seismic significance, as the My Lai massacre and Martin Luther King Jr's assassination became fault lines in the respective histories of the war in Vietnam and the American civil rights movement.

Perhaps because authorities in Australia were relatively restrained, and perhaps because the social and economic circumstances of most Australians – and most protesters – were comparatively comfortable, and perhaps because the political circumstances were comparatively free to begin with, events in 1968 never reached the extremes that they did in other places. But there were episodes of significance. On February 13, while the new prime minister John Gorton was speaking at the Caulfield Town Hall ahead of the Higgins by-election (the one caused by Harold Holt's disappearance), according to the Victorian Council for Civil Liberties, police responded to protesters by punching them in the stomach and burning them with cigarette butts.[1] In March, the president of the Draft Resistance Movement was targeted at his Northcote home by unknown assailants who first assaulted a teenage

"1968" in Australia **135**

boy who was living there and then, just over a week later, set fire to his curtains.[2] Police also reacted violently to a protest in Martin Place on July 2. Two days later, on the US Independence Day, protesters burned flags and threw stones through windows of the US Consulate at Prahran in Melbourne. In response, mounted police were ordered to gallop their horses through protesters engaged in a "sit-in" on the consulate driveway. On August 2, two NSW special branch police officers were detained and held hostage in their own car for more than two hours after Sydney University students discovered them tape-recording a campus meeting. The officers were only allowed to leave after they signed a statement declaring that police spying on campus would end.

As much as students in Australia were protesting "causes" – Vietnam, democratic reform, Aboriginal rights, racism – it was the fact of conscription more than any other that underpinned the radicalism of middle-class university students. Since 1965, the National Service Act had provided for conscripted soldiers to serve overseas.[3] There had been disruptive demonstrations in support of conscientious objectors who were detained, fined or imprisoned for breaching the National Service Act or other laws. Some young people were sentenced to jail terms for refusing to pay fines incurred at protests. Notorious Monash University radical Albert Langer defended himself – successfully – after he was arrested at the US Consulate on July 4. Others were court-martialled by military tribunals, placed in solitary confinement at Holsworthy military prison and beaten.[4] Journalist Simon Townsend became one of a handful of *causes célèbres* in 1968 when he was sentenced to 28 days at Holsworthy.

In May 1968, the Gorton government introduced a new bill that would provide for two years' jail for draft resisters. Students ramped up their protests, staging a sit-in outside the Lodge on May 19 at which 69 people were arrested, and invaded the offices of the Department of Labour and National Service at Chifley Square and its minister, Les Bury, a number of times. In the event, the government withdrew the information-sharing clause from the bill before it passed both houses in June. But the two-year sentences became a focus for renewed protest activity.

A 21-year-old postman, John Zarb, became the first to be sentenced and jailed under the new regime in October. Later, Amnesty International "adopted" him as a recognised prisoner of conscience.[5] His and others' jailing in Pentridge prompted broader sections of civil society – churches, singers and writers (including the journalists Craig McGregor and Allan Ashbolt, *Oz* founder Richard Walsh and author Thea Astley) – to join students and unionists in public demonstrations. Days after Christmas, a conference in Carlton resolved to roll out a major "Don't Register" campaign for the coming draft registration period.[6]

In Australia, 1968 was but one year in a brief period that was described by Donald Horne as a "time of hope" – one of overdue cultural change which promised to usher in a new spirit of democratic openness and a society modelled on the values of the progressive, educated new middle class. In the half century since, "1968" has become symbolic shorthand for the student movement and for the historical moment of turmoil and tragedy that defined it, and which came to be known as the cultural revolution in the west.[7] Students were the bearers of this hope, and by 1968 had formed a radical New Left through which small groups were aiming for fundamental social and political transformation. During the next few years, ideas and tactics developed throughout 1967–68 were adapted in various radical directions, including Black Power, Women's Liberation and Gay Liberation. This is no less true in Australia where, although the year 1968 was perhaps no more significant than any of the years between about 1965 and 1972, students made similar demands of authorities. A history of "1968" in Australia, then, should be less a blow-by-blow narrative of the events of that year than an examination of the brief period of dissent and resistance that surrounded it.[8] When had this new left emerged, and why? This is the history of "1968" in Australia.

★★★

The largely campus-based radicals of the New Left can be seen as the youthful representatives of an increasingly frustrated and swelling section of the Australian middle class who were, as Judith Brett writes, "impatient with the slowness of political change" as "the old pre-war elites held on to power by Menzies' coat tails".[9] This frustration is perhaps best expressed in Horne's books *The Lucky Country* (1964) and *Time of Hope* (1980). Rapidly revising his Cold War identity as that era made way for the Sixties, Horne himself was sympathetic to the broad policy objectives of the Immigration Reform Group, which formed in 1959 as "a small organisation of mainly middle-class professionals, many of whom had a close association with the University of Melbourne" to debate and oppose the issue of the "colour bar" in immigration policy.[10] As well as immigration reform, the growing new middle class was particularly vocal on questions of racism, censorship, the extent of democratic participation and procedural fairness in decision-making, and capital punishment.

Associated with the rise of the new middle class was a new kind of individualism. The post-war boom – the basically unbroken increase in gross material wealth between the war and the late 1960s – occurred at a time when technological advancement made possible the privatisation of individuals' lives to an unprecedented extent. As more and more of the old working class households began to amass enough savings to entitle them to middle class demographic status, the cultural effect of affluence was a widespread "cultural individuation" to an extent not possible during the previous long boom between the 1850s and 1890. More individuals than ever before began to believe that there were fewer limitations on the level of control they possessed over their own futures, above and beyond the future of their class or community or society or family.

This growing sense of control over their own lives and futures accelerated the notion that individuals had a responsibility to their own consciences, rather than to an external structure of authority such as a church, a family or indeed a political party. "The whole direction of my intellectual development" was such that "you reacted to the world in terms of your own morality", recalled draft resister Rowan Cahill four decades later.[11] Conventional morality could be challenged by other moral codes. Jennifer Clark argues that "the finding of voice is an essential indicator of the emergence of the 60s phenomenon in Australia", and that a large part of the "finding of voice" among marginalised groups – "young men conscripted to fight in Vietnam; student radicals advocating university reform; young women who resented male hegemony" – was in the confidence with which they expressed their own experiences.[12]

"The Sixties" can be seen as the site of a hegemonic battle between defenders of an older liberalism and advocates of a newer version. The first major expression of Sixties' student activism following a decade of relative Cold War quiet on campuses was the conscience-based anti-racist politics of what was called the "new" middle class.[13] The standard of the new morality was an international one, as against the national standard of racial hierarchies. Following the massacre in Sharpeville, South Africa, in March 1960, Robert Menzies responded with a defence of the convention of "domestic jurisdiction" – a principle which held that countries would avoid involvement in other countries' affairs unless international peace was threatened. The new middle class responded with moral outrage.[14] "Thousands" of students demonstrated in Martin Place in line with protests around the world.[15] Significantly in terms of the history of the non-ALP (Australian Labor Party) left, the Martin Place protest was not organised by the Communist Party. The violent response by police encouraged the view among some dissenting middle class students that the police – and by extension the state – were hardly the neutral institutions they presented as.[16] David Ferraro, the editor of the Sydney University student newspaper, *honi soit*, drew attention to the "police brutality" which accompanied the demonstration, and asked readers to leave donations with the Student Representative Council to help those who had been arrested pay their fines.[17]

In October the following year, Melbourne University student Bill Thomas formed a group called "Student Action". Thomas, who was associated with the ALP Right, could see that the approaching federal election would be fought on "purely economic issues" following a brief credit squeeze in late 1960 that had temporarily driven up unemployment.[18] Thomas wanted Student Action to force "moral issues" like "racialism" in foreign and immigration policy – including the "white Australia" policy, to which both Labor and the Coalition remained committed – onto the agenda.[19] Indeed, senior Australian politicians – including ALP leader Arthur Calwell – had explicitly advocated a clear distinction be maintained in people's minds between South African apartheid and the legal discrimination faced by Indigenous people in Australia.[20] Student Action organised for groups of students to disrupt the campaigns of both Prime Minister Robert Menzies and Calwell by yelling anti-racist slogans at meetings and wearing "blackface".[21]

In May 1964, white students organised a demonstration in support of the American civil rights movement outside the US Consulate in Sydney. Twenty-five of them were arrested,[22] but the protest was covered in the international press, where the obvious irony was highlighted: white Australian students demonstrating against racial discrimination elsewhere while saying nothing about the increasingly notorious White Australia policy or the legal discrimination against Indigenous people.[23] Writers in *honi soit*, went looking for racial discrimination in Australia, and found plenty. Protests were arranged for July 1964.[24] Later in the year, Student Action for Aborigines (SAFA) was formed, with Charles Perkins as its chair. In February the following year, Perkins and 33 other SAFA students – including future Supreme Court Chief Justice Jim Spigelman and future journalist Darce Cassidy – piled onto a bus bound for country towns in New South Wales to highlight examples of racism and segregation.[25] Modelled on the American "Freedom Rides" which began when seven black and six white volunteers left Washington DC in May 1961 to protest against segregation laws in southern states, the February 1965 Freedom Ride was SAFA's first major political act.[26] Their focus was everyday discrimination faced by Aboriginal people; their target, the attitudes of white Australians, some of whom reacted violently when SAFA rolled into town.

By then, Menzies had announced the re-introduction of national service, intended as a measure to ward off what he called "aggressive communism". A new National Service (Conscription) Act required all males to register with the Department of Labour and National Service upon turning 20. Where public concern translated into dissent, that dissent was restricted to groups like the ALP-oriented Youth Campaign Against Conscription (YCAC, formed at the end of November 1964), the Communist Party's Eureka Youth League and other communist and fellow-travelling Peace groups.[27] Those 20-year-olds eligible for National Service were largely compliant. The first "registration period" in January and February 1965 saw all but one per cent of eligible young men register. Melbourne draft resister Michael Hamel-Green later compared this figure with the 50 per cent which had not registered for the earlier 1911 scheme.[28] Hamel-Green and Rowan Cahill were among future radicals who did register during this first period.

The first "birthday ballot" was held in March 1965.[29] The following month Menzies announced that Australians would be sending combat troops into Vietnam, and Calwell quickly declared the ALP's opposition to the move. With the government about to lose control of the Senate in July (following a December Senate election at which conscription was a major issue), Menzies rushed through amendments which allowed conscripts to be sent overseas. Meanwhile alarmed mothers formed the Save Our Sons (SOS) protest group in Sydney and then elsewhere, Bob Gould (a Trotskyist in the ALP Left) formed the Vietnam Action Committee (VAC), and the first arrests of the growing anti-war movement took place after a sit-down demonstration during an Australian Student Labor Federation (ASLF) conference in Canberra.[30] This was apparently the first major student anti-war demonstration; students held an even larger one in Sydney in October, which occasioned 51 arrests.[31]

It is often suggested that the left-liberal politics of conscience of the early 1960s "could conceivably have been the full extent of student dissent in Australia", had it not been for the Menzies government's decision to introduce conscription for Vietnam.[32] It seems likely that students would have demonstrated in favour of participatory democracy, especially on campuses, had conscription not been introduced – though it is a matter of historical record that conscription provided the

"1968" in Australia **139**

catalyst for the more radical "dissent events" between 1966 and 1972.[33] Demonstrations escalated during the period leading up to the 1966 federal elections, particularly after Prime Minister Holt announced in March that year that conscripts would be sent to Vietnam, and especially after the first conscript was killed. During this time protest groups advocated that potential conscripts apply for "conscientious objector" (CO) status as provided for in the National Service Act, open to a conscriptee whose conscientious beliefs did not allow him to engage in any form of military service, provided those beliefs were sincerely held. "Draft cards" (an American terminology) were publicly and sensationally burned, but at this stage "few, if any, of the burners carried their resistance further into non-compliance with registration procedures, compulsory medical examinations, or army call-up notices".[34]

By the mid-1960s, the participant-observer and future Walkley-awarded journalist Warren Osmond later argued (in the Marxian language of the later movement), students had developed a self-consciousness of their own potential political potency and their self-proclaimed role as "the conscience of society".[35] The "Cold War mould" had begun to crack under the late 1950s efforts of the Campaign for Nuclear Disarmament which, while never developing the momentum of its British parent, nevertheless spread the idea that "the primary reality of the Cold War was not a struggle between democratic West and totalitarian East, but an arms race which threatened to wipe out both".[36] Osmond argued that the decisive break with Cold War mentality among radicals occurred only after conscripted 20-year-olds began going to Vietnam.[37] The first to be killed was 21-year-old Errol Wayne Noack, on 24 May 1966.[38]

Student protesters focused their efforts on getting the Coalition out of government. But in the second half of 1966, things were not looking good. Holt declared Australia to be "all the way with LBJ" while he was visiting Lyndon Johnson in Washington in June; when Johnson repaid the visit in October (just over a month before the election), the protests were overwhelmed by the rapturous applause he received in all cities. Infamously, NSW premier Robert Askin was reported to have urged his driver to "run over the bastards".[39] Twenty-one-year-old schoolteacher Bill White had been sacked in July after he became the first person to publicly declare CO status. Four days before the election, after a standoff which was being covered nationally and which was causing growing embarrassment for the government, White was sensationally dragged from his Sydney home and through a throng of protesters by three police officers, who forced him into a car and conveyed him to Holsworthy military prison. The photographs of White's arrest became iconic for protesters. Within his first week at Holworthy he was charged with ten offences, ranging from failing to salute and failing to polish brass.[40]

But until the 1966 election, student protesters continued to believe that the issue could be "won" if they could just make people see the "truth": their faith in the liberal democratic system remained strong. For many of the leading thinkers and activists of the student movement, that faith was shattered by the result of the federal election on November 26. A Gallup Poll a week earlier had estimated the support for conscription at 68 per cent, but White's arrest had evoked much public sympathy and made it seem feasible that Australians would vote against the war and for Labor in the upcoming November elections.[41] The result was deeply shocking: Labor *lost* nine seats in a landslide. The students could not have known it then, but that election also became a turning point inside the ALP. Evatt had died the previous year; Calwell's leadership did not last much longer. It was this loss which provided Whitlam with the opportunity he needed for his program of modernisation. The 1966 election defeat was, in hindsight, the last gasp of Old Labor.

It is difficult to overstate the shattering effect of the 1966 election outcome on the minds of student activists. That so many voters could have been hoodwinked by what the activists saw as simplistic appeals to fear (this was the election of the "domino theory" and giant red arrows pointing inexorably from China to Australia) and appeals to American righteousness despite what they saw as the obvious reality that young men were dying for an unjust cause could only mean that the system itself was broken. Their faith in parliamentary representation collapsed.[42] Students needed more than the theory of liberal democracy to explain why Labor lost in 1966. Before long, students on campuses across the country radicalised their belief systems in a range of different directions. Activism thereafter shifted from anti-racism and peace to more radical attacks on mainstream culture and the existing political system.[43]

Dissenting students who rejected parliamentary reformism following the election became increasingly receptive to radical ideas, many of which were filtered through the United States. The war became the prism through which young people were able to see the "horrifying contrast between the expressed ideals of Western bourgeois democracy, and its actual policies".[44] Turning to Herbert Marcuse's *One-Dimensional Man* (1964) – as interpreted through an American lens – this newly "conscious" youth was able to see the war, together with other instances of "hypocrisy", as functional symptoms of the "politico-economic power system" of the West. Rather than attempt to shame their governments into behaving according to their expressed ideals – that would be a liberal/reformist response, which was consistent with how they had engaged until the election – radicalised students concluded that the only solution was to overhaul the entire system itself.

There were two main repositories of radical social criticism available to students seeking revolutionary social change: the US-based Students for a Democratic Society (SDS) and its founding Port Huron Statement (1962); and the long tradition of Marxist socialism. A third set of ideas, encapsulated in the then-ubiquitous phrase "the counterculture" and popularised by Theodore Roszak among others, was also available to radicals, though these ideas tended to float in the background in Australia rather than form the direct basis for activism.[45] During the late 1960s and especially the 1970s, the new spirit of radicalism found expression in a set of "new social movements", which began as demands for "liberation" from the oppressive social structures which had been established around such concepts as gender, sexuality and race.

Chapters of Students for a Democratic Society (SDS), inspired by the American network, were established by radicals in Melbourne, Sydney, Adelaide, Hobart and Brisbane. Like the Draft Resistance Movement (DRM), SDS advocated direct, non-violent, conscience-based action in order to raise awareness, galvanise public opinion and effect political change.[46] For participants, the radical nature of SDS was reflected in its members' propensity for being arrested and imprisoned for fine defaults, which one participant-historian likened to Rosa Parks' refusal to pay her fine after she illegally remained in her bus seat in December 1955 despite the driver requesting that she vacate it for a white passenger, an act commonly understood as a catalyst for the Civil Rights movement in the United States.[47]

Perhaps the most significant centre of this kind of direct, non-violent action was Brisbane, and in particular the University of Queensland at St Lucia. The University of Queensland had received a number of American scholars who had been involved in New Left radicalism in the United States during the 1960s, among them Ralph Summy, who had fled the United States in early 1962 after being ordered to appear before a McCarthyist government inquiry in his role as the full-time paid director of an anti-nuclear organisation.[48] One participant-historian of Brisbane radicalism argued that Summy was vital in transferring American SDS ideals to University of Queensland students after he became a staff member there in May 1964, and in providing the New Left there with a "Port Huron" flavour (namely non-violence, individual liberty and disarmament) that did not emerge to the same extent on other campuses.[49] With the encouragement of Summy and others, students and staff who formed the first anti-war protest groups – VAC and YCAC – combined with a large number of social justice Catholics who made up the relatively strong Newman Society and the University Reform Group to form, in mid-1966, a "Society for Democratic Action" (SDA).[50]

Perhaps the most controversial aspect to the more militant, left-wing anti-war movement was in the support some groups advocated for the National Liberation Front in Vietnam. The NLF (National Liberation Front), or *Việt cộng*, was a front of Hanoi-oriented groups committed to the defeat of both the South Vietnamese government and its US allies during the war. The prospect of supporting a foreign – and communist – guerrilla force against Australian troops was much more controversial than simply opposing Australia's military presence in Vietnam. The Australian Student Labor Federation (ASLF), dominated by Trotskyists, expressed "moral support" for the National Liberation Front in 1965. In March 1966, the ALP and Labor Clubs at the University of Sydney established a fund which would direct medical aid monies to the NLF.[51] A meeting of the Monash Labor Club on 24 July 1967 set up a committee whose function was to raise funds for "unspecified support" to the Liberation Front.[52] The Monash Labor Club's decision made front-page news in most capital cities; the club was now dominated by militant Maoist radicals. Also in 1967, Maoist radicals planned to conduct a ceremonial burning of the American flag outside the US Consulate on American Independence Day, but the provocative gimmick was prevented by the official organisers of the July 4 protest, the Vietnam Day Committee, which threatened to notify police.

The campaigns and movements around "draft resistance" were perhaps the most effective of the entire spectrum of New Left radicalism. In early 1967 Mike Matteson (a Sydney anarchist), Chris Campbell (a Sydney pacifist) and Errol Heldzingen (a radical Melbourne socialist), influenced by White's ordeal and by the growing draft-resistance movement in the United States, announced publicly that they would not comply with National Service Act procedures. By the following year the list of active "resisters" had grown to eighteen.[53] There were attempts to organise "resistance" to conscription into an identifiable movement. Perhaps the most visible of these attempts was the short-lived Draft Resistance Movement, which was formed in early 1968 out of the cooperation of a number of youth organisations including YCAC. The DRM encouraged draft resisters to refuse to comply with their *National Service Act* obligations – and risk jail – rather than to merely apply for conscientious exemption under the Act.[54]

In January 1969, SDS (which later changed its name to the Radical Action Movement) along with other conscience-based pacifist groups launched a "Don't Register" campaign to convince 20-year-olds not to register for National Service, which they were required to do under the National Service Act. The campaign was itself a bold statement of civil disobedience – the conscious contravention of what radicals saw as illegitimate laws. In inciting others to break the law, campaigners were in breach of the Victorian Crimes Act and faced a maximum 12 months' imprisonment. It was also an attempt to persuade individuals to act on their own conscience, rather than on the will of the State. This appeal to conscience was not limited to prospective registrees: the system of registration, ballot and conscription depended "on the tacit consent of the many who are exempt", and the Don't Register campaign asked those who were exempt from conscription (including full-time students) to involve themselves in civil disobedience on the basis of a common humanity.[55] Two SDS radicals – Mike Jones (chair of Sydney SDS) and Nick Beams (secretary, Hobart SDS) – were arrested and charged with incitement under the *Crimes Act* on the opening day of the campaign, and another five were charged with breaches of the Melbourne City Council's By-Law 418, which prohibited the distribution of unsanctioned leaflets. These arrests provoked an immediate reaction among Melbourne's radicals, and the following weekend Hamel-Green recalls that five hundred people handed out Don't Register pamphlets. Whereas the Commonwealth Police were only interested in charging the "student 'ringleaders'" under the Crimes Act, the Melbourne Council booked as many as they could under the By-Law – including, as it turned out, Jim Cairns. Many students fined under the By-Law refused to pay and served a week in prison. With the number facing gaol growing larger every week, the Council was effectively forced into repealing the By-Law.[56]

Between January and April 1969 more than three hundred students were arrested across the country on various charges relating to radical dissent. During the middle of the year civil disobedience spread from students to academics and then to the broader community. A senior Minister called for them to face disciplinary action and prepared to prosecute them for incitement, but this only prompted

"1968" in Australia **143**

further expressions of support – and by the end of June there had been over five hundred signatures collected from Australian academics in support of Don't Register. This led to the formation of a more widely based Committee in Defiance of the National Service Act (CDNSA) in July which pledged "whole-hearted support, encouragement and aid" to draft resisters. The CDNSA, faced with a government retreating from filing prosecutions (eight thousand individuals had signed the statement of incitement by the end of 1969), went so far as to prosecute itself for incitement over the 1969–70 summer. Faced with three national Moratorium demonstrations between May 1970 and June 1971 and the prospects of prosecuting hundreds of individuals under either the Crimes Act or the National Service Act, governments adopted various delaying tactics, made minor shifts in policy and applied selective prosecution. As Hamel-Green notes, "[d]espite the dramatic increase in draft resisters during 1969–70 only four resisters received call-up notices in the whole of 1970."[57]

Perhaps inevitably, radicalised students soon began to direct their new-found "voice" toward their own university structures, which were perceived by radicalised students as symptomatic of the wider refusals of autonomy. The Sixties' catchcry, "participatory democracy", demanded that, at the very least, people be afforded the opportunity to participate in decisions which would affect them. University students, among the loudest of those demanding participation, believed they should have a say in university policymaking. The idea also trickled down to some secondary school students. University administrations found themselves the targets of substantial protests, either in response to particular decisions or because of more general sentiments against traditional authority structures. At the University of Sydney in 1967, what became known as the Humphreys Affair – on the face of it a minor dispute over the charging of library fines – became the catalyst for a wave of sit-ins, teach-ins and other protest activities designed to further the goal of participatory democracy and real student involvement in decision-making.[58] In cases such as this one, the universities became proxies for students whose larger target was the system of government which was conscripting 20-year-old men to fight in Vietnam while denying them even the courtesy of a vote. Occasionally, the link between university administrations and the wider structures of power which were held responsible for conscription and Vietnam were explicit, as in 1968, when Sydney University's administration installed steel bars on the windows and doors of its file room to prevent students burning files (in anticipation of pending National Service Act amendments that would have required universities to share information about enrolled students with authorities) and when the Vice Chancellor of Monash University, Louis Matheson, intervened to prohibit the Monash Labor Club from collecting funds intended for the NLF.[59]

The Student Power phenomenon initially appeared to confirm a prediction made by Geoff Sharp, a Marxist thinker who had founded the New Left journal *Arena* earlier in the decade: that the world was witnessing what he and others were calling a revolution of a "new class" – the emergence, with "students acting as catalyst", of a genuine social movement for change which would spread "intellectual" values – rationalism, universalism, humanism and autonomy – throughout society. For Sharp, Student Power was not merely a "temporarily sharpened expression of restlessness" among young people with time on their hands. It was, he believed, a genuine response among the intellectually trained to their experience of an increasingly hypocritical and stiflingly bureaucratic society.[60] Not every left-wing theorist felt this way. Those whose Marxism led them to hold onto a theory of history which saw the working class as the true agents of revolutionary change, such as schoolteacher Humphrey McQueen (later the author of *A New Britannia*), were critical of the idea that students, acting by themselves and without developing a coherent theory of action, could form any sort of sustainable revolutionary vanguard.[61] McQueen came to see "Student Power" as inherently non-revolutionary and derivative of US practice.[62] For different reasons, conservatives also reached negative conclusions about the student movement, and emphasised its violence, its "anarchy" and its lack of novelty.[63]

In the end, McQueen was more prescient than Sharp. The radicalism of Student Power and the New Left only ever captured a minority of the student population. Maybe the students helped galvanise public opinion against conscription and the war, or maybe that would have happened anyway. Whatever the case, many of the most radical aims of the student vanguard were swallowed by, respectively, the antiwar movement and the rapidly individuating broader culture. The first "Moratorium" against the war took place on Friday 8 May 1970. Following the model established in the United States the previous October, the idea was that "normal" activities "be suspended on this day and the time used to discuss the issues of Vietnam, conscription and their implications for Australian society".[64] The centrepiece of the Moratorium was a large march, to take place simultaneously in all capital cities. Organised largely by the Melbourne-based Vietnam Moratorium Campaign and the broader peace movement, it brought together churches, unions and other elements of civil society (including student groups) Additional, less well-attended Moratorium marches took place in September 1970 and June 1971, and marches continued under the "Moratorium" banner until 1975.

★★★

What Sean Scalmer has termed the "dissent events" are one thing, but the radical quality of the New Left in Australia is impossible to understand without an awareness of the radical *ideas* which emerged after 1966. The demands of "participatory democracy" as expressed by groups like SDS and SDA, and the radical forms of civil disobedience like draft resistance – to the point of risking arrest, imprisonment and outcast status among broader society – informed some of the more visible events of the anti-war and anti-conscription movements.

Some of the young thinkers involved in these movements discovered Marxist theory. Marxism encompasses an enormous body of thinking about the nature of social relations, and covers various schools, traditions and approaches which together make up the largest and most significant repository of coherent radical thought available to an "anti-Establishment" twentieth-century thinker. At the heart of Marxist analysis is a highly critical understanding of the way modern capitalism

"1968" in Australia **145**

produces workers who are necessarily alienated from their work, through a set of industrial relations that is inherently exploitative. Once Australian New Left intellectuals discovered that the war in Vietnam and, say, "police brutality" were symptoms of an underlying structure of oppression (rather than exceptions to the rule of harmonious social and international relations within liberal democracies), the various traditions of Marxist thought were, for many, natural places to turn. But mostew left Marxists did not make their way into the Communist Party, as an earlier generation had. They were either "revisionists" who tried to rescue Marxist theory from its association with Stalinism and return to the more humanistic philosophy said to be found in Marx's earlier writings,[65] or they sought to rescue the communist ideal from both the debasement of Stalinist totalitarianism *and* the trend toward humanistic socialism.

Revisionists of the first New Left – the post-war generation who left the CPA in the wake of 1956 – formed their own journals, including *Overland, Outlook, Labour History* and *Arena*. These provided platforms for many of the younger New Left thinkers of the late 1960s, whose Marxism was often even more "revisionist" than that of the ex-communists. Radical intellectuals who finished school during the very late 1950s and 1960s, and after, never had a sense that the CPA was the sole repository of Marxist thought, and so they were, perhaps naturally, more willing to experiment with the Frankfurt School's fusion of Marx and Freud, Sartre's existentialist Marxism, and broader socialist ideas which claimed only general, historical links with the specifics of Marx's thought.

Given the problems created for communism by Stalin, the attempt by some radicals to revive communism after 1966 was perhaps the most surprising development of New Left thought. Particularly after 1966, young radicals joined Trotskyist and militant Maoist groups, or found in Maoist theory permission for their own militant urges. As the Communist Party of Australia liberalised during the second half of the 1960s under Laurie Aarons' leadership, some Trotskyists joined, concerned to influence the Party's de-Stalinisation in the direction of the Fourth International. During the early 1970s, groups of radical intellectuals who were influenced by the French structuralist thinker Louis Althusser's recent critique of the humanist trends in Marxist thought also joined the CPA, hoping to arrest its liberalising trend and return it to a more "correct line".

These efforts at reviving Marxist theory on the left contributed to some intellectual trends within the academy as well as the more influential "liberation" movements – women's, gay, black – which emerged from about 1969. Young women had participated in the conscience-based demonstrations against racism, conscription and war during the early-to-mid 1960s. Some were involved in the non-violent campaigns of civil disobedience after 1966–67. Very few described themselves for very long as "revolutionary socialists", and almost no women agitated for explicit violence in their dealings with the state and university administrations. The story of Women's Liberation, which emerged in Australia by the end of 1969, is that of the development of a radical critique which rejected both the prevailing social organisation of capitalist society *and* what radical women came to

146 Russell Marks

see as the overwhelmingly masculine politics of the New Left.[66] Flowing from the idea that racial minorities and women could be oppressed by a dominant (white, masculine) culture, activists for Gay Liberation emerged in Australia around 1970 after the movement launched in Berkeley the previous year, and following the establishment of the Homosexual Law Reform Society in Canberra in 1968.[67] And building on the Freedom Rides, the Gurindji walkoff at Wave Hill and the constitutional referendum, young, urbanised Aboriginal and Torres Strait Islander activists in Sydney, Melbourne and Brisbane drew ideas and tactics from the Black Power movement in the United States, especially between 1968 and 1972.[68]

While the radical Women's and Gay Liberation movements eventually settled into the liberal-democratic "identity politics" of the new social movements – they ultimately demanded "equality" more than any fundamental restructuring of Australian society – Aboriginal activism continued its radical demands, particularly toward the twin aims of Land Rights and Treaty. This reflects the relative starting positions of each social group: whereas most of the concerns of women's and gay movement activists – and indeed most anti-racist activists – in modern, liberal-democratic Australia could be met with the simple removal of formal and cultural discrimination, Aboriginal justice required a fundamental reorganisation of the constitutional, social and economic structures of modern society.

All these movements and strands of the New Left bore lasting influence on left-wing and progressive politics in Australia, if not the political culture more broadly. Among the most enduring of all influences was in the way progressives thought – and continue to think – about Australian nationalism. While nationalism was a key component of the radical politics of generations until the 1960s, almost every strand of the New Left (with the notable exception of the Maoist radicalism of the early 1970s) rejected the very idea that Australian nationalism could ever inform a progressive politics. Anti-nationalism has continued as a trope of left-of-Labor politics since the 1960s, arguably opening the space for the new right to adopt a nationalist politics for its own ends during the 1980s and beyond.[69]

★★★

During the Australian Sixties, there were no episodes of mass state violence of the kind that met protesters in South Africa or France or Mexico. But there was trauma – because of state activity (the conscription scheme which caused 184 young men to be killed in action in Vietnam and the domestic crackdowns against those who resisted it) but also of the kind associated with the shattering of illusions and the breakdown of relationships that happens when people adopt radically different ideologies from those into which they were socialised. It was also a moment of enormous intellectual and cultural energy. It seems clear that the Sixties changed Australia: the question is how, and to what extent. The Sixties certainly transformed the Australian left, and heralded the new social movements which have made significant gains – both formal and social/cultural – for women and for other minority groups, beginning most notably when the first of the demands were picked up by the Whitlam government.[70] Feminism of second and subsequent waves; LGBTIQ rights; disability rights: all these and more have their immediate

"1968" in Australia **147**

origins in the ideas and tactics of the Sixties. For this reason conservatives often nominate the Sixties as a period of major cultural ruin, and one from which many continue to attempt rescue.[71] But on one view the "equality"-based social movements have taken from the Sixties only those elements that can be most assimilated to capitalism. Or, put another way, capital has allowed only those elements of the Sixties' compatible with liberal capitalism to endure. Other movements, like the green movement and those for Aboriginal and Torres Strait Islander Land Rights and Treaty, are perhaps more in keeping with the *radical* nature of "1968" in that they attack fundamental tenets of the liberal-capitalist "system". Perhaps the best answer is that the legacy of 1968 is in both an extension of liberalism's promises *and* a radical critique of the status quo toward socially progressive ends. While some have actively resisted them, no government since Whitlam's has been able to ignore these demands.

Notes

1 As reported in the CPA's *Tribune* newspaper, no. 1546, 21 February 1968, p. 1: "Vic Big Stick Won't Stop Viet Protests".
2 As reported in *Tribune*, 20 March 1968, p. 12: "Violence and Threats for Protesters".
3 It is (and was) commonly believed that the 1966–72 period was the first in Australian history to see conscripted soldiers sent overseas. However, following the passage of the *Defence (Citizen Military Forces) Act 1943* one group of conscripts served in what is now Indonesia in 1943–44, though it never saw action.
4 *Tribune* no. 1558, 15 May 1968, p. 1: "Big Actions this Weekend".
5 *The Age*, Melbourne, 16 April 1969, p. 13.
6 Michael Hamel-Green, "The Resisters: A History of the Anti-conscription Movement, 1964–1972". In Peter King, ed., *Australia's Vietnam: Australia in the Second Indo-China War* (Sydney: George Allen & Unwin, 1983), p. 100 at p. 114.
7 Appropriating the original usage of the term, as it applied to Mao Zedong's Great Proletarian Cultural Revolution in China between 1966 and 1976.
8 In a very broad sense, this chapter takes an approach consistent with Arthur Marwick has termed "the long sixties": that is, it situates the "moment" of 1968 in the context of a cultural revolution whose first roots appeared in the late 1950s and which probably extended to the mid-1970s: Marwick, *The Sixties: Cultural Revolution in Britain, France, Italy and the United States, c.1958–c.1974* (Oxford: OUP, 1998). This chapter retains a primary focus on the student and anti-war movement, however, and does not extend very far into a broader examination of what Eric Hobsbawm called the "profound, and in many ways sudden, moral and cultural revolution, a dramatic transformation of the conventions of social and personal behaviour": to do so would, as he did, account for the enduring and transformative social, cultural and economic developments of the era (for instance, in youth culture, individuation, identity): Hobsbawm, *The Age of Extremes, 1914–1991* (London: Michael Joseph; New York: Viking Penguin, 1994). Ultimately the approach I have taken in this chapter – to go looking in Australia for evidence of New Left radicalism of the kind found elsewhere – is one I have also criticised: Marks, "Towards an Intellectual History of the Australian New Left: Some Definitional Problems". *Melbourne Journal of Politics* (2009–10), no. 34 at p. 83.

Recent substantive histories of "the long sixties" in Australia include: Jon Piccini, *Transnational Protest: Australia and the 1960s* (London: Palgrave Macmillan, 2016); Sean Scalmer, *Dissent Events: Protest, the Media and the Political Gimmick in Australia* (UNSW Press, 2002); Clive Hamilton, *What Do We Want? The Story of Protest in Australia* (Canberra: NLA, 2016); Jennifer Clark, *Aborigines and Activism: Race, Aborigines and the Coming of the Sixties to Australia* (UWA Press, 2008).

9 Judith Brett, *Australian Liberals and the Moral Middle Class* (Cambridge; New York: Cambridge University Press, 2003), p. 141.

10 Gwenda Tavan, *The Long, Slow Death of White Australia* (Carlton North, Vic: Scribe, 2005), pp. 121–128. See: Tavan, "Immigration: Control or Colour Bar? The Immigration Reform Groups, 1959–1966". *Australian Historical Studies* (October 2001), no. 117, p. 181; Kate Darian-Smith and James Waghorne, "Australian-Asian Sociability, Student Activism and the University Challenge to White Australia in the 1950s". *Australian Journal of Politics and History* (June 2016), vol. 62, no. 2, pp. 203–218.

11 Cahill, interviewed by the author, 2008.

12 Clark, *Aborigines and Activism*, pp. 106 and 120.

13 The "new" middle class of the postwar era is generally distinguished from its "older" counterpart by its high levels of formal education, especially at university level. It was its qualifications which provided the basis for its earning capacity and many of its moral attitudes. By contrast, the "old" middle class of the earlier twentieth century, stretching back into the nineteenth, was much more recognisably *petit-bourgeois*, with its economic foundation less dependent on formal education (though doctors and lawyers were certainly part of it) and its morality more tied to churches and other community institutions. For a general discussion, see: Judith Brett, *Australian Liberals and the Moral Middle Class*.

14 Clark, *Aborigines and Activism*, pp. 76–80 and 23–25.

15 Ann Curthoys, *Freedom Ride* (Crows Nest, NSW: Allen & Unwin, 2002), p. 2.

16 On the culture inside police forces during the 1960s, see: Peter Fairchild, *The Victorian Police Force's Vietnam: An Illustration of the Fragility of Hegemonic Policing* (MA thesis, Criminology, La Trobe University, 1988).

17 "Police Give a Hand in Protest on Sharpeville". *honi soit*, 7 April 1960 at 1.

18 See: Greg Whitwell, *The Treasury Line* (North Sydney: Allen & Unwin, 1986), pp. 129–143.

19 Thomas (as "Vladimir Ulyanov"), "Students as a Moral Force?". *Farrago*, 6 October 1961, p. 2.

20 See: Commonwealth of Australia Parliamentary Debates (*Hansard*), House of Representatives, 31 March 1960, p. 779 (per Arthur Calwell).

21 See: "Blackface Students Boo, Jeer". *Sydney Morning Herald*, 23 November 1961, p. 7.

22 Curthoys, *Freedom Ride*, pp. 1–8.

23 Curthoys, *Freedom Ride*, pp. 8–9; Sean Scalmer, *Dissent Events: Protest, the Media and the Political Gimmick in Australia* (Kensington, NSW: University of New South Wales Press, 2002), p. 18.

24 See: Scalmer, *Dissent Events*, p. 18.

25 For more on SAFA, see: Curthoys, *Freedom Ride*.

26 GW Ford, "The Student Bus: SAFA Interviewed". *Outlook* (April 1965), vol. 9, no. 2, p. 4.

27 See the EYL's referendum call in the CPA's *Tribune*, 20 January 1965.

28 Hamel-Green, "The Resisters: A History of the Anti-Conscription Movement, 1964–72". Ch. 6 in Peter King, ed., *Australia's Vietnam: Australia in the Second Indo-China War* (Sydney: George Allen & Unwin, 1983), pp. 102–107.

29 Concise descriptions of the lottery-style ballot process can be found in: Roy Forward and Bob Reece, *Conscription in Australia* (St Lucia: University of Queensland Press, 1968), esp. ch. 4 ("Conscription, 1964–68") at p. 79; and Sue Langford, "Appendix: The National Service scheme, 1964–72" (n.d.), Australian War Memorial website, <www.awm.gov.au/Encyclopedia/viet_app.asp>, accessed 10 April 2011.

30 Curthoys, "Mobilising Dissent: The Later Stages of Protest" in Gregory Pemberton, ed., *Vietnam: Remembered* (Sydney: Weldon, 1990), p. 138 at 140.

31 Ralph Summy, "Militancy and the Australian Peace Movement, 1960–1967". *Politics* (November 1970), vol. 5, no. 2, p. 148 at 155.

32 See for instance: James Walter, *The Perception of Conflict: Profiles from Student Politics* (MA thesis, La Trobe University, 1974), pp. 45–47.

"1968" in Australia 149

33 Scalmer, *Dissent Events*.
34 Hamel-Green, "The Resisters", p. 109.
35 Osmond and Richard Gordon, "An Overview of the Australian New Left", Ch 1 in Gordon, ed., *The Australian New Left: Critical Essays and Strategy* (Melbourne: William Heinemann, 1970), pp. 3–39 at 19–21.
36 Osmond and Gordon, "An Overview of the Australian New Left". p. 23, quoting Perry Anderson, "The Left in the Fifties". *New Left Review* (1965), no. 29, p. 12.
37 Osmond and Gordon, "An Overview of the Australian New Left", p. 24, citing Summy's (then uncompleted) thesis, *Australian Peace Movement, 1960–67: A Study of Dissent* (MA thesis, University of Sydney, 1971).
38 John Knott, "Noack, Errol Wayne (1945–1966)". *Australian Dictionary of Biography*, vol. 15 (Melbourne University Press, 2000).
39 In 1968, Askin told a luncheon that he had actually said something closer to "it's a pity we couldn't run over them," but he never corrected the journalist who had misquoted him because he believed it had done him no political harm.
40 *Canberra Times*, 24 December 1966, p.1: "White Exempted from Service".
41 Hamel-Green, "Vietnam: Beyond Pity" (1969), *Melbourne Uni Magazine*, 56 (reprinted in *Australian Left Review* (April–May 1970), vol. 24 at 53; also in *Dissent* (Winter 1970), p. 25 at 30.
42 Hamel-Green, "Vietnam: Beyond Pity".
43 Graham Little, *Faces on the Campus: A Psycho-Social Study* (Carlton: Melbourne University Press, 1975), p. 57; James Walter, *The Perception of Conflict: Profiles from Student Politics* (MA thesis, Politics, La Trobe University, 1974); Hamel-Green, *The Legitimacy of the 1964–72 Australian Conscription Scheme* (MA thesis, University of Melbourne, 1975).
44 Hamel-Green, "Dissent on the War to Protest at the System". *Tribune*, 10 July 1968, p. 6.
45 For an analysis which focusses largely on the significant but narrow story of the conceptual disagreement between New Left Marxists in Melbourne and the more American "countercultural" ideas, as represented in a published debate in *Arena* between Kelvin Rowley and Dennis Altman respectively, see: John Docker, "'Those Halcyon Days': The Moment of the New Left", ch. 13 in Brian Head and James Walter, eds, *Intellectual Movements and Australian Society* (Melbourne: Oxford University Press, 1988), p. 289.
46 See various issues of *Inscape*, the organ of the Melbourne SDS, especially during 1968 and 1969. See especially: SDS, "The Principles of a Democratic Society". *Inscape* (December 1968), vol. 1, no. 1, p. 1.
47 Hamel-Green, "The Politics of Passivity I: Apolitical Radicals in a Political Society". *Farrago* (University of Melbourne), 4 October 1968, vol. 46, no. 22, p. 18.
48 Philip R. Lawler, "Radicalism at Queensland University". *Social Survey* (March 1973), vol. 22, no. 2, p. 56; Summy, interviewed by the author, Brisbane, 4 July 2008.
49 Prentice, *The New Left* (MA thesis, University of Queensland, 1972), pp. 188–189.
50 Lawler, "Radicalism at Queensland University" (March 1973), *Social Survey* 22(2) at pp. 56–57; Prentice, *The New Left*; Rootes, *Australian Student Radicals: The Nature and Origins of Dissent* (BC Hons thesis, University of Queensland, 1969), pp. 56 ff.
51 Osmond, "Shock Therapy". *Dissent* (Spring 1967), no. 21, p. 31 at 32.
52 Ian Turner, "Monash and the NLF". *Outlook* (October 1967), vol. 11, no. 5, p. 24.
53 Hamel-Green, "The Resisters", pp. 111–12.
54 Hamel-Green, "The Resisters", p. 113.
55 Hamel-Green, "The Politics of Commitment: Resistance to Conscription". *National U*, 24 March 1969, p. 10.
56 Hamel-Green, "The Resisters", p. 114.
57 Hamel-Green, "The Resisters", pp. 114–120.
58 Cahill and Irving, "The Student Mood: Sydney University" (Spring 1968), *Dissent* vol. 23, p. 19.
59 Humphrey McQueen, "A Single Spark". *Arena* (1968), no. 16, p. 50.
60 Sharp, "A Revolutionary Culture". *Arena* (1968), no. 16, p. 2.

61 McQueen, "Three Tactics for Student Power". *Arena* (1969), no. 18, p. 16.

62 McQueen, "The Suckling Society". Ch. 1 in Mayer and Nelson, eds, *Australian Politics: A Third Reader* (Melbourne: Cheshire, 1973), p. 5 at 6–7 [amended version of "The Suckling Society". *Review* (Melbourne), 30 June 1972, p. 1020].

63 See: Colin Hughes, "The Marching Rule in Brisbane" (Nov–Dec 1967), *Quadrant* vol. 11, no. 6, at p. 29; Patrick Morgan, "The Trouble with Student Power" (July–Aug 1968), *Quadrant* vol. 12, no. 4, at p. 12; Horne, "Anarchism: What do the Students Want?". *The Bulletin*, 8 July 1968 at p. 24; Gerard Henderson, "How 'New' is the Australian New Left?". *Broadside*, 29 May 1969 at p. 9; Henderson, "The New Left in Australia: A Rejoinder". *Broadside*, 24 July 1969 at p. 17.

64 Part of a motion put to a general meeting of the student body at the University of Sydney. See: Haydn Thompson, "The May Moratorium". *honi soit*, 12 March 1970, p. 7.

65 Interest in the "early" or "young Marx" flourished during the 1960s. See: Erich Fromm, *Marx's Concept of Man* (New York: F. Ungar, 1961); Loyd D Easton, ed., *Writings of the Young Marx on Philosophy and Society* (Garden City, NY: Anchor Books, 1967).

66 See: Ann Curthoys, "'Shut up, you Bourgeois Bitch': Sexual Identity and Political Action in the Anti/Vietnam War Movement". In Joy Damousi and Marilyn Lake, eds, *Gender and War: Australians at War in the Twentieth Century* (Cambridge; Melbourne: Cambridge University Press, 1995), p. 311.

67 See: Graham Willett, "Marxism and the New Social Movements: The Case of Gay Liberation", in Carole Ferrier & Rebecca Pelan, eds, *The Point of Change: Marxism/Australia/History/Theory* (Australian Studies Centre, Department of English, University of Queensland, 1998), p. 201.

68 Gary Foley, "Black Power, Land Rights and Academic History". *Griffith Law Review* vol. 20, no. 3, 2011; Alyssa Trometter, *"The Fire in the Belly': Aboriginal Black Power and the Rise of the Australian Black Panther Party, 1967–1972* (PhD thesis, University of Melbourne, 2014); Naima Green, *Black and Bloody Beautiful* (BA Hons thesis, Harvard University, c.2007).

69 Russell Marks, *Rejection, Redemption, Ambivalence: The New Left and Australian Nationalism* (PhD thesis, La Trobe University, 2011).

70 See generally: Verity Burgmann, *Power and Protest: Movements for Change in Australian Society* (St Leonards, NSW: Allen & Unwin, 1993).

71 See for instance: Tony Abbott, *Battlelines* (Carlton, Vic: Melbourne University Publishing, 2009).

PART 3

The 1960s and 1970s: The valences of liberation

8

CHANGING CONSCIOUSNESS, CHANGING LIFESTYLES

Australian women's liberation, the left and the politics of 'personal solutions'

Isobelle Barrett Meyering

On 15 August 1976, a special meeting of Melbourne women's liberation, one of the 'liveliest' in years, was held to debate the movement's future. Attended by over a hundred women, it was prompted by a motion passed at a previous general meeting proclaiming women's liberation to no longer be a 'functioning' political body.[1] While the vast majority agreed to rescind the earlier motion, the meeting illuminated significant discontent over the state of the movement. Among those concerned about its direction was Barbara Wishart, who had issued a thirty-page document purporting to diagnose the 'problems' and 'potential' of women's liberation.[2] The paper was damning, pronouncing that the movement had become 'fragmented' and marred by 'mutual fear and suspicion'.[3]

According to Wishart, the movement's predicament stemmed from the failure to adequately develop and apply feminist theory. Among her chief objections was the alleged distortion of the phrase 'the personal is political', one of the best-known dictums of women's liberation. In its correct 'liberationist' interpretation, she explained, 'the personal becomes political for a feminist when she ... can see the relevance of her actions to the lives and actions of other women'. Wishart lamented that this phrase had, however, come to be misunderstood as a validation of 'personal solutions' rather than producing a commitment 'to work with other women to change the system'.[4]

Wishart could not have been more emphatic in her denunciation of 'personal solutions'. However, while her paper was especially impassioned in its critique, the position itself was not a new one. The paper formed part of a long-running debate within women's liberation over the place of what I will refer to here as 'personal change' or 'lifestyle change' in its revolutionary politics. This debate emerged from two competing tendencies within the 'new feminism'. On the one hand, like other parts of the Australian left in the 1970s, women's liberationists emphasised the centrality of collectivism to feminist struggles, a position powerfully expressed in the concept of 'sisterhood', as well as the movement's emphasis on collective action and protest.[5] On the other hand, women's liberation was founded on the recognition that women's personal lives and relationships were a key site of oppression and that contesting 'personal politics' necessitated attention to change at an individual as well as structural level. Indeed, as historian Marilyn Lake notes, the concept of personal transformation was central to the movement's revolutionary politics, influenced as much by the countercultural ethos of 'personal renewal' as Marxist-inflected critiques of capitalism.[6] This emphasis on personal change in turn presented women's liberationists with a persistent and seemingly insoluble dilemma. At what point did the individual's pursuit of change become a 'personal solution' rather than a contribution to a wider collective struggle?

As this chapter will show, this question was one that women's liberationists struggled with across the 1970s. Although most agreed that some degree of personal change was important, there was open and sometimes vehement disagreement over the appropriate weight to be given to efforts at the individual level and, furthermore, over the effects that such efforts would have on the movement's political cohesion and growth. This debate can be traced to the formative years of women's liberation in Australia but intensified over time and, from the mid-1970s, played into an increasingly pronounced split between those identifying themselves as radical feminists and socialist feminists.[7]

These debates were not unique to Australian women's liberation. Writing about the British movement, Lynne Segal, for example, has alluded to conflicts over lifestyle change and 'personal liberation' that at times played into sectarian divisions within socialist feminist politics.[8] Meanwhile, US historian Alice Echols has outlined – and ultimately endorsed – criticisms of 'cultural feminism' for privileging alternative institution building and lifestyle change, arguing that the dominance of this paradigm in the second half of the 1970s 'aggravated the tendency towards exclusivity' and promoted 'withdrawal from political struggle'.[9] Echols' position that a focus on lifestyle change reduced the capacity of feminism to function as a mass movement has, in turn, been countered by others who argue instead that such efforts helped to sustain activist communities.[10]

These arguments are ones that this chapter similarly identifies as playing out in the Australian context, yet they have so far tended to be overshadowed by other strategic debates, not least of all over the movement's relationship to the state. As has been well documented, the emergence of the new phenomenon of the 'femocrat' or feminist bureaucrat under the Whitlam Labor Government (1972–1975), and the allocation of government funding to feminist projects, such as refuges and women's health services, provoked significant debate within the movement over the dangers of 'cooption'.[11] Reflecting its leftist origins, women's liberation was highly sceptical about the risks of 'working within the system' and providing 'bandaid' solutions to women's problems. While seemingly unrelated issues, there are important parallels between the debates over the movement's relationship to the state and those over personal change, particularly as they relate to questions of cooption and movement building. Closer attention to these debates can in turn provide a more nuanced picture of feminist political strategy in this period.

Drawing on a range of feminist periodicals and position papers, this chapter explores the major debates that emerged over the validity of lifestyle change and the different ways in which they were inflected by leftist concerns. I begin by considering how women's liberationists presented their commitment to personal politics as a point of departure from the 'male left'. Following this, I discuss the importance accorded to consciousness raising in facilitating the process of personal transformation and point to some of the changes that women made in their own lives, focusing on two of the most important (and contested) arenas of feminist politics: the family and sexuality. This discussion is necessarily brief and can only address a small sample of the ways in which personal change translated into feminist praxis in these arenas, aspects of which have been described in more detail elsewhere.[12] In the remainder of the chapter, I focus on the debates that accompanied these developments, tracing three main lines of critique that emerged: first, that a focus on personal change was an 'individualist' and therefore 'elitist' strategy; second, that it led to unwarranted scrutiny of activists' personal lives; and third, that it represented a 'retreat' from politics.

Personal politics, women's liberation and the 'male left'

Like its overseas counterparts in North America and Britain, women's liberation in Australia had a fraught relationship with the left.[13] On the one hand, women's liberation emerged out of the left and identified itself as part of a wider struggle against capitalism and Western imperialism.[14] Notably, many of the movement's early members gained their political training in the left, in most cases through involvement in the anti-war and student movements in the late 1960s, but also as members of the Communist Party of Australia (CPA), other socialist groups and the trade union movement.[15] Moreover, theoretically, women's liberation was indebted to the New Left's language of 'oppression' and 'liberation', as well as its practices of participatory democracy and non-hierarchical political structures.[16] Many women's liberationists also continued to participate in related political struggles through the 1970s, including the anti-apartheid, indigenous rights, gay liberation and environmental movements.

On the other hand, women's liberation saw itself as rejecting 'male left' politics and demanded that it be recognised as an 'autonomous' movement. For those who maintained their connections to the organised left, this proved to be a point of ongoing friction. As women's liberation expanded, some self-described 'political women' within the movement complained that they were treated as suspect due to their allegiances to socialist groups.[17] These debates reached their apogee with proposals to expel Spartacist League members from women's liberation in Melbourne in 1973 and Sydney in 1977, prompted by complaints that they were 'disruptive' and not genuinely committed to women's liberation. The proposals were the subject of significant controversy, with only the Melbourne motion succeeding.[18]

The feminist critique of 'male left' politics that underpinned this fraught relationship had several components. Women's liberationists alleged sexist treatment within the left. As later recalled by poet Kate Jennings – who delivered a scathing critique in her infamous Front Lawn speech at the University of Sydney in September 1970 – women were reduced to subordinate roles within the left, considered 'good for typing and tea-making, scutwork and screwing'.[19] Moreover, women's liberationists pointed to the left's inadequacies when it came to personal politics. Domestic relationships remained determined by conventional expectations about gender roles, with housework and childcare left to the women while men performed 'revolutionary work'.[20] Meanwhile, the sixties' ethos of sexual liberation had mainly advanced male interests, with women still treated as 'sex objects' by their male comrades, as Jennings' comments suggest.

This identification of personal politics as a source of women's oppression contributed to a noticeable wariness about the movement's interactions with the 'male left'. Even in Adelaide, where men continued to attend women's liberation meetings for a longer period than in other parts of the country, there was considerable scepticism about the attitude of the 'male left' to women's liberation. Writing in the New Left journal, *Arena*, in 1970, Anna Yeatman, a sociologist and founding member of the Adelaide movement, sounded a warning that 'radical male-dominated groups will merely *use* women's liberation as a radicalizing instrument', while failing to integrate its precepts in 'the way they conduct their personal lives'.[21]

The following year, at a women's liberation conference held in Sydney from 30 January to 1 February 1971, Ann Curthoys and Lyndall Ryan went further, identifying the left's inadequate attention to personal politics as the source of a deeper political malaise. Leftists were, they argued, too quick to 'employ as their *means* social relationships and manipulative styles which we see as having no part of their ideal society'.[22] Such an approach was inimical to the cause of women's liberation which, they reasoned, could not be achieved solely through a 'change [in] the state by election or political revolution', but rather required an emphasis on 'social and individual change' for women's oppression stemmed as much from cultural institutions as state and corporate power.[23] Curthoys and Ryan explained:

> If a revolution is not a quick seizure of power but a long social revolution with a political aspect... then the means *are* the ends. Immediate behaviour constitutes the revolution itself. For women's liberation this means daily attack on sex roles is one of the most fundamental ways in which the liberation of women will occur.[24]

That Curthoys and Ryan felt a need to outline how their approach differed from that of the left speaks to their own political trajectories. Both women had been active in the student movement, especially anti-war activism, and both also came from left-wing families.[25] Curthoys has explained that she was initially sceptical of women's liberation; when she received a pamphlet announcing the first meeting of women's liberation at an anti-war demonstration in December 1969, she dismissed it as 'rather trivial, people are dying in Vietnam'.[26] However, a year later, she and Ryan confidently defended the movement against criticisms of those 'leaders of the Left' who saw them as a group 'whose personal concerns had broken class lines'. Women had, they concluded, been left with 'no choice' but to 'go our own way'.[27] Not only that, but in committing themselves to the task of restructuring personal relationships and lifestyles, they would offer a corrective to the prevailing style of left politics.

'Changing ourselves': personal transformation in practice

Two months after the Sydney conference, in March 1971, Curthoys and Ryan were part of the collective that produced the city's first women's liberation newspaper, *Mejane*. The 'statement of intent' that appeared in the inaugural edition was unambiguous in its endorsement of personal change as a political strategy. Women's liberation would, the collective asserted, involve 'both political and economic change and a revolutionary change in consciousness'. Conceding that this process would 'not be immediate', the group nonetheless asserted that 'we want to start now, changing life styles, changing the family and above all, changing ourselves'.[28] Their impatience was unmistakable.

As hinted at in the *Mejane* collective's statement, the practice of consciousness raising was accorded a crucial role in this process of personal transformation. Meeting together in small groups, women undertook the task of interrogating their life experiences, discussing wide-ranging topics, from their upbringing to their first sexual experiences to their feelings about having children.[29] The objective was to recast the individual's experience as part of a wider social experience. As *Mejane* collective member and long-time communist Joyce Stevens explained, consciousness raising enabled women 'to realise that personal problems are indeed shared problems and arise from social conditioning and conditions'. Ideally, it would also provide an impetus for action. 'A vital part of this process is the development of actions aimed at changing the oppressive conditions in which women find themselves', Stevens explained.[30]

An early Australian exposition of the transformative potential of consciousness raising can be found in the paper given by Sydney activist Camille Guy at the 1971 conference in Sydney. '[T]his personal revolution in thinking and assumptions is both highly contagious and the strongest possible impetus to sustained action', she asserted.[31] Her enthusiasm stemmed in part from her wider thinking about the organisational practices of women's liberation. Guy firmly believed that a commitment to decentralisation was a key source of its strength. Accordingly, she rejected the idea of establishing a list of movement 'aims' on the basis that women's liberation should avoid developing a single 'line' and affirmed the importance of small group action involving 'more discussion, more detailed analysis and more dissent'.[32] Consciousness raising was consistent with this framework.

Guy's interest in consciousness raising appears to have come from her recent reading of Germaine Greer's *The Female Eunuch* (1970). The book was a 'powerful and perceptive analysis of woman's condition' but 'significantly short on reference to campaigns and demands', Guy noted.[33] Far from seeing this as a failing, Guy welcomed Greer's alternative suggestion that women start not by 'changing the world' but 'reassessing' themselves. According to Greer, such an approach was much more likely to give 'motive and cause for action' than 'conventional political methods', including those of the left. 'The housewife who must wait for the success of world revolution for her liberty might be excused for losing hope', she quipped.[34] Endorsing this view, Guy was adamant that 'as more and more women attempt such re-assessment... change will inevitably follow'.[35]

The changes precipitated by women's participation in consciousness raising – in conjunction with their involvement in feminist activism more broadly – could indeed be profound. Some of the most significant related to family life, notably an arena that the *Mejane* collective had singled out in its March 1971 'statement of intent'. As I have argued elsewhere, the imperative to 'put feminist ideals into practice' was profoundly felt by many mothers in the movement, as they sought to reconcile their new-found desires for autonomy with their obligations to their children. Women sought to renegotiate their domestic arrangements, insisting that men contribute to household chores and take part in childcare. Some also made more radical changes, establishing new communal households that prefigured the kinds of family life they imagined would form the basis of a future, sexually egalitarian society.[36]

Importantly, this interest in creating new forms of family was not limited to younger members of women's liberation or those who had broken ties with the organised left. In early 1972, Joyce Stevens, along with fellow communist, Mavis Robertson, moved into an eight-bedroom house in Roseville, a suburb on Sydney's affluent north shore, with their teenage children, Robertson's husband and four others. Their commune soon featured in a profile on the future of the family in *The Sydney Morning Herald*, in which they were introduced as an example of a living experiment 'based on a desire to evolve a new kind of society'.[37] Ultimately the commune proved to be short-lived and, despite their professed aims of reallocating domestic roles, much of the burden of running the household fell on the two women.[38] As we will see, Stevens would become increasingly critical of 'personal solutions' over time, yet notably she never dismissed lifestyle change outright.

While mothers experimented with new family forms, other women made firm decisions not to have children, a commitment enacted in some cases by undergoing sterilisation. Very few doctors were willing to perform sterilisation procedures on young (white) women – by contrast, Aboriginal women were seeking restrictions on sterilisation in this period[39] – and this prompted some activists to publish accounts of their efforts to navigate the medical system or articles providing advice on the process. In some cases, these writers also made claims for the political consequences of this decision. In an article on 'The Politics of Childlessness' in the Melbourne journal, *Vashti's Voice*, published in Autumn 1975, Karen Lindsay drew an analogy between remaining childless and open lesbianism; both represented 'a declaration against the patriarchal structure of the family … [and] a rejection of reproductive sexuality as the only legitimate sexual base', she argued.[40]

The comparison was a powerful one, for sexual politics represented another intense focus of lifestyle change. Demands for sexual autonomy precipitated significant changes in women's relationships with male partners and their sexual practices. US women's liberationist Anne Koedt's 'The Myth of the Vaginal Orgasm' (1970), for example, is frequently cited as one of the most personally transformative pieces of feminist writing of the period.[41] Moreover, women's liberation – in conjunction with the rise of gay liberation – provided a space in which many women came to openly identify as lesbian for the first time, albeit not without considerable contestation over their 'invisibility' within the movement.[42]

Lesbian activists would in turn play a key role in the formulation of the radical feminist position in Australia, which brought new urgency to the process of personal transformation, emphasising the need for new lifestyles as part of a 'women's culture'. In July 1973, the Melbourne group Radicalesbians organised the first national lesbian feminist conference, held at Sorrento.[43] In a paper on 'Feminist Culture', Chris Sitka set out the radical feminist position, explaining:

> Radical feminism stands so completely in opposition to all the male culture demands that it necessitates a whole new lifestyle. It means changing the way we live and relate all day, every day… we must build a way of life; a way of living out our primacy with women in our every day lives.[44]

This vision of a new women's culture gradually came into fruition during the mid-1970s, with the proliferation of women-only households, the establishment of women's only cultural spaces, and the creation of several women's lands, most famously Amazon Acres in northern New South Wales, established in 1974.[45] Made possible by the financial contributions of women in Sydney and Melbourne, its founders' objective was to create a self-sustaining community where 'women could work towards gaining control of their lives'.[46]

During this period, the argument that political lesbianism was a necessary step to revolutionary change also gained some traction. Its central proposition was that lesbianism might be chosen as an expression of one's 'political commitment' to other women, rather than on the basis of sexual desire per se.[47] As Sharon explained, writing in the Adelaide journal, *Liberation*, in early 1975, 'any woman, "straight" or gay, who is prepared to exert her energies on women to the largest extent' could be considered 'a lesbian'. In recognising herself as such and refusing to 'compromise' with men, she would be better placed to advance the feminist cause. 'Our sympathies must not lie with them but with our sisters and that's where my energies will flow, hopefully yours will too', Sharon declared.[48]

Political lesbianism took the concept of lifestyle change to its logical extreme, with its claim that a total commitment to other women could produce revolutionary change. As I discuss below, it was the source of considerable controversy within women's liberation, including amongst lesbian activists. Nonetheless, the

160 Isobelle Barrett Meyering

premise that personal change represented a political act was a common thread throughout the discussions traced here. The forms and degree of change pursued varied, but the underlying principle remained the same: that as well as providing benefits to the individual, lifestyle change had wider strategic value for the movement. The pursuit of personal change was necessary in order to bring feminist theory and practice into alignment, and as a form of resistance to the existing system of patriarchal relations. Furthermore, activists saw themselves not only as implementing more liberated lifestyles for themselves, but as modelling these new ways of living to others. At the same time, these claims for the strategic value of lifestyle change were countered by a series of criticisms, starting with the charge that it perpetuated an 'individualist' ideology.

Lifestyle change and the dangers of individualism

When Curthoys and Ryan presented their paper at the 1971 Sydney conference, they were careful to emphasise that the strategy they were advocating was one of 'individual *and* social change' (italics added). Women's liberation was not, they stressed, simply a 'social and personal movement which is essentially apolitical'.[49] Nonetheless, a report on the conference that appeared in *Mejane* in March 1971 noted that Curthoys and Ryan's paper had 'provoked basic disagreement' among conference participants, including criticisms of their approach 'as personal and individualistic, confining liberation to a small elite'.[50]

As the initial response to Curthoys and Ryan's paper suggests, the charge of individualism was a particularly potent one as it raised fundamental questions about the mechanisms and beneficiaries of the social changes envisioned by women's liberation. The charge comprised two main components. In a basic sense, the pursuit of lifestyle change was contrasted with efforts to address wider structural inequalities; where Curthoys and Ryan's paper presented these as mutually constitutive, critics tended to pit them against each other. Perhaps even more importantly, lifestyle change was depicted as a strategy that could only be pursued by those already in a relatively privileged position. The critique of lifestyle change as 'individualist' thus came to form part of a wider debate within women's liberation over its alleged middle-class orientation.

Variations of this argument quickly appeared. The charge of elitism was, for example, raised almost immediately with respect to consciousness raising. In its early phases, advocates were forced to defend the practice from critics who 'seem to view "personal talk" as somewhat of an indulgence'.[51] Furthermore, even those who recognised the value of consciousness raising warned that it could reinforce a limited view of 'individual liberation' that could dilute the impetus for wider social change. In the same article in *Mejane* in which Stevens highlighted its role in enabling women to challenge oppression in their own lives, she also cautioned that consciousness raising would 'not necessarily lead all women in the direction of radical or revolutionary solutions' and could 'lead to a mistaken belief that women can liberate themselves through libertarian agreements in their personal lives', an approach that benefited those in 'more privileged positions'.[52]

The traction of this critique of elitism is similarly reflected in the apologetic tone evident in some women's accounts of their efforts to pursue more 'liberated' lifestyles. For example, four months earlier, in March 1971, fellow Sydney activist Lesley Gray had written in *Mejane* about the childcare arrangements she had made for her son so that she could keep working. Gray was emphatic about her 'right both to have children and to continue my life outside the house in much the same way as before I had them'. Yet she was also at pains to acknowledge that, in sourcing childcare, she had benefited from her middle-class status and connections.[53] Gray was the first to acknowledge the limitations of this 'personal solution'.

The argument persisted in various forms over the years in the form of recurrent warnings that 'individual liberation' was not a sufficient political strategy. It was made with particular force in an article by Ann Game, 'Some Criticisms of the Women's Liberation Movement', published in a special edition of *Liberation* produced by the Socialist Women's Group in May 1973. Later a well-known feminist sociologist, Game offered a scathing assessment of the movement: women's liberation 'has become something of a sacred cow', she began, and for too long this had allowed various 'inadequacies' in its theory to go unchallenged. One of its major flaws, she argued, was to seek solutions at the individual level. While 'not criticising the idea that we should attempt to change our personal relations now', Game objected that 'to centre one's political activity on a personal level will not change structural conditions of the position of women'.[54] Furthermore, Game suggested that a focus on personal politics and lifestyle change revealed the middle class basis of the movement. 'It is clear that to talk of such things to working class women would be absurd. Only people like us in a privileged position have the time for such things', she asserted.[55]

Game framed her analysis of the limitations of lifestyle change as part of a wider critique of the movement's emphasis on 'sex roles' and the psychological foundations of women's oppression, an approach she was far from alone in noting 'theoretically and politically' privileged the 'individual'.[56] In particular, Game took aim at US feminist Kate Millet's *Sexual Politics* (1970), which had provided one of the most influential examinations of women's 'conditioning', along with an early manifesto by Yeatman, which Game criticised for advocating a 'political practice' focusing on the individual, even if it recognised roles as 'socially imposed'.[57]

Not surprisingly, given its forthright attacks on these foundational writings, Game's article met with significant resistance. A letter from fellow Adelaide women's liberation and communist Pat Vort-Ronald rejected her suggestion that the movement concentrated on 'individual solutions', asserting that this was the 'opposite' to what she had experienced. The phrase 'the personal is political' implied that 'women's unhappiness is not individual' and, concomitantly, that 'there can be no individual liberation'.[58] Notably though, Vort-Ronald's letter was less a defence of lifestyle change than an attempt to correct what she saw as Game's misrepresentation of the movement's political emphasis.

162 Isobelle Barrett Meyering

Another respondent, Barbara Jones in Melbourne was similarly troubled by Game's 'total failure to grasp what WLM is really all about'. Jones declared that Game's article 'could have come straight from the pen of any or all of the young males of Melbourne's branch of the Spartacist League', a group that, as noted earlier, was the source of ongoing acrimony.[59] Game had anticipated – indeed, arguably provoked – this very response, having opened her article with the disclaimer that criticisms of women's liberation were often seen as a 'betrayal' and sign of being 'indoctrinated by the "male left"'.[60]

As the responses to Game's article indicate, the charge of individualism was one that activists were highly sensitive to, all the more so when it was joined with criticism of their middle-class orientation. By the time her article appeared, debate over the politics of 'personal solutions' had also intensified, amidst concerns about the 'policing' of other activists' lifestyles. This criticism was also inflected by wider left politics, with its proponents framing their concerns in terms of the implications that such a tendency posed for mass movement building.

Policing lifestyles: dogmatism and personal scrutiny

While the search for new lifestyles could be one of the most exhilarating aspects of women's liberation, it was also accompanied by what many considered to be a worrying tendency for increasing scrutiny of the personal lives of other activists. There had already been signs of this tendency in the formative stages of the movement. For example, writing in *Mejane* in March 1973, Anne Summers, a founding member of Adelaide women's liberation, recalled having been 'abused' for wearing make-up when she attended the first national women's liberation conference, held in Melbourne in May 1970.[61] However, it was in the mid-1970s, when Summers was writing, that these concerns became more persistent. A satirical piece in the *Sydney Women's Liberation Newsletter* in April 1974, outlining 'ten commandants' for feminists, encapsulated activists' concerns about a growing dogmatism when it came to women's personal lives.[62]

To critics, it increasingly seemed that women were not simply encouraged to pursue changes in their personal lives pursuant with their own liberation, but rather expected to adopt an 'ideologically sound' lifestyle in order to demonstrate their commitment to the movement. As Lake notes, there was significant irony in this: 'A movement that had been born in the desire to be free from the imposition of social roles had quickly developed its own set of prescriptions'.[63] These developments inserted further heat to debates about the strategic merits of personal change. According to critics, it was not simply that a focus on developing new lifestyles was misguided in its perpetuation of 'personal solutions'. Rather, the focus on lifestyle change was damaging to movement cohesion and morale, and could, at its worst, risk dividing women within the movement and alienating others from taking part.

The dangers of this increasing scrutiny of activists' lives were outlined forcefully in a paper by Barbara Bloch and Kerryn Higgs presented at the Feminism and

Anarchism Conference held in Canberra in October 1975 and later reproduced in *Scarlet Woman*, a new socialist feminist journal that reflected the increasing attempt to demarcate radical and socialist feminist camps in this period.[64] A critique of 'feminist conformity', the paper argued that feminist thinking had become 'hedged by expectations of ideological soundness'. As a result, feminism risked becoming 'dogmatic and intolerant' and imposing new norms of its own. 'In the process of claiming what we see as our rights, we turn those rights into obligations for others', they warned.[65]

Both lesbian activists, Bloch and Higgs were particularly concerned about the emergence of a new 'sexual conformity'. While agreeing 'in principle' that women's relationships with each other represented a 'threat to male supremacy', Bloch and Higgs did not believe that lesbianism was a precondition of being a 'true' feminist nor a foundation for a wider political strategy of change. 'We are not prepared to prescribe lesbianism either as a necessary interim strategy for all women – still less as a permanent panacea for all women', they wrote.[66] Bloch and Higgs' objections were multiple. In expecting all women to become practising lesbians, feminists risked establishing expectations that were 'no less oppressive than the societal heterosexual norm'. Crucially, such a norm was dangerous for all women: the idea that 'a true feminist has to be a lesbian' not only put pressure on heterosexual women, but on women who had lesbian relationships 'never to deviate again', they argued.[67] In short, it was, they asserted, 'unfeminist' to place such expectations on other women.[68]

Where Bloch and Higgs focused primarily on the unnecessary guilt and pressure this 'new conformity' created for activists, others raised concerns that the new norms of behaviour would distance feminists from other women. The debate that ensued in the Perth women's liberation journal, *Sibyl*, in 1975 over an article by local activist Maureen Davies, setting out her reasons for choosing to be sterilised, is a prime example.[69] While some praised Davies for her honesty in describing her lack of desire to have children, others objected that sterilisation did not provide a solution for the majority of women who were mothers. A lengthy and particularly critical response from Perth mother Madelon Wilkens retorted that the role of women's liberation was 'to propose feasible changes and thus new choices for women' and described her own efforts to establish shared care for her 12-month old with her male partner.[70] Davies responded that Wilkens had 'missed the point' of the article which had not been to 'lay down guidelines and rules as to family relationships, but to appeal to women who secretly felt they didn't want children'.[71] The extended exchange reflects the high stakes invested in discussions of activists' personal lives that in turn flowed into debates about the movement's relevance to 'ordinary' women.

Such concerns continued to persist into the second half of the 1970s, when they dovetailed with anxieties about the movement's lack of political momentum. For example, at the Marxist-Feminist Conference, held in Sydney in June 1977, a paper by the *Scarlet Woman* collective queried the relevance of the lifestyle changes pursued by activists to the 'mass of women'. It asked:

164 Isobelle Barrett Meyering

> What is the political implication of what we are doing in our relationships? What has this got to do with the personal lives of the mass of women? Are we developing revolutionary models appropriate for us but irrelevant to most women?[72]

The paper, entitled 'Afternoon Tea or Revolution...', suggested the need for a reassessment of the strategic merits of personal change. While the lifestyle changes pursued by activists might indeed be 'revolutionary', the collective implied that they would not necessarily prepare them for the wider 'revolution' required to 'smash patriarchy'.[73]

'Retreating' from politics

The collective's paper was consistent with a new line of critique that entered debates about personal change in the second half of the 1970s: that 'personal solutions' represented a 'retreat' from politics. This argument was, in a sense, a variation of the idea that lifestyle change represented an individualist approach. However, it was now more explicitly framed in terms of the politics of separatism, and the growing division between radical feminists and socialist feminists, with 'personal solutions' often serving as a euphemism for 'women's culture'. In addition, this criticism corresponded with what Katy Reade has described as a growing discourse of 'crisis' and 'panic' within the movement in this period, reflective of a broader sense of despondency within the left following Whitlam's dismissal.[74]

Indeed, this criticism of activists' retreating into 'personal solutions' was one of the key ones raised by Wishart in her paper in August 1976, an exemplary of this 'crisis' discourse.[75] In her analysis of the problems of 'personal solutions', Wishart rejected separatism as leading to a 'ghetto approach... a lifestyle and way of relating [that] is based on a withdrawal from the system'. According to Wishart, this 'withdrawal' was a product of a misconceived view that the creation of self-sufficient feminist communities represented a 'viable' strategy of change. On the contrary, she argued that separatism was 'destructive' to women's liberation, representing an 'idealistic red-herring, because all women will never leave the system or stop relating to men'.[76]

The 'retreat' into 'personal solutions' was similarly represented in the language of 'crisis' by activists describing the state of the movement in other cities. Writing in Adelaide's *Liberation* in mid-1976, Sally Jackson declared that a sense of 'defeat' had led activists to 'move away from our collective struggle' and 'look for personal solutions in feminist households or feminist relationships'. Jackson's language was particularly hyperbolic. She despaired that this process of retreat only compounded the lack of morale: as "personal solutions" fail one by one defeat after defeat, I die a little more and I don't know what to do next', she wrote.[77]

An assessment of Canberra women's liberation by Susan Eade (later Magarey), published in *Refractory Girl* in March 1977, was somewhat more tempered, but the sentiments expressed were similar. She described the 'prevailing mood' as 'bewildered, irritated, and weary'[78] and identified the movement as having become 'fragmented', with groups and individuals 'isolated' from and 'sometimes antagonistic' towards one another. This state of affairs was exemplified in some women having 'carried the "personal is political" argument to the extreme of opting out of the feminist struggle altogether, turning inward to sole concern with dwellings and personal relationships', a trend that she equated with the success of the 'anarchist-reformist' mode of feminism over the 'feminist-socialist' mode.[79] Looking back on this piece, Magarey has recently reflected that her concern about the movement's 'diminishing allegiance' to socialist principles was overstated.[80] Even so, her diagnosis of a crisis in the movement caused in part by activists 'opting out' and seeking 'personal solutions' were hardly unique.

Alongside notions of 'crisis', the criticism of 'withdrawal' was linked to a number of other arguments about lifestyle change and 'ghetto politics'. The views presented in *Scarlet Woman* through this period provide an indication of some of the key concerns. One was that the movement had become too insular and complacent. Writing in the special 'lesbian issue' of *Scarlet Woman* in July 1976, Melbourne activist Dianne Otto worried in particular about the state of lesbian feminist politics:

> For those of us who are almost totally ensconced in the lesbian-feminist ghetto, this means that we seldom get it together to discuss and organise around lesbian-feminist issues… We seem to settle smugly into a network of parties, ups and downs of relationships and household organisation, and not get ourselves much further…[81]

Others suggested that time and energy was misdirected into these activities. In the same issue, Lyn Hovey noted the concerns of fellow Melbourne activist Zelda D'Aprano regarding lesbian activists' involvement in a food co-operative. 'Is this the way we see the solution in changing society, dissipating our women's energy to save a few dollars', D'Aprano queried.[82]

Yet these critical views were not the only ones presented in *Scarlet Woman*. Indeed, Otto went on to suggest that one way to address activists' complacency was for feminism to be more 'fully' incorporated into 'our lifestyles and ways of relating to each other', thereby stimulating greater political discussion.[83] Meanwhile, D'Aprano's disparagement of the co-op was countered by Hovey who defended 'ghetto politics' as productive in so far as they created a space for 'action, protection and communication'.[84] Hovey's response was precipitated by the intense debates that had recently ensued within Melbourne circles after a letter by D'Aprano expressing qualms about lesbian women's presence at the women's centre was published in the *Melbourne Women's Liberation Newsletter*.[85] Five months earlier, however, Sydney activist Janet Wahlquist had made a similar defence of 'ghetto politics', this time in relation to the value of communal living to provide the 'necessary emotional support to fight a revolution'. Far from a misdirection of energy, she argued that addressing their personal circumstances was all the more important given the 'impending backlash' from the Liberal Government.[86]

166 Isobelle Barrett Meyering

As Wahlquist's article suggests, while the criticism of 'personal solutions' as a 'retreat' from politics was one that fit well with narratives of 'crisis' in the second half of the 1970s, it was also still possible to make a case for lifestyle change as a productive dimension of feminist politics, including for socialist feminists. Indeed, if the 'crisis' faced by the movement was blamed in part on activists' withdrawal into 'personal solutions', then it was also seen as partly resolvable through a renewed attention to their own lives, in the interests of creating a stronger activist culture and a movement that could sustain itself.

Personal change as revolutionary politics?

By the late 1970s, arguments about the limitations of 'personal solutions' had been well rehearsed in *Scarlet Woman*, but no resolution had been found. In March 1977, Joyce Stevens summed up the position well. In an article purporting to address the 'future' of women's liberation, Stevens lamented the emerging view that 'personal solutions... could suffice'.[87] Yet, Stevens, whose feminist involvement had, as we have seen, precipitated significant changes in her own life, was also careful not to be seen as rejecting personal change outright. 'Personal politics and consciousness raising have been, and are, important weapons in changing women's passive acceptance of their allotted roles', she acknowledged. What she objected to, she stressed, was the view 'that personal solutions can be *the* way to change society'.[88]

The following year, when Stevens and fellow *Scarlet Woman* collective member Sarah Gibson proposed setting up a new group that would bring together socialist feminists in Sydney with varying allegiances, they were once again at pains to emphasise that lifestyle change had a place in socialist feminism. While a strong political movement of women could not be achieved 'through sole emphasis on personal change and life-style', they defended a 'concern for personal politics, for new life-styles within a women's culture, or the relationship of women to women' as 'an important part of our revolutionary politics'. 'The impetus gained from personal politics', they warned, 'must not be lost as socialist feminists examine traditional revolutionary theories'.[89]

That the question of what position personal change should occupy within socialist feminist politics had emerged as a pressing dilemma for Stevens and Gibson is not surprising. It not only speaks to the part that debates about 'personal solutions' had played in the increasingly pronounced split between radical and socialist feminists that had emerged in the preceding years, but the recurring influence of left politics on debates about personal change as a feminist political strategy across the decade. As we have seen, from the beginnings of women's liberation, attention to 'personal politics', including in the context of their own lives, was presented as a corrective to 'male left' politics. Yet the movement's origins in the left also had an enduring impact on arguments about the merits and limitations of efforts to transform individual consciousness and lifestyle.

All three lines of critique directed at 'personal solutions' traced in this chapter were, in some form, inflected by leftist concerns. The early charge that an emphasis

Australian women's liberation **167**

on personal change was individualist and elitist touched a raw nerve as it brought into question the movement's class politics. Meanwhile, later criticisms that a focus on personal change produced new feminist norms that were alienating to 'ordinary' women and led to a 'retreat' from politics were variations on wider debates about strategies of mass movement building. Furthermore, underlying these arguments was a concern about the possibility of cooption. Yet, for all these concerns, Stevens and Gibson still felt a need to recognise a place for personal change in socialist feminist politics, albeit with the qualification that it could not be their 'sole emphasis'. Attesting to the profound and enduring impact of early critiques of 'personal politics', the question they posed was not whether personal change had a place in revolutionary politics, but what emphasis it should be given.

Notes

1 For a full account of the meeting, see Jean Taylor, *Brazen Hussies: A Herstory of Radical Activism in the Women's Liberation Movement in Victoria 1970–1979* (Melbourne: Dyke Books, 2009), 444–446.
2 Barbara Wishart, 'Women's Liberation: The Problems and the Potential', 1976, written with Zelda D'Aprano, Joan R. and Anna C., file 70/01/042, box 1, Laurie Bebbington Collection, Women's Liberation Centre Collection, 2000.0166/VWLLFA no. 70, University of Melbourne Archives (UMA).
3 Ibid., 3.
4 Ibid., 6.
5 Susan Magarey, 'Sisterhood and Women's Liberation in Australia', *Outskirts: Feminisms Along the Edge,* 28 (2013), www.outskirts.arts.uwa.edu.au/volumes/volume-28/susan-magarey
6 Marilyn Lake, *Getting Equal: The History of Australian Feminism* (Sydney: Allen and Unwin, 1999), 232-233.
7 For a brief discussion of this split with reference to debates about lifestyle politics, from the perspective of socialist feminists, see Margaret Penson, *Breaking the Chains: Communist Party Women and the Women's Liberation Movement 1965–1975* (Sydney: Breaking the Chains Collective, 1999), 78, 80-81.
8 Lynne Segal, *Is the Future Female?: Troubled Thoughts on Contemporary Feminism* (London: Virago, 1987), 50.
9 Alice Echols, *Daring to Be Bad: Radical Feminism in America, 1967–1975* (Minneapolis: University of Minnesota Press, 1989), 281.
10 Anne M. Valk, 'Living a Feminist Lifestyle: The Intersection of Theory and Action in a Lesbian Feminist Collective', *Feminist Studies* 28, no. 2 (2002), 303–332; and Nancy Whittier, *Feminist Generations: The Persistence of the Radical Women's Movement* (Philadelphia: Temple University Press, 1995).
11 This literature is extensive. For a recent discussion of women's liberation's views of the state, see Susan Magarey, 'Women's Liberation Was a Movement, Not an Organisation', *Australian Feminist Studies* 29, no. 82 (2014), 378–390. For an overview of key developments relating to femocrats and government funding, see Lake, *Getting Equal,* chap. 11.
12 On family life, see for example Isobelle Barrett Meyering, '"There Must Be a Better Way": Motherhood and the Dilemmas of Feminist Lifestyle Change', *Outskirts: Feminisms Along the Edge,* 28 (2013), www.outskirts.arts.uwa.edu.au/volumes/volume-28/isobelle-barrett-meyering; and Rebecca Jennings, 'The Boy-Child in Australian Lesbian Feminist Discourse and Community', *Cultural and Social History* 13, no. 1 (2016), especially 67–71. On sexuality, see for example Rebecca Jennings, *Unnamed*

168 Isobelle Barrett Meyering

Desires: A Sydney Lesbian History (Clayton, Victoria: Monash University Publishing, 2015), 85–88; and Sophie Robinson, 'Bar Dykes and Lesbian Feminists: Lesbian Encounters in 1970s Feminism', *Lilith: A Feminist History Journal,* no. 22 (2016), especially 59–62.

13 For a recent discussion of how this relationship has been historicised and, the author argues, often misunderstood, see Sara M. Evans, 'Women's Liberation: Seeing the Revolution Clearly', *Feminist Studies* 41, no. 1 (2015), 138–149.

14 Ann Curthoys, 'The Anti-War Movement', in *Vietnam: Myth and Memory: Comparative Perspectives on Australia's War in Vietnam,* Sydney, ed. Jeffrey Grey and Jeff Doyle (St. Leonards, NSW: Allen & Unwin, 1992), 103.

15 For example, on communist women in the Sydney movement, see Penson, *Breaking the Chains.*

16 Curthoys, 'The Anti-War Movement', 103.

17 An early example is the 'Manifesto: On the Rights of Political Women within Women's Liberation', paper presented at the Sydney Women's Liberation Conference, 10–12 June 1972. Republished in *Mejane,* no. 8 (August 1972), 4.

18 The Spartacists were first expelled from Melbourne women's liberation meetings in 1973. The issue was revisited on multiple occasions in subsequent years and the position was maintained, including at a meeting on 7 May 1977 prompted by the Sydney motion. Taylor, *Brazen Hussies,* 215–217. The Sydney meeting took place on 17 April 1977 and the motion lost 100 votes to 85 votes, with between 30–40 women abstaining. Sue Wills, 'Seventies Chronology, Part II, 1973–1979', *Australian Feminist Studies* 23, no. 55 (2007), 146.

19 Kate Jennings, *Trouble: Evolution of a Radical: Selected Writings, 1970–2010* (Melbourne: Black Inc., 2010), 4. For a more general discussion of these concerns, including Jenning's 1970 speech, see Lake, *Getting Equal,* 220–221.

20 Mavis Robertson, 'Victims of Double Oppression', *Australian Left Review,* no. 28 (December 1970–January 1971), 6.

21 Anna Yeatman, 'The Liberation of Women', *Arena,* no. 21 (1970), 22.

22 Ann Curthoys and Lyndall Ryan, 'Up from Radicalism: Problems of Organisation in Sydney Women's Liberation', paper presented at the Sydney Women's Liberation Conference, 30 January to 1 February 1971. Reprinted in Ann Curthoys, *For and Against Feminism: A Personal Journey into Feminist Theory and History* (Sydney: Allen & Unwin, 1988), 12.

23 Ibid., 11.

24 Ibid., 12.

25 Curthoys was the daughter of Barbara and Geoffrey Curthoys, both members of the Communist Party in Newcastle, while Ryan's parents, Edna and Jack Ryan, were Labor Party activists and former communists, having been expelled from the party in the early 1930s. Curthoys and Ryan have written about their political upbringings on multiple occasions, including most recently in Ann Curthoys and Joy Damousi, *What Did You Do in the Cold War, Daddy? Personal Stories from a Troubled Time* (Sydney: NewSouth Publishing, 2014), 18–19; and Lyndall Ryan, 'Caught Out: Edna and Jack Ryan and the 1951 Referendum', in *What Did You Do in the Cold War, Daddy?,* 72–86.

26 Ann Curthoys, 'History and Reminiscence: Writing About the Anti-Vietnam-War Movement', *Australian Feminist Studies* 7, no. 16 (1992), 129.

27 Curthoys and Ryan, 'Up from Radicalism', in Curthoys, *For and Against Feminism,* 11.

28 'Statement of Intent', *Mejane,* no. 1 (March 1971), 2.

29 For an account of one such group, see Kristin Henry and Marlene Derlet, *Talking up a Storm: Nine Women and Consciousness-Raising* (Sydney: Hale & Iremonger, 1993).

30 Joyce Stevens, 'Male Liberation?', *Mejane,* no. 3 (July 1971), 6.

31 Camille Guy, 'Some Thoughts on Women's Lib.', paper presented at the Sydney Women's Liberation Conference, 30 January to 1 February 1971, box 31, First Ten Years of Sydney Women's Liberation (First Ten Years) Collection, MLMSS 9782, State Library of New South Wales (SLNSW).

32 Ibid.

33 Ibid.

34 Germaine Greer, *The Female Eunuch,* paperback edition (London: MacGibbon & Kee, 1970; London: Paladin, 1971), 14.

35 Guy, 'Some Thoughts on Women's Lib'.

36 For an extended discussion, see Barrett Meyering, 'There Must Be a Better Way'.

37 Julia Orange, 'Just One Big, Happy Family', *Sydney Morning Herald, Look!,* 13 July 1972, 3.

38 Canberra activist Julia Ryan, who visited the household, later recalled that it struck her that the Sydney women now had 'the burden, a much greater burden of responsibility, of this conglomerate' rather than a single household. Julia Ryan, interview by Sara Dowse, 26 September 1990, ORAL TRC 2651, NLA.

39 Aileen Moreton-Robinson, Talkin' up to the White Woman: Indigenous Women and Feminism (St Lucia, Qld: University of Queensland Press, 2000), 171.

40 Karen Lindsay, 'The Politics of Childlessness', *Vashti's Voice,* no. 10 (Autumn 1975), 7.

41 Anne Koedt, 'The Myth of the Vaginal Orgasm', 1970. Reprinted in Leslie Tanner (ed.), *Voices from Women's Liberation* (New York: Signet Book, 1971), 158–166. For a discussion of its impact, see Susan Magarey, 'The Sexual Revolution as Big Flop: Women's Liberation Lesson One', *Dialogue* 27, no. 3 (2008), 24–25.

42 A widely cited critique of lesbian invisibility was made by the Hobart Women's Action Group in their paper at the Mt Beauty conference in January 1973. For an overview, see Jennings, *Unnamed Desires,* 84.

43 On the Radicalesbians, see Robert Reynolds, *From Camp to Queer: Re-Making the Australian Homosexual* (Carlton South, Victoria: Melbourne University Press, 2002), 142–146 and Robinson, 'Bar Dykes and Lesbian Feminists', 63–64.

44 Chris Sitka, 'Feminist Culture', paper presented at the Radicalesbian Conference, Sorrento, 6–8 July 1973. Last accessed 21 July 2017, http://users.spin.net.au/~deniset/a lesfem/s2radlesps73.pdf

45 Jennings, *Unnamed Desires,* 88. On women's households, see Lake, *Getting Equal,* 244– 245. On women-only spaces, see Louise R. Mayhew, '"Volatile, Feral and Glamorous": Australian Women's Warehouse', *AM Journal of Art and Media Studies* 8 (2015), 29–34. On women's lands, including Amazon Acres, see Judith Ion, 'Degrees of Separation: Lesbian Separatist Communities in Northern New South Wales, 1974–95', in *Sex in Public: Australian Sexual Cultures,* ed. Jill Julius Matthews (St Leonards, NSW: Allen & Unwin, 1997), 97–113.

46 Cited in Graham Willett, *Living out Loud: A History of Gay and Lesbian Activism in Australia* (St Leonards, NSW: Allen & Unwin, 2000), 69.

47 Barbara Baird, 'Lesbian Identities', in *Australian Feminism: A Companion*, ed. Barbara Caine, et al. (Melbourne: Oxford University Press, 1998), 198–199.

48 Sharon, 'Lesbianism and the Adelaide Women's Movement', *Liberation,* no. 1 (c. March/ April 1975), 10. Note the numbering of *Liberation* changed for a period in 1975.

49 Curthoys and Ryan, 'Up from Radicalism', 11.

50 Camille Guy, 'NSW Women's Lib Conference', *Mejane,* no. 1 (March 1971), 14.

51 Guy, 'Some Thoughts on Women's Lib'.

52 Stevens, 'Male Liberation?', 6.

53 Lesley Gray, 'Child Care Centres – Part One: A Personal Account', *Mejane,* no. 1 (March 1971), 5.

54 Ann Game, 'Some Criticisms of the Women's Liberation Movement', *Liberation,* no. 19 (May 1973), 1–2.

55 Ibid., 3.

56 Ibid., 1. For a recent discussion of Millet's influence see Victoria Hesford, *Feeling Women's Liberation* (Durham; London: Duke University Press, 2013).

57 Game, 'Some Criticisms', 2.

58 'Criticisms of the Criticisms', *Liberation,* no. 20 (June 1973), 6.

59 Ibid., 7.

60 Game, 'Some Criticisms', 1.
61 Anne Summers, 'Where's the Women's Movement Moving To?', *Mejane*, no. 10 (March 1973), 6.
62 'Is This Our Religion', *Sydney Women's Liberation Newsletter* (April 1974), 17.
63 Lake, *Getting Equal*, 237.
64 On the history of the journal, see Sue Williamson, *Refractory Girl and Scarlet Woman: Contributions to Counter-hegemonic Feminism* (Masters thesis, University of New South Wales, Sydney).
65 Kerryn Higgs and Barbara Bloch, 'Beyond the Cliches: A Reappraisal of Feminism', *Scarlet Woman*, 3 (February 1976), 24.
66 Ibid., 21.
67 Ibid.
68 Ibid., 22.
69 Maureen Davies, 'Child Free', *Sybil*, no. 2 (March 1975), 18.
70 'Forum', *Sybil*, no. 3 (April 1975), 38.
71 'Forum', *Sybil*, no. 4 (May-June 1975), 30.
72 Sydney Scarlet Woman Collective, 'Afternoon Tea or Revolution....', paper presented at the Marxist-Feminist Conference, 11–13 June 1977, box 32, First Ten Years Collection, SLNSW.
73 Ibid.
74 Katy Reade, 'The Discourses of Crisis in the Women's Liberation Movement and the Women's Electoral Lobby in Melbourne in the Late 1970s', *Lilith: A Feminist History Journal*, no. 9 (1996), 125–145.
75 For a closer analysis of Wishart's paper and its deployment of 'crisis' language, see Reade, 'The Discourses of Crisis', 137–139.
76 Wishart, 'Women's Liberation', 7.
77 Sally Jackson, 'Dear Sisters', *Liberation*, no. 35 (c. June 1976).
78 Susan Eade, 'Now We Are Six: A Plea for Women's Liberation', *Refractory Girl*, no. 13–14 (March 1977), 3.
79 Ibid., 8.
80 Susan Magarey, *Dangerous Ideas: Women's Liberation – Women's Studies – around the World* (Adelaide: University of Adelaide Press, 2015), 5.
81 Dianne Otto, 'Bars, Ghettos and Dykes', *Scarlet Woman*, no. 4 (July 1976), 24–25.
82 Cited in Lyn Hovey, 'Melbourne', *Scarlet Woman*, no. 4 (July 1976), 30.
83 Otto, 'Bars, Ghettos and Dykes', 25.
84 Hovey, 'Melbourne', 30.
85 These debates are recorded in Lake, *Getting Equal*, 243 and Taylor, *Brazen Hussies*, 404, 418–419, 436–439.
86 Janet Wahlquist, 'Living Collectively', *Scarlet Woman*, no. 3 (February 1976), 9.
87 Joyce Stevens, 'Some Questions on the Future of the Women's Movement', *Scarlet Woman*, no. 5 (March 1977), 4.
88 Ibid., 3.
89 Sarah Gibson and Joyce Stevens, 'Into the Socialist Swamp', *Scarlet Woman*, no. 7 (August 1978), 16.

9

BLACK POWER AND WHITE SOLIDARITY

The Action Conference on Racism and Education, Brisbane 1972

Lewis d'Avigdor

On Friday 28 January 1972, 350 white, predominantly student activists, and 50 Aboriginal activists gathered at the Action Conference on Racism and Education. The Conference ran for six days at the University of Queensland. On the opening night, Aboriginal activists, led by Australian Black Panther leader Denis Walker, seized control of the Conference. The Aboriginal activists challenged the "friendly" paternalism of their white New Left allies, embracing the principle of the American Black Power leader, Stokely Carmichael (later Kwame Ture) and political scientist Charles Hamilton, who asserted that

> Black people must lead and run their own organizations. Only black people can convey the revolutionary idea – and it is a revolutionary idea – that black people are able to do things themselves.[1]

While the majority of the white New Left, broadly defined, may have agreed in principle with this "revolutionary idea", the assertion of black leadership became contentious in practice. This chapter takes the assertion of black control as its central concern, revealing the ways in which Black Power activists experienced racism and paternalism, not only from the state and society writ large, but more insidiously, from their allies on the New Left.

The Conference took place in a context of transnational radicalism that defined the long sixties in Australia.[2] Race was central to this decade, especially the global anti-colonial and Black Power movement.[3] Australia was experiencing a surge in pan-Aboriginal militancy, as the long running movement for Aboriginal rights adopted the language of Black Power.[4] Queensland in particular, widely regarded in international terms as an apartheid state or Australia's "deep north" in reference to America's "deep south", was a hotbed of dissent.[5] Recent protests against apartheid and the tour of the South-African Springboks

Rugby team, and proposed amendments to the Aboriginal and Torres Strait Islander Affairs Acts in Queensland put race firmly on the protest agenda, although there remained a disconnect between white protest against foreign and domestic racism.[6]

The Black Caucus, which included all the Aboriginal activists present but was largely dominated by the recently formed Brisbane based Black Panther Party of Australia, posed three challenges to the white activists at the Conference.[7] First, the Black Caucus sought to take control of the Conference, as they contested the overly academic nature of the proposed agenda, which failed to address their demands for immediate action. Secondly, Black Power activists questioned the Marxist privileging of class over race as the analytical category through which to understand their ongoing dispossession. Despite Black Power's dominant discourse concerning economic oppression, many white activists viewed Black Power as Black Nationalism and thereby a deviation from class struggle. Thirdly, Indigenous women refused the overtures of the Women's Liberation activists, whom they saw as failing to acknowledge the structural differences between the positions of Aboriginal and white women in society. The Conference provides a window through which to view and untangle these tensions, which were simultaneously ideological, practical and personal in nature.[8] Black Power activists refused to be viewed paternalistically as objects in preconceived schemes of liberation, either liberal or Marxist, and demanded to be considered as subjects prefiguring their own decolonisation.

This chapter seeks to provide an analysis of this event, highlighting the gritty politics of Aboriginal Black Power activists seeking to build a broader movement. The first part of this chapter will investigate the sudden emergence and contested meaning of Black Power in Australia. Black Power was a shared political consciousness that emerged between 1968 and 1972 amongst a vibrant if loose network of Aboriginal activists from inner suburbs of Melbourne, Sydney and Brisbane.[9] Aboriginal Australians developed their own interpretation of Black Power that became yoked to both Aboriginality as an identity and to the land rights movement. While it is easy to overemphasise the extent of generational rupture in this period and to elide linkages with previous struggles for civil rights, this period nonetheless saw the assertion of new demands as well as new forms of protest, but above all a new intensity. I highlight two key moments when Aboriginal activists sought to take control of two organisations, the Victorian Aborigines Advancement League (VAAL) and the Federal Council for the Advancement of Aboriginal and Torres Strait Islanders (FCAATSI). Symbolically, these takeovers signalled broad disillusionment with the efficacy of multi-racial coalitions. Practically, they led to the organisations' demise. Activists regrouped to establish exclusively Aboriginal organisations such as the Brisbane Tribal Council, the National Tribal Council and the Black Panther Party. The second part of this chapter will turn to the Conference itself, in order to explore the three aforementioned tensions, namely, Black Control, Marxism and Women's Liberation. This chapter attempts to tell the story of Black Power as a self-conscious attempt to decolonise the settler-state.[10] In so doing, Black Power posed a challenge to the white New Left and revealed the limits of its self-assured radicalism.

The Conference has received little scholarly attention, perhaps due to the fact that it was overshadowed by the emergence of the Aboriginal Tent embassy. Established on the same Australia Day weekend, the Tent Embassy was a powerful assertion of land rights, Aboriginal sovereignty and Black Power in the nation's capital, garnering significant media attention to become one of the most well-known Indigenous protests.[11] The emphasis on this contemporaneous protest, however, can only partially explain the lack of academic focus on the Conference. Echoing anthropologist W.E.H. Stanner's famous reference in 1968 to the "The Great Australian Silence",[12] Aboriginal activist and academic Gary Foley, who attended the Conference, said in 2001, that historians have "trivialized, marginalized and dismissed" the achievements and historical influence of the Australian Black Power Movement.[13] While Stanner's silence has arguably been shattered,[14] the historiography of Black Power in Australia is only recently growing,[15] particularly through a transnational lens.[16] Significant work has been done on Aboriginal activism with reference to civil rights,[17] land rights,[18] the involvement of white people,[19] and longer regional studies that include the Black Power movement.[20] I want to highlight Black Power as an essential component of this era, to recover the political structure of this moment and in particular the possibilities and limits of black and white solidarity.

In popular memory, one reason for the continued trivialisation is that Black Power cannot be assimilated to the triumphalist narrative that the settler-state tells about itself, even in its most liberal and multicultural guise. Sandwiched between campaigns for civil rights in the early sixties and later claims based on indigeneity, it is a past that resists historicisation.[21] Black Power activists rejected the policies of assimilation and integration, considered merely different slogans for the same programmatic dispossession. Aboriginality and Black Power may have emerged at the same time, but became decoupled in the later 1970s, resulting in consequences for how we understand Aboriginal politics in the present, and the perceived failure of the bi-partisan policy of self-determination from the election of the Whitlam Government in 1972 until 1996.[22] On the one hand, the Australian nation has sought to appropriate Aboriginality to fill the "commendable emptiness" left by Australia's gentle but forced decolonisation from the British imperial metropole.[23] On the other hand, Black Power is regarded at most as a historical but irrelevant curiosity, and at worst as a violent and imported ideology. If Black Power is considered in U.S. historiography as part of a declension narrative, from the "good" to the "bad" sixties, in Australia it is simply a dismissed narrative.[24] For the very reason that Black Power remains discomforting to the Australian nation, it demands careful and considered attention. It may contain resources for the ongoing but always incomplete project of decolonisation, and a more meaningful politics of solidarity.

The emergence of Black Power

"Every time there is a meeting of people concerned with Aboriginal Affairs I hear the term Black Power expressed. Could this be an omen of things to come?" asked

VAAL's then liaison officer, Bruce McGuinness in the pages of the newssheet he edited, *The Koorier.* [25] "If so, in what form will it appear as violent or non-violent; or will it be in the form of an organisation made up entirely of Aboriginal radicals?" McGuinness did not have to wait long for an answer as "over the latter months of 1969, Black Power emerged from overseas to hit Australian with a thud that was heard all over the world".[26] The "thud" came in the form of a visit by Bermudan parliamentarian and Black Power advocate Dr Roosevelt Brown in August 1969. Brown gave a widely reported press conference on Black Power in Melbourne. Brown advocated "the empowerment of coloured people to decide their own destiny" and spoke of Aboriginal Australians as being part of the global struggle for black liberation. While Brown acknowledged land as being a unique problem faced by Aboriginal peoples, he also warned of Australian Black Power Leaders being "rubbed out", like as anyone who "fought for black people", referring to a varied political genealogy that spanned Marcus Garvey, Patrice Lumumba, Medgar Evers, John F. Kennedy, Malcolm X and Martin Luther King Jnr.[27] For McGuinness, Brown's invocation that black people must make decisions for themselves, forced him to rethink, but not entirely forgo, his faith in black–white coalitions as the best strategy to counteract the "dispossession from the Aborigine of his land and identity."[28] McGuinness, who would soon become co-director of VAAL, disparaged "parasitical nothings" who "usually start off by telling all and sundry about how much they help the Aborigines and finish up by telling Aborigines how to manage their own affairs".[29] Brown's words resonated with Aboriginal activists frustrated with the slow pace of change. The thud that hit Australia from overseas soon reverberated to a national roar.

Days after Brown's visit, VAAL held its annual meeting and issued the following statement on Black Power, heralding the acceptance of black power by Aboriginal advancement organisations. The statement began by quoting Jean-Paul Sartre's famous preface to what became known as the Bible of Decolonisation, *The Wretched of the Earth*, written by Martinique-born psychiatrist and revolutionary Frantz Fanon,

> Not so very long ago, the earth numbered two thousand million inhabitants: five hundred million men, and one thousand five hundred million natives.
> That is white power.
> Since the end of World War II, many of the coloured peoples who lived under white colonial rule have gained their independence and coloured minorities in multi-racial nations are claiming the right to determine the course of their own affairs in contradiction to the inferior state under which they had lived.
> That is Black Power.[30]

Following historian Jon Piccini's analysis, this statement demonstrates the inventive manner in which Indigenous activists drew upon both Black Power and anti-colonial emancipatory traditions,[31] which were always in conversation with each other. The Aboriginal Black Power movement read African-American literature on Black Power, particularly titles such as Carmichael and Hamilton's *Black Power*, Bobby Seale's *Seize the Time* and Malcolm X and Haley's *The Autobiography of Malcolm X*. Australian Black Power activists also saw themselves in the context of the Third World decolonisation struggles taking place in Asia, Africa and beyond.[32] Yet neither tradition quite fit the predicament of Aboriginal activists. They understood that for African Americans, the internal colony paradigm ascendant within both activist and scholarly circles in 1960s America[33] was an evocative and useful analogy, while in Australia colonialism was a literal and lived reality.[34] Australian Black Power groups also recognised that Fanon's Manichean vision for decolonisation, which required the complete evacuation of the colonisers, was inapplicable to Australia where, "The colonizers come to stay – invasion is a structure not an event."[35] Accordingly, Indigenous activists drew inspiration from the Red Power take-over of Alcatraz in 1969 as well as thinkers of what became known in the mid-1970s as the fourth world such as Vine Deloria Jnr.[36] Creatively appropriated into Indigenous forms of protest, Black Power and anti-colonial imaginaries proved portable, modular and productive.

The conservative criticism that Black Power was an irrelevant import from America largely misses its mark.[37] Aboriginal activists creatively appropriated Black Power for their own political ends, emphasising the commonality of experience shared between Aboriginal Australians and Black Americans, and other oppressed groups in the third and fourth world. Aboriginal Australians faced similar structures of colonialism, capitalism and racism, and consequently Black Power and broader anti-colonial discourses were resonant and meaningful for Aboriginal Australians. Paul Coe, member of the Redfern Black Power Caucus, insisted that their minority status should not overshadow the fact that the Aboriginal movement "should be classified as a liberation movement rather than a civil rights movement or a land rights movement".[38] Key to understanding the Aboriginal Black Power movement was that it had begun to reject the entire edifice of "the system"; that meaningful change could be achieved through parliamentary channels.[39]

Brown's visit prompted not only a revolution in consciousness, but also the push for Indigenous activists to take over the leadership positions of VAAL. Bob Maza offered words of encouragement:

> Nothing ventured, Nothing lost
> Gubbah helper, Koorie Boss![40]

In November 1969, activists led by Harry Penrith stormed into the meeting of the black–white management committee, demanding the resignation of the League's white Director, Rev. Bruce Silverwood. The activists faced opposition from both Aboriginal and white members, and after losing the vote to turn complete control of the organisation to Aboriginal members, a compromise motion was passed where a majority of Aborigines would sit on the Management Committee.[41] VAAL's operational capacities, however, were soon curtailed by the Federal

Government's decision to withhold its annual $40,000 in funding. The State had made its position on Black Power evident. The push for Aboriginal control, however, signalled a major symbolic victory. The black takeover of VAAL heralded the first concrete expression of Black Power in Australia, firmly convincing activists that black people must lead and run their own organisations.

The opening of horizons to the global black freedom struggle stimulated the creation of a pan-Aboriginal cultural identity and national political consciousness. An explosion of Indigenous media circulated news of Black Power and Aboriginal activism, whose very titles *Smoke Signals, National Koorier, Origin* and *Identity*, indicate the issues at stake. Aboriginality was no longer something imposed by anthropologists, but was reclaimed with pride.[42] With reference to establishing black studies courses, Paul Coe said, "It's only when we find an identity, as a group, as a race, and only until then can we possibly sort of mobilize action on the scale which I think could change this country for the better".[43] Although never sharply demarcated, Black Power activists did, however, draw a distinction between Black Power as political resource, and Aboriginality as a cultural basis of identity. Following the Conference, Denis Walker was asked by ABC reporter-cum-activist, Darce "Jon" Cassidy, "Do you see yourself primarily as black or as an Aboriginal?" Walker said that he might have been "over-reacting" when he said that he was "first black and then Aboriginal", but to identify as Aboriginal would be to "cut off all global links".[44] For this reason, the Australian Black Panther Party did not use the name "Black Emus". Black Power activists, and especially the Australian Black Panther Party, deliberately adopted the glamour and sartorial trappings of their American counterparts, decked out in Afros, black berets, leather jackets, sunglasses and badges. When pressed by Cassidy in the same interview, both Walker and the Black Panther Minister for Information, Susan Chilly, said that they understood Black culture as Aboriginal culture, rather than as the culture of a global black diaspora. Both Chilly and Walker believed it was vital to educate Aboriginal children in their culture and history, and above all, to have a connection to the land. For this reason, urban Black Power activists became involved in land rights struggles such as the Gove Land Rights Case in 1971.[45]

If Black Power supplied the global language of dissent, it was the disillusionment with the "success" of the 1967 referendum that catalysed Australian Black Power activism. The 90.77% yes vote, which gave the Federal Government responsibility for Aboriginal affairs, was immediately mythologised as a foundational moment for Aboriginal rights, part of a broader Australian redemption narrative of racial progress.[46] The referendum was seen as the crowning achievement of FCAATSI, and the Federal Government's subsequent disinclination to legislate pursuant to its newly acquired constitutional power saw resentment shift to the multi-racial coalition that had worked so hard for equality. For Aboriginal activist and poet Kath Walker (later Oodgeroo Noonuccal) the referendum was of little benefit to Aboriginal Australians, although it "eased the guilty conscience of white Australians in this country and overseas".[47] At the July 1969 meeting of FCAATSI, Walker presented a critique of existing multi-racial coalitions, which circulated widely.

Walker argued that multi-racial coalitions are pervaded by a sense of white paternalism, and "If black Australians are to become masters of their own destiny, white Australians must recognise them as being capable of formulating their own policy of advancement".[48] In views that would be echoed by her son, Denis, at the Conference, Kath Walker took a disdainful view of white Australians, "especially intellectuals such as students, who want to 'come alive' through black organisations".[49] Like McGuinness, Walker's understanding of the role of white supporters and multi-racial coalitions had shifted dramatically from her earlier backing of unqualified white support and guidance.[50] Although a generation older than many of the Aboriginal activists in the Black Power movement, Walker embraced many of its ideals. If the adoption of Black Power in Australia can be described as a "new mood"[51], it is one that spanned generations.[52]

The tensions identified by Walker played out at the FCAATSI Easter Conference in 1970.[53] Until this time, FCAATSI, founded in 1958, had been the peak Aboriginal body demanding both civil rights and Aboriginal political participation.[54] Affiliates from hundreds of organisations, including those concerned exclusively with Indigenous affairs but also an eclectic mix of organisations sympathetic to Aboriginal issues such as communist, labour, and church organisations, all sent delegates to FCAATSI's annual conferences. If the black takeover of VAAL was the first organisational assertion of black autonomy, the splintering of FCAATSI was the most public and dramatic fight over black leadership. Repeating the demise of VAAL, the super-majority vote to amend the constitution, allowing only those of "Aborigine or Island descent" to vote and hold executive positions, failed. The 1970 Conference and FCAATSI itself immediately fractured, with those in favour of black control resolving immediately to form a rival organisation, the Aboriginal-led National Tribal Council (NTC).[55]

This split marked the culmination of a trend towards black control, which shaped both the content and form of later demands. Indigenous activism did not entirely embrace separatism,[56] as within organisations such as the NTC and the Panthers whites could play a supportive role. Yet a significant shift occurred as the emerging Black Power movement began to emphasise Aboriginality over civil rights that "ran towards a homogeneous assimilated Australia".[57] Kath Walker contested the idea that Aboriginal people should work towards integration into the Australian nation, highlighted by her "Black Commandments" published in 1969.[58] Paul Coe and Bobbi Sykes went as far as to suggest the formation of a Black State in the Northern Territory that would function as a "Black Mecca".[59] While such pronouncements may indicate that liberation was conceived of in cultural terms,[60] Foley insists that Black Power was never about spirituality, but was about political and ultimately economic demands.[61] Further, for the Black Power activists who were present at the FCAATSI Conference, many of whom would later attend the Action Conference in Brisbane, the difficult experience of multi-racial coalitions in the 1960s enshrined their belief in black control as a necessary foundation for effecting meaningful change. In 1970 and 1971, Black Power organising only increased and Foley claims that by the end of 1971, everyone had heard of Black Power.[62] Black Power was no longer an overseas phenomenon. While Aboriginal activists drew inspiration from overseas sources, and indeed travelled overseas in search of transnational solidarity, they also began to look to their own history of concrete actions asserting black control, that began with the takeovers of VAAL and FCAATSI and led to the formation of political organisations such the Brisbane Tribal Council, NTC and the Black Panther Party.

Action Conference on Racism and Education

The Conference was advertised throughout Australia in a series of provocative leaflets such as "The Wild Colonial Boong" and "A Racy Anti-Racist Race-Off". The latter leaflet referred to the recent anti-Springbok riots, during which many New Left activists protested the touring South African Rugby Team in 1971 as a symbol of the apartheid regime. Foley recalls strong alliances forming between anti-apartheid protestors and Aboriginal activists, even as the latter criticised the former for being myopic to the racism in their own backyard.[63] In this vein, the leaflet criticised those who did not join the anti-Springbok protests, but also, those who did,

> No wonder all those hypocrites came up to you and accused you of being hypocrites. I mean, there you were, practically jacking yourself off about [South-African] blacks in your psyche and here were all those blackfellers in your own country and you never joined any riots about them.[64]

Indeed not since the Australian Freedom Rides had students taken part in a widely known protest concerning Aboriginal issues.[65] The leaflet's author was Dan O'Neill, a lecturer at the University of Queensland and high profile radical activist associated with the Society for Democratic Action. Alongside Tony Lawson, the ABSCHOL National Director, the pair organised the Conference. ABSCHOL, which began as a student run scholarship scheme for Aboriginal students under the umbrella of the National Union of Australian University Students in the early 1950s but soon developed a more expansive radical agenda, provided the majority of the funds, with the National Tribunal Council, the Brisbane Tribal Council and the Act Confrontation Movement providing limited support.[66]

The Conference aimed to analyse racism, particularly within educational institutions, and to plan action to combat it.[67] There was always an anxious relationship between action and theory. According to the agenda, Saturday, the first full day, was to explore theoretical and practical aspects of racism, with topics such as "The Struggle for Black Liberation" and "Race, Sex, Class". The second day included panels of high-school students and teachers, with the aim of educating the teachers on racism in schools. The third day was devoted to universities and the failure of liberalism to combat racism. The final two days were set aside for discussion on black and white alliances, and further proposals for joint action against racism.[68] But the Conference did not run according to the advertised agenda. Detailed ASIO

Black Power and white solidarity **179**

accounts and subsequent media reports record a lively debate around three issues. Two of these three tensions were inextricably linked: the first involved attempts by Black Power activists to take control of the Conference and the agenda; the second, involved Black Power resistance to the emphasis of class over race. Both these issues became immediately apparent as the opening lecture unfolded, and would continue to play out over the course of the Conference.

Black leadership

Dr Neil Eddington, a visiting American lecturer, gave the opening lecture on Friday night, comparing racial activity in Australia to the United States.[69] Although he was in favour of Indigenous activists asserting control, he believed that replicating the Black Panther Party experience in Australia would be detrimental.[70] Unsurprisingly, Eddington's judgement on the recently formed Australian Black Panther Party was not well received. Denis Walker interrupted Eddington, asserting, "You don't have the pigs on your back like we do. You can go into a hotel for a beer without being victimized."[71] O'Neill, however, who was acting as chairman, asked Walker to refrain from interrupting the speakers. Perhaps sensing the mood of the crowd, Eddington concluded his lecture, but took a parting shot at Walker, whom he said could better direct his energies towards helping black people if he left the Black Panther Party. This exemplified the essence of the problem of black–white coalition building as Aboriginal people saw it: white Australians showing Aboriginal activists a better way of doing things.

Walker then introduced that very Party, which heralded its first public appearance, via its "Platform and Program" as well as a Manifesto written for the Conference, which began with a hopeful tone:

> We believe that this Conference has the potential to set the stage for the forthcoming year of 1972 for blacks and whites to wage their struggle effectively against the present systematic forces arraigned against us...[72]

The statement drew a less hopeful picture of the condition of Aboriginal people in Queensland, noting, "You are gathered here in perhaps the most racist state in Australia". This racism was exhibited by "the number of Blacks held in institutions such as prisons, homes and reserves" and the fact that the Queensland Government refused to legislate on "the problem of urban Blacks". Such circumstances, the statement continued, "prove that it is impossible to work through the present fascist system to alleviate racism". The system would not listen to "appeals to a sense of fair play". Since such an Australian sense of equality was not on the cards, the Black Panthers, "as a vanguard of any revolutionary struggle" must instead "link up with our Black Brothers and sisters throughout the world, as well as revolutionary whites within Australia to smash this decadent system" and replace it "with a system of control by the people". The statement demanded that the Conference focus on "Action Programmes", and approve "Actions which will give power back to the people" such as "community control of courts, police business etc".[73] Echoing the views of his mother, Walker said, "You go home to your nice little home and say "I've helped these poor Black bastards out." That's as far as it goes."[74] The Manifesto concluded by threatening, "If this Conference refuses to deal with these problems, then we will state here and now that there will be confrontation on any and all issues."[75]

Walker's intervention set the tone for the Conference, which was characterised by a continuous negotiation for control between the Black Caucus and the white participants. Towards the end of the Friday night, the motion that the Conference should be turned over to the Black Caucus was approved unanimously. The Black Caucus retained the basic agenda with two qualifications: that speakers must include open discussion on action programmes to combat racism, and to use clear language, as Aboriginal people had been systematically denied access to the same educational opportunities afforded to white students.[76] New Left intellectual Warren Osmond suggests that because Black Power activists sensed that the white left did not genuinely accept black leadership, meaningful discussion of theory and practical action was often stymied.[77] Indeed, the Black Caucus only had to look as far as the organisers of the Conference, ABSCHOL, whom they criticised as failing to accept black leadership in practice. Interrupting ABSCHOL co-director Bryan Havenhand's talk on Saturday, the Black Caucus demanded that all ABSCHOL positions be vacated in favour of electing an all black executive.[78]

Reflecting similar cynicism, by Saturday afternoon the Black Caucus accused whites of again attempting to take over the meeting.[79] Len Watson said after the Conference that the antagonism "arose out of the fact that the whites gave the blacks leadership and the blacks wanted to conduct the procedure as they felt was best and this didn't quite fit in with white meeting format".[80] White activists were often blind to the fact that insisting on organisational procedure was considered a form of colonialism, echoing a similar critique levelled at FCAATSI.[81] When O'Neill, suggested that more would be achieved by breaking into smaller groups, many Indigenous activists felt that they would not be able to mix freely with whites in small groups, where they would be outnumbered.[82] One white student from Monash dismissed this concern, suggesting, "Until Blacks can learn to mix freely with the white people then there is nothing that can be done for them. They will always feel the underdog."[83] Such debate encouraged white activists to confront their own subtle racism, what Denis Freney, reporting in *Tribune*, the Communist Party of Australia newspaper, referred to as "unvoiced, even sub-conscious opposition among whites" to accepting the principle of Black leadership.[84] John Alford, reporting in the Monash University student newspaper *Lot's Wife* was far more biting, "More people exposed themselves at the Action Conference on Racism and Education... than at a National Perverts Convention." Alford continued, "For the first time in the history of the Australian Left, some white socialists saw the black man and comprehended the accusing finger pointed at them from the depths of the Aborigine's oppression."[85] As the Conference continued white activists were confronted by a formidable group of Black Power activists who were as critical of their white allies as they were of the white establishment. White activists were forced to come to terms with the fact that they were not as radical as they believed, that when faced with concrete demands, their anti-racism was not absolute.[86]

Colonialism by concept: Marxism

The opening night of the Conference also revealed ideological differences between the black and white activists. Many Marxist activists and New Left activists conceived of the struggle against racism as subordinate to the struggle against capitalism. Despite the fact that the Australian Black Panthers and the Australian Black Power movement in general embraced the elements of anti-imperialist, anti-capitalist Marxist thinking, they refused to be lectured to by white activists on the correct Marxist line, far removed from their lived experience of racism. Black Power activists viewed the white students' ability to manipulate Marxist theory, derived from the privilege afforded them by higher education unavailable to them, as yet another attempt to subjugate the Aboriginal people.

The Sydney-based Labour Press voiced this Marxist line most zealously. The group asserted that Aborigines were first and foremost members of the working class. On the "Nationality Question" they pushed a Leninist line, arguing that the overthrow of capitalism is "a task designated by history to the working class, be it black, yellow or white".[87] The Labour Press decried the "lack of theory" with which the New Left approached the "Aboriginal question", including its failure to correctly locate this national minority in its historic world context. The right to self-determination for Aboriginal people was seen as bourgeois and reactionary. Further they opposed the importation of Panther vanguardism into Australia. They accused the Black Caucus of being manipulated by the Communist Party of Australia and the New Left, "now that the issues of Vietnam and anti-apartheid were dead".[88]

The Marxist perspective voiced by the Labour Press was on the far left of the ideological spectrum and was opposed by the more theoretically eclectic elements of the New Left. Such a "more radical than thou" attitude was nonetheless present in a muted form amongst many white radicals. Alford continued his report in *Lot's Wife*, highlighting "the exposures of great lefties":

> Every single white socialist who got onto the rostrum laid down his Universal Panacea for the Liberation of Blacks: the local Maoist debating club... 13 odd different brands of Trotskyite... the CPA... etc... In all of these schema, the blacks figured as objects, as the recipients of a white strategy, as mere pawns to be used in the overall glorious white revolution.[89]

Black Power activists were but bit players in the fight against "the system", irrespective of whether the system was Marx's Capitalism or Marcuse's one-dimensional society. Indeed, the New Left was also stimulated to rethink whether students were

182 Lewis d'Avigdor

really agents of emancipation and that targeting the university, as a site for social change, was in fact truly radical.

On Friday night, it was student Richard "Dick" Shearman, leading member of the Revolutionary Socialist Student Alliance, who would bear the brunt of the Black Power activists' anger, when he took the stage to argue that "capitalism and big business" were keeping both the white and black man down:

> We have White people living in the slums without adequate medical aid because they can't afford it. What we need to do is to band together and fight the common enemy, i.e., capitalism.[90]

Challenging both the Marxist thinking, and refusing to be an object of white strategy, Walker interrupted Shearman, declaring that the Conference was called to deal with racism, and "not the bullshit Dick Shearman is handing out on the problems of the White man" which were incomparable to those of the Black man.[91]

> How many times do we have to tell this bloody meeting that the conditions of the Black man are intolerable? The Black man has been suppressed right from the first landing on Australian soil and has been down-graded ever since.

The Black Caucus concurred. That Aboriginal people were not part of the worker's struggle as they were not even in the lumpenproletariat, was a commonly expressed view. Australian trade unions were not viewed as avenues of change. Black power activists viewed themselves as fundamentally outside the white, capitalist system. One unidentified Aboriginal person, told Cassidy, after the Conference, "We can't take any part in a class struggle until we can stand up there with the lowest white man."[92] Linking land rights, with a racialised identity, he concluded, "we haven't got land, we've got nothing to participate in your system with. We haven't got anything. We've only got our blackness and that's been taken from us."[93] Black Power activists considered Marxism a white ideology forced upon Aboriginal people. Paul Coe, who had arrived from the Tent Embassy in Canberra, said, "Two hundred years ago your missionaries came out here and rammed your white Christian religion down our throats. Now you want to shove white Marxism down our throats."[94] Sammy Watson, summed up the Black Power demands succinctly when he asserted, "We want help, not direction."[95] Following the Conference, Paul Coe released the following statement:

> The concept of white capitalism and white communism is not applicable to the black man because the black man is trapped first and foremost by the colour of his skin. He is then, perhaps, trapped in an economic circumstance. He must develop his own concepts with his own theories in order to solve his own problems, problems which face the black race, which have not before existed in the concepts of capitalism and communism.[96]

Theirs was not a rejection of economic or structural thinking. Rather the Black Power Movement was influenced by Fanon's idea that every single category of Marxism would have to be stretched when applied to a colonised people. As Fanon wrote, "in the colonies the economic infrastructure is also a super-structure".[97] While activists gestured towards new categories and even to a "New Man",[98] Osman bemoaned that little of this intellectual work was developed at the Conference, which was dominated instead by black and white conflict.[99]

The issue of black control of the Conference was intimately intertwined, both theoretically and practically, with debate over the role of race and class as the dominant cause of repression of Aboriginal people. Black Power activists adopted Marxist inspired anti-imperialist rhetoric, yet their demands were shaped by their concrete experiences in Australia of colonialism and dispossession.

"Splitting the movement": Black Power women and Women's Liberation

Debate erupted late on Saturday morning, when Merle Thornton, a white Women's Liberation activist and postgraduate student, spoke to the sexism faced by Aboriginal women within Aboriginal communities. Thornton was renowned for having chained herself to the bar at the Regatta Hotel in 1965 to protest the fact that women could not drink alcohol in public in Queensland. Garnering much media attention, Thornton's direct action "presaged a new phase in the history of feminism".[100] She struggled, however, to make a positive impression on the Black women present at the Conference.[101] In Thornton's view, Aboriginal women faced the same problem as white women, namely, their domination by their male counterparts. According to the ASIO report, Denis Walker interrupted Merle Thornton, yelling, "Get off the stage you lying b....!" Despite this overtly offensive language, Aboriginal women joined in the chorus, with one woman denouncing Thornton in the following terms, "Listen here you white b.... No one stands over us. We think for ourselves."[102] She continued, "he [Denis Walker] may be our leader and spokesman, but we are not afraid of him". Merle Thornton replied, "If they are free to do what they want to do, why did he have to force her to come up here?" Thornton was shouted down until she left the stage.

Following the conference, Susan Chilly, the Black Panther Minister for Information, released a statement about the confrontation, "Panthers speak":

> ... when Denis Walker was accused of dominating the sisters within the Panther Party by the Women's Liberation Movement, I blew my cool and so did the rest of the Panthers. At first it seemed ludicrous and then downright insulting to the sisters within the party and I said as much in far less refined terminology when I spoke on the matter. I think Women's Liberation needs to get a little closer to the Panthers before they attempt to criticise the status of the women within black social, economic or political structures. I feel they would learn far more than they could teach us.[103]

Women's lib activists conceded little ground on this point as they put forward a familiar critique of the American Black Panther Party as "introducing an emphasis upon male leadership, aggressiveness and physical strength" which undermined any emancipatory possibility offered by the Party's vanguard politics.[104]

Rancorous interaction at the Conference mirrored a broader conflict that developed between Women's Liberation groups and Black Power women. In an interview in the Sydney University student newspaper *Honi Soit*, Chilly was asked by the reporter why she believed that there was no place for Women's Liberation in the Black Movement.[105] Chilly responded by saying that Women's Liberation would "split the movement, the men from the women and we can't afford this now". The fight was against racial oppression first, and sexual oppression second. In the same interview, Walker recognised that "Black men do oppress black women physically" but countered, "you must understand that we're not in a position to oppress the black women economically; we can't oppress them politically or socially".[106] Demonstrating a concern with black men's masculinity Chilly opined: "Black men have been trodden down by the system, perhaps the only way they can assert themselves is to slap their women."[107]

Many indigenous women shared Chilly and Walker's outlook. The documentary *Ningla A-Na*, filmed in Canberra three months after the Conference, records a meeting aimed at identifying points of support Women's Liberation activists could offer Black Power. The scene captures the competing perspectives of the two movements and the lack of shared understanding. Sitting under a banner for the Black Moratorium, Isabel Coe, flanked by Marlene Cummins and Alana Doolan told the white Women's Liberation group,

> You women talk about liberating yourselves while blacks are going through violence everyday of your lives. And all you talk about is women's liberation... We can't afford to split at the moment.[108]

Defiantly, Alana Doolan added, "the place of the black woman is behind her man". One frustrated white women said, "As I understand it, the support you want is anything we can give in terms of money or support, physical support. But it is you who is leading the movement, you who is pressuring our society. What can we as individuals do?" Coe responded by saying, "You can educate your own white people about our problem, our struggles."[109] This exchange was not atypical, as many Aboriginal women felt alienated from Women's Liberation groups, viewing them as yet another white dominated movement with white values, ideologies and concepts.[110]

In her 1975 article, "Black Women in Australia: A History", Sykes rejected the weak overtures made by women's organisations, and "the lack of understanding of the reasons why black women do not wish to join these groups".[111] As Sykes wrote, in the realm of sexuality, the sexual liberation sought by the white woman was the right to say "yes", to have sex without opprobrium. For Aboriginal women, it was the right to say "no", "to explode the myth of the over-sexed black woman".[112] The slogan "Smash the family" was anathema to Aboriginal women, who had battled for many decades against Australian policies that removed Aboriginal children from their families.[113] By "asking Aboriginal women to stand apart from Aboriginal men, the white women's movement was", as Aboriginal activist and historian Jackie Huggins argues, "unconsciously repeating the attempts made over decades of welfare administrations to separate Aboriginal women and use them against their communities".[114] As Marilyn Lake explains, "the very radicalism of Women's Liberation", with its attack on traditional motherhood, made for "inappropriate politics" for Aboriginal women.[115] Women's Liberation groups also failed to appreciate white women's own complicity in the history of colonisation.[116]

On the one hand, the desire not to split the movement reflects the Black Power movement's prerogative to close ranks, painfully highlighted in Rachel Perkin's 2014 documentary *Black Panther Woman*, which explores the sexual abuse suffered by Marlene Cummins within the movement. Cummins reflects upon the fact that the "Sacrifices that we [women] made was the backbone of the struggle that never gets looked at".[117] On the other hand, "splitting the movement" went beyond the strategic recognition that racism was a greater threat to Aboriginal women than sexism, reflecting instead the deep solidarity between Aboriginal men and women that stemmed from a shared history of colonisation, and not simply from a lack of, or false, sexual consciousness.[118] As Aboriginal lawyer Larissa Behrendt writes, "Aboriginal women fought beside Aboriginal men for the right to vote, the right to keep our children, the right to get our land back and have our sovereignty recognised."[119] The experience at the Conference was one moment in this recognition of deep political and structural differences, as Women's Liberation groups sought to bring Aboriginal women into their fold.[120] Black Power Women's resistance to the Women's Liberation movement compelled the latter to reflect upon their own radical limitations; that the very emancipatory analysis which conceived of women as being colonised by men contained within it colonising tendencies.[121]

Conclusion

In a talk given in 1999, Gary Foley explored a question constantly asked of him by Koori people, "why does it often seem that some of our best white friends behave like some of our worst enemies?"[122] Foley noted that many non-Kooris are unintentionally "patronising and paternalistic" and present themselves as little different from those who oppose justice for Aboriginal Australians. Most importantly, they fail to understand the importance of "Aboriginal control of Aboriginal affairs." The Action Conference on Racism and Education provides historical reflection on answering just this question. Black Power activists forced New Left and Marxist students to rethink the basis of their own radicalism, to counter a challenge not from the left or right, but from outside their European categories of critique.

Despite the heavily contested debate that characterised the Conference, most Black Power and white participants viewed the Conference as a success. White radicals were forced not only to "come to grips with their own racism", as Denis Freney reported, but also to see "the struggle against racism not in terms of liberal "do-goodism" but as Black self-determination and liberation."[123] The words "surprise" or "stunned", referring to the unified militancy of the Black Caucus, litter many reports of the Conference.[124] White radicals were given a practical lesson in viewing Aboriginal Australians not as mere objects, but as agents of their own liberation, decolonising their country and mind. Sue Chilly reported that the "conference as a whole was a worthwhile exercise", but noted that there were many whites including, 'Women's Lib, Marxists, Trotskyites, and the Church", who refused to view "The problems and effects of Racism through our black prism." Nonetheless, the Conference provided a space to "compare notes with blacks interstate" and to "feel out any alliances which could be formed with black and white revolutionary individuals and groups."[125] Foley claims that awareness of Aboriginal struggle fostered by the Conference fostered crucial student support for the Tent Embassy during the winter of 1972.[126]

Finally, it is easy to lose sight of the radical undercurrent of agreement between the principle antagonists in this story. Both sides conceived of oppression as deeply structural: race, sex, and class required a radical shift in society, not simply, or only, a politics of recognition. Black Power invoked blackness and Aboriginality as an identity-based politics, yet at the same time made profound demands against the settler-state in terms of land rights, self-determination, and sovereignty. Although both white radicals and Black Power activists disagreed with how modes of oppression intersected – and at times refused to discuss it – all sides agreed that accepting these stakes was necessary for a meaningful and decolonised politics of solidarity.

Notes

1 Stokely Carmichael and Charles Hamilton, *Black Power: The Politics of Liberation in America* (New York: Vintage, 1992 [1967]), p.46.
2 Jon Piccini, *Transnational Protest, Australia and the 1960s* (Palgrave Macmillan, 2016).
3 Jennifer Clark, *Aborigines and Activism: Race & the Coming of the Sixties to Australia* (Crawley: UWA Press, 2008).
4 Gary Foley, Black Power in Redfern, 1968–1972 Honours Thesis, The University of Melbourne, 2001. Accessed at: www.kooriweb.org/foley/essays/essay_1.html
5 Kevin Gilbert, *Because a White Man'll Never Do It* (Sydney: Angus and Robertson, 1973), pp.18–20.
6 Clark, *Aborigines and Activism*, p.232; John Chesterman, *Civil Rights: How Indigenous Australians Won Formal Equality* (Brisbane: University of Queensland Press, 2005), p.171.
7 After completing this draft I read Warren Osmond's analysis of the Conference in *Arena*, which similarly identified these "three areas of conflict". But Osmond viewed the Conference as a failure in producing a new intellectual analysis of Australian racism or a broad programme of action and "the chances of blacks and whites joining in a common struggle as 'very slight'." Warren Osmond, "Black Militancy and the White Left, *Arena* 28 (1972), pp.12 and 16.
8 Denis Freney, "Q'land Racism Conference a Milestone", *Tribune*, 8–14 February 1972, p.10.

9 Clare Land, *Decolonizing Solidarity: Dilemmas and Directions for Supporters of Indigenous Struggles* (London: Zed Books, 2015), p.41.
10 This argument is further elaborated in "Black: Internalizing Decolonisation and Networks of Solidarity" in Tracey Banivanua Mar, *Decolonisation and the Pacific: Indigenous Globalisation and the Ends of Empire* (Cambridge: Cambridge University Press, 2016).
11 That many of the main figures of the Redfern Black Power caucus chose to attend the Conference rather than the initial days of the Tent Embassy, underscores the fact that "the key leaders of the Black Power movement in Sydney, Melbourne and Brisbane" considered the Conference an important opportunity to both pressure the McMahon Government, as well as to "join forces to confront, challenge and test the mettle of white student activists". Gary Foley, "A Reflection of the First Thirty Days of the Embassy", in Andrew Schaap, Gary Foley, and Edwina Howell (eds), *The Aboriginal Tent Embassy: Sovereignty, Black Power, Land Rights and the State* (New York: Routledge, 2014), p.28.
12 W.E.H. Stanner, *The 1968 Boyer Lectures: After the Dreaming* (Sydney: ABC, 1969), pp.24–25.
13 Foley, "Black Power in Redfern".
14 Ann Curthoys, "Stanner and the Historians", in Melinda Hinkson and Jeremy Beckett (eds), *An Appreciation of Difference: WEH Stanner and Aboriginal Australia* (Canberra: Aboriginal Studies Press, 2008), p.247.
15 Clark, *Aborigines and Activism*; Kathy Lothian, "Seizing the Time: Australian Aborigines and the Influence of the Black Panther Party, 1969–1972", *Journal of Black Studies* 35, no. 4 (2005), pp.179–200.
16 Piccini, *Transnational Protest, Australia and the 1960s*; Alyssa Trometter, "Malcolm X and the Aboriginal Black Power Movement in Australia, 1967–1972", *The Journal of African American History* 100, no. 2 (2015), pp.226–249; Ravi de Costa, *A Higher Authority: Indigenous Transnationalism and Australia* (Sydney: University of New South Wales Press, 2006); Banivanua Mar, *Decolonisation and the Pacific*.
17 Chesterman, *Civil Rights*; Sue Taffe, *Black and White Together: FCAATSI: The Federal Council for the Advancement of Aborigines and Torres Strait Islanders, 1958–1973* (Brisbane: University of Queensland Press, 2005).
18 Miranda Johnson, *The Land is Our History: Indigeneity, Law and the Settler State* (Oxford: Oxford University Press, 2016); Heidi Norman, *'What do we want?': A Political History of Aboriginal Land Rights in New South Wales* (Canberra: Aboriginal Studies Press, 2015).
19 Land, *Decolonizing Solidarity*; Deborah Wilson, *Different White People: Radical Activism for Aboriginal Rights, 1946–1972* (Perth: UWA Publishing, 2015).
20 Heather Goodall, *Invasion to Embassy: Land in Aboriginal Politics in New South Wales, 1770–1972* (Sydney: Allen and Unwin, 1996); Bain Attwood, *Rights for Aborigines* (Sydney: Allen & Unwin, 2003).
21 This concept is Dipesh Chakrabarty's, explored by Bain Attwood in "Unsettling Pasts: Reconciliation and History in Settler Australia", *Postcolonial Studies: Culture, Politics, Economy* 8, no. 3 (2005), p.244.
22 Gary Foley, "An Autobiographical Narrative of the Black Power Movement and the 1972 Aboriginal Embassy", Ph.D., University of Melbourne, 2012, p.9.
23 Donald Horne, *The Bulletin*, 20 January 1968, p.22. Quoted in James Curran, "Australia Should Be There", *Australian Historical Studies* 39, no. 1 (2008), p.76.
24 Peniel Joseph "The Black Power Movement: A State of the Field", *The Journal of American History* 96, no. 3 (2009), p.751.
25 Bruce McGuinness, *The Koorier* 1 no. 7, p.2.
26 Bruce McGuinness, *The Koorier* 1, no. 13, p.3.
27 "Roosevelt Brown Meets the Press", *Smoke Signals* 8, no. 3, September 1969, p.9.
28 Editorial, *The Koorier* 1, no. 12 p.3.
29 Editorial, *The Koorier* 1, no. 9, p.3; McGuinness, "Don't Go it Alone!", *Aboriginal Quarterly* 1, no. 4, December 1969, p.15, reprinted in *Smoke Signals* 8, no. 3., March 1970, p.7.

30 Aboriginal Advancement League Newsletter, reprinted in *Smoke Signals* 8, no. 2, September 1969, p.3.
31 Piccini, *Transnational Protest, Australia and the 1960s*, p.154.
32 Foley, "Black Power in Redfern".
33 For one of the first and most influential statements, see Harold Cruse, "Revolutionary Nationalism and Afro-Nationalism", in *Rebellion or Revolution* (New York: William Morrow and Company, 1968).
34 Carmichael and Hunt *Black Power*, pp.6 and 191. Although proponents of the colonial analogy, including Carmichael, refer to Indian dispossession, as Chickasaw scholar Jodi Byrd persuasively argues, the analogy repositions "African American bodies as the foundational site of colonization rather than American Indian lands". Accordingly, the internal colony analogy masks the continual erasure of the settlement of American Indian land and instead "services the construction of the United States as a multi-cultural nation that is struggling with the legacies of racism, rather than as a colonialist power engaged in territorial expansion since its beginning". Jodi A. Byrd, *The Transit of Empire: Indigenous Critiques of Colonialism* (Minneapolis: University of Minnesota Press, 2011), pp.125 and 135.
35 Patrick Wolfe, *Settler Colonialism and the Transformation of Anthropology: The Politics and Poetics of an Ethnographic Event* (London: Cassell, 1999), p.3.
36 George Manuel and Michael Posluns, *The Fourth World: An Indian Reality* (New York: Free Press, 1974); Bobbi Sykes, "Parallels", *Identity* 1, no. 2, October 1971, pp.31–32.
37 This argument was put forward by the conservative Liberal-Country Senator Neville Bonner, the first Aboriginal man elected to an Australian parliament, in Ann Turner, ed., *Black Power in Australia: Neville Bonner vs. Bobbie Sykes* (Melbourne: Heinemann Educational Australia, 1975), p.68.
38 Paul Coe, quoted in Gilbert, *Because a White Man'll Never Do It*, p.111. Coe's argument here ought not overshadow the fact that Black Power was intertwined with land rights, as the front page of the *Aboriginal Quarterly* December 1969 headline read, "Black Power is Land Rights Now!"
39 Kevin Gilbert, "Of Black Patriots and Black Intelligentsia", *Alchuringa* Jan–March 1973, p.4.
40 *The Koorier* 1, no. 12, p.8. *The Koorier* defines "GUBBARIGINAL" as a "white man concerned with Koorie affairs". *The Koorier* 1, no. 7, p.23.
41 "Night of Black Power Failure", *The Age,* 29 November 1969.
42 *The Koorier* 1, no. 5, p.5.
43 Paul Coe and Bobbi Sykes, "Monday Conference", ABC television, 20 March 1972.
44 Darce Cassidy, "The Conference on Racism in Australia", *Fact and Opinion*, ABC, 9 February 1972, pp.6–7.
45 Attwood, *Rights for Aborigines,* p.321; Gilbert, *Because a White Man'll Never Do It*, p.7.
46 Bain Attwood and Andrew Markus, *The 1967 Referendum: Race, Power and the Australian Constitution* (Canberra: Aboriginal Studies Press, 2007), p.47.
47 Kath Walker, "Coalition of Black and White Australians – July 1969", Walker, Denis Bruce Volume 1, 1972, A6119, 4877.
48 Ibid.
49 Ibid.
50 Taffe, *Black and White Together*, p.252.
51 Attwood, *Rights for Aborigines*, p.321; Lothian, "Seizing the Time", p.183.
52 Russell McGregor, "Another Nation: Aboriginal Activism in the Late 1960s and Early 1970s", *Australian Historical Studies* 40, no. 3 (2009), p.348.
53 See Barrie Pittock, "Easter 1970 and the Origins of the National Tribal Council: A Personal View", available at http://indigenousrights.net.au/__data/assets/pdf_file/0008/392039/f102.pdf
54 Clark, *Aborigines and Activism*, p.81.
55 Pittock, "Easter 1970 and the Origins of the National Tribal Council", p.4.
56 Cf. Taffe, *Black and White Together*, p.266.

57 Peter Read, "Cheeky, Insolent and Anti-White: The Split in the Federal Council for the Advancement of Aboriginal and Torres Strait Islanders – Easter 1970", *Australian Journal of Politics and History* 81 (1990), pp.73–83.
58 Kath Walker, "The Black Commandments", *The Koorier* 1, no. 10, 1969, p.25.
59 Paul Coe and Bobbi Sykes, "Monday Conference".
60 McGregor, "Another Nation", p.345.
61 Foley, "An Autobiographical Narrative", pp.30 and 8.
62 Ibid., p.162.
63 Ibid., pp.145–147.
64 "Anti-Racist Race-off", Dan O'Neill Collection, UQFL132, Box 6, Folder 10, Fryer Library, University of Queensland Library.
65 Ann Curthoys, *Freedom Ride: A Freedom Rider Remembers* (Sydney: Allen and Unwin, 2002).
66 Action Conference on Racism and Education – Flyer, Dan O'Neill Collection, UQFL132, Box 6, Folder 10; Clark, *Aborigines and Activism*, p.140.
67 "Wild Colonial Boong", Action Conference on Racism and Education, 1972, F2181, Fryer Library.
68 "Action Conference on Racism and Education", 1972, F2181.
69 "400 at Opening of 'Race' Talks", *Courier Mail*, 29 February 1972.
70 "Dr Neil Eddington – ASIO Report", The Black Panther Party of Australia 1972 A6122, 2292, National Archive of Australia (NAA).
71 As if to demonstrate the Black Power activists' central point about "getting the pigs off our backs", on both Friday and Saturday night, activists clashed with police outside the "Open Door Club", with reports indicating that several were beaten. Freney, "Q'land Racism Conference a Milestone", p.10.
72 "Manifesto: 28/1/72", The Black Panther Party of Australia Volume 1, 1972, A6122, 2292.
73 Ibid.
74 "Denis Freney – ASIO File", The Black Panther Party of Australia Volume 1, 1972, A6122, 2292.
75 "Manifesto: 28/1/72".
76 "Panthers Speak", The Black Panther Party of Australia Volume 1, 1972, A6122, 2292.
77 Warren Osmond, "Black Militancy and the White Left, *Arena* 28, 1972, p.14.
78 "Blacks Take Over Conference", *Woroni*, February 1972, p.3; "ABSCHOL Meeting Elects Blacks", *Semper Floreat* 42, no. 2, 16 March 1972, p.6.
79 "Walker ASIO File", Walker, Denis Bruce, Volume 3, 1972, A6119, 4877.
80 Cassidy, "The Conference on Racism in Australia", p.4.
81 Read, "Cheeky, Insolent and Anti-White", p.80.
82 Freney, "Q'land Racism Conference a Milestone", p.10.
83 "Walker ASIO File", Walker, Denis Bruce Volume 3, 1972, A6119, 4877.
84 Freney, "Q'land Racism Conference a Milestone", p.10.
85 John Alford, "Racism Conference", *Lot's Wife*, 28 February 1972.
86 Henry Mayer, "The Racist Lurking inside all of us" *The Australian*, 9 November 1971.
87 "Labour Press Supports the Struggle for the Eradication of Racial Discrimination", Dan O'Neill Collection, UQFL132, Box 6, Folder 10.
88 Ibid.; Freney, "Q'land Racism Conference a Milestone", p.10.
89 Alford, "Racism Conference".
90 "Walker – ASIO File", Walker, Denis Bruce Volume 3, 1972, A6119, 4877.
91 Ibid.
92 Cassidy, "The Conference on Racism in Australia", pp.6–7.
93 Ibid.
94 Alford, "Racism Conference".
95 Ibid.
96 "Paul Coe, Statement to the Press: Conference on Racism", Dan O'Neill Collection, UQFL132, Box 6, Folder 10.

97 Frantz Fanon, *The Wretched of the Earth* (New York: Grove Press, 2004 [1967]), p.5.
98 See Chapter 15, "Towards a New Black Man", in Gilbert, *Because a White Man'll Never Do it.*
99 Osmond, "Black Militancy and the White Left", p.19.
100 Marilyn Lake, *Getting Equal: The History of Australian Feminism* (Sydney: Allen & Unwin, 1999), p.214.
101 "Merle Estelle Thornton", Walker, Denis Bruce Volume 3, 1972, A6119, 4877.
102 Ibid.
103 "Panthers Speak".
104 Osmond, "Black Militancy and the White Left", p.15.
105 "Australia's Black Panthers: An *Honi Soit* Interview", *Honi Soit*, 16 March 1972, p.7.
106 Ibid.
107 Ibid.
108 Alessandro Cavadini (director), *Ningla A-Na*, 1972.
109 Ibid.
110 Meredith Burgmann, "Black Sisterhood: The Situation of Urban Aboriginal Women and Their Relationship to the White Women's Movement", *Australian Journal of Political Science* 17, no. 2 (1982), p.32.
111 Bobbi Sykes, "Black Women in Australia: A History", in Jan Mercer, *The Other Half: Women in Australian Society* (Ringwood, Victoria: Penguin, 1975), p.318.
112 Sykes, "Black Women in Australia" – A History, p.319.
113 Burgmann, *Power and Protest*, p.121; Marilyn Lake, "Women, Black, Indigenous: Recognition Struggles in Dialogue", in Barbara Hobson (ed.), *Recognition Struggles and Social Movements: Contested Identities, Agency and Power* (Cambridge, 2003), p.150.
114 Jackie Huggins, "A Contemporary View of Aboriginal Women's Relationship to the White Women's Movement", in Norma Grieve and Ailsa Burns (eds), *Australian Women: Contemporary Feminist Thought* (Oxford: Oxford University Press, 1994), p.71.
115 Lake, *Getting Equal*, p.249.
116 Larissa Behrendt, "Aboriginal Women and the White Lies of the Feminist Movement: Implications for Aboriginal Women in Rights Discourse", *Australian Feminist Law Journal* 1, no. 1 (1993), p.31.
117 Rachel Perkins (Director), *Black Panther Woman*, 2014.
118 Burgmann, "Black Sisterhood", p.23.
119 Behrendt, "Aboriginal Women and the White Lies of the Feminist Movement, p.32.
120 Lake, "Women, Black, Indigenous", p.152.
121 Anne Summers, *Damned Whores and God's Police: The Colonization of Women in Australia* (Ringwood, Vic: Penguin, 1975).
122 Gary Foley, "Whiteness and Blackness in the Koori Struggle for Self-Determination", Paper for Winter School on Advocacy and Social Action 16–18 July 1999, Trades Hall, Melbourne. Accessed at: www.kooriweb.org/foley/essays/essay_9.html. Quoted in Land, *Decolonizing Solidarity*, p.7.
123 Freney, "Q'land Racism Conference a Milestone", p.10.
124 "Blacks Take Over Conference", *Woroni*, p.3; Osmond, "Black Militancy and the White Left", p.12.
125 "Panthers Speak".
126 Foley, "An Autobiographical Narrative", p.197.

10

THE AUSTRALIAN LEFT AND GAY LIBERATION

From 1945 to 2000s

Liz Ross

"Historically, sex has been a compelling issue for the left", writes Rosemary Hennessy.[1] Others agree, writing about the rise of lesbian and gay voices in tandem with revolutionary movements from the French Revolution to the present. Revolutions, such as that in Russia in 1917, brought about real change to the laws and rights of lesbian and gay men. Lenin commented: "Sexual and marriage reforms in the bourgeois sense will not do. In the sphere of sexual relations and marriage a revolution is approaching – in keeping with the proletarian revolution."[2] In Russia these were times which saw a flowering of theoretical explorations of human relationships, sexuality and the role of women. Not to mention material changes to the laws on homosexuality, divorce and marriage.

Fast forward to the 1960s and in a time when "revolution was in the air", once again, the voices of lesbians and gays were heard in the explosive birth of the Gay Liberation Movement (GLM). A movement that started with a riot had no hesitation in calling for revolution.

"Gay Liberation has a perspective for revolution based on the *unity of all oppressed people*. There can be no freedom for gays in a society that enslaves others through male supremacy, racism and economic exploitation (capitalism)." These were the words of the Australian Gay Liberation Front's first leaflet in 1972. It is no surprise then that the demands of Gay Liberation would mesh with those of the radical left, the newly formed Trotskyist groups and the evolving Communist Party of Australia (CPA), as well as some in the left unions.[3]

While it has been argued that the new movement arose from a new middle class – university students, intellectuals and the like – the strongest social movements, including GLM, always had connections with the labour movement and left-wing political groups. Tellingly it was the organised working class which was amongst the first to support gay rights very early in the movement's history in Australia.[4]

Overall, it was Marxism, through the left political organisations, which brought all those issues into a coherent world view and outlined a strategy for change; that linked the fight of all the oppressed with class struggle against the system of capitalism. Ken Davis joined the Socialist Youth Alliance (SYA, youth group of the Socialist Workers Party, SWP) as well as the local Labor Party branch in 1972 while he was still at school. Despite SWP/SYA support for gay liberation, Davis initially questioned why sexuality would be of interest to working class or left-wing groups. It was the Marxism he encountered in the SWP that "taught me that…our sexual lives were socially constructed and it was not a question of personal blame". The CPA-led Builders Labourers Federation (BLF) NSW Branch support for gay students Jeremy Fisher and Penny Short in 1971 was also important in changing his views. Davis came out in 1972 on the day the left had organised a rally in support of the Allende government in Chile. It was also Sydney's first Gay Pride demonstration. He went to both, commenting that "there was a tremendous intersection between a whole lot of issues, whether we liked it or not".[5]

The strength of the communist position, adds then-CPA member Phil Carswell, was that it drew "this *absolute* connection between homosexuality and feminism and the fight for gay rights *and* the fight against capitalism… [that they were] inextricably linked… It gave people a chance to have a world view and an organised political response…"[6]

This period also brought big changes to the main left-wing party, the CPA and saw the formation of two new Trotskyists groups – the Socialist Workers Party (1967) and the International Socialists (1970).[7] The CPA, responding to the revolts in the Soviet bloc and the rising social movements, split into three.[8] Of these, only one, the majority Eurocommunist-line CPA, supported the new gay rights movements.

The other two, taking a harder Stalinist line, supported women's and Indigenous rights, but not for gays. The pro-China CPA(Marxist Leninist) or Maoists, which split from the CPA in 1963, was influential on some campuses and unions. Though its members opposed the persecution of homosexuals, they actively (sometimes violently) opposed gay groups on campus, claiming Gay Liberation was a tool of US imperialism and a distraction from the class struggle. In particular, in 1975 when the peak student union body, AUS, put a pro-homosexual motion to all campuses, it was the CPA(ML) which spoke out against the motion; at Monash joining future Liberal politician Peter Costello and the Christian Right in opposition. However the Maoists at La Trobe University, who were more openly hostile to Gay Liberation and other left groups on campus, put up a counter-motion to adopt "a policy of opposing the legal and especially, the social persecution of homosexuals" while opposing the rest of the AUS motion.

The pro-Russia Socialist Party of Australia (SPA), a later split from the CPA in 1971, did not support gay rights and did not take part in any activities or debates, but was less actively hostile. In October 1979 the Victorian Gay Trade Unionist Group sent a letter to the SPA requesting information on the party's attitude to homosexuality. Their reply was: "So far the Socialist Party has not determined a policy on this question, nor have we published any articles in *The Socialist* or elsewhere relating to it..."[9]

In much of the commentary on the role of the Australian left in Gay Liberation and Lesbian, Gay, Bisexual, Transgender and Intersex (LGBTI) struggles, it is the examples of these groups – the CPA(ML), the SPA – that is used to describe the left as uniformly homophobic or at best indifferent. While it is fair to say these two groups were homophobic and their influence on a couple of campuses and within the union movement undoubtedly had a negative effect on the fight for gay rights, they were not the voice of the left within Gay Liberation or other LGBTI struggles, as this chapter will show.

On the left it was the CPA, the SWP and the International Socialists, who were the active and significant part of the struggle in the workplaces and unions, the campuses and in the radical movements, influencing many of the activists and campaigns.

The Communist Party

The biggest of the three, the CPA was the first party to respond to the new movements of the 1960s – even before a Gay Liberation group had formed in Australia. As Denis Freney notes in his autobiography he had been reading reports of the new movement in the Trotskyist papers from the US and "found the militancy and leftism of Gay Liberation in the USA much more to my liking (than the more reformist CAMP)".[10] *Tribune* carried the first serious article in the Australian press, left or otherwise, on Gay Liberation, by Freney on 26 May 1971.

In reaching its position of support for Gay Liberation, the Party could look back to a history – despite the influence of Stalinism – of standing up for the rights of oppressed peoples.

The first organised socialist current in Australia was the Socialist Party (1905–1923). The party's paper, *The Socialist*, regularly referred to key Marxist texts such as Frederick Engels' *Origin of the Family, Private Property and the State*, as well as August Bebel's *Women and Socialism* and the writings of outspoken Bolshevik Alexandra Kollontai. They also reviewed and sold such books as Edward Carpenter's *Love's Coming of Age*.

However, for all the party's coverage of relations between the sexes and other social questions, homosexuality only appeared in an indirect way. There was no call for ending the criminalisation of homosexual behaviour or other proposals for change. The need for change was clear from the many reports in the mainstream press of the time. These included men charged with a variety of homosexual crimes, a few about lesbians, some on women who cross-dressed or even married other women, and an article on a "remarkable theory" of homosexuality.[11]

It was the 1917 Russian Revolution which was to bring issues such as homosexuality to the fore with decriminalisation and a freeing up of sexual relations more generally. The year 1917 inspired socialists in Australia. Victorian Socialist Party (VSP) member Amelia Lambrick observed in *The Socialist*, that it was "a time of rapid movement. Old methods, old ideas, old conceptions are in the crucible. Changes vital and far reaching are making themselves felt."[12]

It also led to a new type of political party – the Communist Party, which quickly replaced many of the socialist parties around the world, including Australia. Party member Ella Morgan argued that communism would mean "the very taste of life" and "if women become rebels, the revolution is in sight".[13] From its foundation in 1920 to its dissolution in 1991, the Communist Party of Australia dominated far left politics.

Despite the promise of the Russian Revolution, victory for the working class was not to be – either in Russia or other countries. In the wake of World War I and revolutions, the 1920s had started out as a time of experimentation, of mass social change – a time of hope. It turned to ashes as the European revolutions were defeated, Stalin took power in a counter-revolution in Russia, while capitalism crashed into recession. As Depression, the rise of fascism and then War engulfed the world during the 1930s, mass impoverishment, political polarisation and the barbarity of war shook society to its core. These massive changes, while negative on many levels also opened a new world and new opportunities, including for homosexuals, many of whom met others like them for the first time in their lives.

Unlike the 1920s and 1930s, the 1940s decade did not end in war or financial chaos, but rather saw the beginning of the biggest economic boom in world history. Post World War II, the left had expected a different outcome, a re-run of the revolutionary post-WWI period. The ruling class fearing just such a revolution engaged in a Cold War and arms race, as well as attempting to crush working class dissent, in a period of paranoia and conservatism with the demonisation of communism in the West, alongside a strong focus on the family. Australia, the UK and US all cracked down on homosexuals as part of this pro-family, anti-communist push. In Eastern Europe and Russia, Stalinism played a similar role. There the state vigorously promoted the capitalist nuclear family, with medals for motherhood, tighter divorce laws, restrictions on abortion and in March 1934, the re-criminalisation of homosexuality.

However, too much had changed to keep the lid on completely, especially in the West. Women were not forced out of the workforce as they had been after WWI, but entered it at an unprecedented rate, while the sexual freedoms of the war years were not completely reversed. Some in the Eastern bloc did not follow Stalin in re-criminalising homosexuality. And, despite widespread anti-communist sentiment fuelled by ruling class propaganda, Australian government attempts to ban the Communist Party failed.

In the face of these threats the CPA did not stop its progressive campaigns to challenge censorship and the fight for women's rights especially in the areas of birth control and wages. While the fight against censorship was vital to the Party's survival – many of the censored publications were their own – Peter Murphy, a party member from the 1970s, notes that much of the literature that the Party defended in their anti-censorship and free speech campaigns was banned on the grounds of obscenity because of its sexual content.[14]

Tribune regularly published reviews of plays, books and even poetry, which challenged conservative views of society and personal relationships, including homosexuality. Particularly in the 1930s and 1940s a number of the Communist Party members were noted – and notorious – authors and playwrights, performing in radical theatre and joining in the literary debates of the day. While *Tribune*'s reviews of the time never referred to the homosexual content, neither did they condemn it. Thousands must have read the books, seen the plays and discussed what it all meant.[15]

Where the Party failed was in its uncritical acceptance, even glorification, of the views of the family during the Stalinist era. This led it – in the absence of a mass movement campaigning for gay rights – into its more negative view of homosexuality from the 1930s to the mid-1960s. That is when they addressed rhe issue of homosexuality at all.[16]

The CPA came to embody, as Phil Griffiths argues, a "profound contradiction". The Party was way out in front of the rest of society on the question of women and other oppressed groups, but the heavy hand of Stalinism was to lead it in a socially conservative direction.[17] Stalinism, it cannot be denied, played a key role in holding back the fight for sexual liberation in a large part of the world for many decades.

From the hardships of the war years to the increasing prosperity of the boom, the 1950s was a transition decade into the radicalising 1960s. Often portrayed as the dullest and most conformist of eras, the 1950s were for some the most exciting times of their lives. Times when they were involved politically in campaigns against censorship and nuclear bombs, a defence of the CPA and a range of other causes. Rebellious young people, partly through the flamboyant Rock and Roll culture and resistance to Menzies' militarisation, were beginning to be heard – and joining the Party.

By the end of the 1950s, several homophile groups had been established in the US and UK. In Britain, in response to scandals, there had been the Wolfenden Enquiry into the so-called victimless crimes of homosexuality and prostitution. Its report in 1958 recommended law reform and resulted in the formation of a public homosexual law reform group. Attempts by CPA member Laurie Collinson to establish a similar group in Australia failed, despite private support. He did not seek support within the Party, though it is clear his moves were known about, nor was he censured. Collinson left soon after for the UK and never returned.[18]

Would Party support for law reform have made a difference? Despite constant Party backing for abortion law reform, it was not achieved until the early 1970s and even now faces challenges. It was the changed political environment of the 1960s that made it possible to build a sizeable campaign. It was then that the Communist Party (and others on the left) could seize the opportunity to set up and build the liberation movements and more effective campaigns for reform. Homosexual law reform itself, even with the radicalisation of the 1960s, took from 1972 to 1997 to be implemented Australia-wide.

Throughout the 1960s, as the Communist Party welcomed the global youth rebellion, the references to sex and, for the first time, drugs, increased in its publications and the Party started having meetings about these topics. Homosexuality itself, though, only rated four explicit mentions in *Tribune*, and only one was positive.[19]

To bring the Party in Australia back to a more progressive stance would take three developments: first among homosexuals themselves, then changes in the political climate and finally within the CPA itself.

First there was the development of the homophile groups as homosexuals came to know themselves as a group with shared interests, a group which could recognise it had rights and could organise to fight for those rights. While it had long history overseas, this awareness was slower to develop in Australia, but then took only a few short months over 1969 to 1970 to move from having no self-identifying political groups, to the formation of two groups understanding they needed to fight for their rights.

The political climate was changing too, coming from the rising working class challenges to capitalism and students radicalising on the campuses. In Australia student numbers had increased exponentially, including the biggest intake from the working class. The party recruited a number of young activists – students and workers – especially from the anti-Vietnam War campaign and the early women's and gay liberation movements.

Finally, support for gays did not come without other political developments inside the party. The CPA was in trouble as it entered the 1970s, smaller and more divided than it had been for decades, so it needed to cohere a new politics and grow if it was to survive. It also began to face challenges from the new Trotskyist groups that were forming. Critical to transforming the Party's position on gays was its new political stance in relation to Stalinism, as well as to students and the new liberation movements. The Party had split over these issues and though the fragmentation was disruptive it opened the CPA up to the wave of radicalisation and enabled it to grow again.

The Communist Party adopted its first pro-gay resolution in 1972. Moved by Lance Gowland and Denis Freney, it read in part: "The CPA believes that the legal basis for police persecution and prosecution of homosexuals and social and economic discrimination against them must be ended and homosexuals accepted as full citizens". By 1973 Freney was putting a more radical line in public, talking about oppression, liberation and revolution. In *Tribune* during Gay Pride week he argued that oppression was systemic and just changing the law could not end it.[20]

At the Party's 1974 Easter Congress a more substantial policy expressed the importance the CPA gave to winning the working class to fight against all oppression. The resolution rejected the notion of homosexuality as a disease, or a product of "decadent capitalism" that would be "cured" by socialism. Homosexuality was a "valid form of sexual expression". The links between the fight against homosexual oppression and women's oppression were emphasised.

The Party took its gay organising as seriously as its other work, with a Gay Collective meeting regularly to plan and review its work. A Collective report gives a picture of CPA activities. They held a reading group to form a "principled

Marxist position on sexuality" and contributed to a debate in *Tribune*. There was also a "Wednesday night at the CPA" series on sexuality. The Collective helped develop national congress policies and members were active in the Gay Trade Unionist Group, Young Gays and Gay Youth Accommodation. The report concluded that members were "increasingly influential in the gay community because of their principled position, ability and consistency of work".[21]

It was not always a case of winning every battle, of making advances, either for the Party or the Movement. There was always debate about which was the way forward, a debate which became more focussed and heated when campaigns reached both their high and low points.

Gay Pride Week 1973 marked both the highpoint and the end of the first, exuberant, optimistic and revolutionary phase of Gay Liberation. A time when "we believed we were making a new revolution; a clearly social revolution in which masculinity, femininity and institutionalised heterosexuality would all disappear".[22]

There had been gains from two years of gay activism, including a shift in public support for law reform. But the tide was turning worldwide and as the working class struggle ebbed, the capitalist class went on the offensive.

In Australia, Gay Liberation, which had started its rise towards the end of the period of revolt, could not sustain its early level of activism as the political situation began to turn down. The election of the Labor Party to federal government in 1972 encouraged the politics of lobbying in the halls of power, rather than demonstrating on the streets, co-option rather than confrontation.

It was an uneven shift, however, and in 1975 a new wave of student radicals, many members of left-wing groups, took up the battle for gay rights. Included in this were the National Homosexual Conferences, eleven in all, where a battle of ideas was fought out. Marxism, radical feminism, patriarchy theory and the primacy of class were the main debates.

The year 1978 represented another such time. In response to a right-wing backlash in the US and a request from activists there for a day of international solidarity on Stonewall Day, SWP members Ken Davis and Annie Taylor called a meeting. Out of that came a day-time rally, a forum and an evening Mardi Gras, the latter particularly promoted by CPA members on the organising committee. Some 500 turned up for the rally, while around 2,000 took part in the Mardi Gras. Spectacularly attacked by the police, it became Australia's Stonewall.[23]

The Communist Party was in the throes of another change of direction and Mardi Gras provided apparent vindication of a shift to the "community" rather than a class-centred strategy, when more joined the night time protest and parade than the morning rally. Although the party was committed to a range of campaigns, Peter Murphy says: "We felt like we were doing the same thing over and over again, but getting nowhere, not even getting bigger...we had to do something new." Lance Gowland pushed for community coalition politics, the type of politics he claimed the CPA stood for, that the other groups opposed. "We believed in working with the green movements, the social movements", whereas for the other left groups, "the idea was to get massive strikes and things and bring down the capitalist society... [their] focus was only on the trade unions".[24]

But there was still debate within the Party. The Gay Collective's proposed position for the party's 1979 program seemed to emphasise a more class-based approach. Craig Johnston wrote that they aimed to develop a Marxist–feminist analysis, to show that challenging homophobia can broaden and strengthen the movement for socialism. It was to be a "tool for action".[25] But this did not last.

By 1981 most of the gay men in the Party had all but abandoned this approach and had moved solidly behind the shift to community politics. Some were arguing that "a task for radicals is to make alliances with independent small business as part of our efforts to build an effective and broad gay rights movement".[26]

However, this was not the CPA's initial approach to building the movement and building the Party. In 1974 Denis Freney described their position. He said it was about organising an activist minority that could bring people in around more left-wing demands and build a stronger, fighting movement. The main job then was to go out and confront those institutions that oppress us, involving mass work such as demonstrations. "We've got to find those demands which are really challenging (not the lowest common denominator)... We've got to start from real, felt oppression and at the same time link it to the real causes."[27]

More than the future of the struggle for gay rights was at stake for the CPA. Its own future was at risk more generally. The Party had been shrinking since the end of World War II and Denis Freney wrote in his 1991 autobiography that after a short reprieve in the wake of the sacking of Whitlam, by 1977 the CPA was losing members again. "We had sought to get rid of the dross of the Party's Stalinist past", he said, "and to adapt our ideas to feminism and other new movements, but to no avail."

In the last decade of the Party, while the fight for law reform continued, the community was hit hard by the HIV-AIDS crisis. CPA members threw themselves into the committees and other support activities set up in Australia, rather than having to use the more outward activism needed against the homophobic governments of the US and UK. By 1990, as drug accessibility became more of an issue, gays did turn to the activism of earlier days. Copying their US and UK counterparts they formed ACT-UP (AIDS Coalition to Unleash Power) and engaged in public stunts like abseiling in chambers in federal Parliament, replacing flowers with white crosses in public places, or setting up pickets with union support.

Party activists were important in both committee and ACT-UP style activism; however, by 1991 the CPA's downward spiral was completed, with members voting to dissolve the Party. The Communist Party was no more.

The Socialist Workers Party and the International Socialists

Although both the Socialist Workers Party (SWP) and the International Socialists (IS) came from the Trotskyist tradition, there were significant differences between the groups which mirrored political schisms internationally. The SWP belonged to the Fourth International (an international grouping of Trotskyists groups representing those who saw Russia as a degenerated workers' state and the Eastern bloc countries as socialist). Initially the SWP closely followed the American SWP in its pro-Cuba, pro-women's and gay liberation politics and its industrial stance. The group also saw work within the Australian Labor Party (ALP), entrism, as critical to its activities. This came to an end when the ALP named the SWP as a proscribed organisation, but the group retained this policy for future use. Later the SWP dropped Trotskyism, though still seeing Trotsky as an important figure in the Russian Revolution and theoretically.

By contrast the International Socialists saw Russia as state capitalist (i.e. no longer any sort of workers' state or socialist), and did not see countries in the Eastern bloc, China and Cuba as socialist, or even on the way to socialism, while recognising China and Cuba had had revolutions which overthrew feudal or corrupt capitalist regimes. In this they followed the British Socialist Workers Party and its group of sympathising parties in the International Socialist Tendency. The group has never abandoned Trotskyism, but continues to hold a critical attitude to his analysis, for example, disagreeing over the analysis of Russia after Stalin's counter-revolution. Entrism into the ALP was never attempted, though not through political opposition to such a tactic in certain circumstances.

While the politics of each group meant different priorities, their activism in Gay Liberation and other LGBTI struggles was similar, though the IS was the more militant of the two. (The SWP would describe this as ultraleftism.) However, a significant difference between the groups was the position on patriarchy theory and autonomous organising. The IS argued strongly against patriarchy theory – a theory that the oppression of women pre-dates class society and will remain after a socialist revolution – on the grounds that the oppression of women, as Engels wrote, arose with class society and will end after a working class revolution smashes capitalism. For the SWP, if Russia, the Eastern bloc countries and Cuba were some sort of workers' state or socialist, the continuing presence of women's and gay oppression proved a fundamental theoretical problem, only resolvable by arguing that socialism cannot bring an end to oppression, but that another revolution would be necessary.

A lesser issue, flowing in part from patriarchy theory and then identity politics, was the support by the SWP for autonomous organising as a timeless principle. The IS on the other hand, saw autonomous organising – the self-organisation of an oppressed group – simply as a tactic, useful at times during a struggle for rights. The Communist Party until its demise took a similar position to the SWP.

Socialist Workers Party

In the 1930s the CPA could have taken a different direction to Stalinism. Leon Trotsky, one of the Russian Revolution's leaders was a fierce opponent of Stalin and the degeneration in Russia. Particularly scathing of Stalin's valorisation of the family, Trotsky charged that: "the leaders are forcing people to glue together again the shell of the broken family...to consider it, under the threat of extreme penalties, the sacred nucleus of triumphant socialism. It is hard to measure...the scope of this retreat."[28]

Exiled, he kept up his opposition and called for the formation of new communist parties to recover the real legacy of the Revolution. He found followers around the world, including Australia. But the group in Australia, formed in 1933, was banned, had members jailed, split frequently, was hounded by the CPA and stayed too small to be influential. The 1940s and 1950s were particularly hard on the groups. But the small groups did start to revive in the early 1960s, only to be outmatched by a new group of mainly student activists who claimed the Trotskyist mantle.[29]

John Percy wrote of the group's politics. "Our roots were the IWW [International Workers of the World], the CPA and the early Trotskyist group [the Australian group headed by Nick Origlass], but the direct links were tenuous, so the lessons and experiences of overseas revolutionaries, the [Trotskyist] Fourth International and especially the US Socialist Workers Party, became more important for us."[30]

The Cuban Revolution of 1959 was an inspirational event for young students like Percy and fed into their support for the Vietnamese struggle against Western imperialist intervention in the mid-1960s. An audience of 400 at a meeting on Cuba at Sydney University illustrated the Third World radicalism of the time.

The campuses provided the emerging group with most of its new members, while it also attracted some high school students. Ken Davis remembers an SYA-planned national school strike in 1972, where 800–1,000 students protested at Sydney Town Hall for political rights and against discrimination. At least four gay groups were set up in high schools, including one at Davis's school where there were also prominent gays on the school staff. The groups joined protests but also invited speakers and on one occasion Davis's school group invited the SYA's Nita Keig and author and activist Dennis Altman.

Resistance was the first of the SWP-related organisations to be established, in 1967, though its founding conference was not until 1970 when 45 members attended. 1972 saw the formation of the Socialist Workers League, as the SWP was then called. So during the beginnings and rise of the Gay Liberation movement, the SWP itself was forming and consolidating.

The group's newspaper *Direct Action*, appeared in September 1970, the year CAMP was formed. The first article about homosexuality, in July 1971, was an attack on a homophobic, anti-Trotskyist piece in the Maoist paper *Vanguard*. The first comprehensive analysis of Gay Liberation appeared in *Direct Action* in September 1971 and included references to the Russian Revolution, declaring that for the Bolsheviks, "it was quite simply the responsibility of the revolution to eliminate all forms of oppression and discrimination".[31] As *Direct Action* (and much later *Green Left Weekly*) the paper reported and analysed the movement's activities and history, with the frequency (high or low) of articles providing a rough barometer of Gay Liberation's fortunes. The SWP often fielded candidates in federal and state elections and party policy on homosexuals was reprinted in the paper as part of the general election platform.[32]

The SWP undertook assessments of its role within GLM. The National Committee's 1973 *Memorandum on the Gay Liberation Movement*, emphasised the importance of linking the gay struggle with that of the working class. While Gay Liberation was not a key national sphere of work at that time for the group, a number of members had been involved and it was noted that Gay Pride Week activities had "demonstrated the ability of the movement to mobilise significant numbers in action".[33] The movement had given the SWP an opportunity to engage with lesbians and gay men and win new people to the group and its socialist analysis. The National Committee proposed that branches be prepared to intervene in future activities.[34] Its analysis at this time proved over-optimistic, as Gay Liberation slumped by the end of 1973.

After some time in the doldrums, the movement started to revive in 1975. SWP student members were part of the gay "push" in the AUS that year, backing the AUS campus motions on homosexuality and later the organising of the First National Homosexual Conference. The conference was a forum for debate over questions of liberation, radical feminism and the like, that were to dominate the movement over the coming years. SWP members were active contributors at the conference, arguing the case for a Marxist perspective. Their involvement continued over the intervening years, and they were well-placed to play an important role when the movement reached a second peak in 1978. SWP members were part of the proposal to set the theme of "Gays at Work" for that year's National Homosexual Conference. They were also crucial in establishing the Sydney Gay Solidarity Group to organise the International Day of Solidarity on June 24, which ended with the Mardi Gras. Party activists played a major role in the successful anti-Mary Whitehouse (anti-Festival of Light) national campaign that same year.

The SWP took 1978 very seriously indeed; its lesbian and gay membership had grown from around 14 activists in 1975 to the high 40s in 1978. The upsurge of 1978 saw the SWP buoyant, predicting a vibrant movement poised for victories. Allen Myers, one of the party's leaders, wrote that they wanted the SWP to be an integral part of the movement, with a more organised party intervention, providing political leadership. "As a minimum target, every branch should be working towards the establishment of a functioning gay fraction."[35] The SWP leadership argued that the GLM was moving left, organising to build mass actions rather than relying on parliamentarians, seeking allies in the organised working class and overall adopting a militant program. Lobbying was a strategy for defeat. Instead lesbians and gays needed "a fighting program" to defend their rights, especially in the face of any prospective right-wing offensive. The Party expected sharpening class conflict under the Fraser government to bring a test of strength between workers and the ruling class. Every victory by the bosses, whether it was against gays or any other oppressed group, Myers argued, would be a defeat for the working class just as much as a wage cut or a rise in unemployment. The struggle for homosexual liberation was part of the workers' struggle.

The SWP saw itself as politically positioned between what the group described as the left reformism of the CPA and ultra-left tactics of groups such as the International Socialists.

The SWP was confident it could reach out to new social layers and draw them into action and into its project of building for a revolutionary party. During the course of such struggles the group believed that masses of gays would accept the Party's explanations of the "profound stake which homosexuals have in the socialist revolution".[36]

However a combination of the SWP's sharp turn to industry, its rapid reallocation of many members to work in the growing anti-uranium movement, and a significant drop in gay activism put paid to such optimistic predictions. There was an exodus of gay members and the Party's work around lesbian and gay issues fell dramatically. Again, as with the CPA, the AIDS crisis took its toll both of members and activism more generally, but it did propel others into action later in the 1980s, and new gay members were won to the SWP.

The politics of the movement, however, had turned inwards with the rise of "identity politics", a theory of individual change and of endlessly divisible oppressed groups. Sherry Wolf explains Marxists argue for solidarity amongst oppressed groups as essential for a united struggle against capitalism. For supporters of identity politics all straights benefit from queer oppression, all whites benefit from racism and so on, meaning that "the prospects for unity are at best slim and unity is neither possible, nor desirable".[37]

The late 1990s saw the beginnings of a world-wide anti-capitalist movement, which not only brought new young activists to left parties and Marxism, but also saw LGBTI activists build a left 'Queer' politics. The SWP grew, as did the International Socialists and the newly formed Socialist Alternative.

Throughout the 1990s the SWP went through various transformations, abandoning its Trotskyist positions and following an international trend on the left to form a broad left party, the Socialist Alliance. LGBTI activism, particularly around the Equal Marriage Campaign and Community Action Against Homophobia (CAAH) in NSW, remain key activities for the Alliance.

International Socialists/Socialist Alternative

The smallest of the three significant groups and the latest onto the political scene was the International Socialists (IS).

The IS formed as a small discussion group at the end of 1971, and during 1972 its membership stayed at around 20–30. While there was quick turnover, the group had started to clarify its political stance. By November 1975 membership was still low (circa 20), but in the wake of the November 11 constitutional crisis, the numbers went up fairly rapidly to around 70. The group was still thinly spread across south eastern Australia, but it felt politically confident enough to establish itself as a national organisation with agreed upon politics.[38]

Most important initially for the group was the small, but politically coherent, student club at Monash University, the Revolutionary Communists or RevComs (1972). Although not formally part of the IS at the beginning, they shared opposition to Australian nationalism and support for workers' struggles. Their anti-nationalist stance, as well as their support for Women's and Gay Liberation brought them into conflict with the more prominent Maoist students. However, as Tess Lee Ack recalls, "There was only ever a handful of RevComs, but we had quite a lot of influence among left-wing students and by 1974 were pretty much the leading group on the campus left." Tess helped write and put out the RevComs newsletter *Hard Lines* and gained a reputation as a leading student activist.

Hard Lines supported Gay Liberation, with the RevComs standing on joint election tickets alongside Gay and Women's Liberation candidates. The newsletter advertised Sexuality Week events, sexual liberation forums and promoted 1973 Gay Pride week. More generally the club campaigned against the homophobia and sexism of the administration and right-wing students. Promoting Gay Pride, *Hard Lines* talked of the nationwide events which would involve "more homosexuals in Australia than any other organised activity". The week would involve those heterosexuals "who identify with the gay movement against the oppression of homosexuals – that's important as it is too easy to view all heterosexuals as our oppressors when these are people who are questioning and changing their attitudes towards us".[39] *Hard Lines* also campaigned for the AUS pro-gay motions in 1975.

The RevComs were involved in initiating the country's first "Homosexuals and Society" course on campus. The course so outraged Vice Chancellor Matheson, that he claimed it was a threat to the very core of university values.[40]

One of the founding members of the IS, Janey Stone, had been involved in Women's Liberation in the USA, at Berkeley, as well as being briefly in Paris during some of the 1968 upheavals. Along with other women, she initiated Women's Liberation at Melbourne University. With the holding of a Sexuality Week, "We felt like we were breaking new ground." Both Lee Ack and Stone were at Melbourne's first gay demo on Swanston Street in December 1972. It was a politically charged time, with the prospect of a Labor government coming to power after 23 years of conservative rule.

Off-campus, the IS was slowly building a base. Initially it had a strong trade union and workplace focus. However, in the first issue of its paper *The Battler* in November 1972 there was a full page article, "What is The Party Line on Love?" In it Janey Stone wrote of the rich humanitarian tradition of revolutionaries such as Alexandra Kollontai and the lessons of the Russian Revolution, as well as welcoming the contributions of Women's and Gay Liberation. She added, "We believe that revolutionaries should be *sex-affirming*."[41]

Having overstretched resources somewhat, the next issue of the paper did not appear until October 1974, coinciding with a period of downturn in the gay movement. However members of the IS were active in their unions. Tess Lee Ack and Tom O'Lincoln were in the rank and file group, Teacher Action. This group successfully argued for the Victorian Secondary Teachers Association to establish women's and later, homosexual subcommittees. These subcommittees helped form the union's pro-gay, pro-women policies.

In1977 *The Battler* began to include articles about gay liberation, starting with reports on the Greg Weir campaign. When the movement hit its peak in 1978, *The Battler* ran articles on Mardi Gras, the "Gays at Work" national homosexual conference, and the protests against Mary Whitehouse.

The year 1978 was also the first that the group had a number of lesbian and gay members who could attend many of the gay-only groups. With the increase in membership, the IS could stage a serious intervention into the 1978 protests and Homosexuals at Work conference, as well as the 1981 Socialism and Homosexuality forum. In Melbourne, as part of the campaign against Mary Whitehouse, Janey Stone chaired the public meeting and IS members were part of the demonstrations around the country. At the Melbourne anti-Festival of Light campaign forum, Tom O'Lincoln challenged the ALP speaker Gareth Evans to come to the rally. To much uproar Evans replied that unfortunately he could not attend as he would be addressing a meeting in Ballarat on "the future of socialism"! The group held public branch meetings on Gay Liberation and at one time ran a debate, "Which way forward for the Australian gay movement?", in its theoretical journal. Contributions came from independent activist Michael Hurley, Phil Carswell from the CPA and Graham Willett, then an IS member.[42] Coverage of lesbian and gay issues continued in the paper until 1985. After a break of three years while the group turned the paper into a more theoretical publication, HIV-AIDS and ACT-UP protests, many involving IS activists, saw greater coverage in *The Socialist*.

What was significant about the IS, as compared to the CPA and the SWP, was its more critical view of autonomous organising. In a paper to the Socialism and Homosexuality Conference, then member Alison Thorne put the IS position:

> In the early 1970s the autonomous gay movement played a vital role in advancing the struggle for gay liberation. It contributed to the growth of gay pride...it explored and advanced the understanding of sexual politics, especially of the relationship between gay liberation and socialism.[43]

As the movement declined, however, it became more inward looking and lost direction. Clinging to autonomous organising "always and everywhere", the IS argued, closed off possibilities for the movement to grow.

The group favoured more united front work in the vein of the anti-Festival of Light campaign, including opposing the later de-politicisation of Mardi Gras. The IS pointed to the missed opportunity arising out of the "Drop the Charges" campaign against the police arrests at Mardi Gras. The July demonstration in Sydney immediately after Mardi Gras was the biggest protest for gay rights that the country had seen and it was joined by trade unionists, straights (heterosexuals), political groups and other campaign groups. The arrests of gays were seen as an attack on everyone's rights. Then International Socialist member Di Minnis explained that in building for the demonstration, activists (gay and straight) were able to win over fellow workers to the need to fight for gay rights.

The IS, like the other left groups, argued for building support within the unions through gay caucuses, rank and file groups and solidarity work with other struggles. Important as these were, IS members argued at the Socialism and Homosexuality conference, more than reforms were needed if the system was to be fundamentally changed. Reforming capitalism could only go so far, the struggle for reforms had to be turned into revolt. IS members argued that if real liberation was the goal, then the group would need to build for revolution, build a revolutionary party that could unite the different areas of struggle into one force.[44]

As the movement crumbled, the class struggle declined and HIV-AIDS took its toll, the International Socialists, like the rest of the left, proved too weak to hold most of its lesbian and gay members against the rightward pull. The IS was also caught up in two major splits in 1985 (Socialist Action, which re-united with the IS in 1990) and 1995 (Socialist Alternative). Socialist Alternative has since become the biggest group on the left, with the anti-capitalist movement of the late 1990s to early 2000s as well as the Equal Love same-sex marriage campaign, from 2004, coming mainly from the campuses, solidifying the gains for the group.

It took consistent theorising around the questions of gay liberation, autonomous organising and identity politics, as well as significant involvement on the campuses, for Socialist Alternative to rebuild a layer of committed left-wing LGBTI activists, people committed to building both the campaigns and a group of revolutionary socialists, throughout the 1990s and 2000s.

Battle of ideas

Activism is key for the left – building the protest groups, the marches on the street, the focus on organising within the unions, on the campuses. But activism on its own, without a political underpinning, leads nowhere. Struggle, informed by Marxist theories of change, of oppression, of resistance, its ultimate goal the overthrow of the system, was what the left brought to Gay Liberation and other movements – as it continues to do today.[45]

Debate about activism and theory were part of the development of Gay Liberation, with the GLM borrowing heavily from the Women's and Black Liberation Movements and the anti-Vietnam war campaign. Marxism too was seen as critical for understanding oppression and building resistance.

At meetings and conferences, the role of capitalism, and the need for radical change were regularly discussed, with much of the theoretical material drawn from Gay Lib and Marxist groups in the US or UK. At the beginning of 1973, for example, a mixed bunch of labourers, seamen, university lecturers, high school and university students as well as old age pensioners, 80 in all, collected at the CPA camp, Minto. Papers by Dennis Altman and Pam Stein were a call to radically restructure society, while Barry Prothero and Lance Gowland discussed "Vanguard group or mass group?" and relations with the left, especially the CPA.[46]

As the world-wide struggle turned down, increasingly ideas of patriarchy theory, identity politics and autonomy gained traction. Patriarchy theory was a clear attack on Marxism, that Marxist politics was somehow lacking in its analysis and needed feminism to "repair" it. Autonomous organising became a principle, instead of a tactical question.

Within Gay Liberation, not only were these ideas gaining currency, but notions of a gay community began to surface. Initially the left could see the problems with such an approach. Craig Johnston pointed out that it watered down ideas of class difference, that "what we have in common, our sexuality, is supposed to take priority".[47] Di Otto added that, "We make the mistake of assuming that lesbianism, in itself, is a radical position...it is conservative to ignore the differences such as class and political perspective."[48]

Identity politics and separatism meant that the socialist politics of working class alliance and mass struggle was marginalised. Appeals across class lines, rather than solidarity with the working class became dominant. Of the left, only the IS (and later Socialist Alternative) openly opposed this shift, arguing against patriarchy theory, identity politics and putting up a strong defence of Marxism itself.[49]

Overall though the movement was in decline and groups like the IS were not able to counter this politically, nor stop the exodus of LGBTI members. A situation that was mirrored internationally as the movement took on a more rightward shift in response to the changing political situation world-wide.

By the late 1990s world politics began shifting leftwards with an anti-capitalist movement, a combination of the "Teamsters and the Turtles" (a reference to coalitions of unions and environmentalists) took to the streets against the dominant neoliberalism.

LGBTI people were quick to join in, especially on the campuses, forming groups such as QUEER (Queer United to Eradicate Economic Rationalism) and QuACE (Queers Against Corporate Exploitation) in Australia. These groups argued for direct action and blockades and the importance of being activists against the system that oppressed them.

Queer, a term usually used abusively was re-appropriated by the young activists. Its strength lay in a sense of unity in struggle, as against the separateness of identity politics. But with queer theorists still seeing identity as the main battleground for oppressed groups, they had no way of arguing for future organising as the anti-capitalist movement declined and the politics of a "war on terror" took hold and neoliberalism withstood the anti-capitalist challenge.

Nonetheless, it was an important step forward politically and the far left did grow out of the movement, recruiting another layer of activists and gave currency to class politics once more.

Spurred by the homophobic push against same-sex marriage, another round of activism and growth for the far left began after the 2004 amendment to Australia's Marriage Act; a move that redefined marriage as only between a woman and a man and was supported by both major political parties.

Marriage for LGBTI couples in the days of Gay Liberation was seen as a reactionary adaptation to the capitalist family. It was a demand primarily of the

Christian gay groups, seeking equality within the church. By the late 1990s, early 2000s, however, denial of the right to marry became a question of equal rights. It was a contested analysis as many were critical of the institution of marriage, but the two main left groups, Socialist Alternative and Socialist Alliance argued to support the issue as one of civil rights. The major debates since then, as tens of thousands have protested, have been over the tactics of action on the streets, winning the active support of the organised working class versus lobbying conservative politicians and the like; in other words what will take the campaign further, how can it be won?

In the fight for gay liberation, the left brought analysis, organisation, class politics and a focus on what united LGBTI people in the struggle against the common enemy, capitalism. It has continued to argue the case for total social change – for revolution not just reforms. And for a revolution led by a working class united around questions of race, sex and sexuality, which as the Socialist Homosexual Manifesto wrote, "is the only class with the potential to lead a revolution because of its size, organisation and base at the point of production".[50]

Notes

1 Hennessy, Rosemary. "Queer theory, left politics", in Makdisi, Saree, Cesare Casarino and Rebecca Karl, Eds, *Marxism beyond Marxism* (New York, Routledge, 1995), p.214.
2 Zetkin, Clara. "Lenin on the women's question". www.marxists.org/archive/zetkin/1920/lenin/zetkin1.htm. See also Healey, Dan. *Homosexual desire in revolutionary Russia. The regulation of sexual and gender dissent* (Chicago, University of Chicago Press, 2001); Carleton, Gregory *Sexual revolution in Bolshevik Russia* (Pittsburgh, University of Pittsburgh Press, 2005).
3 Symons, Beverley and Rowan Cahill, Eds. *A turbulent decade. Social protest movements and the labour movement* (Sydney, ASSLH, 2005).
4 Willett, Graham. *Living out loud: a history of gay and lesbian activism in Australia* (Sydney, Allen & Unwin, Johnston, 2000); Burgmann, Verity. *Power and Protest. Movements for change in Australian society* (Sydney, Allen & Unwin, 1993), pp.6–7; and O'Lincoln, Tom, *Years of rage. Social conflicts in the Fraser era* (Melbourne, Intervention, 2012) for discussion on the new middle class.
5 Ken Davis 2005. "Sexual Politics: Gay and Lesbian Rights", pp.38–46 in Symons, Beverley and Rowan Cahill, Eds. *A turbulent decade. Social protest movements and the labour movement* (Sydney, ASSLH, 2005); Interview with author as are future quotes.
6 Phil Carswell interview with Graham Willett. Held at Australian Lesbian and Gay Archives (ALGA).
7 Like the other two Trotskyist groups, the Spartacist League supported the liberation movements, but played only a cameo, and not always welcome, role in the campaigns.
8 O'Lincoln, Tom. *Into the mainstream. The decline of Australian Communism* (Sydney, Stained Wattle Press, 1985).
9 The CPA(ML) and SPA (now the Communist Party) have changed and, while not active around LGBTI issues, they oppose discrimination and support demands for Equal Marriage.
10 Freney, Denis. *A map of days* (Sydney, Heinemann, 1991), pp.329–333; CAMP – the Campaign Against Moral Persecution formed in 1970.
11 "Remarkable theory", *Adelaide Advertiser*, 5 September 1908, p.5.
12 Amelia Lambrick wrote a two-part article on the times; the quote is from 24 January. "The changing world – on post-war problems", *The Socialist*, 17 January 1919, p.3 and 24 January 1919, p.2.

13 Morgan, Ella. *The Communist*, 5 August 1921, p.6.
14 Ross, Liz. "Love's coming of age: Australian socialist and communist parties and sexuality", *The La Trobe Journal*, no.87, May 2011, pp.107–115. http://latrobejournal.slv.vic.gov.au/latrobejournal/issue/latrobe-87/t1-g-t10.html; Ross *Revolution is for Us. The left and gay liberation in Australia* (Melbourne, Interventions, 2013), p.94.
15 Peter Murphy. Interview with author; "Gay and lesbian existence under socialism. 'Pink love under the red star'. Gay Laboratory Leningrad speak out", *Tribune*, 26 June 1985, pp.8–9.
16 See Ross, *Revolution is for Us*, for *Tribune* coverage.
17 Griffiths, Phil. "Women and the CPA: 1920–1945". 1998 www.philgriffiths.id.au/writings/Aust_hist_old.html
18 Willett, Graham. "Moods of love and commitment: Laurie Collinson in Melbourne. *La Trobe Journal*, no.83, 2009 pp.77–83 http://latrobejournal.slv.vic.gov.au/latrobejournal/issue/latrobe-83/t1-g-t8.html; See Anderson, Roderic. *Free Radical. A memoir of a gay political activist* (Self published, 2013) for experience in the CPA. Ross, *Revolution is for Us*, pp.94–5. Homosexuals had mixed experience within the CPA, from acceptance to expulsion.
19 "Sniggers for Sister George", *Tribune*, August 1966, p.6. Despite the title, the review was a positive take on the lesbian play *The killing of Sister George*. Author listed as D.M.
20 Freney, Denis. "Are homosexuals oppressed?" *Tribune*, 11 September 1973, p.8.
21 Gay Collective report to 1981 CPA State Conference, NSW.
22 Melbourne Gay Liberation nd – c.1972.
23 Carbery, Graham. *Mardi Gras: a history of Sydney Gay and Lesbian Mardi Gras* (Melbourne, ALGA 1995).
24 Peter Murphy. Interview with author; Lance Gowland. Interviews held at Sydney Pride History Group.
25 Draft document for CPA 26th Congress, 1980; Johnston, Craig "What is this document for?" *Australian Left Review*, no.75, 1980, p.80.
26 Johnston, Craig. *A Sydney gaze. The making of gay liberation* (Glebe, Wild & Woolley 1999), pp.82–83.
27 Freney, Denis. "Comments on Gay Liberation", *Gay Liberation Press*, August 1974, pp.16–18.
28 As quoted in German, Lindsay. *Material Girls. Women, men and work* (London, Bookmarks 2007), p.180.
29 Percy, John. *Resistance: A history of the Democratic Socialist Party and Resistance. Volume 1: 1965–1972* (Chippendale, Resistance Press, 2005).
30 Ibid., p.49.
31 Joliffe, Jill. "Vanguard on homosexuality", *Direct Action*, no.8, July 1971, p.15; Ferguson, Jenny. "Homosexual Liberation", *Direct Action*, no.10, September 1971, p.14.
32 Ross, *Revolution is for Us*, for *Direct Action* coverage.
33 Memorandum on the Gay Liberation Movement. Adopted by the SYA National Committee at its October 13–14 plenum, 1973; Adopted by the SWL Political Committee on 20 October 1973
34 Ibid.
35 Socialist Workers Party "Gay Liberation report" *SWP Party Organiser*, vol.1, no.7. August 1978.
36 Ibid.
37 Wolf, Sherry. "Unite and fight: Marxism and identity politics", *International Socialist Review*, no. 98, 2015. http://isreview.org/issue/98/unite-and-fight
38 See O'Lincoln, Tom. *The highway is for gamblers. A political memoir* (Melbourne, Interventions, 2017); and Armstrong, Mick. "The origins of Socialist Alternative: summing up the debate", *Marxist Left Review*, no. 1, 2010. http://marxistleftreview.org/index.php?option=com_content&view=article&id=77:the-origins-of-socialist-alternative-summing-up-the-debate&catid=34:issue-1-spring-2010&Itemid=77
39 Tess Lee Ack, personal communication

Gay liberation from 1945 to 2000s **209**

40 Left-wing scientist and lecturer at Monash, Lesley Rogers, played an important role in running the course. She has since written several books and articles about sex and sexuality. Rogers, Lesley. *Sexing the Brain* (London, Weidenfeld & Nicolson 1999).
41 *The Battler*, vol. 1, no.1, 17 November 1972, p.6.
42 "Controversy: Which way forward for Australian gays", *International Socialist*, no.12 1981–82, pp.3–7.
43 Thorne, Alison "Where should the Gay Liberation Movement be going...to the working class: in "ISO Statement on socialists and the Gay Liberation Movement", Socialism and Homosexuality Conference. Collected Papers, 25–26 April 1981.
44 "ISO Statement on socialists and the Gay Liberation Movement", Socialism and Homosexuality Conference. Collected Papers, 25–26 April 1981.
45 Bloodworth, Sandra. "Marx and Engels on gender and sexuality and their legacy", *Marxist Left Review*, no.1, August 2010, pp.65–109.
46 Gowland, Lance. Sydney Gay Lib papers 1973, p.8; Program for the conference. (Held at ALGA.)
47 Johnston, Craig. "Civil disobedience by the gay and lesbian movements: fashion, media, glamor? (notes from an investigation, or an archeology of tactics)" Australian Homosexual Histories conference. Collected Papers. 19 November 1999, p. 82.
48 Otto, Di. *Lesbian Newsletter* (Melbourne) October 1980.
49 Stone, Janey. *Perspectives for Women's Liberation. Radical feminism, reform or revolution?* (Melbourne, Redback Press 1978); Bloodworth, Sandra. *The poverty of patriarchy theory* (Melbourne, Socialist Alternative 2006).
50 Socialist Homosexuals. "Manifesto of the Socialist Homosexuals", reprinted in *Lot's Wife*, 2 August 1976, pp.15–18.

11

BEATING BHP

The Wollongong Jobs for Women Campaign 1980–1991

Diana Covell

In 1980, a multi-cultural group of unemployed women in Wollongong made history when they challenged the 'Big Australian' BHP over sex discrimination in employment at the Port Kembla steelworks. They took up a political campaign that won hundreds of jobs for women in the steelworks and also became a major legal test case – the first class action of its kind in Australia. Despite all the odds, the women's case succeeded from the NSW Equal Opportunity Tribunal right through to the High Court of Australia and brought about changes to employment policies and practices and to workplace health and safety legislation affecting all Australian workers. After the High Court victory, negotiations began on behalf of 709 additional complainants in a representative action that was finally settled out of court in 1994.

This chapter is in two parts. Part 1 provides an account of the Wollongong Jobs for Women Campaign (WJFWC) in the political and industrial context of the 1980s; Part 2 examines the controversial role of the Socialist Workers Party (SWP)[1] in the WJFWC and the impact of the SWP's challenge to the leftwing Rank & File leadership in the Port Kembla Federated Ironworkers' 1982 elections.

Part 1: the Wollongong Jobs for Women Campaign in the 1980s

Wollongong, on the New South Wales coast south of Sydney, is a city built by immigrants. It developed as a boomtown around the industries of coal and steel, which since 1927, when the Hoskins brothers from Lithgow established the first blast furnace at Port Kembla,[2] have employed an overwhelmingly male workforce. One of the long-standing problems in the Illawarra region has been the shortage of employment opportunities for women.[3]

The Australian Government's post-war migration programs from the 1950s to the 1970s were primarily intended to bring skilled and non-skilled labour from

Britain and Europe to work on big engineering projects such as the Snowy Mountains Hydro-Electric Scheme and to boost the expansion of the steel industry in BHP's plants at Port Kembla, Newcastle and Whyalla. From the 1960s the majority of unskilled migrant labourers who came to work at Port Kembla and settled in Wollongong were from the former socialist republic of Yugoslavia.[4] However there were no jobs offered to women relatives who migrated with the men or soon afterwards.

Australia's biggest company, the Broken Hill Propriety – better known as BHP and now amalgamated with the British corporation Billiton – acquired its major subsidiary Australian Iron & Steel – now known as Bluescope Steel – in 1935 and from that time it steadily consolidated its monopoly control over the steel and coal mining industries. According to its own estimates, BHP accounted directly and indirectly for 71.6 per cent of the pay packets in the Illawarra in 1980–81.[5]

In April 1980, Australian Iron & Steel (AI&S) had a total workforce of 20,635. Of this number only 1,037 were women, including canteen workers, cleaners, typists, clerks, apprentices, cadets and professional staff. At the time, the company employed 15,518 production ironworkers and trades workers, the rest being clerical, professional, and consultant staff.[6] The steelworks had not retrenched workers at that point, and although a dirty and dangerous industry, it was widely regarded at the time as the most secure workplace in the Illawarra.

Furthermore, in production ironworker classifications, men and women were paid the same rate for the job, and AI&S was the only employer in the region still advertising for labour and hiring people every day. That is, they were hiring men. Although 2,061 women had applied to work at the steelworks from 1973 to 1980 they were routinely rejected, while men applying at the same times were regularly hired.[7]

On 20 April 1980, in response to higher than national average unemployment rates[8] for women and youth in the Illawarra region and the exploitation of this situation by unscrupulous employers, such as a take away chicken shop owner who sexually molested 41 teenage girls he had employed over a period of six months,[9] the Wollongong Working Women's Charter Committee[10] held a seminar on Women, Unemployment and Sexual Harassment. It was at this public forum that the Wollongong Jobs for Women Campaign was officially launched.

In the weeks that followed, 34 complaints were lodged with the NSW Anti-Discrimination Board (ADB) and the women began a campaign to win jobs at the Port Kembla steelworks. Most of these women were migrants from Macedonia, Croatia, Turkey, Chile and Greece.

The movement into non-traditional jobs

From the early 1970s the women's liberation movement called renewed attention to the marked sex segregation of the workforce and the inequalities experienced by women in terms of job opportunities, pay and promotion in Australia and in other OECD countries such as Canada and the United States.

In the United States, following the displacement of women by men returning from WWII, it took an affirmative action court order filed on 15 April 1974 before jobs would once again be opened up to women in the steel industry – this time on an equal footing with men.[11] However there were no similar sweeping affirmative action provisions that took into account women's exclusion or displacement and opened up blue-collar jobs in the steel industry or any other non-traditional occupations to women in Canada and Australia.

During the 1970s and early 1980s women in many countries around the world were challenging prevailing notions of 'femininity' and gender divisions in the workforce and taking up jobs in occupations and industries and public office that were traditionally regarded as men's jobs. The slogan popularised by the women's movement at the time was 'A woman's place is everywhere!'

Efforts to gain steelworks jobs in the 1970s

In 1973, a feminist group that had been formed the previous year in Wollongong protested against the refusal by AI&S to open up production and trades jobs for women. In one demonstration, women chained themselves to the fences inside the steelworks employment office gates. In another, four women slipped past the security guards and entered the works illegally half a mile away. With the help of men in the Communist Party of Australia (CPA), they stayed in the steelworks for a shift overnight, emerging next day with fists held high before the Fairfax press. A week later, AI&S employed the first women production ironworkers since the war.[12]

Slobodanka Joncevska and Rosika Tot, who both migrated from Macedonia and joined the WJFWC in 1980, gained jobs as labourers in the Port Kembla steelworks following the earlier women's protests in 1973. But the onset of the recession from 1976, combined with a lack of maternity provisions in awards, the absence of anti-discrimination laws, and propaganda suggesting married women were depriving their sons and daughters of jobs, forced most of the women who had recently gained jobs, including Rosika and Slobodanka, out of the steelworks.

Differences between the 1970s and 1980s campaigns

The 1973 campaign set an important precedent. As Illawarra campaigner Ruby Makula pointed out, "it raised local women's political consciousness and opened up the eyes of a lot of men, workers, husbands, to women's employment issues".[13] Yet there are certain key differences between the 1970s and 1980s campaigns worth noting.

Firstly, while the earlier women's protests took place in the economic boom period of the early 1970s when there was a shortage of labour, the Wollongong Jobs for Women Campaign began in early 1980 during an economic recession. Secondly, the 1980s campaign was able to utilise a greater range of political resources and infrastructure to empower its challenge to BHP following the introduction of the NSW Anti-Discrimination Act in 1977. Thirdly, unlike the

1973 protests, the 1980s campaign involved many culturally diverse women, with 28 of the initial 34 complainants being immigrants and all but one of those from non-English speaking countries. A further significant difference is that, unlike the earlier feminist protestors in 1973, all the women involved in the 1980s WJFWC sought and took up jobs in the steelworks themselves.

The SWP's 'turn to industry'

While the steelworks was an obvious target as the major employer in the region still advertising jobs but refusing to employ women, the decision to campaign for blue-collar jobs in steel in 1980 came about due to the ambitions of a small far left group, the Socialist Workers Party (SWP), which had recently embarked on a full scale "turn to industry", a radical change in focus from its previous anti-war, anti-nuclear, social liberation movement orientation.

Like its North American counterparts – the Socialist Workers Party USA and the Canadian Revolutionary Workers League – the Australian SWP was part of the Trotskyist Fourth International (FI United Secretariat), so-named to distance itself from the atrocities committed in the name of communism under Joseph Stalin and his followers in the Third International or 'Comintern'. At its world congress in 1979, the FI predicted that major class battles of the future would likely take place in 'basic' or 'heavy' industries that were strongly unionised and traditionally combative. Anticipating this scenario, the North American and Australian sections of the FI encouraged their existing members to get jobs in the steel, metal manufacturing, coal and transport industries and to recruit new members from these industries in order to participate more effectively in the struggles of the working class.[14]

The WJFWC was led from the outset by several committed socialist feminists, however most of these women resigned from the Socialist Workers Party by 1984 but continued to help lead the Campaign until the final outcome of the High Court ruling in 1991.

Labour movement and community support

The WJFWC gained strong support from the Port Kembla branch of the Federated Ironworkers Association (FIA) and the South Coast Labour Council, even though the women were unemployed and not union members at the time. In addition to eleven Members of Parliament and numerous individuals, over sixty organisations supported the Campaign including many unions, women's organisations, ALP branches and the peak national body, the Australian Council of Trade Unions (ACTU).

Among the far left organisations in 1980s Wollongong, the CPA and Socialist Party of Australia (SPA) branches as well as the SWP allowed the campaign group to add their party names to the list of Jobs for Women supporters in a leaflet produced at the time of mass sackings in 1983.

The Jobs for Women Tent Embassy

One of the highlights of the WJFWC in 1980 was the Jobs for Women tent embassy outside the steelworks opposite the AI&S employment office held on 3–5 July. A bright hand-painted banner demanding 'JOBS FOR WOMEN: OPEN THE GATES BHP' stretched across the footbridge linking the steelworks to Cringila railway station over the six-lane Five Islands Road. Information tables and tents were set up. Leaflets in English, Macedonian, Serbian, Turkish, Spanish and Greek were handed out at the two main steelworks gates at every shift change and over 2,500 signatures were collected from male steelworkers on a petition supporting women's right to work in the industry and condemning BHP's discriminatory hiring policies. Miners' union members brought a stove of coals to keep the protestors warm and the South Coast Labour Council (SCLC) organised a night security patrol. There was a poster advertising the public meeting planned to take place on 17 July 1980 at the Ironworkers Hall in Crown St, Wollongong and also a sign saying HONK FOR SUPPORT! AI&S was forced to close the employment office due to the rush of women applicants and the noise of horns from passing cars and trucks. Women who had been rejected at the employment office came across the road and joined the Campaign. As well as generating tremendous publicity and community support, the tent embassy was successful in pressuring the company into hiring as many as 64 women, although none of the initial complainants were among them.[15]

The 'weight limit' law

A month after the tent embassy, six of the complainants – Slobodanka Joncevska, Diana Covell, Louise Casson, Cheryl Bayford, Robynne Murphy and Lou-anne Barker – were invited to attend a 'conciliation' meeting at the NSW ADB offices in Sydney where attempts to resolve their complaints failed. Also present were AI&S representatives John Thirlwell and Peter Hilton, FIA officials Graham Roberts and Nando Lelli. It was at this meeting on 15 August 1980 that the women first heard the company's defense. AI&S claimed that women could not do most of the steelworks jobs, citing clause 5, section 36 of the New South Wales Factories, Shops and Industries Act (No. 43, 1962), which set a maximum load handling limit for women of 35lb or 16kilos and was introduced in 1912.[16]

The ADB President, Carmel Niland, subsequently commissioned feminist researcher Chloë Refshauge (now Chloë Mason) to conduct a survey of the application of the 'weight-limit' throughout the steelworks. The Port Kembla FIA provided statistics showing that 70% of all injuries at the steelworks were back injuries sustained by men who had no weight limit protection at all. The results of the ADB survey would become crucial evidence for the Jobs for Women complainants' legal action in 1984.

Jobs breakthrough!

By mid-1981, as a result of the political pressure and publicity generated by the Campaign and negotiations by the ADB President, over 300 women gained jobs at the Port Kembla steelworks (and 60 at BHP Newcastle). The Campaign opened up a greater range of classifications and job opportunities for women in the industry than ever before. Women were employed in 152 different job classifications, with men comprising 77% and women 23% of those positions.[17]

Once on the job, new women steelworkers received a mixed but mostly positive reaction from the men. However there were some AI&S managers and foremen who resented the women's 'intrusion' and placed those seen as 'ringleaders' of the Campaign as the only female on all male shifts.[18] Increased mechanisation since WWII had reduced any actual physical impediments to working in steel, but the introduction of new computerised technology, together with international competition, led to major downsizing in the steel industry from late 1982, reducing overall employment including the number of women's jobs.

The question of seniority

The Jobs for Women (JFW) campaigners tried to work out a strategy in relation to seniority that would not undercut their ability to build a united campaign with union support at a time when retrenchments were affecting men as well as women.

Having been denied equal opportunity with men for jobs in the first place, women were among the last to be hired and therefore, according to seniority principles, the first to be fired. So, as well as taking part in the unions' industrial action to defend jobs, the JFW campaigners decided to take BHP to court.

More complaints were filed with the Anti-Discrimination Board, claiming that the company had not only discriminated against them (directly) by denying them jobs but also that they were now suffering the (indirect) effects of previous discrimination in terms of loss of seniority and the threat of, or actual retrenchment. It was decided to demand recognition of retrospective seniority in the form of compensation for lost wages, status and future employment prospects. This strategy was seen as "extremely fair and workable" by the FIA Port Kembla leadership who were relieved that the WJFWC did not join the union as a party to their complaints.[19]

Retrenchments and the unions' fight back

On 18 October 1982, an urgent meeting of the JFW Action Committee voted to participate in the Port Kembla FIA's campaign to oppose BHP's coal and steel retrenchments and also to release a media statement and take food to the picket in solidarity with 31 miners at Kemira Colliery who had refused to leave the mine in protest and had been sacked at 4 am while 5 metres underground.

On 26 October 1982, a group of JFW campaigners, carrying their banner, joined the large contingent of steelworkers and miners from Wollongong who travelled by specially arranged trains to Canberra for the demonstration that became famous as the 'storming of Parliament House'.

AI&S began retrenching workers at the Port Kembla steelworks on 14 November 1982. In the event, retrenchments stopped at those who commenced work after 6 January 1981, so this meant that only eight of the JFW complainants were retrenched but most women who gained jobs as a result of the WJFWC remained employed. More than 100 women's jobs were saved thanks to the Port Kembla FIA's preference clause, which ensured job security for financial union members ahead of non-members, regardless of seniority.

"The fight back against unemployment by Wollongong's working class was so significant", writes Nick Southall, "that as leader of the Opposition, Bob Hawke travelled here on the last day of his election campaign, promising a crowd of 10,000, gathered in the Dapto Showground, that he would save the steel industry within one hundred days of winning office." [20]

The new Labor Government's Steel Plan

The three-term Liberal Coalition Government led by Malcolm Fraser was decisively defeated and Hawke's Labor Government was elected on a platform of 'jobs, jobs, jobs' on 11 March 1983. Less than a year later, PM Hawke and his cabinet claimed they had kept their promise of saving the steel industry, and proof of this was that BHP's steel division had contributed more than $72 million of the company's record $638 million profit in 1984. Hundreds of millions of taxpayers' dollars had been provided to the company, which had then invested in job-displacing technology.

Eight thousand people employed at AI&S in 1982 no longer worked there by early 1984, and although not all were retrenched, all left their jobs in a "climate of fear, threat and uncertainty that was completely without precedent". For the unemployed, the Hawke Government's claims seemed "dishonest at best and cynical at worst" as the Steel Industry Plan appeared to be nothing more than a ratification of BHP's restructuring process.[21]

The battle for legal aid

Following the rejection of their applications for legal aid from 24 March 1983, the JFW campaigners embarked on what would turn out to be a 16-month long battle to gain legal aid in order to be able to run their case against BHP.

After four applications, four rejections, four appeals and an extensive lobbying campaign, including a direct approach to Premier Wran, the NSW Legal Services Commission eventually granted funding for the women's legal action on 19 September 1984, to be effective from 13 September, the day after the first full hearing of the Equal Opportunity Tribunal.

Victory in court

The NSW Equal Opportunity Tribunal (EOT) handed down its decision on 30 September 1985. It upheld all the women's complaints, finding that BHP and its subsidiary AI&S had unlawfully discriminated against women in employment on a systematic basis since 1 June 1977. The Tribunal found that section 36 of the Factories, Shops & Industries Act was not a valid defence, that jobs regarded by the company as 'weight-barred' were not consistently selected and the company had employed women in some 'weight-barred' jobs in any case. It also found that the reverse gate seniority retrenchment system operated to disadvantage women in this case by continuing the effects of past discrimination.[22] All the women who were employed in the steelworks as a result of the WJFWC gained backdated seniority to the time of their original application and women who had been retrenched were reinstated, retaining their seniority. The only men with greater seniority who were retrenched were those who were not union members.

On the evening of the first judgement in favour of the women by the EOT in 1985, PM Hawke announced that Affirmative Action legislation would be introduced for the private sector, making it mandatory for companies employing more than 100 people to incorporate the policies in their employment practices.[23]

BHP appealed the EOT's decision in relation to compensation, estimated to be more than the ceiling of $40,000[24] for eight women who had been retrenched. The NSW Court of Appeal dismissed the company's appeal in 1986. BHP appealed again. The case was then referred to the High Court of Australia where it was heard before the full bench between 3 May and 5 December 1989. Finally, in early 1991, Justices Deane, Dawson and Gaudron announced a majority decision to dismiss BHP's appeal and uphold the women's complaints. The women were awarded a combined total of $1.4 million. Most of this was for lost wages, calculated individually, as well as a small sum each ($500) for damages.

One of the most significant outcomes of the test case was to bring about changes to section 36 of the NSW Factories, Shops and Industries Act. As a result of the Wollongong Jobs for Women challenge to BHP's discriminatory hiring practices, the law that had been designed and used to prevent women's entry into male dominated industries was transformed and neutralised into workplace health and safety guidelines that now provide equitable manual handling protection for all Australian workers, regardless of gender.

Part 2: the role of the SWP in the 1982 Port Kembla Federated Ironworkers' elections and the Jobs for Women Campaign

A consistent feature of Wollongong's history has been its association with industrial militancy and an unusually strong leftwing regional peak trade union body, the South Coast Labour Council (SCLC). Most unions that became well established in the region from the 1930s were either communist or left-ALP led and the CPA maintained a strong branch in the region from the 1930s to 1990.[25]

The Federated Ironworkers' Association (FIA)[26] has a colourful history among unions in the Illawarra with sharp swings from left to right and back again. In 1951, the national Communist leadership of Ernie Thornton's team was captured by Laurie Short's rightwing ALP Industrial 'groupers'. In 1952 Short entrenched his control of the FIA with election defeats for communist officials in every branch. The SCLC lost its largest affiliate until December 1970 when a left-ALP Rank & File team won control of the FIA Port Kembla branch. Ferdinando 'Nando' Lelli, an Italian migrant who was part of the successful left challenge, became Secretary of the Port Kembla FIA from 1972–1990 and was the first from a non-English speaking background to achieve a leadership position in any Australian union.[27]

By the time of the 1982 elections, the Port Kembla Rank & File team led the only leftwing branch of the FIA and by far the largest, with 280 delegates. In contrast to the 'activist' nature of the Port Kembla branch, the FIA nationally and in the Newcastle and Sydney branches was seen as a 'company union' to the extent of actively collaborating with BHP in submissions to the Industrial Commission.[28]

The new SWP branch in Wollongong

In 1978, following the 'turn to industry' decision of the annual SWP conference, Andrew Jamieson, Chris Jones and Diana Covell moved to Wollongong to set up a new branch of the party. Both Jamieson and Jones were employed at the steelworks within days of their first application. Covell, finding herself among many other women being regularly rejected for jobs at the steelworks and elsewhere, set about establishing contacts for what would become the Jobs for Women Campaign and joined local women's organisations such as the International Women's Day Committee and the Wollongong Working Women's Charter Committee. By early 1980, the SWP branch numbers had grown with a couple of new recruits and more inter-city arrivals including Louise Casson, Robynne Murphy and Lou-anne Barker who also helped to build the Jobs for Women campaign following its launch on 20 April that year.

Phillip Walker arrived in Wollongong in early 1979 and got a job in the steelworks straight away. He worked mainly in the Plate Mill for five years and led a successful four-week strike to bring about equitable roster conditions, known as the '6-day' dispute. As a result, he earned a good reputation as a union militant and became part of the Port Kembla FIA R&F Committee. By early 1981, Peter Davison, Andres Garin, Chris Jones and Diana Covell had also been elected as FIA delegates and the WJFWC had won more than 300 women's jobs in the industry, gaining support within the steelworks and in the wider community.

The activities of this small influx of Trotskyists into the highly industrialised and strongly unionised city were observed by the established local labour movement with both curiosity and wariness, although some of the younger CPA set were openly hostile from the start. Gradually, as it became clear that the SWP branch leaders were willing to work with and accept advice from more seasoned local unionists and to help build local industrial and women's campaigns and events in a constructive way, the general attitude towards the Wollongong SWP branch activists changed to "acceptance and in some cases, respect".[29]

In 1982, when restructuring had begun ahead of the announced retrenchments, the Port Kembla FIA R&F team approached some of the SWP delegates to join their ticket in the forthcoming FIA elections and strengthen their fight against the sackings. It is fair to say that the SWP members who joined the Port Kembla FIA R&F Committee were broadly in agreement with the industrial policies of the Lelli-Roberts leadership. One area where there was disagreement concerned protective tariffs on steel, which the SWP opposed. However in relation to other issues, including total opposition to retrenchments and the need to mount a fight back campaign, support for nationalisation of BHP, opposition to sex discrimination in employment and support for rank and file union control, any differences were "matters of detail rather than principle".[30]

The SWP's 'Militant Action Campaign'

Suddenly, in the midst of efforts by the steel and mining unions to organise mass meetings at Wollongong Showground and protest the retrenchments in coal and steel through a series of rolling stoppages and 'lightning' strikes, the SWP national leadership "threw a political bombshell"[31], announcing that the SWP would run a ticket against the Port Kembla FIA R&F leadership in the 1982 union elections.

A leaflet headed *ONE OUT, ALL OUT*, written by the SWP national secretary, Jim Percy, was delivered in bundles to the Wollongong branch with instructions to hand it out at the next mass meeting. The leaflet attacked "the phoney Rank-and-File group in Port Kembla" stating "our union officials are getting in the way of our unions standing up to the BHP". It called for mass meetings of steelworkers at Port Kembla to support *an indefinite stoppage for nationalisation of the steel industry under workers' control* to resist the retrenchments.

Aside from the dishonest and abrasive style of this leaflet, the possibility of getting mass support for an indefinite strike was unlikely. As Phillip Walker has pointed out, the tactic of an indefinite strike was "unsustainable – but the fact that the SWP raised it in such a sectarian way meant that it was not a tactic anyone would support".[32]

The SWP Political Committee met in late August 1982 to consider the party's intervention in the FIA elections. The discussion took place over a period of three days and only SWP 'full' national committee members took part. This excluded most of the Wollongong steel fraction, including the fraction leaders, Phillip Walker and Diana Covell. Some of the Wollongong steelworker members were opposed to standing against the Port Kembla R&F ticket from the outset, pointing to possible negative repercussions for the Jobs for Women Campaign, while others expressed strong reservations about what seemed such an obviously contrived political stance. However most were too intimidated to speak at the national steel fraction involving Wollongong, Newcastle, Adelaide and Sydney members in a meeting with Jim Percy on 12 September when the final decision was made. In the end, a majority voted to run a ticket called 'the Militant Action Campaign' in Port Kembla when the SWP leadership agreed to also stand candidates against the rightwing FIA officials nationally and in Newcastle in the union postal ballot (17 November – 6 December, 1982).

The Militant Action Campaign (MAC) did not develop as any rank and file or grassroots movement among steelworkers. It was essentially a platform for the SWP national leadership to intervene in the Port Kembla FIA elections. It was obvious that the MAC ticket put together by the SWP national committee was not a serious challenge to the Port Kembla R&F team. Even the most unquestioning and thick-skinned Wollongong comrades flinched with embarrassment when the lead MAC candidate for national secretary, a hastily recruited Turkish immigrant with limited political or industrial experience and hesitant English, participated in a live debate with Nando Lelli on local radio.

Nevertheless, a speech given by SWP national secretary Jim Percy to a plenum of the National Committee on 11 October 1982, indicates just how seriously he regarded the MAC and, at the same time, how removed his view was from the actual alignment of forces at Port Kembla:

> This may not be the decisive battle in which the ruling class tries to smash the FIA, that's for sure. But how we do in this battle that the FIA is engaged in today, or how we do in trying to get the FIA to engage in a battle and the role we play in that is going to be very important in terms of our standing in the working class and in terms of the development and training of our cadre, in terms of how we move ahead on both levels in regard to other tendencies. It is going to have a very big impact on what sort of role we are going to play in the decisive battles down the road and therefore on the outcome of the big battles down the road. So these preparatory battles are very important for us. Our general task in this period, of course, is to win hegemony of the workers' vanguard.[33]

The MAC election broadsheet headed *WHY OUR UNION NEEDS A NEW LEADERSHIP* claimed:

> Twelve years of the Lelli bunch is enough. Their policies may have been acceptable as far as they went in the past but in the difficult years ahead, they will be disastrous. They have stopped fighting for us and have done little more than follow the lead of the national officials. Our problem is that it's hard to fight the boss when our officials are against us. That's why we need to change the leadership at the Port Kembla branch as well as get rid of our current national officials.[34]

It's not surprising that the R&F team were livid. As Phillip Walker points out, "When you look back at the jobs crisis, the only place where there was a fight back was in Wollongong. There was a democratisation of the union membership in the process – but the party and the comrades who'd been working in steel lost the ear of the FIA officials and the delegates." Walker's view is that the MAC was an act of "political suicide". The SWP "could have extended its support base and could have influenced the Port Kembla FIA leadership from within the Rank and File team" he says, in terms of tactics and in helping to organise the members, but instead "the SWP blew the work that was being done effectively in an act of ultra left stupidity".[35]

FIA Port Kembla R&F Organiser, Paul Matters, regarded the SWP's electoral challenge as being "totally the wrong strategy at the time" and says "it was quite obvious after a while that there was a political agenda being driven by the external national SWP leadership itself and that was the big thing that was impermissible. We had to run an election campaign against two opponents – which was a nightmare".[36]

The South Coast Labour Council made a unanimous decision to support the Rank and File ticket against the Militant Action Campaign. The apparent left split in the Port Kembla FIA delighted the rightwing national leadership. The outcome of the ballot was that the R&F team swept the board in Port Kembla. The best few of the MAC candidates received 20% of the vote at the Port Kembla branch committee level. Only about 300 R&F supporters voted for the MAC nationally and 2,400 preferred the right wing to the MAC. In Newcastle the right won by about six to one against the MAC. The margins in favour of the right were even bigger nationally, allowing the Short–Hurrell leadership to claim their "greatest union election victory ever".[37]

As a result of its sectarian role in the FIA elections, the SWP was isolated and regarded as 'wreckers' by the Wollongong left. Worse still, the developing national opposition to the Short–Hurrell rightwing leadership of the FIA was disrupted due to time and resources being diverted to respond to the unexpected MAC ticket, and, in a relatively short time, all but one of the SWP steelworkers left the industry and by early 1984, most of the Wollongong SWP branch, including the JFWC coordinator, had left the Party. Clearly, it was not the outcome the SWP national leadership had sought.

Veteran Illawarra MP George Petersen's stinging rebuke of the SWP/DSP for its actions in the 1982 Port Kembla FIA elections, written in 1998 and later posted on the *Ozleft* website[38] reflects the sense of outrage of the region's left. He asks: Why did the SWP do it? The reply on behalf of the SWP/DSP national executive and published in *Green Left Weekly* six months later does not really answer this question. Allen Myers writes: "No one in the Militant Action Campaign expected the ticket to win. The campaign was not about getting union offices, but about building a fight-back against BHP."[39]

Petersen's next question is: "If that was the case, why did all the SWP members except Robynne Murphy give up employment at the steelworks after the elections?" The answer to that is that almost every other Wollongong comrade at the time felt undermined by the party leadership's decisions, from which they had been largely excluded, and exasperated that the years of work they had carried out in good faith in the steelworks, together with the good will and cooperation they had established with the most leftwing elements in the union and the local labour movement had been so recklessly and needlessly destroyed. It was the Wollongong branch members who bore the brunt of the fallout from the SWP leadership's ultra left intervention in the Port Kembla FIA elections and, as a result, the party lost a number of capable, experienced union militants and hitherto dedicated cadres. With their departure, the party lost its main base in the steel industry and with one isolated member remaining in the steelworks it was unable to carry out effective work.

The whole 'top down' operation of the MAC, driven by the SWP national secretary and endorsed by the national committee, was in many ways indicative of more general problems within the party and its approach to other sections of the labour movement.

A post SWP/DSP assessment

In July 2002, around 30 former members of the SWP/DSP and several other leftists with a Trotskyist background met to discuss and attempt to develop a collective assessment of the SWP/DSP's role in the 1982 FIA elections, the WJFWC and other industrial and political experiences. The two day seminar held in Carlton, Sydney, came about because of the SWP/DSP's continuing refusal to acknowledge specific mistakes or take any responsibility for the political, industrial and human costs of its various sectarian grabs for power. After hearing a "bizarre justification" presented at a DSP conference in 2000 regarding the MAC in the 1982 Port Kembla FIA elections, Bob Gould, whose history with the Percy brothers (John and Jim) dates back to the anti-Vietnam war rallies they helped to build in the 1960s, observed: "Internal DSP mythology presents this disastrous piece of industrial adventurism as a great achievement."[40]

Those who attended the 2002 seminar who had been involved in the Wollongong experience were keen to unravel what had motivated the then SWP leadership, and particularly Jim Percy, in forcing on the steelworkers' fraction a course that was clearly going to smash up the working relationship established with the leftwing leaders of the Port Kembla FIA, and would potentially have negative effects on the WJFWC. After a lengthy discussion, the general view was that the self-perpetuation of the 'party' was of paramount concern to its domineering national secretary who was afraid that Wollongong members in the steelworks would be drawn out of party activity into mainly union activity if elected as part of the R&F ticket. So running a ticket against the R&F union leadership was a deliberate way of preventing that from happening as well as providing a propaganda platform. However the departure of all but one SWP member from the Port Kembla steelworks and the virtual disintegration of the Wollongong branch were unforseen and undesired consequences of Percy's political opportunism.

It is also true that there was a disjunction between the national secretary's grandiose vision of the SWP/DSP 'winning hegemony of the workers' vanguard' – an impossible mission with only a few hundred members and no mass base – and the more closely focussed views of the comrades who were engaged in the daily issues confronting them and others in the steelworks and who were developing confidence as union militants that was not reliant on direction from the party hierarchy.

In retrospect it seems clear, as Steve Painter says, that Jim Percy "wasn't willing to trust the main comrades in the steel industry" and sought to maintain control at all costs. As Painter has acknowledged, the SWP national executive, of which he was a member, was strongly influenced at the time by the US SWP, led by Jack Barnes, and the Fourth International, to which the SWP was affiliated. Both sides of the FI had a "quite mechanical" approach to trade unions, he says, and while "it's true that the ranks need to keep an eye on what the union leadership is doing", there was "a feeling that there was something inherently corrupting about being in the leadership of a union". He describes the SWP's 'turn to industry' as "artificial, a messy project" that was "wrong in a whole of ways, particularly when it came to the MAC".[41]

The SWP abandoned both the turn to industry and its association with the US SWP by late 1983 and disaffiliated from the Fourth International in 1985. In a talk given by Jim Percy in January 1986, the following came closest to anything resembling regret for the mistakes made during the 'turn':

> Because our tactics were based on a wrong political assessment, we paid an overhead price. We disoriented and mis-educated comrades, telling them that the political mood of the working class would shift decisively in a relatively short time. When we make a prediction like that and it doesn't happen, comrades naturally lose confidence in the party and perhaps also in the working-class struggle as a whole. Those were the most negative aspects of our experience with the turn.[42]

Apart from Percy's obfuscation of facts and events, the above statement contains the SWP/DSP leadership's habitual dismissive explanation that those who have left the party – whether or not it is acknowledged that they either resigned or were expelled after having raised a variety of political and/or tactical differences – are likely to be 'lost' to the left movement altogether.

Writing in 2002 around the time of the ex-members seminar, 'CW', an SWP/DSP member in Brisbane, addressed the question of 'lost' members rather differently:

> [The] lack of real democracy and the lack of the cut-and-thrust of open debate (without repercussions) has driven a lot of people out of the party, people who should have remained members. Our ex-members now tally in the thousands. I am not saying all of them would have necessarily remained involved but our internal culture has forced a dreadful toll on the size of our membership. We must ask ourselves why we have remained at 300 members for over 30 years?

224 Diana Covell

There has to be an answer and it's not the glib one of members getting too tired or demoralised or becoming bourgeois because they might own a house or a car. An example of this is our continuing preoccupation with our ex-members. We have to accept we are partly responsible for their psychological problems, because of our past rigidity, bureaucratic methods of operation and psychological manipulation of individuals, withholding of information and so on. Let them have their conference on the DSP. They have a right to discuss whatever they feel they have to discuss, who cares? [43].

"In political cults", Tourish and Wohlforth point out, "growth is universally sacrificed in the interests of control."[44] The internal life of the SWP/DSP, as described by 'CW', and the ways in which complaints about sexual harassment by Jim Percy and a few other male leaders were (not) dealt with or how political factions and disagreements were handled within the party – by ostracism or expulsion respectively – substantially matches the criteria for leftwing political cults set out by Tourish and Wohlforth: "authoritarianism, conformity, ideological rigidity, and a fetishistic dwelling on apocalyptic fantasies".[45]

The SWP's controversial role in the WJFWC

Fortunately for the Wollongong women who had worked in the steelworks after winning jobs there through the WJFWC and who continued to help lead the Campaign after leaving the SWP, the transition to life outside the party was eased by friends within the women's and union movements. The main problem these ex-members had to face was the sectarian behaviour of the SWP who, confronted with the fact that they had lost the JFWC coordinator and other leading activists, carried out various attempts to undermine them and divide the JFW Campaign group in order to exert some influence on the Campaign.

In early 1984, for instance, not long before the start of the NSW EOT hearings, the SWP tried to re-gain some influence in the campaign by proposing that an unspecified member of the SWP's national executive should be accepted as a 'proxy' member of the Jobs for Women Action Committee (JFWAC) and allowed to speak and vote in Campaign meetings. When this proposal was explained via interpreters and put to a full meeting of the JFWAC, it was unanimously rejected as it contravened the democratically agreed ground rules for membership accepted by all the women complainants.

In another example of underhand tactics, one remaining Wollongong SWP member involved in the JFW Campaign alleged that the coordinator, the publicity officer and a Macedonian organiser were conspiring to "rip off" Campaign funds. When this was drawn to the attention of the coordinator, a special Jobs for Women Action Committee meeting was called, all the Campaign account keeping records and bank statements were tabled and, with the help of interpreters, the falsified 'evidence' put together by the SWP member was exposed. Once all the campaign members were satisfied that there were receipts for all reimbursements paid to the publicity officer and that no money was missing and the bank account was earning interest, the women were so outraged by the SWP member's trickery that they decided to remove her as one of the account signatories and voted her off the Campaign funds committee.

Despite these and other attempts by the SWP to undermine the ex-members who continued to help lead the WJFWC, the overwhelming majority of the Campaign group held together and kept any sectarian disturbances away from the media and out of the court.

The SWP's sectarian behaviour "certainly created a problem" for steel unions. However, as Paul Matters makes clear:

> We didn't take the view: let's do over the women because of the SWP's intervention in the elections. The FIA Port Kembla branch supported the Jobs for Women campaign because it was the right thing to do. The fact that the majority of women involved were migrants did not in itself change the fact that the branch supported it but it helped to make it possible to justify support for it too.[46]

Conclusion

As many in the broad left may recognise, the WJFWC was never just a front group for the SWP and the SWP was certainly not the main source of expertise when it came to campaign strategy, legal matters and industrial concerns. From the very start, the WJFWC involved seasoned union leaders such as Peggy Errey and Fay Campbell, senior public service feminists, particularly ADB President Carmel Niland, OH&S researcher Chloë Refshauge and solicitors from PIAC who provided constructive advice and helped shape its development. Similarly, the advice and expertise of barrister John Basten was critical to the success of the legal action against BHP. Likewise, the WJFWC benefited from the support of the Port Kembla FIA – an organisation skilled in negotiating, defending its members and doing battle with BHP.

As well as gender and class, ethnicity was a factor that shaped the WJFWC. Essential to its success and sustainability for over a decade was the trust and mutual respect established between the women of different cultural and linguistic backgrounds involved, and the support of local migrant communities. The WJFWC drew on existing migrant support structures and resources, including the Illawarra Migrant Resource Centre, to help provide information and facilitate communication between its different language groups.

Political demonstrations and symbolic acts right outside the steelworks attracted strong media interest. Confronting BHP directly – through the tent embassy in particular – won the WJFWC more support than anything else and pressured the company into employing women as well. The result was not only a social movement protest but also an event that had industrial impact.

The JFWC took on the biggest, most ruthless employer in Australia – so BHP's defeat had "significant implications within the capitalist class". After the JFW case

226 Diana Covell

won, every employer of any size and substance in Australia was put on notice that if there was a way to accommodate any non-discriminatory employment strategy they should include it. As Matters points out:

> BHP fought all the way to the High Court because its whole industrial strategy was not to be seen to be defeated. BHP was fighting for the right of capital to control, to manage. The JFW campaign challenged that directly and even more rarely, BHP was defeated in a straight out confrontation.[47]

The Wollongong Jobs for Women Campaign remains one of the most successful campaigns initiated by members of a far left group in Australia since WWII. So it is not surprising that the remnants of the SWP/DSP, now Socialist Alliance, want to claim it – as evidenced by their book.[48] Yet in reality, the Campaign's success was due to a range of factors almost entirely outside the SWP/DSP. Most important of these were: the collective leadership of the political campaign and legal action; the reciprocal relations negotiated with compatible social networks, agencies and organisations; the specific actions, media events and legal outcomes that changed the perceived balance of power for women and all workers within the workplace; and the political and industrial alignment of forces in Wollongong during the 1980s.

The legacy of the SWP/DSP highlights not only the pitfalls of sectarian ultra-leftism but also the crisis of leadership and dangers of political cultism common to the contemporary far left. As former US SWP member Peter Camejo has written: "Lenin's concept of a 'party' has no meaning without a mass base" and "without differences, debate and a really open, democratic culture a movement can easily adopt positions disconnected from reality".[49]

Notes

1 The SWP changed its name to the Democratic Socialist Party (DSP) in 1989 and then became the Democratic Socialist Perspective in 2003 before merging into the Socialist Alliance in 2010.
2 Erik Eklund, *Steel Town: the making and breaking of Port Kembla*, Melbourne University Press, Carlton, Victoria, 2002, p.19.
3 Marie Flood, Leigh Baker and Helen Meekosha, *Migrant and Refugee Women Outworkers in the Clothing Industry in the Illawarra: A report to the Law Foundation of NSW*, Illawarra Migrant Resource Centre, Wollongong, 1982, p.14
4 Michael Quinlan, 'Immigrant Workers, Trade Union Organization and Industrial Strategy', PhD thesis University of Sydney, 1982, p.485.
5 Julianne Schultz, *Steel City Blues: the human cost of industrial crisis*, Penguin Books, Ringwood, Victoria, 1985, p.15.
6 Australian Iron & Steel Pty Ltd, 'Employment Situation as at month ended April 1980', *Labour Statement No. 1*, Exhibit 44, Najdovska & Others v Australian Iron & Steel, NSW Equal Opportunity Tribunal hearing 1984–85.
7 NSW Anti-Discrimination Board, *Protective Legislation at Work: A case study of the 'weight limit' on manual handling*, April 1984, p.49.
8 ABS 1981 Census figures show Australia's official unemployment rate of registered unemployed stood at 7.8 per cent whereas in the Wollongong electorate of Cunningham, the rate was 39.3 per cent.

9 '41 Girls in Six Months: Unionists accuse shop boss', *Illawarra Mercury*, 30 January 1980, p.1.

10 Local branch of a national network to lobby the ACTU to adopt a Charter of Rights for Working Women, supported by the South Coast Labour Council.

11 Mary Margaret Fonow, *Union Women: Forging feminism in the United Steelworkers of America*, University of Minnesota Press, Minneapolis, 2003, p.7.

12 Megan McMurchy, Margot Oliver and Jeni Thornley, *For Love or Money*, Penguin, Victoria 1983, pp.3, 151.

13 Ruby Makula, quoted in Anne Deveson, *Faces of Change*, ABC Books, Fontana, 1984, p.160.

14 Mary-Alice Waters, 'Fourth International Decides on Turn to Industry', *Major Resolutions and Reports of the 1979 World Congress of the Fourth International*, Intercontinental Press/Inprecor, New York 1980, pp.3–6.

15 Diana Covell and Chloe Refshauge, 'The Biased Australian', in *Scarlet Woman*, no 21, 1986, pp.18–22.

16 NSW Anti-Discrimination Board, *Protective Legislation at Work: A case study of the 'weight limit' on manual handling*, April 1984, p.17.

17 NSW Anti-Discrimination Board, *Protective Legislation at Work*, p.60.

18 For a detailed account of women campaigners' experience in the steelworks see: Diana Covell, 'Who's that in the hard hat? Women into steel in Canada and Australia', in Pierre Actil, André Loiselle & Christopher Rolfe (eds), *Canada Exposed/Le Canada à découvert*, P.I.E-Peter Lang S.A. Éditions Scientifiques Internationales; 1 edition August 2009, pp.101–116.

19 Paul Matters interviewed 31 January 2009.

20 Nick Southall, 'The WOW Factor: Wollongong's unemployed and the dispossession of class and history', https://revoltsnow.wordpress.com/2010/08/23/the-wow-factor-wollongong%E2%80%99s-unemployed-and-the-dispossession-of-class-and-history-2/

21 Julianne Schultz, *Steel City Blues: the human cost of industrial crisis*, Penguin, 1985, pp.ix–x.

22 EOT Ruling, *Najdovska & Ors v. Australian Iron & Steel Pty Ltd* (1985), pp.92–140.

23 Chris Ronalds, *Affirmative Action and Sex Discrimination: A handbook on legal rights for women*, Pluto Press, Sydney and London, 1987, p.23.

24 Following settlement of further JFW complaints in 1993, recommendations by the NSW Law Reform Commission led to the anti-discrimination damages ceiling being raised to $100,000.

25 Raymond Markey and Shirley Nixon, 'Peak Unions in the Illawarra', in B. Ellem, R. Markey, J. Shields (eds), *Peak Unions in Australia: Origins, Purpose, Power, Agency*, The Federation Press, Leichhardt, 2004, p.173.

26 From 1991, the FIA amalgamated with several other manufacturing and engineering unions, merging finally in 1993 with the Australian Workers Union, as it is now known.

27 Robert Murray and Kate White, *The Ironworkers: A history of the Federated Ironworkers Association of Australia*, Hale & Ironmonger, 1982, pp.302–304.

28 Paul Matters, interviewed 31 January 2009.

29 Paul Matters, interviewed 31 January 2009.

30 George Petersen, 'Sectarianism and the Socialist Workers Party', *Ozleft*. https://ozleft.wordpress.com/2002/09/27/sectarianismandswp/

31 George Petersen, Ibid.

32 Phillip Walker, interviewed 20 November 2004.

33 Jim Percy, 'Preparing the Party to Meet the Crisis' in *Building the Revolutionary Party: Selected Writings 1980–1987*, Resistance Books, Sydney, 2008, p.65.

34 Militant Action Campaign FIA election broadsheet, November 1982.

35 Phillip Walker, interviewed 20 November 2004.

36 Paul Matters, interviewed 31 January, 2009.

37 George Petersen, https://ozleft.wordpress.com/2002/09/27/sectarianismandswp/

38 George Petersen, Ibid.

39 Allen Myers, quoted in 'Sectarianism and the SWP' by George Petersen, *Ozleft* website, 27/9/2002.

40 Bob Gould, '*John Percy's Industrial Philosopher's Stone*', *Ozleft*, website 2 April, 2005. http s://www.marxists.org/archive/gould/2005/20050402b.htm
41 Steve Painter, interviewed 2 November 2016.
42 Jim Percy, 'Recent experiences in party building – settling accounts with the turn to industry', speech given at 11th annual SWP Conference, 1986, in *Building the Revolutionary Party: Selected Writings 1980–1987*, Resistance Books, Sydney, 2008, p.88.
43 'CW', 'The future of the Socialist Alliance and our Trotskyist sectarian past', *Ozleft*. http s://ozleft.wordpress.com/2002/12/21/futureofsocialistallianceandourtrotskyist-past/
44 Dennis Tourish and Tim Wohlforth, *On the Edge: political cults right and left*, M.E. Sharpe, New York, 2000, p.152.
45 Tourish and Wohlforth, Ibid., p.213.
46 Paul Matters, interviewed 31 January 2009.
47 Paul Matters, interviewed 31 January 2009.
48 Carla Gorton and Pat Brewer, *Women of Steel: gender, jobs & justice at BHP*, Resistance Books, Sydney, 2015.
49 Peter Camejo, 'Return to materialism', *Ozleft*. https://ozleft.wordpress.com/2003/12/29/returntomaterialism/

PART 4

Mainstreaming the far left

12

HALCYON DAYS?

The Amalgamated Metal Workers' Union and the Accord

Elizabeth Humphrys

We are in the midst of the 30th anniversary of the period of the Accord social contract between the Australian Labor Party (ALP) and the Australian Council of Trade Unions (ACTU), which lasted from 1983 to 1996. The Accord was a national agreement on economic policy that profoundly reshaped the Australian political economy during the Hawke and Keating governments. The parties involved nowadays commonly view the Accord era as the high point of relations between the ALP and ACTU, and as being beneficial to workers in a period marked by the anti-worker policies of the New Right overseas. For many in the ALP and the trade unions these remain halcyon days, awash with electoral successes only dreamed of in a contemporary era of low ALP primary votes, declining party and union membership, and the consolidation of a political challenger to the left of Labor in the form of the Australian Greens. Yet it was also an era where a Labour government, with the direct collaboration of the union movement, introduced a full suite of neoliberal economic reforms while workers acceded to a systematic, government-led program of real wage cuts – a process which bureaucratised, weakened and hollowed out previously powerful and militant union organisation.

In recent years there have been calls for a new social contract between the unions and government from members of the ALP and the labour movement. These calls turn attention to the strategy of the Accord in the 1980s and 1990s, and of the role of far-left unions in backing or fighting it. Support for the Accord on the far left was not universal with a small number of union state branches opposing it, and small numbers of workers and activist organisations publicly campaigning against it.[1] However, dissent was among a minority of workers who were largely disconnected from each other, and unable to alter the direction of the union movement away from supporting the social contract.

The Accord was possible because the Communist Party of Australia (CPA) unions at the centre of the labour movement backed it; with the party by far the

232 Elizabeth Humphrys

most influential far left formation inside the workers' movement in the period leading up to the signing of the social contract. Without the backing, in particular, of the CPA-aligned Amalgamated Metal Workers' Union (AMWU)[2], the most powerful union in Australia during that period, the Accord would not have been possible.[3] As such, analysis of the AMWU's role in the Accord provides a distinctive 'window' for considering the development and implementation of the social contract.[4]

This chapter explores four moments of the AMWU's involvement in the Accord. Section one of the chapter considers why the AMWU broke with its strategy of workplace and rank-and-file militancy to support a centralised state-led economic project. The second section considers the immediate reshaping of the Accord through the 1983 Economic Summit and its Communiqué. Section three details the *Australia Reconstructed* initiative in 1985, which sought to reinvigorate the corporatist element of the Accord within the ALP's roll out of neoliberal policy. The fourth section considers the motivation of the AMWU in seeking the implementation of enterprise bargaining from 1991 to 1993, a strategy on the surface at odds with the Accord's focus on centralised wage setting. The analysis reveals the difficulties for the AMWU in realising the implementation of the original Accord, and the impact on the rank and file organising that was a hallmark of the union through the 1970s.

The context for the Accord

The CPA began as a socialist organisation inspired by the Russian Revolution, and existed from 1920 to 1991. Although the CPA remained small, and had little electoral success, it was by far the largest political formation to the left of the ALP and was influential in trade unions and social movements. The CPA was traditionally closer to the mainstream than similar parties overseas, and by the 1960s it was criticising the Soviet invasion of Czechoslovakia while being increasingly Eurocommunist in orientation.[5] By 1975 the CPA had developed in a more general 'New Left' radical orientation.[6] The CPA viewed the strategy for socialism as one where the state would be transformed from the inside, by becoming 'the instrument for rule of the majority of people led by the working class', beginning to 'wither away because its function to ensure domination of one class over others disappears as class division, exploitation and human oppression are abolished'.[7]

During the long boom following the end of the Second World War, workers' confidence was boosted by steadily increasing affluence and close to full employment. In this period a new generation of union militants had emerged, and between 1967 and 1969 the number of strike days doubled.[8] Laurie Aarons, Secretary of CPA, stated in 1969 that the 'time has come for a determined, militant confrontation with the employer-arbitration-Government class structure'.[9] The CPA won a number of key union elections in the period that followed, and Australia's most intense period of industrial militancy commenced – with the AMWU playing the leading role. The successes of the union movement in the 1970s included an increased wages share of national income, which rose from under 55 per cent (in the late 1960s) to over to 62 per cent by March 1975. Although, as we will see below, the social contract disorganised the labour movement and was detrimental for AMWU, it was initially the union's successes and rank and file power that positioned it as a necessary partner in any national economic program.

The Hawke Government was elected on a platform of implementing the Accord social contract. The agreement sought to address stagflation by tackling upward wage pressure. In return for the labour movement voluntarily moderating wage claims, the government agreed to policies including full wage indexation to inflation, industry policy focused on increasing employment, a more progressive taxation system and an expanded social wage. The social contract set out a broad and comprehensive economic plan. The aim of the Accord was 'to ensure that living standards of wage and salary earners and non-income earning sectors of the population requiring protection [were] maintained and through time increased with movements in national productivity.'[10]

The Accord returned the Australian industrial relations system to centralised wage setting with full indexation, after its breakdown during the Fraser Liberal (conservative) government. The parties agreed that 'government policy should be applied to prices and all income groups, rather than, as has often been the case, to wages alone'.[11] The agreement established a process of continuous consultation between the ALP and the ACTU, to be embedded and supported at all levels of government. The Accord established 'a representative tripartite body [including government, business and unions] which [had] responsibility for advising on the prices and incomes policy and for monitoring and discussing problems associated with the implementation'.[12]

While the agreement – taken as a whole – was broad and covered a range of policy areas, at heart it focused on wage restraint to reduce inflation; increase growth; decrease industrial action; and address unemployment (but not with the aim of restoring full employment in the short term). Its central goal was to ensure that the next period of growth did not lead to a 'wages explosion', and to achieve this through a collaborative process with the trade union movement.

The Accord was signed after a decade of failed attempts, by successive Australian governments, to resolve the economic crisis of the 1970s. Despite unions formally exchanging a promise of wage and industrial restraint for various economic benefits to the working class, in practice these sacrifices were rewarded with aggressive state-led neoliberalisation of the national economy. Many of the promised progressive elements of the Accord were not implemented, and others – such as industry policy – were recast to fit in with the increasingly neoliberal trajectory of the ALP.[13]

Incorporating the AMWU

In the 1970s the AMWU was the largest and most powerful trade union in Australia. The fitter's wage rate in the metals industry acted as the benchmark in arbitration of award wage and condition rates, and the AMWU was at the leading edge of industrial struggle with the gains it made in shop floor industrial action often flowing on to other segments of the workforce. Without the sanction and ongoing support of the AMWU the social contract could not have been implemented.

For the Accord to be agreed to, the left and CPA-aligned unions had to be brought inside the social contract. And for the Accord to be successful, it had to suppress the industrial action of unions characterised by militancy throughout the 1970s and early 1980s. Bringing militant unions inside the Accord required a significant shift in the manner in which these unions approached labour organising, and for the AMWU it involved a radical break with its previous strategy of local organising. In the early 1970s, the AMWU achieved increased real wages through industrial action and this contributed to an increased wages share of national income.[14] The AMWU industrial approach, based around 'hot shops', saw campaigns mounted at the best-organised sites with a 'trickle-down' effect to the rest of the industry.[15] The AMWU was not the only union involved in militant action at this time, and total strike days hit a number of historical peaks in the period from 1973 to 1981. In the early 1980s the AMWU led a national push for 35-hour working week agreements in large parts of the metals industry, in part to address unemployment in the wake of recessions in the 1970s, and achieved 'a 38-hour week and a $39 per week increase in wages'.[16]

This militant strategy was undermined from the mid-1970s onwards by recessions, but most particularly by the recessions of the early 1980s. At the time of the 1981 recession, Australian workers were experiencing 'the worst labour market conditions since the Depression'.[17] The collapse of a short-lived, mining-led economic recovery in 1981 had a dramatic impact on employment, shifting the AMWU and other CPA-aligned unions behind the Accord for several reasons. Job losses and mass sackings in manufacturing increasingly undermined the confidence of the union leadership that it could fight at the shop floor level, and its focus shifted to the national level. A growing number of unemployed workers (both inside and outside the ranks of the AMWU) also drove concerns about the inadequacies of welfare state provisions in a high inflation environment. Thus high unemployment increased the importance of the social wage to the union's leadership.

The 'recession of 1981 destroyed 80,000 jobs in metal manufacturing [but] the upturn later that year and into 1982 restored only 35,000 of them'.[18] When the economy collapsed again in 1982, shedding further positions – including 100,000 in the metals and engineering sector alone – it forced the AMWU to significantly rethink its strategy.[19] The union leadership believed it could not win back the lost jobs without a coordinated plan across the industry, and that an expanded social wage – including an increase to the level of unemployment benefits – was necessary in the context of escalating job losses. This was the crucial background to the AMWU's decision to support a social contract. These economic factors occurred alongside a more contingent reason for the shift in the AMWU, involving the impasse of the militant strategy under Fraser and the lack of an alternative approach in that context.[20]

Although the economic conditions were central to the AMWU's shift, throughout the 1970s the AMWU had argued state planning was needed to resolve Australia's problems. It was not simply that industrially weaker unions were looking to the state to resolve the impact of the crisis on their members, but that industrially militant unions increasingly looked to various European countries for models of corporatist alternative economic programs. Various union and ALP members visited Europe to examine planning models and in 1977 the AMWU brought UK academic and Labour politician Stuart Holland, to Australia.[21] The AMWU leadership had been persuaded by his work – as well as that of other intellectuals in the union movement, ALP and academia – that the only defence against the ideas of the New Right was a centralised national response in the form of an alternative economic strategy.[22] In that sense, the ideas around an alternative economic strategy that the AMWU had been developing for some time were consistent with the Accord when it arose.

A number of AMWU publications in the late 1970s and early 1980s elaborated an alternate economic strategy, including 'The People's Budget'[23], 'Australia Up-Rooted'[24], 'Australia Ripped Off'[25], and 'Australia on the Rack'[26]. These documents provided detailed facts on the state of the economy, emphasising the impact of the crisis and government policy on working people. They highlighted how business was making significant profits in the midst of the crisis, and criticised increasing attacks on labour movement organising. In *Australia Up-Rooted*, the AMWU argued that planning – at both the individual firm level and centrally via the state – was the only solution to protracted economic stagnation. Similarly, at an ACTU Conference on the Manufacturing Industry in 1978, ACTU Senior Vice-President Cliff Dolan argued in favour of increased state planning involving the unions and criticised both the Fraser and Whitlam Governments for their *ad hoc* approach to the crisis.[27]

Over time, key militant unions came to accept the argument that the 'old' approach of industrial struggle contributed to social division and price inflation driven by wage pressures, and that there was a shared national interest in managing the crisis cooperatively. The AMWU was, at the same time, shifting from its approach of intervention at the workshop level (a strategy that sought to increase industrial democracy and worker control) to one centred on industry development and tripartite planning at the national level. In a draft paper entitled 'A Strategy for the 1980s in the Metal Industry'[28], published by metal worker members of the CPA, union activists welcomed the possibility of an Accord with an incoming ALP government. At the 1982 AMWU National Conference, the shift was clear in newly adopted policies stating that:

> Industry plans formed through consultation between capital, labour and the State at a national level, rather than independent union intervention at a workplace level, [were] now the union's primary focus. Rather than workplace intervention being used as a lever to shape investment decisions, it was now quarantined in a separate policy with a reduced focus.[29]

The 'national interest' became progressively more central to the outlook of unions. The focus on planning as a solution to crisis provided fertile ground for those who argued for an Accord, positing it as an alternative economic regime to that of hostile New Right governments in the US and UK. Centralised planning in the national interest was the rhetorical gel that allowed the ALP and a diverse group of unions – including those of the far left – to develop the social contract.

The AMWU played an important role in winning support for the Accord within rank-and-file networks, both within and outside its ranks. In Victoria, just prior to the 1983 federal election, it organised education sessions on the Accord in local areas. These were pitched internally as well as at members of other unions and their spouses.[30] The union's Victorian Special Education Sub-Committee proposed a number of topics for study circles including: the Fraser wages freeze; 'the contending forces amongst employers and the Fraser Government'; the role of protection and tariffs; what incomes policy is and is not; and the experience and history of previous wage and price freezes.[31] The union also printed and distributed copies of the Accord within the labour movement and, after the ALP was elected, distributed speakers' notes to assist with prosecuting arguments in support of it.[32] In this way, it was the union movement's 'left leaders [from the AMWU and BWIU in particular] who, with the help of an ideological framework supplied by the CPA, did most to win support for the Accord among worker militants'.[33]

National Economic Summit and Communiqué

From the earliest days of the Hawke Labor Government's election in March 1983, the union movement raised concerns about how the Accord was being implemented. Immediately after the 1983 election, the direction of economic policy began to move away from the framework outlined in the original Accord statement. Only a month after taking office, Hawke convened the 1983 National Economic Summit, from 11–14 April, at the Commonwealth Parliament House. The Summit included invitees from government, trade unions, business organisations and social welfare organisations. The event culminated in the release of the Summit's Communiqué, which set out an agreed political-economic agenda.[34]

Business was not formally a party to the Accord, but the agreement's content (such as decision-making structures) effectively brought sections of capital inside its framework. The Summit extended this by establishing tripartite bodies to negotiate and implement industry policy, and by gaining a general sanction from the business representatives at the forum to move back to the centralised arbitration of wages. The Summit, in part, *post facto* secured the consent of business to the Accord – a consent to be understood in a dual sense of incorporating capital into the social contract *and* the priorities of the state. While the Accord was prominent at the Summit, the final Communiqué was not entirely consistent with the spirit of the social contract. The Government and business effectively treated the Accord as an ambit claim within the process.

The Summit established ground for the narrowing of the Accord over its subsequent editions (Mark I–VIII) to focus almost exclusively on wages. There was also a 'move away from the social reform tenor of the Accord to a more qualified, more conservative economic language' around prices, wages, non-wage-incomes, taxation and government expenditure.[35]

Other divergences from the Accord included: a watering down of action on prices; changed wording about wages so that it did not necessarily support cost-of-living adjustments; a greater focus on questions of productivity; limitations over the control of incomes not subject to determination by industrial tribunals (i.e. voluntary restraint for non-wage incomes); and a less candid discussion of taxation and government expenditure.[36] The Communiqué resulted in employer representatives acceding to a return to centralised wage fixing, but only on the basis that, if 'profitability increased, real wages would be restrained and only increased "over time", while sectional claims were to be suppressed'.[37] Tom McDonald, Assistant National Secretary of the BWIU, another important CPA-aligned union, summarised the differences in noting that the Accord's main purpose was 'towards protecting living standards and the Communiqué's main [purpose was] to restore profitability'.[38]

While the ACTU leadership was content with the Communiqué, some left unions were not. These unions attacked the elements of the Communiqué that parted ways with the Accord on the basis that the Summit document was non-binding, while the Accord was. The AMWU stated in internal documents that while the Summit 'embraced a number of policy objectives set out in the Accord, the Communiqué from the Summit does not in any way modify the Accord or any of its policy objectives'[39]. Similarly, John Halfpenny, Victorian State Secretary of the AMWU, stated that the Accord 'was the only agreement between the Trade Union Movement and the Labor Government. The Summit was something different [and] ... represents consensus about very little more than shadows.'[40]

Halfpenny's comments illuminate the paradox in the approach of left unions in this period. His statement articulates a concern about the failure of the government to defend the letter and spirit of the Accord so soon after the election, yet also expresses confidence that the Accord (rather than the Communiqué) would be the central and lasting document – notwithstanding the general acknowledgement of tripartite 'consensus' around the Summit agreement. Furthermore, Halfpenny's faith in the Accord is also in spite of the regressive impact of early Labor Government reforms, such as the 1983 budget decision to increase and index many indirect taxes. This was in contrast to the 'well established view in the Labor Movement that indirect taxes are inequitable and impose greater burden on low income earners than they do on high income earners',[41] and the Accord statement committing the ALP to a discernible redistribution of income and a more progressive taxation system. This was far from the only reason for disquiet, as the early years of the Hawke Government also saw significant neoliberal structural adjustment to the economy, including: floating the Australian dollar and abolishing exchange controls; deregulating the financial and banking sectors; and the

238   Elizabeth Humphrys

beginning of dismantling the tariff system. Over time the government promoted 'free trade', engaged in widespread industry deregulation, privatised government-owned entities, marketised the retirement payments system, adopted national competition frameworks, imposed a level of austerity on the working class, and introduced a 'deregulated' labour market in the form of enterprise bargaining.

Although the Summit drew business into the Accord, it must also be understood as more firmly tying the labour movement into the government's agenda – 'cementing' the unions further into the social contract. Leading proponent of trade liberalisation and Hawke economic advisor Ross Garnaut argued that the Summit was one of the early 'instruments of public education, helping to prepare a climate of public opinion that expected and favoured trade liberalisation'.[42] This 'education' was directed at the civil society organisations participating in the Summit, as much as the broader public outside it – but was particularly directed at the unions and labour movement in both cases. Kelty later stated that the Summit 'forced the unions to come to terms with process of government very early'.[43] Thus, the Summit began to 'educate' the unions about what would be possible under the Accord – in educating 'consent' for the emerging neoliberal project, through civil society organisations.

When major components of the Accord were not implemented, union concerns were predominantly expressed privately or in a limited way. The Victorian Branch of the AMWU internally criticised the Economic Summit for parting ways with the letter of the Accord and, as early as June 1983, the AMWU reported 'lack of enthusiasm' on the part of the new ALP government for industry policy.[44][45] Token efforts at mobilising the AMWU membership around Accord issues – such as the August 1983 wage case when the AMWU organised 200 shop stewards and job delegates to attend the court – were short-lived.[46] The AMWU did make threats to break with the Accord or to take action against capital to ensure workers did not bear the brunt of austerity, if the agreement was not implemented.[47] But a mobilisation to impose the labour movement's interests – or simply the agreed terms of the Accord – on capital or on the state, never eventuated. This was not simply a result of the context of the economic crisis, but because there was an impasse of left strategy in terms of defining an alternative project to the social contract – which was increasingly apparent as the full Accord failed to be delivered. Thus, despite union protestations about the implementation of the Accord, and in particular industry policy, Jones has pointed out that the ALP 'never had any intention of taking seriously the underlying spirit of the industry policy section of the Accord'.[48] Many of the Accord's components, such as industry policy and full wage indexation, were viewed simply as a mechanism for drawing the AMWU and others inside the Accord process and keeping them there.

In the first few years of the agreement, the union leadership was increasingly being drawn inside the corporatist project and tied to the state. The shift to the agency of the state was accompanied by a strengthening of the union leaders relative to the rank and file. There was a direct interest for the trade union leadership in maintaining the Accord, even after it was clear that economic policy was moving against working-class interests overall. This interest of the trade union leadership emerged in response to the weakening of the ground-level civil society organisation based on an active rank and file, and, thus, of the union bureaucracy's social weight. That is, the more that union leaders' entry into high-level and state-centric processes led to the hollowing out of union organisation, the more their own influence rested not on the social power of organised labour but on their ability to manoeuvre within the state and political sphere.

Stewart argued in the early years of the Accord that the agreement might be broken if a powerful affiliate had retracted its support, and posited that (in spite of the central role of the AMWU in backing the social contract) its concerns over the direction of economic policy might spill over into open revolt in the mid-1980s.[49] In retrospect, Stewart underestimated both the level of union leader integration into the Accord process and the lack of any alternative strategy within the left unions. In fact, the CPA-led unions looked to deepen the Accord through industry policy in the *Australia Reconstructed* report, rather than change strategy.[50]

Australia Reconstructed

The Australian unions best placed to mobilise large numbers of workers were also deeply nationalist, despite being the most politically radical. Within the Accord process the AMWU and other left union officials

> called for industry plans, reflecting their desire to bolster domestic industry against multinational competition. ... [But over time] hostility to foreign capital, which at least carried some echo of class struggle, was subsumed in the broader notion of national competitiveness which carried none.[51]

Over the period of the social contract the unions sought direct engagement with capital to support its profitability and restructuring. So sharply had sections of the labour movement shifted through the early years of the Accord that the *Australia Reconstructed* report called not simply for efforts to ensure the profitability of local capital, but 'a program ... which encourage[d] productive foreign investment' to ensure Australia's competitiveness.[52]

The original Accord agreed to implement a comprehensive industry development policy with the objective being the 'attainment of full employment' through 'interventionist' planning. Industry planning was a key inclusion to gain the support of the AMWU and fitted with their broader direction of developing a 'European' corporatist model in Australia. In their view, tripartite bodies and industry plans were to be developed and, alongside tariff protection and the use of superannuation funds for national investment, this was to reinvigorate manufacturing and address unemployment. In the period of the first Accord the government established bodies included the Economic Planning Advisory Council (EPAC), the Australian Manufacturing Council (AMC) and the Trade Development Council (TDC) – with such organisations implementing plans in areas including shipping, steel and motor vehicles. However,

240 Elizabeth Humphrys

the plans 'were short-lived and undermined the government's desire for a general reduction in tariffs'.[53] Industry policy was ultimately used to achieve ends contrary to those intended by the trade unions that championed it. These changes often took place with union consent, or in the face of derisory resistance. Social contract clauses related to maintaining tariff protections were ignored, while policy and funding directed at technological adjustment were used to ensure that industries were restructured in the interests of capital in an increasingly less protected environment. Industry planning bodies were in many ways superfluous to government policy development, with economic priorities being set by Treasury and in line with the neoliberal direction of the government.[54]

The left unions often complained that the industry planning elements were not being implemented as per the original Accord statement, or in accordance with the wishes of major employers rather than unions and their members.[55] They actively sought to reinvigorate and redeploy the planning elements of the Accord, through the joint ACTU and TDC fact-finding mission to Europe in 1986. The mission arose because it was believed that although the Accord had been adopted and 'set new policy directions, it provided few details to aid policy implementation [and] the economic crisis of late 1985 and 1986 precipitated renewed concern for policy formulation'.[56]

In the wake of the visit to Europe, the mission released the *Australia Reconstructed* report. The document set out recommendations on macroeconomic, incomes and industry policy, as well as a framework of strategic unionism. The AMWU was central to this process and Ted Wilshire, its former national research officer, was Executive Director of the TDC in this period. The mission and report sought to move government policy away from the neoliberal direction of the ALP – i.e. to shift from financial deregulation and towards industry policy – and promoted the curbing of prices and executive salaries (not only wages). It sought the use of superannuation funds to promote 'productive' investment and promoted greater vocational training and industrial democracy. In many ways, the report echoed the original Accord and highlighted the key components that had not been implemented. The document, and the labour movement more generally, failed to map out a strategy that could see either the Accord or the new recommendations delivered.

The ALP government effectively ignored the recommendations of *Australia Reconstructed* pertaining to industry policy, with few recommendations implemented. John Button, Minister for Industry, Technology and Commerce in the Accord era, highlighted the extent of this in a later interview when he stated: 'I don't think *Australia Reconstructed* got much attention in the Parliamentary Labor Party except from people like myself from whom it had to get some attention'.[57] By 'strategic unionism', the report meant that unions should assume

> greater responsibility for economic conditions in the nation. 'Responsibility' was thought to have two sides: the burden of responsibility, in terms of reducing wage demands as a contribution to a national growth strategy; and

the power of responsibility, in terms of increasing union influence on government economic policy.[58]

In terms of wages policy, this meant tying increases to 'productivity growth and workplace change (which became known as enterprise bargaining), rather than simply to cost of living rises'.[59] The report argued that 'the creation of wealth is a pre-requisite of its distribution and … the appreciation of the importance of wealth creation [needs to be developed] *at the workplace*'.[60] The report argued that through 'strategic unionism, trade unions recognise that wealth creation is as important as its distribution'.[61] The strategic unionism objectives of the report were to be achieved via the 'rationalisation' of union structures, through amalgamations and 'the centralisation of policy control by the ACTU'.

In the absence of recommendations around industry policy being adopted, the strategic unionism objectives – in particular the reorganisation of the trade union movement through union amalgamations – became the key outcome of the mission to Europe. The ACTU believed amalgamation was the way to arrest the decline in union membership. In the first half of the 1990s, the number of unions operating in Australia more than halved, decreasing from 275 in 1991 to 132 by 1996, with more amalgamations occurring in those years than in the previous 50.[62] However, despite the magnitude of this effort, the decline of union density was not halted.

One consequence of the amalgamations was the increased centralisation of policy and decision-making in the ACTU and the state-based union federations, further relegating the rank and file of the Australian labour movement. The *Australia Reconstructed* document and its impact on the direction of the ACTU resulted in the

> competitiveness of individual companies increasingly [being] seen as the way to create employment and secure national economic growth – an agenda at odds with the industry planning program of *Australia Reconstructed*. … In the 1990s competitiveness agenda, it became market forces with union complicity which is the key to profitable industry.[63]

Ultimately, the impact of *Australia Reconstructed* was chiefly on 'the internal affairs of the trade union movement'.[64] The report and process did not effect a break with neoliberalism, but further enwrapped the trade union leadership in the priorities of the neoliberal state. It is not just that the unions were unlikely to succeed in reconstructing industry in Australia 'in circumstances where the leadership of the political and industrial wings of the Australian labour movement were simultaneously conspiring to introduce a panoply of market-oriented reforms',[65] but that by collaborating to maximise the profitability of capital and the productivity of labour this outcome was always the most likely one.

The Italian Marxist Antonio Gramsci developed his theory of molecular transformations 'particularly in relation to absorption of elements of one group by another in the *trasformismo* he saw in the passive revolution of post-Risorgimento Italy'[66]. He also used the term in other contexts to 'describe processes of slow but steady transformation that eventually issue in a dialectical conversion of quantitative into qualitative change'[67] – including in relation to himself while subject to the social circumstances of prison.[68] Gramsci's theory is a useful way in which to understand the transformation of elements of the trade union leadership in the Accord period, demonstrating how – when representatives of subaltern classes become directly incorporated into processes in and around the state – they shift their activities and outlook. At first, modifications can appear barely visible, but over time quantitative becomes qualitative change. The union bureaucracy underwent such a 'molecular' transformation during the Accord period, despite being populated by predominantly the same people.

This dramatic shift can perhaps be seen most clearly in the evolution of Laurie Carmichael – CPA member and Victorian State Secretary, Assistant National Secretary and Research Officer AMWU, and later Assistant Secretary of the ACTU – who was once described as the 'left linchpin in the ALP/ACTU alliance'[69]. Carmichael argued in the mid-1970s that he would have nothing to do with workers' participation in the running of corporations, because it allowed ordinary workers to rise to higher management only if 'they commit themselves body and soul to profit'[70]. He would later state, in a publication of a petrochemical company, that 'in the workplace of the future, everyone is a manager'[71]. The contrast between the two positions could not be starker. The CPA union officials entered the Accord on the understanding that it would be used to pursue the interests of the working class and, as late as the 1985 ACTU Congress, Carmichael was arguing that the social contract was 'a transitional program for socialism'[72]. Carmichael's change of heart about worker participation in management can be explained as the product of being drawn into a state-centred political project, whereby the participation of workers in business direction became subsumed under a progressive political umbrella – and rank-and-file organising fell by the wayside. It is not that Carmichael changed his mind about the social priorities of business. Rather, it was because the state and the unions were at the centre of a political project to reorganise industry, and, therefore, Carmichael came to see business imperatives as subordinate to the wider project of the 'national interest' being implemented through the Accord and state (and, thus, no longer simply driven by private capitalist gain). The processes of the Accord and *Australia Reconstructed* produced greater and greater assimilation of the unions into state-led economic restructuring. This was concurrent with the widespread containment of industrial militancy through the Accord and the policing of union dissent – including by the ACTU and its leading affiliates.

Enterprise bargaining

The shift from centralised wage determinations to enterprise bargaining has been presented in some accounts as a response to pressure by New Right business lobbies like the Business Council of Australia. Yet it was not simply introduced by a neoliberal state, but actively campaigned for by the ACTU and key left unions.[73] Enterprise bargaining was a key element in the neoliberalisation of industrial relations and was, at the same time, both a response to the constraints of the Accord and a greater curtailment of workers' organised power. In the wake of the move to enterprise bargaining, 'industrial relations has moved further and further down the path mapped out by "free market deregulationists"'.[74]

By the late 1980s, intense pressures had built up inside unions because of the heavy cost of wage restraint. Real wages had fallen significantly throughout the Accord, but the sacrifice was unevenly spread because 'minimum rates adjustments, flat rate increases and social wage benefits moderated the impact of aggregate wage discipline on low-income earners'.[75] It was the better-organised, skilled and paid members of key left unions in metals, manufacturing and construction who bore the brunt of real wage cuts; their disciplined adherence to the social contract ironically resulted in them taking the proportionally largest cut in real income.[76]

Interviewed a decade later, a series of trade union leaders attested to their fears at the time that, without a change to the process of wage setting, there was a real threat of militants leading breakaway unions and undermining the Accord process.[77] The success of the Accord in suppressing wages and in increasing the rate of exploitation had, therefore, created a reaction that threatened to fragment the relationship between the Labor government and unions. The layers of workers within the unions that had been best organised and more able to mobilise their social power to gain high wages and good working conditions before 1983 – and whose social weight had been subordinated to the imperatives of the state-led social contract – were now agitating for a return to a pre-Accord situation, where direct bargaining power would determine pay rates.

Leading unions and the ACTU began to campaign for enterprise bargaining in the hope this would allow more strongly organised unions and workplaces to fight for and gain the additional wage increases denied to them under strict centralisation. The Industrial Relation Commission's October 1991 wage decision permitted enterprise bargaining, but dissociated it from the award system. This meant that wage agreements won on an enterprise-by-enterprise basis could *not* be fed back into the next national award determination, as they had been during wage campaigns of the pre-Accord era with the metal industry's fitters' rate. This made it significantly more difficult to use the bargaining power of stronger workplaces to deliver gains indirectly for weakly organised workers. In this sense, the solidarity implicit in past militancy was broken. Strong groups of workers were fighting only for sectional gains. This was a further step in the disorganisation of workers' organised social power, ending their ability to make gains in a class interest beyond a sectional level. As Carmichael later argued, this was not a new phase of the old pattern of 'enterprise bargaining – consolidation, enterprise bargaining – consolidation' but 'a new policy ... very much part of economic rationalist policy'.[78] It was also the outcome of the slow death of arbitration in Australia, ironically delivered through the deepening of corporatism embodied in the Accord process.

244 Elizabeth Humphrys

It is possible that this further labour disorganisation – coming on the back of plummeting union density and militancy – could have been defended against, but the push for enterprise bargaining came at a time when unions were least prepared for the new system's negative consequences and least able to take advantage of any possible gains. The 1991 recession – the worst since the Great Depression – made wages growth virtually impossible. Moreover, the Accord's centralising tendencies had led to passivity and decline at the level of workplace and delegate organisation, so that by that point 'one-third of unionised workplaces had no delegate and only in 26 percent of workplaces was there an "active" union presence'.[79] They were unable to use enterprise bargaining to their advantage, and unions did not foresee how much the loss of a legal framework connecting centralised wages rulings and enterprise level bargaining would work against them.

Thus, the early 1990s saw neither a revival of union fortunes nor a substantial clawing back of lost wages and conditions. There was some recovery of wages for better organised workers who could take most advantage of enterprise bargaining, but the dispersion of wages increased[80] – in part because of the wide variation in enterprise deals, but also because the weakest groups of workers continued to rely on the often sub-inflation award pay rises of subsequent national wage cases. This state of affairs was worsened by the 1993 *Industrial Relations Reform Act*, which left awards as a mere 'safety net' for workers who had entered the enterprise bargaining stream. The introduction of decentralised enterprise bargaining was associated with a sharp drop in the number of strikes, with the agreements limiting industrial action to certain periods and thereby preventing workers from taking advantage of cyclical improvements in economic conditions as had happened under the old centralised system.[81] Rather than enterprise bargaining being a way to reassert workers' organised social weight in their own interests through direct industrial methods, as the ACTU had hoped, it coincided with a further decline in union density.

Conclusion

With the AMWU leading the way, the militancy and organisation of the Australian union movement in the 1970s enabled its leaders to push their way into the highest levels of national political and economic decision-making, in the shape of the Accord. This social contract was central to drawing unionised workers directly into the process of national economic restructuring. However, the cost of this process was the weakening, disorganisation and fragmentation of the union movement. Unions suffered from declining membership they could not reverse, decreased activity and organisation at the workplace level, and an increased focus on local and sectional interests once enterprise bargaining began to take hold. Enterprise bargaining successfully stemmed the threat of open rebellion against the Accord, but its timing and legal framework meant it could not prevent an acceleration of union membership decline. There was a consequential deterioration of the relationship between the ALP and the ACTU, as both sides found diminishing value in cooperation. Whether a sustained pushback by militants forming breakaway unions could have reversed the further decline of worker organisation is impossible to know in retrospect, but it seems likely that the deterioration prior to 1989 had already been sufficient to change the overall balance of forces, and that the shift to enterprise bargaining simply reinforced the downward trajectory of the early 1990s and beyond.

Current ACTU President Ged Kearney has described the Accord's centralised wage system of the early 1990s as 'a yoke and shackle for unions' and that because of this they 'fought for and won direct collective bargaining'.[82] Kearney also argued that union leaders were aware that the election of a conservative government was inevitable, and that there was a 'need to rejuvenate the capacity of the union movement to organise, to bargain and campaign again'.[83] But this is not what enterprise bargaining delivered in practice. Instead, the labour movement was unable to recover its declining workplace density.

The contradictions of the Accord also point to the improbability of a similar social contract being used to drive radical political economic reform in the future. This is because the social organisations that were central to instituting the Accord were hollowed out in the process of the social contract, so much so they can no longer play the same role – and nor can they be as effective in resisting such reforms as they had been in previous decades. During the Accord years there was a substantial fall in the level of unionisation from 49 to 32.7 percent. In the years since, this has fallen by a further 50 percent to under 15 percent. While there is debate about the relationship between the Accord and this decline it is clear that, within the Accord framework and through the ACTU's post-Accord era strategy, there has been no sustained reinvigoration of union activism or organisation across the country.

The failure of the left unions' strategy of industrial militancy and mobilisation to resolve the crisis in favour of labour (in the 1970s and early 1980s) resulted in these unions seeking a political solution through central state planning, and, thus, being brought inside the state and political society. The role of the CPA-led AMWU in the Accord process demonstrates how the social contract incorporated a militant union suffused with radical perspectives into the new political project centred on reviving accumulation and 'modernising' the Australian economy. Central to neo-liberal restructuring was the participation of unions in industry structural adjustment and efforts to increase productivity, which proceeded alongside the attempted reorienting of the Accord in the 1986–1987 *Australia Reconstructed* initiative. The shift from a workplace-focused strategy to a corporatist one facilitated the enwrapment of labour and the trade union leadership by political society and its priorities. This resulted in the molecular transformation of the AMWU – its leaders, members and structures – so that they were no longer capable of playing a significant role in defending, let alone winning, social gains for Australian workers. In the end, the solution the AMWU adopted for the impasse of its previous strategy of industrial militancy hollowed out the union's membership and power – which exacerbated the devastating impact of economy-wide changes on the metals and manufacturing industries. This was a tragic outcome, the consequences of which reverberate well beyond its ranks and are still with us today.

Notes

1 See in particular Jonathan Strauss, 'Opposition to the Accord as a Social Contract in the 1980s', *Labour History* 105 (2013): 47–62.
2 The union representing metal workers has held various names over its existence, including during the Accord period, but the name Amalgamated Metal Workers' Union, or AMWU, is used throughout this chapter.
3 Tom Bramble and Rick Kuhn, *Labor's Conflict: Big Business, Workers and the Politics of Class* (Port Melbourne: Cambridge University Press, 2011): 102.
4 Sean Scalmer and Terry Irving, 'The Rise of the Modern Labour Technocrat: Intellectual Labour and the Transformation of the Amalgamated Metal Workers' Union, 1973–85', *Labour History* 77 (1999): 65.
5 Peter Beilharz, *Transforming Labor: Labour Tradition and the Labor Decade in Australia* (Melbourne: Cambridge University Press, 1994): 98.
6 Bob Catley, 'The Technocratic Labor Thesis Revisited', *Thesis Eleven* 82 (August 2005): 97–98.
7 CPA, 'The Socialist Alternative: Documents of CPA National Congress 1974' (Red Pen Publications, 1974): 3.
8 Tom O'Lincoln, *Years of Rage: Social Conflicts in the Fraser Years* (Melbourne: Bookmarks Australia, 1993): 14.
9 Cited in ibid., 15.
10 ALP & ACTU, 'Accord Mark I: 1983–84', in *The Accord...and Beyond*, ed. Frank Stilwell (Leichhardt: Pluto Press Australia, 1986): 162–163.
11 Ibid., 163.
12 Ibid., 175.
13 Damien Cahill, 'The Contours of Neoliberal Hegemony in Australia', *Rethinking Marxism* 19, no. 2 (2007): 221–233.
14 Nikki Balnave and Greg Patmore, 'The AMWU: Politics and Industrial Relations, 1852–2012', in *Organise, Educate, Control: The AMWU in Australia 1852–2012* (Melbourne: Melbourne University Press, 2013): 25.
15 Tom Bramble, 'Australian Union Strategies since 1945', *Labour & Industry* 11, no. 3 (2001): 11.
16 Balnave and Patmore, 'The AMWU: Politics and Industrial Relations, 1852–2012', 25.
17 Michael Beggs, *Inflation and the Making of Australian Macroeconomic Policy, 1945–85* (Basingstoke: Palgrave MacMillan, 2015): 260.
18 John Halfpenny, 'Victorian State Conference State Secretary's Report 1984' (Amalgamated Metals Foundry and Shipwrights' Union, 1984): 3, 1989.0054, Box 3/3, Melbourne University Archive.
19 Evan Jones, 'The Background to Australia Reconstructed', *Journal of Australian Political Economy* 39 (1997): 18–19.
20 O'Lincoln, *Years of Rage: Social Conflicts in the Fraser Years*.
21 AMWSU, 'Dr Stuart Holland ABC Radio Interview, 8 August 1977' (Amalgamated Metal Workers' & Shipwrights' Union, 1978), 1995.0096, Box 56, University of Melbourne Archive.
22 John Langmore, 'An Economic Strategy for a Labor Government', *Journal of Australian Political Economy* 12/13 (1982): 20–39.
23 AMWSU, 'A People's Economic Program' (Amalgamated Metal Workers' & Shipwrights' Union, 1977).
24 AMWSU, 'Australia Up-Rooted' (Amalgamated Metal Workers' & Shipwrights' Union, 1977).
25 AMWSU, 'Australia Ripped Off' (Amalgamated Metal Workers' & Shipwrights' Union, 1979).
26 AMWSU, 'Australia on the Rack' (Amalgamated Metal Workers' & Shipwrights' Union, 1982).
27 Cliff Dolan and Laurie Carmichael, 'ACTU Conference on Manufacturing Industry (cassette Recording)', April 5, 1978, Z282A, Box 701, Tape 3, Side A, Noel Butlin Archive.

28 'A Strategy for the 1980s in the Metal Industry' (Communist Party of Australia, 1982).
29 Scalmer and Irving, 'The Rise of the Modern Labour Technocrat: Intellectual Labour and the Transformation of the Amalgamated Metal Workers' Union, 1973–85', 74.
30 AMFSU, 'Victorian State Council Minutes 2 February 1983' (Amalgamated Metals Foundry and Shipwrights' Union, 1983), Z102, Box 515, Noel Butlin Archive.
31 Ibid.
32 John Halfpenny, 'Briefing Notes: The Accord, The Summit, Wages, Prices and Industry Policies' (Amalgamated Metals Foundry and Shipwrights' Union, May 17, 1983), Z102 Box 990, Document NRC-F-M692–0048, Noel Butlin Archive.
33 Bramble and Kuhn, *Labor's Conflict: Big Business, Workers and the Politics of Class*, 102.
34 Commonwealth of Australia, 'National Economic Summit Conference Communiqué' (Canberra: Commonwealth of Australia, April 14, 1983).
35 Larry Sonder, 'The Accord, the Communiqué and the Budget', *The Australian Quarterly* 56, no. 2 (1984): 157.
36 Ibid., 156–157.
37 Michael Rizzo, 'The Left and the Accord' (Master of Arts (Research), La Trobe University, 1991): 90.
38 Cited in ibid., 91.
39 AMFSU, 'Victorian State Council Minutes 16 May 1983' (Amalgamated Metals Foundry and Shipwrights' Union, 1983): 7, Z102, Box 515, Noel Butlin Archive.
40 Halfpenny, 'Victorian State Conference State Secretary's Report 1984', 9–10.
41 Ibid., 1–2.
42 Ross Garnaut, 'Australia: A Case Study of Unilateral Trade Liberalisation', in *Going Alone: The Case for Relaxed Reciprocity in Freeing Trade*, ed. Jagdish Bhagwati (Massachusetts Institute of Technology, 2002): 139–166.
43 Cited in Pam Oliver and Janet Collins, 'Labor in Power' (Sydney: Australian Broadcasting Corporation, 1993).
44 AMFSU, 'Victorian State Council Minutes 16 May 1983', 7.
45 AMFSU, 'Victorian State Council Minutes 20 June 1983' (Amalgamated Metals Foundry and Shipwrights' Union, 1983): 8, Z102, Box 515, Noel Butlin Archive.
46 AMFSU, 'Victorian State Council Minutes 22 August 1983' (Amalgamated Metals Foundry and Shipwrights' Union, 1983): 8, Z102, Box 515, Noel Butlin Archive.
47 John Halfpenny, 'For Adequate Promotion, Implementation and Development of the Accord: Prices Surveillance (Joint Union Seminar Briefing Paper)' (Amalgamated Metals Foundry and Shipwrights' Union, February 22, 1984): 6–7, Z102, Box 620, Folio 'Economy and the Accord', Noel Butlin Archive.
48 'The Background to Australia Reconstructed', 22.
49 'The Politics of the Accord. Does Corporatism Explain It?', *Australian Journal of Political Science* 20, no. 1 (1985): 30.
50 ACTU/TDC, 'Australia Reconstructed: ACTU/TDC Mission to Western Europe' (Canberra: ACTU/TDC Mission to Western Europe, 1987).
51 Rick Kuhn, 'The History of Class Analysis in Australia', 2005, 6–7, https://openresearch-repository.anu.edu.au/bitstream/1885/42700/2/clan.pdf
52 Quoted in ibid., 7.
53 Balnave and Patmore, 'The AMWU: Politics and Industrial Relations, 1852–2012', 29.
54 Mark Beeson, 'Organised Labour in an Era of Global Transformation: Australia Reconstructed Revisited', *Journal of Australian Political Economy* 39 (1997): 64.
55 Nick Southall, 'Working for the Class: The Praxis of the Wollongong Out of Workers' Union' (Honours, University of Wollongong, 2006); Julianne Schultz, *Steel City Blues: The Human Cost of Industrial Crisis* (Melbourne: Penguin, 1985).
56 Edward M. Davis, 'Australia Reconstructed: A Symposium; Australia Reconstructed: An Ambitious Report', *Prometheus: Critical Studies in Innovation* 6, no. 1 (1988): 151.
57 Dick Bryan, 'Interview with John Button', *Journal of Australian Political Economy* 39 (1987): 8.
58 Mike Rafferty, 'Union Amalgamation: The Enduring Legacy of Australia Reconstructed', *Journal of Australian Political Economy* 39 (1997): 100.

59 Ibid., 101.
60 ACTU/TDC, 'Australia Reconstructed: ACTU/TDC Mission to Western Europe', 169.
61 Ibid., 172.
62 John Buchanan, 'Union Amalgamations as a Basis for Union Renewal in Australia: Insights from Unfinished Business', *Just Labour* 2 (2003): 54–56.
63 Rafferty, 'Union Amalgamation: The Enduring Legacy of Australia Reconstructed', 103.
64 Frank Stilwell, 'Australia Reconstructed: Oops, Missed the Turning', *Journal of Australian Political Economy* 39 (1997): 43.
65 Beeson, 'Organised Labour in an Era of Global Transformation: Australia Reconstructed Revisited', 68.
66 Peter Thomas, *The Gramscian Moment*, Historical Materialism Book Series (Leiden: Brill, 2009): 398.
67 Ibid.
68 Antonio Gramsci, *Letters From Prison*, trans. Lynne Lawner (London: Jonathon Cape, 1975): 137.
69 Brian Aarons and Peter Murphy, 'Labor's Five Years: Counsel for the Defence. An Interview with Laurie Carmichael', *Australian Left Review* 109 (1989): 21–25.
70 Tim Dare, 'Join In? But Nobody Wants to Know', *The Australian*, February 1, 1974.
71 Kemcor, 'Work Training Forum Comes to Kemcor' (Kemcor, July 1993).
72 Liz Ross, Tom O'Lincoln, and Graham Willett, 'Labor's Accord: Why It's a Fraud' (Socialist Action, March 1986): 13.
73 Tom Bramble, *Trade Unionism in Australia: A History from Flood to Ebb Tide* (Melbourne: Cambridge University Press, 2008): 161.
74 Chris Briggs, 'Australian Exceptionalism: The Role of Trade Unions in the Emergence of Enterprise Bargaining', *The Journal of Industrial Relations* 43, no. 1 (2001): 27.
75 Ibid., 32.
76 Ibid.
77 Ibid., 34.
78 Cited in ibid., 36.
79 Ibid., 38.
80 David Peetz, 'The Impacts and Non-Impacts on Unions of Enterprise Bargaining', *Labour & Industry* 22, no. 3 (2012): 245.
81 Ann Hodgkinson and Nelson Perera, 'Strike Activity Under Enterprise Bargaining: Economics or Politics?', *Australian Journal of Labour Economics* 7, no. 4 (2004): 455.
82 'Address to 'The Accord 30 Years On' Symposium' (The Accord 30 Years On, Macquarie University Sydney Campus, May 31, 2013), www.actu.org.au/actu-media/ speeches-and-opinion/ged-kearney-address-to-the-accord-30-years-on-symposium-31-may-2013
83 Ibid.

13

READING AND CONTESTING GERMAINE GREER AND DENNIS ALTMAN

The 1970s and beyond

Jon Piccini and Ana Stevenson

Two books, published within a year of each other in 1970–71, were to have profound effects on the 'liberation' movements of that decade. Both emerged from their writers' experiences as Australian outsiders: members of the political and cultural community of the far left in a nation still in the grips of conservative hegemony. As such, both looked abroad for answers to questions which animated their lives – Why were women and gay people ('queer' had not yet been appropriated) stigmatised, trivialised and stereotyped by a society which denied them full sexual lives, not to mention political and social rights? Both found different answers in the United States – and particularly the emerging black power movement – and both were to have resounding, global impacts which continue to this day.

Germaine Greer's *The Female Eunuch* (1970) and Dennis Altman's *Homosexual: Oppression and Liberation* (1971) are now viewed as epoch-making texts. Greer's is perhaps only challenged by Kate Millett's *Sexual Politics* (1970) in its remembered place as a foundational manifesto of second-wave feminism, while one reviewer called Altman's work "A 'Sexual Politics' for the gay liberation movement".[1] Anniversaries of the publication of both are marked by new editions, commentary and conferences.

Yet, in many ways, these are actually very different books, written by very different people and received in very different ways. Much recent scholarship surrounding Greer has focused on celebrity feminism and her heterosexual sex appeal, often charting the pros and cons of her resultant (mis)engagement with the mainstream media.[2] Scholarship about Altman, however, is much more limited, with a 2014 collection of conference papers – mixing scholarly engagement with personal reminiscences and reproduced primary sources – the only sizable contribution to date.[3] Historian of Australian sexuality Frank Bongiorno places both authors within the expatriate tradition in Australian writing – they "spoke (and wrote) in a language the metropolis could understand, but with an Australian accent".[4]

This chapter draws on archival and published sources to tell the story of the origins of these works, both in Australia and overseas, how they interrelated or opposed each other thematically, and how these 'Australian accents' were received – both by the mainstream press, public opinion and the radicals to whom both at least imagined themselves to be writing. In so doing, Greer and Altman's works emerge as in no way equal contributors to the movements they are remembered as feeding. Instead, the works of these far-left exports have had very separate and controversial 'lives'.

Origins

Germaine Greer grew up in Melbourne's bayside suburb of Elwood and graduated from The University of Melbourne in 1959. Upon moving to Sydney during the early 1960s, she became involved with the Sydney Push and then the Sydney Libertarians, an anarchist group. After further study at The University of Sydney, she was awarded a Commonwealth Scholarship for doctoral studies at the University of Cambridge. There, Greer became the first woman to gain full membership to the Cambridge Footlights theatrical club. A Shakespearean scholar, Greer worked at the University of Warwick in Coventry, England between 1968 and 1972 as an assistant lecturer.

During 1968 and 1969, Greer contributed to emerging publications which celebrated the sexual revolution. Her articles in Richard Neville's London-based *Oz* Magazine covered topics such as the sexual culture of groupies and the theory of "cunt power".[5] As one of the co-founders of *Suck*, an Amsterdam-based magazine Kate Gleeson describes as "more straightforwardly pornographic" than *Oz*, Greer served as editor and appeared naked in photographic spreads. The freedom and sexual licence Greer expressed herein had its foundations in the anarchist and libertarian traditions earlier celebrated by the Sydney Push.[6]

The degree to which Greer's academic research into Shakespeare's early modern plays shaped her approach to women's liberation during this same period is only just being revealed.[7] This and other insights are due to the sources available via the new Germaine Greer Archive, recently acquired by The University of Melbourne.[8] For example, Marilyn Lake uncovers how the book proposals Greer penned for *The Female Eunuch* reveal a fascination with "radical American admirers of Black urban machismo", including Norman Mailer, Eldridge Cleaver, Abbie Hoffman, and Jerry Rubin. Hence, a transnational awareness of civil rights and black power in the United States shaped Greer's understanding of women's oppression much more clearly than the contemporaneous efforts of other feminists or the British New Left.[9]

Greer was also largely contemptuous of Australian social movements – in a 1972 discussion with Melbourne socialist Ian Turner she remarked that Australians had less engagement with revolutionary struggles in China, Cuba or Chile "than anywhere else in the world", and as such lacked "an open, reverberant Marxist dialogue".[10] Britain, France and the United States were, for her, where true radicalism lay. Even so, Bongiorno detects echoes of early-twentieth-century Australian sex reformer William Chidley in Greer's theory of "cunt-power", and positions her admittedly few rhetorical allusions to "colonisation" as a precursor to Anne Summers' feminist blockbuster, *Damned Whores and God's Police: The Colonisation of Women in Australia* (1975).[11]

On the other hand, Dennis Altman participated as a leading intellectual of the Australian 'New Left'. His frequent travel to the United States imbued him with the authenticity of someone 'in the know'. Altman grew up in the island state of Tasmania, where he completed undergraduate study before departing for the United States to undertake graduate work in 1964. It was here, Altman recalls, that he matured "both politically and sexually".[12] Altman studied at Cornell University in upstate New York, where he encountered such intellectual luminaries as philosopher Hannah Arendt and South-East Asia expert George Kahlin, both of whom influenced his early involvement in the campus anti-Vietnam war movement.[13]

Yet, Altman was equally influenced by the burgeoning civil rights and, later, black power movements. Much like Greer, Altman was fascinated by the evolving politics of race in the United States. The title of Greer's book was based on writings of Eldridge Cleaver, who described how white Americans had denied the black man "his masculinity, his energy and his virility".[14] Altman's influences from the Black American scene were different, however. In a 1968 article for Australian student newspaper *National U*, Altman reviewed Martin Luther King's *Chaos or Community* (1967) and the seminal text *Black Power* (1967), by Stokely Carmichael and Charles Hamilton. He found the latter the more useful, as it looked beyond questions of political organisation to those of an "emotional quality" – freeing the black man from "his inferiority complex and from his despair and in-action…restor[ing] his self-respect".[15]

Altman also found potentially even more influence in gay African-American author James Baldwin, whose erotic work exploring the colour line in the United States was banned in Australia. A former student at Monash University remembers Altman suggesting a reading of Baldwin's essays to "understand the men and their humiliation, despair, anger and search for identity" as representative of the broader struggle of black people. As Altman wrote, Baldwin and gay writer Christopher Isherwood were "the two writers most important to me in making sense of my sexuality, which is reflected in the heavy reliance on their writings in my first book".[16]

Altman's trips to the United States not only proved educational for him, but made him someone the Australian left respected and turned to for opinions. Altman spoke at many student and activist conferences, and was involved in much activism at the famously radical Monash University. Two of his pre-*Homosexual* essays proved particularly influential in Australian far-left circles, helping to mainstream the ideas of Marxists Herbert Marcuse and Errich Fromm. "Students in the Electric Age", first published in the Marxist journal *Arena* in 1970, spoke of student protest as the harbinger of a new post-industrial age, harkening a new set of values without "the restraints on human behaviour necessary in previous cultures".[17]

252 Jon Piccini and Ana Stevenson

Drawing heavily on Marshall McLuhan, as well as the Frankfurt School, Altman argued that the American 'counter-culture' – with its rejection of morality, capitalism, imperialism and violence – was the only set of ideas that could govern a post-industrial world. In another piece, entitled "The Politics of Cultural Change", presented at the 1970 Socialist Scholars Conference in Sydney, Altman argued that Australia resembled the "repressive society" theorised by Marcuse, arguing that "our society is based on the most severe restraints on gratification of pleasure in the name of duty, responsibility [and] decency". "The real revolution", Altman argued, "would be a change in men's perceptions that can lead to freedom from repression".[18] Such language saw him roundly criticised by fellow New Left thinker and historian Kevin Rowley, who termed the counter-culture a "passing fad" and condemned what he saw as the "mechanical determinism" of Altman's approach.[19] Yet, such ideas presaged those that were to appear in *Homosexual*.

Reading

Both Greer and Altman's work appeared in the same moment of rebellion and change, yet they are very different books in composition and style. Borne of personal experience and peppered with disgust for the misogynistic views of not just a few early modern male philosophers, *The Female Eunuch* argued that women had been rendered sexually powerless eunuchs because of the demands of marriage, the nuclear family, and consumerism. "The world will not change overnight", Greer contended, "and liberation will not happen unless individual women agree to be outcasts, eccentrics, perverts, and whatever the powers-that-be choose to call them."[20] First published in Britain in October 1970 and then in the United States early in 1971, the book soon became an international bestseller. Famously, Greer was interviewed by – and featured on the cover of – *LIFE* Magazine, which described her as the "Saucy Feminist That Even Men Like".[21]

Many of the women who read *The Female Eunuch* enthusiastically engaged with Greer's feminism. Its impact on the women's movement was "first felt in the United States and elsewhere overseas; then, as a recirculated effect, within Australia itself."[22] In response, Greer received thousands of letters.[23] In June 1971, she acted as guest host for a popular American Broadcasting Company late-night talk show, *The Dick Cavett Show*. This highly successful appearance prompted further audience response. As Rebecca J. Sheehan suggests, access to these women's voices via their letters demonstrates their positive reaction to feminism when mediated by Greer. Her "willingness to work with the media was critical to the role she played in moving feminist issues into the American mainstream". Greer was able to convey "an inspiring model of complex and empowered womanhood", giving voice to key feminist issues – namely, abortion and rape – so as to school American audiences in some of the tenets of women's liberation.[24]

Altman's book, in turn, was written after a six month stay in the United States in 1970, during which he lived in a flat with the "editorial collective of the first Gay Lib paper in New York", a setting which provided "a very easy ride" into the emerging movement. Here, Altman collected the material and experiences he used to write *Homosexual* back in Australia, as "nothing very much was really happening" back home.[25] The book he produced was not easily definable, part radical manifesto, sociological investigation and a precursor to 1990s Queer Theory.[26] Altman's contention, expanding on the work of Reich and Marcuse, was that identities of 'homo' or 'heterosexuality' resulted from capitalist society, which had constructed binaries to police enjoyment and desire. The work of the nascent gay liberation movement, in Altman's view, was not so much to demand 'rights' for homosexuals – though he notes the importance of this in press interviews – but to lead a cultural and sexual revolution. As the book's closing lines state: "Gay Liberation as a new consciousness...can only add to growth in the acceptance of human diversity, of the realization that we all possess far greater potential for love and human relationships than social and cultural structures allow us to reveal."[27]

Commenting on an early draft, Altman's long-time mentor, University of Sydney politics professor Henry Mayer, voiced concerns that Altman's approach, steeped in European Marxism and American liberationism, would treat "the gay experience...as treated as just another 'role'". The editor was concerned that the literary fad of the time – "endless analogies a la [Frantz] Fanon with the Colonizers/Colonized" – would "hide what is different in different types of stygmitisation", adding that "Women, Chicanos, Blacks...have or had to hide their specific identity but nowhere near to the extent that gays have had to do this".[28]

Altman shopped around for prospective publishers, but had trouble selling the idea, until it was picked up by the tiny American publisher Outerbridge & Dienstfrey. Despite experiencing initially disappointing early sales in the United States, *Homosexual* received a "lukewarm review" in *Time* magazine and a more positive one in the *New York Times*, encouraging publishers in Britain and Australia to pick it up. Richard Walsh, who had worked alongside Neville and Greer at *Oz* Magazine and had taken over as Managing Director of Angus & Robertson in 1971, negotiated rights for the Australian edition despite the opinions of his "fairly conservative staff[:] Frankly they were appalled".[29] The *Sydney Morning Herald* commissioned a review only to pull it at the last minute.[30] But not all mainstream opinion condemned or conveniently ignored Altman's proclamations. Sydney's *Daily Telegraph* reviewed the work, noting it had earned the author "something of the status of the homosexual's Germaine Greer".[31] The *Canberra Times* published a very favourable review of Altman's work, in which the book is described as part of "the necessary consciousness-raising of an oppressed and victimised minority"; while "liberals will get a jolt from Mr Altman", no one "concerned with the sort of society we live in...should bypass" him.[32] One reader thought differently, however. Frances West felt "nauseated by the idea of colonies of homosexuals... being allowed to stroll hand-in-hand among more wholesome citizens", and hoped they be sent "to live together on a desert island...and in time, thank heaven, they would all die out or kill one another". While West reported feeling "pity, even tolerance" for homosexuals, she felt the need to "protest...the latitude allowed these pitiful misfits" in the mainstream media.[33] Despite – or perhaps because of – the work's controversial reception, it sold very well: hitting second place in the non-fiction listings in September 1971. Yet, perhaps the best marker of the book's success was Altman being interviewed by *Vogue* magazine.[34]

West's anger at the media's so-called latitude emerged in part from Altman's widely publicised July 1971 appearance on the Australian Broadcasting Corporation's (ABC) current affairs program *Monday Conference*. Altman's appearance was quite well received, with a *Canberra Times* columnist noting he appeared "with excellent effect", showing "anyone who did not know it already that dignity, sensitivity and integrity are as wholly compatible with the homosexual condition as with any other".[35] The author's appearance was not so much about his book, though it received quite a bit of publicity on the program, but more about the politics of gay liberation. Altman fended off questions from two conservative panellists, Liberal parliamentarian Peter Coleman and Methodist minister Rev. Roger Bush, about whether decriminalising homosexuality would simply "lead to more homosexuals". Altman remarked that he "thought not... [b]ut there might be a decline in the number of people who were miserable, some committing suicide, because they could not accept their homosexuality."[36]

Altman noted that his appearance was only made possible because of his positive reviews in *Time*: "We still have this colonial cringe mentality that if someone has made it in *Time*, that has somehow sanctified them and made them respectable."[37] He believed that this was the reason for the ABC's controversial decision not to screen a documentary featuring Altman and other gay liberationists on the channel's premiere program, *This Day Tonight*. Sparking protest outside the ABC offices in Melbourne, Altman put the program's cancellation down to the fact that the other liberationists slated to appear were not "respectable", holding neither official positions at universities nor positive reviews in respectable magazines.[38]

Yet, Australians appear to have responded more positively to gay liberation than one might have expected, with West's homophobic letter to the *Canberra Times* sparking a flurry of responses. "Rarely has an Australian paper published a more vile and outrageous attack on a minority group", "Homosexual" angrily wrote, concluding that gay liberation "does not want the kind of toleration Miss West is offering; hers is of a kind we can do without", with "misfit" adopting a similar tone.[39] Other letter writers took the opportunity to critique contemporary understandings of marriage and biology, or to propose homosexuality as a solution to ever-growing populations.[40] Annabelle Clynes of Dickson, Canberra took a more sarcastic note in her response, suggesting that Australia should also "attempt to eliminate those other groups who have become the misfits of our society: our Aborigines, unmarried mothers, the physically and mentally handicapped, and the aged".[41]

A similar, if less censorious and violent, response awaited the publication of Greer's work in Australia. Sue Matthews, a prominent Australian feminist activist, described its publication as sparking "a frenzy of literary outrage, amusement and condescension". The anger and humour Matthews reported was from the "'I don't want to be liberated' ladies", whose conservatism was "warming the hearts of the terror-stricken bra and cosmetics manufacturers".[42] Yet critical discussion of Greer's work was not limited to respectable ladies – feminist and radical circles in the United States and elsewhere equally read and debated *The Female Eunuch*.

If Australian women's reactions to Greer were mixed, she was – perhaps surprisingly – judiciously welcomed by the *Australian Women's Weekly*. A 1971 article by Nika Hazelton appeared ahead of her 1972 press tour of Australia. It underscored the discrepancy between expectation and reality, femininity and women's liberation. Hazelton discussed her conversation with "Miss Greer (I balk at calling her Dr. Greer since she certainly does not conform to the popular notion of a female Ph.D.)", recalling her "trepidation" prior to the interview. Alongside some fairly laudatory commentary upon Greer's feminism, Hazelton described her femininity (apparently abundantly clear in person but hidden from the media), her appearance (specifically her "generous mouth"), and her wardrobe. If Hazelton could not fully agree with Greer, she did hope for the adoption of "a new set of values and joyful ways of living to produce a true human liberation".[43] Underneath this article appeared a quiz – "HOW LIBERATED ARE YOU? By Lawrence S. Baker, Ph.D., and Louise Kreisberg [sic]" – which asked readers to answer loaded questions about mothering, marriage, and careers.[44]

In February 1972, during Greer's Australian press tour, the *Australian Women's Weekly* featured a more explicitly celebratory article. Journalist Kay Keavney described Greer as "the free soul who won freedom the hard way".[45] But in the coming years, the magazine would capture a greater multiplicity of women's voices responding to women's liberation. In 1974, the *Australian Women's Weekly* published letters to the editor about Greer and her supposed "arch enemy", Arianna Stassinopoulos, many of which held greater sympathy for the latter.[46]

Greer, unlike Altman, did appear on ABC's *This Day Tonight* in a March 1972 report by Caroline Jones. This segment captured impressions of *The Female Eunuch* in a way that was supposed to be representative of all Australian women. Lukewarm at best, hostile at worst, and also simply confused, a cache of interviews suggested that young and older women – none of whom had read the book – did not embrace Greer or her philosophy. As Jones editorialised, the book's success overseas did not mean it would "incite many Australian women to revolution". The camera lingered on Greer's cigarette as she gave voice to her personal feeling of being sensationalised by the Australian media.[47]

Overall, however, *This Day Tonight* aimed toward some objectivity. When a group of seniors from the Sydney Church of England Girls' Grammar School – all of whom had read the book – were interviewed, they enthusiastically embraced Greer's message and offered thoughtful responses shaped by knowledge of current events. One spoke of the gendered conditioning little girls experience; another rejected her father's worldview. Australian historian Ann McGrath, reflecting on what she wrote in her own personal diary from 1972, corroborates the embrace with which many teenaged girls responded to Greer.[48] "Does Germaine Greer's book *The Female Eunuch* offer *you* a way of life that would appeal to *you*?" Jones asked the seven teenagers. "Yes," they enthusiastically responded in chorus.[49]

256　Jon Piccini and Ana Stevenson

These diverse grassroots voices reveal the variety of responses Greer provoked, from warm to questioning to unsympathetic. Years later, in a book review of Christine Wallace's unauthorised biography *Germaine Greer, Untamed Shrew* (1997), Laura Miller captured a similar sentiment:

> An Australian contemporary of [Greer's], Susan Ryan, reminded Wallace that "women who were housewives, who were pretty miserable...felt inspired by her book and their life changed. They didn't become megastars, but they became a librarian or something. I've heard women say again and again when the subject of Germaine comes up: 'Well, her book changed my life for the better.' And they'll be modest women living pretty ordinary lives, but better lives." Women entirely unlike Germaine Greer, the feminist who improved the world in spite of herself.[50]

Contesting

In the 1970s and beyond, a number of voices in Australia and the United States engaged in an ongoing critical dialogue about Greer and Altman, their pathbreaking works, and their current endeavours. While as diverse an audience as radical feminists and feminist theologians debated Greer's ideas, the radical community received Altman's work as both a pathbreaking manifesto and an overblown failure. The later writings of both featured in Gloria Steinem's famous and widely circulated *Ms.* Magazine.

Perhaps the first contestation the books engendered was between the authors themselves. Altman acknowledged his debt to Greer in *Homosexual*, but was critical in equal measure. Overall, Altman found Greer's work limited both through its exclusions and missed opportunities. "*The Female Eunuch*...largely ignores the lesbian", Altman commented, "though whether because she is in Greer's view not a female or not a eunuch I am not sure", he added pithily. Altman suggested that Greer's calls for women to "love themselves" is weaker for not dealing with those women whose sexual preferences already carried this sentiment to its logical conclusion.[51] At a Sydney forum on Sexual Liberation in 1972, where both were in attendance, Altman asked: "Where is the lesbian in *The Female Eunuch*?"[52] Equally, Altman expressed concern that Greer's calls for "women [to] humanize the penis" left out the role men need to play in this process. "Women alone can hardly achieve this", Altman concluded; it was instead necessary for men to "learn to relate to each other with the same love Greer would have them show for women".[53] Greer responded to Altman's "gentle chiding" at the Sexual Liberation forum by declaring the women's and gay liberation as "part of a continuum".[54]

Greer faced her own contestations in the United States. As editor of *Ms.* Magazine, Steinem reportedly sought original contributions from Greer, but without success.[55] Based on the (sometimes competing) initiatives of its editorial staff, *Ms.* prided itself on being an open forum for the articulation and popularisation of a variety of feminist ideas.[56] When *Ms.* published Greer's "Down with

Panties" in July 1972, it was actually a reprint (under a new title) from a 1971 column in London's *Sunday Times*. [57] Greer was often constructed as "exotically Australian" in the American media, and indeed, her article appeared in *Ms.*'s "Notes from Abroad" section.[58] "The famous feminist says 'knickers' must go", an added subtitle read, underscoring Greer's idiosyncratic Australian-British English. "Once warmth is no longer appropriate as a reason for wearing knickers", Greer succinctly asked, "what else is there?"[59] As Greer later commented, such frivolous journalistic pieces "were the only ones anyone ever remembered."[60]

Due to its appearance in the *Sunday Times* and *Ms.*, Greer's flippant call for women to abandon their underwear gained circulation – and inspired mixed responses – among feminists of varying stripes. "Despite the proselytizing of the Gloria Steinems and Betty Friedans, black women and their Third World sisters have yet to join the organized women's movement in significant numbers", Emily F. Gibson observed in the *Rochester Democrat and Chronicle* in 1975. "We are hardly 'libbing it up'." Drawing on her personal disengagement with feminism, Gibson emphasised, "I didn't burn my bra, nor did I yield to the temptation of Germaine Greer's shortlived 'Down with panties' campaign".[61] In spite of the inspiration Greer gained from the writings of black liberation, African American women did not always see themselves reflected in her theories. The concerns raised in *The Female Eunuch* did not necessarily speak to the intersectional experiences of black women.

But Greer also received condemnation – and, perhaps surprisingly, a measure of support – from commentators of an arguably competing ideological perspective. Australian feminist theologian Barbara Thiering could agree with Greer on some points, while rejecting the premise of her argument on others. Like Greer, Thiering undertook higher education in Sydney and Britain; she would later publish ground-breaking and controversial scholarship in Biblical exegesis.[62] From the late 1960s, increasing secularisation and the emergence of women's liberation meant Christianity in Australia struggled to transcend the gulf between religion and feminism.[63] The spectre of marriage was used to obstruct emerging claims about the ordination of women in the Anglican Church. "I believe marriage is still more attractive to most women, despite what Germaine Greer says", Anglican deaconess Elizabeth Alfred concluded.[64] Thiering, who would advocate women's ordination, was one of the few Australian women to be early concerned with feminist interpretations of the Bible.

Thiering objected not to the liberation of female sexuality per se, but to why Greer rejected the institution of marriage. "Germaine Greer argues that woman has become a castrate by being defined as sex object", she wrote, "her own aggressive sexuality being denied in the process". Thiering perceived Greer to be concerned with power, a perspective she viewed as antithetical to the Christian conceptualisation of love. "The opposite of being a sex object is to be a sex subject, and for [Greer], subjectivity consists in dominance." Rather than seeking power through sexuality, since "[e]xperiments in promiscuity lead to the re-objectification of women", Thiering believed that women and men alike should seek to maintain "the subjectivity of both the lover and the loved" so as to remain "fully human". Greer's own emphasis on the liberation men could enjoy in consequence of women's sexual empowerment thus paralleled feminist theological attention toward the beauty of shared sexual experience. But Thiering concluded: "A woman's power lies in the ability to give or withhold at will. ... This power is lost where there is no contract of fidelity. But the promiscuous male does not lose any power."[65] If emergent aspects of feminist theology could coexist with some tenets of women's liberation, others remained completely at odds with attitudes toward women's bodily and sexual autonomy.

Altman's reception was equally contested, both in Australia and America. Warren Blumenfeld, who would later become an eminent queer academic, wrote to Altman in 1972. *Homosexual* "is by far the best book written about the social ramifications of the gay movement", Blumenfeld remarked, adding, "I am sure it will catch on and be read throughout this country". Blumenfeld enclosed a copy of Southern Illinois University's first gay liberation newsletter, *InterCHANGE,* clearly expressing the transnational nature of this movement.[66] Prominent American gay activists Allen Young also wrote to Altman in 1971, describing *Homosexual* as "the book we have all been waiting for", while another activist from Rochester University, New York, reportedly hoped to pen his own book on gay liberation, only to read *Homosexual* and find "that you said everything I wanted to say, only better than I could have said it".[67] Such commentary is remarkable given Altman acknowledges *Homosexual*'s lacklustre reception in the United States, as opposed to in Australia.

Yet, critical voices were heard, from both liberal and radical opponents in the transnational gay movement. Altman's "all-too-familiar slip into leftist cant" was critiqued by gay activist John Mitzel in Boston's *Advocate*, which along with his desire to "show how Gay Liberation relates to struggles of black people [and] feminists" means that "Altman writes about this commodity called Gay Liberation as a piece of the social movement without having fully explored what it is that Gay Liberation is all about".[68] Thus, Altman's associations with the far left and its exciting ideological world was not always well received. Altman was even criticised by some of his compatriots for abandoning the radical cause. In one stinging piece from 1973, Simon Kronenberg wrote in *National U* that Altman's recent appearance on the Australian Broadcating Corporation's popular talk show *With Gerald Stone* meant he "no longer has any credibility as a radical". Altman's appearance was likened to "a questionnaire for 'Woman's Day'", and he was condemned for professing admiration for Martin Luther King – "Where are your Huey Newton's and Angela Davis", Kronenberg retorted – and for fitting into "the safe niche as house poofter". The criticism itself recalled the inspiration white Australian radicals such as Greer and Altman received from the black power movement. "Gay Liberation isn't about winning acceptance through absorption", the article concluded.[69] The role of the far-left celebrity, it seems, was always a contested one.

Greer, in turn, never regained the celebration or controversy garnered by *The Female Eunuch*. "Germaine, at 40, is still the world's best-known women's libber,

Reading Germaine Greer and Dennis Altman **259**

and one of the world's most maligned women", the *Australian Women's Weekly* stated in 1979. "She does not write on or talk much about the women's movement now", Rosemary Munday continued. The article quoted Greer's reply: "People are always asking me what I think of it, but I don't think my role is to pontificate on others' struggles."[70] Perhaps unfairly, *Ms.* featured Greer in a 1981 article entitled "Is There Life After Notoriety?" At least it answered in the affirmative, noting her involvement in "an astonishing range of scholarly activities that span the globe – from teaching in a women's college in Bombay, India, to currently directing the Tulsa University (Oklahoma) Centre for the Study of Women's Literature".[71] But Greer's engagement with feminism had not actually ceased. *Ms.* featured an excerpt from her new book, *The Obstacle Race: The Fortunes of Women Painters and Their Work* (1979), in November 1979. A far more academic monograph than *The Female Eunuch*, it was clearly grounded in the feminist project of historical recovery. "We cannot but marvel that so many works by women painters have simply rotted away", Greer wrote, alongside stunning reproductions of the seventeenth-century paintings of Judith Leyster. The short author biography that followed emphasised that this book was "the result of seven years' work".[72] Clearly, Greer had not been idle since the early 1970s.

Yet Greer continued to create consternation among readers. In April 1984 *Ms.* published "The Uses of Chastity and Other Paths to Sexual Pleasures", a feature article based on another new book, *Sex and Destiny: The Politics of Human Fertility* (1984). Reflecting upon the sexual revolution and women's liberation, Greer conjectured: "What we campaigned for was the right to say yes: what we may be pardoned for not having understood…was that the right to say yes is not freedom in the absence of the right to say no[.]" Asking whether or not women should be primarily responsible for fertility, Greer gave culturally relativistic examples of societies in which celibacy was not unusual. Hoping not to be "construed as advocating sexual repression", Greer desired "for young women…to regard themselves as hard to get, and their bodies as far too precious to bloat with steroids and bury [birth control] gadgets in".[73]

As some *Ms.* letters to the editor would reveal, readers could not decide whether they found this article controversial or humdrum. One woman found it "very disturbing". Questioning the logical outcome of such thinking, she concluded, "Greer seems to have lost sight of the feminist goal of enabling women to be autonomous and self-actualized."[74] A male reader, on the other hand, couldn't see what all the fuss was about:

> I'm surprised that *Ms.* labelled Germaine Greer's new book "controversial." All Greer seems to be saying is:
>
> - women ought not risk their health or their sanity in the pursuit of ephemeral pleasures
> - if orgasm is the goal, there are many ways to reach it without having to use contraceptive devices

- men are more easily sated than Old Husbands' Tales suggest
- the emotional and physiological hazards of continence have been greatly exaggerated

So what is to controvert? It all seems sensible and liberating; indeed, rather grandmotherly.[75]

Though in no way homogenous, the *Ms.* readership was sympathetic to a wide range of feminist perspectives, suggesting that these later responses to Greer were likely more beneficent than that of mainstream audiences.

Altman, too, wrote for *Ms.* during the 1980s. His September 1986 article, "The Tragedy of AIDS: More Than Lives Have Been Lost," was part of the magazine's unfolding editorial concern about the epidemic. "I am lucky", Altman began. "None of my lovers and only a few of my friends have died over the past several years." Unlike the media's often sneering attitude toward homosexual men, *Ms.* sympathetically concerned itself firstly with the situation of women and secondly with men. This editorial focus did not represent a latent homophobia; instead, it sought to reclaim rather than overlook the voices and experiences of the women who were affected but may otherwise have been silenced. Altmam, too, offered a wider perspective, emphasising that AIDS affected "gay men", but also "drug users and hemophiliacs". Mourning human and cultural losses alike, Altman reflected: "Too many of the gay men I know in New York, Los Angeles, San Francisco, yes, and Sydney and London as well, are numb[.]" Advocating for safer sex and denouncing "voyeuristic stories about the end of 'fast-lane sex'," Altman made it clear that AIDS was not a moral disease; nor had it only affected the gay community in the United States.[76]

The author biographies *Ms.* published alongside Greer and Altman's writings offer insight into the relative durability of their radical celebrity in the United States. *The Female Eunuch* was always cited as Greer's seminal achievement. While its American year of publication was usually dated correctly, ironically "Is there life after notoriety?" erroneously stated 1969.[77] "[Greer] taught in a provincial English university, clowned in a popular television show, and wrote 'The Female Eunuch' all at more or less the same time", *Ms.* editorialised alongside "The Uses of Chastity", continuing: "She was married for only three weeks, is unintentionally childless, and lives in London and Italy where she raises medicinal plants."[78] Since authoring this seminal feminist text, it was suggested, she had perfected unconventionality and potentially even become a purveyor of marijuana. Did being "unintentionally childless" make her more relatable than her intentionally childless peers, such as Steinem? In contrast, *Ms.* made note of Altman's academic appointments at the University of California, San Francisco and, in "his native Australia", La Trobe University. It referenced his recent book, *AIDS in the Mind of America* (1986), but not *Homosexual* − likely out of obliviousness rather than as a purposeful slight.[79] Clearly, *Ms.* was more literate in the particulars of Greer's life, achievements, and idiosyncrasies than those of Altman.

Reading Germaine Greer and Dennis Altman **261**

In contrast, *Homosexual* retained greater interest for Australian activists in later decades. The book's republishing in 1993 saw activists who came to political maturity in the 1980s recall its continuing importance. Rodney Croome, leading activist in Australia's marriage equality campaign of the 2010s, reviewed the republished work in Tasmania's *Island* literary journal. "When, as a frightened, closeted undergraduate, I first read *Homosexual* in 1986 my views on sex and sexuality were profoundly shaped", Croome recalled. "[I]t was Altman's exposition on gay identity, more than any other text on homosexuality, which helped me make sense of my profound alienation from a world disfigured by heterosexual chauvinism".[80] As Jeffrey Weeks wrote in his introduction to the 1993 edition, *Homosexual* was very much a product of its time – laden with vernacular and utopian hopes that emerged from the 1960s.[81] Even so, it still influenced those, like Croome, whose activism had much more limited horizons.

In 2010, upon the 40th anniversary of *The Female Eunuch*, Australian Sex Discrimination Commissioner Pru Goward observed that until its publication, "most of us hadn't thought of ourselves as oppressed, we just thought that was the way it was".[82] On Greer's 75th birthday in 2014, *The Guardian* chronicled a number of women's remembrances of – and more recent responses to – *The Female Eunuch*. "Today's feminists shouldn't airbrush her legacy into something we find more palatable", Helen Lewis emphasised. Anna Holmes found herself unmoved by Greer, while Bidisha astutely situated her as "a defining voice in western feminism, alongside Susan Brownmiller, Andrea Dworkin, Kate Millett and others". For Zohra Moosa, Greer's "culturally relativist approach to human rights violations such as female genital mutilation, as well as her transphobia, [is] abhorrent".[83] A multiplicity of perspectives characterised initial responses to and memories of Greer and Altman's writings. This diversity clearly continues today.

Conclusion

It is often remarked as peculiar that so many of the 1970s radical manifestos originated in Australia. Germaine Greer and Dennis Altman are here often placed alongside Peter Singer, whose work on animal liberation continues to inspire.[84] Yet, this chapter has demonstrated how placing these writers within a purely Australian context is misconceived in two key ways. Firstly, it ignores the importance of the language of the transnational far left, and its particular Australian idioms, for both Greer and Altman's work. Neither were expressly Marxists – Greer describes herself as an 'anarchist-communist' and Altman wrote as much in opposition to the limitations of Marxism as in its defence. Still, the Left's language of liberation, of challenging racial, gender and sexual divides and the system of profit and exploitation that drove them, was implicit in their work. While these writers found meaning and ideas within the far left – anarchism for Greer and the Frankfurt School for Altman, and both were inspired by black power – their radicalism was a key factor in why they were criticised by both mainstream audiences and fellow activists. And yet, voices from across the political spectrum also emerged in support of their radical writings. Both, if to varying degrees, were embraced by mainstream audiences. It is important and revealing to uncover the grassroots celebration of these manifestos as well as the ongoing questioning and critical responses they garnered from prominent feminists and gay liberationists alike.

Secondly, to pigeonhole these writers as 'Australian' ignores how much both their writing processes, inspiration and, importantly, reception and contestation, were transnational. Greer wrote her work in Britain in opposition to local second-wave feminism, while Altman wrote his in Australia after a lengthy stay in the United States, yet specifically dismissed the Australian context. And both works were first published overseas, before being hugely successful in the antipodes.

Today, both authors maintain their global, controversial lives. For Greer, this arises not from her feminism and ongoing emphasis on liberation, but for her sensationalistic style and objectionable comments about transgender women.[85] Interestingly, the genesis for these comments is clearly laid out in *The Female Eunuch*, now an oft-cited foundational text for second-wave feminism.[86] Altman, on the other hand, has been a critical supporter of the marriage equality movement, the aims of which seem at complete odds with his 1970s sexual utopianism. The fact that both have stuck to their foundational ideas – of binary gender oppression and opposition to the bourgeois institution of marriage – also helps to cement them as erstwhile members of a far left which today still doubts and debates the veracity of 'identity politics'. Placing both in a transnational context, as activists and celebrities of differing degrees, reveals the competing legacies of *The Female Eunuch* and *Homosexual* in the histories of Australia, the United States, and beyond.

Notes

1 Donn Teal, "Dennis Altman: Hip Scholar from Down Under", *Gay Magazine*, 7 February 1972, 8.
2 Mary Spongberg, "If She's So Great, How Come So Many Pigs Dig Her? Germaine Greer and the Malestream Press", *Women's History Review* 2, no. 3 (1993): 407–419; Marea Mitchell, "Beyond the Fragments Again: Germaine Greer and the Politics of Feminism", *Journal of Interdisciplinary Gender Studies* 5, no. 1 (2000): 67–77; Sandra Lilburn, Susan Magarey, and Susan Sheridan, "Celebrity Feminism as Synthesis: Germaine Greer, *The Female Eunuch* and the Australian Print Media", *Continuum: Journal of Media & Cultural Studies* 14, no. 3 (2000): 335–348; Anthea Taylor, "Germaine Greer's Adaptable Celebrity: Feminism, Unruliness, and Humour on the British Small Screen", *Feminist Media Studies* 14, no. 5 (2014): 759–774; Anthea Taylor, Maryanne Dever, and Lisa Adkins, "Greer Now: Editorial", *Australian Feminist Studies* 31, no. 87 (2016): 1–6; Petra Mosmann, "A Feminist Fashion Icon: Germaine Greer's Paisley Coat", *Australian Feminist Studies* 31, no. 87 (2016): 78–94.
3 Carolyn D'Cruz and Mark Pendleton (eds.), *After Homosexual: The Legacies of Gay Liberation* (Crawley, WA: University of Western Australia Press, 2014).
4 Frank Bongiorno, "Sensational Sexualities: Germaine Greer's *The Female Eunuch* and Dennis Altman's *Homosexual: Oppression and Liberation*", in Tanya Dalziell and Paul Genoni (eds.), *Telling Stories: Australian Life and Literature 1935–2012* (Melbourne: Monash University, 2013): 299.
5 See: Megan Le Masurier, "Resurrecting Germaine's Theory of Cuntpower [sic]," *Australian Feminist Studies* 31, no. 87 (2016): 28–42.

6 Kate Gleeson, "From *Suck* Magazine to *Corporate Paedophilia*. Feminism and Pornography – Remembering the Australian Way", *Women's Studies International Forum* 38 (2013): 86–87. See also: Megan Le Masurier, "Photograph: Germaine Greer", in Margaret Henderson and Alison Bartlett (eds.), *Things That Liberate: An Australian Feminist Wunderkammer* (Newcastle upon Tyne: Cambridge Scholars Publishing, 2014).

7 Rachel Buchanan, "How Shakespeare Helped Shape Germaine Greer's Feminist Masterpiece", *The Conversation*, 27 May 2016, https://theconversation.com/friday-essa y-how-shakespeare-helped-shape-germaine-greers-feminist-masterpiece-59880 (accessed 17 March 2017); "Germaine Greer's Shakespeare: Early Writing", *The University of Melbourne Library*, https://digitised-collections.unimelb.edu.au/handle/11343/91820 (accessed 15 July 2016).

8 Rachel Buchanan, "The Record Keeper", *Australian Feminist Studies* 31, no. 87 (2016): 22–27.

9 Marilyn Lake, "'Revolution for the Hell of it': The Transatlantic Genesis and Serial Provocations of *The Female Eunuch*", *Australian Feminist Studies* 31, no. 87 (2016): 8 and 12.

10 Germaine Greer in conversation with Ian Turner and Chris Hector, "Greer on Revolution; Greer on Love", *Overland* 50/51 (Autumn 1972), www.takver.com/history/sydney/greer1972.htm (accessed 17 March 2017).

11 Bongiorno, "Sensational Sexualities", 299. See: Anne Summers, *Damned Whores and God's Police: The Colonization of Women in Australia* (Ringwood: Allen Lane, 1975).

12 Dennis Altman, *Defying Gravity: A Political Life* (St Leonards, NSW: Allen & Unwin, 1997): 27.

13 Dennis Altman interviewed by Jill Matthews, 18–19 December 1991, ORAL TRC 2771, National Library of Australia (NLA).

14 Lake, "'Revolution for the Hell of it'", 14.

15 Dennis Altman, "King vs Carmichael", *National U*, 8 July 1968, 8.

16 Cameron Forbes, "Is Homosexuality a Sickness or a Terrible Sin?" *The Age*, 22 July 1972, 12.

17 Altman, *Defying Gravity*, 57.

18 Dennis Altman, "Students in the Electric Age", in Richard Gordon (ed.), *The Australian New Left: Critical Essays and Strategy* (Melbourne: William Heinemann, 1970): 131.

19 Dennis Altman, "The Politics of Cultural Change", Paper presented at the Socialist Scholars Conference, 21–24 May, 1970, in Altman, Dennis Patkin, Volume 1, A6119, 3692, National Archives of Australia, Canberra.

20 Germaine Greer, *The Female Eunuch* (London: MacGibbon & Kee, 1970), 328.

21 "Saucy Feminist That Even Men Like", *LIFE*, 7 May 1971.

22 Henry S. Albinski, "Australia and the United States", *Daedalus* 114, no. 1 (1985): 407.

23 Buchanan, "The Record Keeper", 22.

24 Rebecca J. Sheehan, "'If we had more like her we would no longer be the Unheard Majority': Germaine Greer's Reception in the United States", *Australian Feminist Studies* 31, no. 87 (2016): 64.

25 Kevin Rowley, "Ideology in the Electric Age", in Richard Gordon (ed.), *The Australian New Left: Critical Essays and Strategy* (Melbourne: William Heinemann, 1970): 148, 161.

26 On *Homosexual* as a precursor to Queer Theory, see Bongiorno, "Sensational Sexualities".

27 Dennis Altman, *Homosexual: Oppression and Liberation* (St Lucia, Queensland: University of Queensland Press, [1971], 2012): 248.

28 Henry Mayer to Dennis Altman, March 1971, Box 1, Dennis Altman Papers, MS 5402, National Library of Australia (NLA).

29 Richard Walsh, "From Ulan Bator to Literary Fame", in Carolyn D'Cruz and Mark Pendleton (eds.), *After Homosexual: The Legacies of Gay Liberation* (Crawley, WA: University of Western Australia Press, 2014): 16.

30 Dennis Altman interviewed by Lisa Whitehead, "Forty Years On: Australian Remembers Role in Gay Liberation Movement", Broadcast 6 February, 2012, www.abc.net.au/7.30/content/2012/s3424275.htm (accessed 17 March 2017).

31 Walsh, "From Ulan Bator", 17.
32 James Grieve, "A jolt for the liberals", *Canberra Times*, 2 September 1972, 12.
33 Frances West, "Homosexual Liberation", *Canberra Times*, 5 September 1972, 2.
34 Walsh, "From Ulan Bator", 18.
35 D.W. Rawson, "Gay Liberation Tests the ABC", *Canberra Times*, 19 July 1972, 2.
36 "CAMP in all States", *Canberra Times*, 4 July 1972, 3.
37 "Altman on Himself", *Woroni*, 24 August 1972, 8–9.
38 Ibid., 8–9.
39 "Homosexual Liberation", *Canberra Times*, 12 September 1972, 2; "Homosexual Liberation", *Canberra Times*, 7 September 1972, 2.
40 Anne Westbrook and Sylvia Passioura, "Homosexual Liberation", *Canberra Times*, 9 September 1972, 2.
41 Annabelle Clynes, "Homosexual Liberation", *Canberra Times*, 6 September 1972, 2.
42 Sue Matthews, "Female Eunuch: Reviewed by Sue Matthews", *Lot's Wife*, 28 February 1972, 16.
43 Nika Hazelton, "Germaine Greer Talks," *Australian Women's Weekly*, 24 November 1971.
44 Lawrence S. Baker and Louise Kreisberg, "How liberated are you?" *Australian Women's Weekly*, 24 November 1971.
45 Kay Keavney, "The Liberating of Germaine Greer", *Australian Women's Weekly*, 2 February 1972.
46 "Arianna or Germaine?: Readers' views on woman's role in society today", *Australian Women's Weekly*, November 6, 1974. See further: Isobelle Barrett Meyering, "Germaine Greer's 'Arch Enemy': Arianna Stassinopoulos' 1974 Australian Tour", *Australian Feminist Studies* 31, no. 87 (2016): 43–61.
47 "*This Day Tonight*: 22.3.1972", in "Publication of Germaine Greer's *The Female Eunuch*", *80 Days that Changed Our Lives: ABC*, 19 January 2012, www.abc.net.au/archives/80days/stories/2012/01/19/3411580.htm (accessed 17 March 2017).
48 Ann McGrath, "The Female Eunuch in the Suburbs: Reflections on Adolescence, Autobiography and History-Writing", *Journal of Popular Culture* 33 (1999): 177–190.
49 "*This Day Tonight*: 22.3.1972".
50 Laura Miller, "Germaine Greer", *Salon*, 22 June 1999, www.salon.com/1999/06/22/greer/ (accessed 17 March 2017).
51 Altman, *Homosexual*, 100.
52 Dennis Altman, *Coming out in the Seventies* (Sydney: Wild & Woolley, 1979): 18.
53 Altman, *Homosexual*, 235.
54 Christine Wallace, *Germaine Greer, Untamed Shrew* (Sydney: Pan MacMillan, 1997): 255.
55 Ibid., 199–200.
56 Amy Erdman Farrell, *Yours in Sisterhood: Ms. Magazine and the Promise of Popular Feminism* (Chapel Hill: University of North Carolina Press, 1998): 39 and 42.
57 Germaine Greer, "Going Without", *Sunday Times*, 26 September 1971.
58 For "exotically Australian", see: Sheehan, "'If we had more like her'," 65.
59 "Germaine Greer: Down With Panties", *Ms.*, July 1972 (Special Collections, Hillman Library, University of Pittsburgh).
60 Germaine Greer, *The Madwoman's Underclothes: Essays and Occasional Writings* (New York: Atlantic Monthly Press, 1986), xxv. See: Rachel Buchanan, "Foreign Correspondence: Journalism in the Germaine Greer Archive", *Archives and Manuscripts* 46, no. 1 (2018): 18–39.
61 Emily F. Gibson, "A Black Woman's View of Equal Rights", *Rochester Democrat and Chronicle*, 21 November 1975.
62 See: Barbara Thiering, *Jesus and the Riddle of the Dead Sea Scrolls: Unlocking the Secrets of His Life Story* (Harpercollins, 1992, 1993).
63 Peter Sherlock, "Australian Women Priests? Anglicans, Feminists and the Newspapers", *Lilith: A Feminist History Journal*, no. 10 (2001): 137–138.
64 *Sun-Herald*, 27 May 1973, in Sherlock, "Australian Women Priests?" 143.

65 Barbara Thiering, *Created Second? Aspects of Women's Liberation in Australia* (Sydney: Family Life Movement of Australia, 1973): 54–55 and 61.

66 Warren Blumenfeld to Dennis Altman, undated, Box 1, Dennis Altman Papers, MS 5402, NLA.

67 Allen Young to Dennis Altman, 27 December 1971, Box 1, Dennis Altman Papers, MS 5402, NLA; Larry Fine to Dennis Altman, 15 April 1972, Box 1, Dennis Altman Papers, MS 5402, NLA.

68 John Mitzel, "Altman Fails to Explain what Gay Lib really is", *Advocate*, 19 January 1972, 20.

69 Simon Kronenburg, "Altman, Man of the Year", *National U*, 5 March 1973.

70 Rosemary Munday, "Germaine Greer: Why Have Australians Stopped Caring about People?" *Australian Women's Weekly*, 14 February 1979.

71 Jill Storey, "Is There Life After Notoriety?" *Ms.*, October 1981. See: Germaine Greer, "The Tulsa Center for the Study of Women's Literature: What We Are Doing and Why We Are Doing It", *Tulsa Studies in Women's Literature* 1, no. 1 (1982): 5–26.

72 Germaine Greer, "In Search of Lost Women Artists", *Ms.*, November 1979. See: Germaine Greer, *The Obstacle Race: The Fortunes of Women Painters and Their Work* (London: Tauris Parke Paperbacks, 1979, 2001).

73 Germaine Greer, "The Uses of Chastity and Other Paths to Sexual Pleasures", *Ms.*, April 1984. See: Germaine Greer, *Sex and Destiny: The Politics of Human Fertility* (London: Secker & Warburg, 1984).

74 Millea Kenin, Oakland, Calif., *Ms.*, July 1984.

75 George Dusheck, Albion, Calif., *Ms.*, July 1984.

76 Dennis Altman, "The Tragedy of AIDS: More than Lives Have Been Lost", *Ms.*, September 1986. See: Dennis Altman, *AIDS in the Mind of America* (Garden City: Anchor Press/Doubleday, 1986). This was written when "AIDS" was the predominant terminology. Altman makes one reference to HTLV-III/LAV (discovered in 1983); HIV was only announced by the International Committee on the Taxonomy of Viruses in May 1986 to be the descriptor for the newly renamed human immunodeficiency virus.

77 Greer, "In Search", 1979; Storey, "Is There Life", 1981.

78 Greer, "Uses of Chastity", 1984.

79 Altman, "Tragedy of AIDS", 1986.

80 Rodney Croome, "Pride, Visibility and Courage", *Island Magazine*, Winter 1994, 56–7.

81 Jeffrey Weeks, "Introduction to the 1993 Printing", *Homosexual: Oppression and Liberation* (St Lucia, QLD: University of Queensland Press, 2012): 1–15.

82 Pru Goward, "An Inconvenient Truth", *The Drum*, 28 September 2010, www.abc.net. au/news/2010-03-08/34278 (accessed 17 March 2017).

83 "What Germaine Greer and The Female Eunuch Mean to Me", *Guardian*, 25 January 2014, www.theguardian.com/books/2014/jan/26/germaine-greer-female-eunuch-feminists-influence (accessed 17 March 2017).

84 Gonzalo Villanueva "'The Bible' of the Animal Movement: Peter Singer and Animal Liberation, 1970–1976", *History Australia* 13, no. 3 (2016): 399–414.

85 Germaine Greer, "Caster Semenya Sex Row: What Makes a Woman", *Guardian*, 20 August 2009, www.theguardian.com/sport/2009/aug/20/germaine-greer-caster-semenya (accessed 17 March 2017); British Broadcasting Corporation, "Germaine Greer: Transgender Women are not Women", *BBC Newsnight*, 24 October 2015, www. bbc.com/news/uk-34625512 (accessed 17 March 2017); Tara John, "Germaine Greer Defends Her Controversial Views on Transgender Women", *TIME*, 12 April 2016, http://time.com/4290409/germaine-greer-transgender-women/ (accessed 17 March 2017).

86 See also: Laurie Penny, "The Female Eunuch 40 Years On", *Guardian*, 27 October 2010, www.theguardian.com/books/booksblog/2010/oct/27/female-eunuch-40-years-on (accessed 17 March 2017). For other examples, see: Malia Schilling, "Outing a Rapist", *Ms Blog*, 10 April 2013, http://msmagazine.com/blog/2013/04/10/outing-a-rapist/ (accessed 17 March 2017); Michele Kort, "Jill Johnson Taught Me to be a Lesbian", *Ms Blog*, 11

October 2010, http://msmagazine.com/blog/2010/10/11/jill-johnston-taught-me-to-be-a-lesbian/ (accessed 17 March 2017); Susan J. Bandy, "Curious Tension: Feminism and the Sporting Woman", *Ms Blog*, 2 May 2012, http://msmagazine.com/blog/2012/05/02/curious-tension-feminism-and-the-sporting-woman/ (accessed 17 March 2017).

14

THE CULTURAL FRONT

Left cultural activism in the post-war era

Lisa Milner

Australian cultural life in the decades following World War II is notable for a flourishing of activity amongst creative people on the far left of the political spectrum. The landscape of left cultural activism has left a rich and generally unacknowledged legacy for contemporary Australian creatives and intellectuals, and provides an important case study in left cultural politics and networking. This chapter explores the rich diversity of Australian left cultural activist groups in the post-war period and analyses their motivations and legacy.

Left cultural activist Norma Disher remembered that 'we were part of the whole upward surge in creative work that was going on in the progressive movement of the time'.[1] Here she identifies her work as part of a definite formation. In a discussion of working-class identity and crowd behaviour, EP Thompson employed the concept of 'moral economy' to understand activism.[2] There was a shared moral economy amongst the left cultural activists. People with strongly held opinions on the nature of social justice, and faith in the utility of collective action, drove their groups. They mobilised their own creative resources to establish and sustain their groups, relied on formal as well as informal networks of communication, and aimed to provide not just artistic but broader educational, and sometimes political, training. They used the technologies and forms of existing art forms for oppositional purposes, and their activities inspired and supported the upsurge in cultural production of the period.

As two forms of protest, political activism and artistic activism fed into each other most notably in post-war Australia through the Communist Party of Australia (CPA). From its earliest times the organisation had attracted and encouraged the energies of creative people, and culture in its broadest sense was a topic which engendered much debate. Its vitality is evident in the ways that it supported a wide range of cultural activities: Stuart Macintyre describes how early Party work 'sustained a whole spectrum of alternative cultural activity',[3] whilst Frank Farrell explains that 'around the CPA sun rotated a bewildering array of organisations which reflected its light and extended its field of gravity'.[4]

A source of inspiration for comrade-artists was the work of AA Zhdanov, Secretary to the Central Committee of the Russian Communist Party and cultural critic of the 1930s, who urged writers and painters to draw their subjects from the working class. His work led to the refinement of the Party directive on cultural production, the tenets of which became known as socialist realism. Its basic ideal was a development of the view of art as a weapon, where art had a directly political purpose: the propelling of society towards communism. Socialist realist work emphasised ideological correctness over the individual freedom of the artist in the creative process. Zhdanov believed that artists should be propagandists. 'Create works of high attainment, of high ideological and artistic content', he advocated. 'Actively help to remould the mentality of people in the spirit of socialism. Be in the front ranks of those who are fighting for a classless socialist society.'[5] While its basis was in literature it soon spread to other disciplines, including drama, the visual arts and cinema.

One of the earliest manifestations of the CPA's involvement in creative work was the establishment of the Workers' Arts Club (WAC). Both New Zealand-born, communist and writer Jean Devanny was its most prominent founder in August 1932, whilst visual artist George Finey (not a Party member) was President. The WAC was 'completely democratic', according to one of its members, Eddie Allison.[6] The movement did much to encourage alternative cultural production, as a response to the high unemployment and poor living conditions of the Depression.

Since the early days of the WAC, Australian communists had adopted Lenin's advice which followed Zhdanov's: 'we must not put our hands in our pockets and let chaos ferment as it pleases. We must consciously try to guide its development, to form and determine its results … for art is a weapon.'[7] This was his exhortation to use creativity as a political tool, to harness the fruits of artistic production with the intention of mobilising the audience to act. He believed that for socialists, the cinema was the 'most important' of the arts.[8]

From 1935, the WAC was replaced by other organisations, some detailed in this chapter. Many of these groups reported to the CPA's Arts Committee, where they received advice, direction, criticism, and censorship. Although the ideals of the philosophy had been in common use, the term 'socialist realism' was not specifically employed in Australia until the post-war period. CPA executives and comrades, notably those on the Arts Committee, pursued and debated the expression of the theory. One document from this group expressed the foremost aim of the Party's movement towards communism, in which artist-comrades were urged to ask themselves:

> to what extent is our work in artistic fields part and parcel of this movement? The struggle, the correct presentation of Marxist-Leninist views, whilst simultaneously finding a basis for common action on the demands of creative workers, is an urgent task for all communists, both personally and through the collectives.[9]

From the end of WWII the CPA lent a heightened level of support for artistic production, as long as it was according to the tenets of socialist realism. In a policy speech at the 1945 National Congress, CPA leader Harry Gould claimed that 'art, in its origins and functions, can be understood only by relating it to the labour process'.[10] An important goal was, he argued, to 'unite art and science with the labour movement'.[11] With these sentiments, he expressed the aim of the Party leadership to harness all areas of culture towards the attainment of a socialist state. Like the Party's relationships with the trade union community, those with artists were important, and the realm of culture was not to develop on its own, but under the guidance of the Party. Journalist and labour leader Edgar Ross was the embodiment of the Party line in this aspect.[12] Throughout the 1950s and 1960s he was an executive of the CPA Arts Committee, and was convinced that 'the arts constitute one of the most important spheres of activity in the deep-going ideological struggle between decadent capitalism and the forces making for human liberation'.[13]

In this Australian exposition of socialist realism, there was a contradiction between the CPA's nationalism and a wholesale adoption of the Moscow line. The paradox was a reflection of many of the Party's ideologies: there was an intriguing relationship between the explicit internationalist basis of communism and its manifestation in the Party as an Australian structure. Robin Gollan claims that 'Communists were internationalists but this was held in tension with an Australian nationalism which grew out of opposition to imperialism but settled into a nationalism which took its colour equally from specifically Australian experience and Russian chauvinism.'[14] This contradictory dialogue is reflected in one of the Party's aims in 1951, which was to 'take steps to develop our own specific Australian culture, while at the same time accepting all that is best in world culture'.[15] The notion of 'our own' culture was an assumption that there was a single, united culture, a debatable idea at any time in any country's history. Nevertheless, this ongoing and intricate dialogue between nationalism and internationalism occurred in many aspects of radical politics and culture in post-war Australia, as other chapters in this collection indicate – and this was reflected in the radical nationalist idiom of many left cultural activists and Communist Party members. Like all forms of nationalist rhetoric in Australia in the 1950s, it assumed the existence of a unified view of Australian history.

Dissent from canon is not uncommon in any organisation, and not everyone shared the Party line on socialist realism. Many left cultural activists viewed it as an overly restrictive doctrine, which increasingly narrowed the scope of what was officially possible for communist artists and writers to produce. The viability of socialist realism as an artistic practice was hotly debated, and it was seen by some as a bureaucratic approach to art. In her autobiography *Artist of the Left*, Evelyn Healy, CPA member and artist, writes on the problems of 'working within a party climate which narrowed the role of culture to working class politics'.[16]

One of the most important aspects of social realism as manifested in post-war Australia was its encouragement of a collective approach. In 1958 John Pringle rather romantically suggested that Australian cultural workers were doomed to lead lonely lives, isolated … from their fellow writers. There is no Bloomsbury or Left Bank; no life of the cafe or the salon. They rarely meet anyone who has read their work or who can discuss it intelligently. Like the first pioneers who plunged into the wilderness with a bullock-cart, the Australian writer must 'plod on and keep his [sic] passion bright' alone.[17]

Pringle did not consider organisations outside the mainstream, the left cultural activist groups. The collectivist impulse in these groups was as strong as the political impulse in the CPA, or in the militant labour movement. Following the WAC, the groups were often established and administered by comrades, but membership was by no means restricted. They extended the Party's aims to interest, entertain and educate a wide spectrum of society, including ALP members, rank and file workers, intellectuals, and artists. Evelyn Healy remembers that 'I used to go at night to Victoria Artists Society, that's where I came across left politics.'[18]

The groups thrived as social and political as well as creative collectives, and in all these groups the solidarity and support of members were important. As artist-workers, left cultural activists often chose to stand up for their politics and resist conservative views. Their efforts exposed them to counter-attacks and isolation from other artists and the wider community, and against this, the comradeship of their own circle was an important sustaining element. Their output – literature, prose, drama, painting or cinema – was often imbued with this sense of the collective strength of working-class solidarity.

The form of national identity embraced by left cultural activists often adopted the historicist view exemplified in Russel Ward's *The Australian Legend*, in reviving and renewing what were identified as uniquely Australian traditions and themes. According to them, these were more authentic manifestations of Australian identity than those embodied in the 'Australian way of life'. There had been support to investigate local traditions since the times of the WAC in the 1930s, but the post-war decade brought with it a much more energetic invigoration of these ideas; John Docker identifies the Party's moves to establish 'a cultural offensive' in this period.[19] The New Theatre performed newly written as well as older Australian plays, on explicitly antipodean themes. The Realist Writers looked to Lawson and Furphy for inspiration, and the wharfie filmmakers helped to produce the Wattle films. A revival of interest in anti-authoritarian themes contributed to radical nationalism. Convicts, bushrangers, and the rebels of Eureka were in vogue, as were activist workers and unionists who fought bitterly for their rights, militant Australians all. Left writer Len Fox remembers this era:

Writers, musicians, dancers and others created new Australian songs, music, dances and plays in or around the tradition of the pioneers. The early 1950s became for the Communist Party and to some extent for the Left in general a period of exploration of what it means to be an Australian … it was an exciting period, a time of Reedy River, of the early Bushwhackers and the

Bush Music Club, of Margaret Walker's dance group, of the Australasian Book Society, and of many other cultural activities exploring not the Russian or Chinese tradition but our own.[20]

Here, Fox conveys the enthusiasm and energy of these organisations. Like the CPA's declarations on socialist realism, he assumes a unity of national identity in 'what it means to be an Australian'. This was a selective exploration; while the 'tradition of the pioneers' was seen as the rightful working-class formation of the Australian national heritage, it generally ignored women, migrants, and indigenous Australians. Gollan has noted this proclivity:

> it seemed natural to Australian communists that they should be the leading proponents of an aggressive, militant, democratic stance which was believed to be the most characteristic quality of Australian workers. Thus they looked for origins in those who had resisted the authority of the upper classes: convicts, bushrangers, gold-diggers, and the unionists who had fought the bitter battles of the 1890s. In doing so they idealised the past and censored out or muted those parts of it, in particular the xenophobia and racism which were inherent in the Australian working-class outlook, which were in conflict with basic communist ideology.[21]

Looking back on the left-wing artists of 1950s Australia, it is true that whilst they shared a collectivist impulse which valued their relationships with other artistic and political activists and a great interest in peace and equality, so too did they share frequent omission of women, immigrants and indigenous Australians.

This chapter introduces the most prominent left cultural activist groups in post-war Australia in the disciplines of theatre, literature, visual arts, film and music; there were many other groups, however.

Theatre

Perhaps the most well-known left cultural activist organisation during the 1950s was the New Theatre, also the country's oldest continuously performing theatre. It began life as the WAC theatre group in 1932, with inspiration from the British Unity Theatre and similar groups in the USA.[22]

The New Theatre's foundation objectives were:

- To express through drama, based on the Australian tradition of freedom and democracy, the progressive aspirations of the Australian people.
- To cultivate a theatre free from commercialism, capable of developing a native drama, and of educating all sections of the people to appreciate a high standard of contemporary and classical drama.
- To secure the widest possible co-operation with all associations aiming at social justice.[23]

The New Theatre, still active in 2018, has had over four hundred plays produced, written by Australian and overseas dramatists. Non-professional actors were the mainstay of productions, although many well-known performers were to come out of the New Theatre family. Perhaps more significant were its writers, who constituted an important contribution to Australian literature. The theatre's strong tradition of performing socially and politically relevant work attracted a predominantly working-class following, both artist and audience. Often contemporary industrial and political situations were the inspiration. Anti-war and anti-oppression themes were the staple, and topical reviews were common.

The New Theatre's commitment to broadly socialist ideas extended to their performative style, and was unique in its range of performance sites. Theatre members would perform at parks and beaches, next to dole queues, and from trucks.[24] During the 1949 coal strike, for instance, a concert party travelled from the Sydney New Theatre to the Newcastle area to entertain the strike-bound workers and their families. And in 1952 two plays were performed to striking miners down a mine at Glen Davis, west of Sydney. Requests for performances came from factories, rural and regional localities and country towns. Their presentations on street corners, union and trade halls, large factories and workplaces such as railway yards and wharves were remembered long after the applause died away.

The highlight of their popularity came with the season of the Dick Diamond musical *Reedy River* in 1953 which, through its championing of Australian folk music, became very well known.[25] It proved to be a critical factor for the ongoing success of each of the New Theatre branches around Australia. Its popularity, with music performed by the Bushwhackers Band, was the crest of a wave of nationalist interest in folk and bush music, amongst the most lyrical manifestations of a radical nationalist movement.

New Theatre members would very often produce plays or short sketches for unions or other left organisations. An example lies in the strong connections between the New Theatre and communist-led trade unions, especially the Waterside Workers Federation (WWF).[26] In particular, the Sydney New Theatre and the Sydney branch of the WWF enjoyed a long-standing alliance. New Theatre member Betty Roland wrote *War on the Waterfront* in response to the 1938 pig-iron dispute, which played in Sydney to appreciative audiences – and to police who stopped performances and arrested actors.[27] Artists from WWF art groups worked in the Theatre, and from 1954 to 1968 the New Theatre operated within the WWF Federal offices in Phillip Street and performed regularly at the Sussex Street hall, under the auspices of the WWF Cultural Committee. When the New Theatre lost its permanent premises in Sydney's central business district, the wharfies offered their Sussex Street premises to the New Theatre on the Friday, Saturday and Sunday of each week, for a number of years.[28] Mona Brand writes:

> it was a two way relationship with the WWF and the New – the New Theatre giving something of itself whenever possible, from handing out

strikers' leaflets to performing daytime fundraising sketches and on one occasion writing the twenty minute operetta, *Butcher's Hook*, for members of the WWF Women's Committee to perform.[29]

New Theatre member Jock Levy has spoken of 'the role the Communists played within the Theatre. They gave it vigour, a commitment and undoubtedly played a vital role in the development of the Theatre presenting a working class perspective'.[30] In the 1950s, when Party membership was at its peak of 23,000, the New Theatre was seen, at least by one of the leading members of the CPA's Cultural Committee, as 'the party's main and foremost enterprise in that area of cultural activity'.[31] Ray Clarke, a member of the Committee, said that 'every three or four years we went to these meetings there'd be a time set aside for a report from the Literature and Arts Committee on what they were doing, and how they were doing it'.[32] The committee hosted many discussions and arguments about the role of culture and the arts within a progressive movement; for Edgar Ross, whose membership of the Committee in the 1950s and 1960s was 'one of the most traumatic periods' in his party life, the committee was a 'disarmingly innocent-sounding name covering incredible complications and potential for divisiveness'. Ross discusses the committee's main problems arising through 'basic differences of viewpoint on the role of the artist'.[33]

Like the CPA and other left cultural groups, the New Theatre also attracted the attention of governments and security services anxious about the 'insidious' influence of left-wing workers' theatre.[34] Australian Security Intelligence Organisation (ASIO) workers raided theatre premises, arrested thespians and confiscated scripts on more than one occasion. The mainstream press rarely reviewed New Theatre performances because of their political content: like many left cultural groups, the organisation was dismissed as a communist front whose work was merely propaganda.

Literature

The Realist Writers' Association (RWA) was formed in 1944, initially in Melbourne, by Frank Hardy, Stephen Murray-Smith and Eric Lambert. In his meticulous study of the RWA Ian Syson notes that it 'incorporated twin aims: the encouragement and development of worker-writers and the continuation of a perceived national, democratic and realist tradition'.[35] Syson also writes that 'the Realist Writers and earlier groups had important roles in arguments establishing the existence and worthiness of Australian literature'.[36] Other RWA writers included Jack Coffey, Judah Waten, Edgar Ross, Len Fox, Roger Milliss, Mona Brand, Dorothy Hewett, Oodgeroo Noonuccal, Ralph de Boissiere, Rodney Hall, Denis Kevans, Rupert Lockwood, and Gavin Casey.

The RWA noted its inspiration in 'the image of an Australian tradition of mateship, of standing together against the exploitation of tyrants... [social realist writers will] write as a partisan, a spokesman' for the working class.[37] Frank Hardy claimed that the initial task of the RWA was to promote literature 'written about the working class, by the working class, for the working class'.[38]

The Sydney RWA was formed in 1954. Dorothy Hewett was pleased that this group gave her 'the necessary support system for a new left-wing writer struggling to survive in a hostile environment'.[39] The RWA's important journal *The Realist Writer* was first published from the Melbourne group in 1952. It became *Overland* in 1954, but the Sydney and national groups continued to publish the *Realist Writer* until 1970. The organisation was a national movement by the early 1960s, and some branches were active until 1970.

Out of the energies of the Melbourne RWA came the Australasian Book Society (ABS), a co-operative publishing house established in 1952, and led by Frank Hardy, George Seelaf and Eric Lambert. Inspiration also came from the UK's Left Book Club. CPA Arts Committee leader Ray Clarke recalls the Party's move to establish the ABS:

> That was a deliberate Communist Party decision to set up the outfit, because there were so many people that couldn't get published. The hard reality was that in the immediate post-war years any communist or near-communist or progressive person who wrote a book couldn't get it published in Australia. It didn't matter that you weren't a communist, but if you were regarded as one, or even a party sympathiser, or some bloody thing, you couldn't get published.[40]

Hardy believed that 'it is among trade unionists that the Society expects to get its main support … writers interested in the Society aim to develop discussion groups around the books and to conduct readings in factories, libraries and halls seeking criticism of their work'.[41] The membership requirement was a commitment to buy six books a year for fifty shillings.

The ABS featured Australian novels by RWA members, and also supplied international works of a broadly left-wing nature. They also produced a journal for their members, *Readers and Writers*. Whilst its aims were explicitly leftist, Party member Bert Keesing noted that the ABS 'should try to be a broader organisation, and not seek to impose political qualifications on its membership … I mention this matter because it is apparent that so far the CP organisation is the principle vehicle of distribution'.[42]

Jack Beasley made the successful networking skills of left cultural activists explicit:

> ABS people saw their responsibilities as going far beyond ABS's own books or even literature generally. When ABS arranged such things as the public receptions for playwrights Ray Lawler and Richard Beynon, commissioned William Dobell to do Mary Gilmore's portrait, now on permanent exhibition in the NSW Gallery, initiated and participated in, during Ian Turner's

secretaryship, the Australian Book Fairs and when it recognised Harry Watt's contribution to the cinema, then it was cultivating an appreciation of our national culture. And for many thousands of people it may have been their first realisation that such a thing existed.[43]

Branches were formed in other states, with the enrolment of thousands of members, and in 1958 the CPA moved the ABS head office from Melbourne to Sydney, in some eyes for tighter political control.[44] The ABS continued to publish up to 1978 and did not completely wind up till 1981.

Visual arts

The Studio of Realist Art (SORA) was established in the basement of 171 Sussex Street, Sydney, in March 1945. Rod Shaw recalls that the group:

> came out of, and after, a meeting at the Contemporary Art Society, where there was quite a lot of argument about attitudes to painting and so on … we went away then and we decided that the Contemporary Art Society wasn't really for us. We, like many other painters and artists throughout the world after the war, felt that the "art for art's sake" idea was just not for us … the foundation members of the Studio of Realist Art were Bernard Smith, Roy Dalgarno, Roderick Shaw, James Cant, Adrian Galjaard, Hal Missingham was drawn into it.[45]

SORA artists included Noel Counihan, Dora Chapman Herb McClintock, Dore Hawthorne, Sali Herman, John Oldham, Nan Hortin, Clem Seale, Newton Hedstrom, Marjorie Penglaze and Jean Kelly. Quickly needing more space, SORA soon moved to larger premises on the third floor of 214 George Street. As well as a working artists' studio, the space was used for art classes of all kinds and meetings.

Art critic Bernard Smith believed that SORA was formed 'to promote an art which has been at the best of times regarded as a sort of heresy by the majority of post-impressionist moderns', but admitted its successes:

> The studio has been a success since its inception. Regular art classes in advanced and elementary drawing and in painting are well attended. A series of fortnightly lectures has been most successful. With its well-stocked art library and the regular monthly bulletin SORA it is fast becoming the most vigorous art centre in Sydney … what is most impressive about the studio is the vigour of its activity and production, and the tolerance of its principles.[46]

The working-class viewpoint was central to socialist realism in the SORA studio, where members often used the working-class Australian as a subject, whether it was the miner and his lamp, the wharfie heaving a sack of wheat, or the Surry Hills child playing in the slum lane. For these people workers and their lives were

276 Lisa Milner

important subjects for exploration. One of the most well-known SORA artists was Noel Counihan, seen as the 'only social realist to purpose his popular-unpopular art from one decade to the next'.[47]

Like other cultural activists, SORA artists often worked with trade unions and assisted striking workers, so as to acknowledge 'the unity of artists' problems with those of the working people'.[48] In his important critical history of Australian art, *Place, Taste and Tradition*, Bernard Smith defends the work of socialist realist artists:

> The fundamental issues for these painters, both as artists and as 'men-in-the-street' have been social and political questions. They have felt these issues, not as abstractions for the purpose of discussion, but as material forces at the threshold of existence, moulding their lives. They have realised that Australia is a part, and not an insignificant part, of world movements; that it cannot be separated from these movements. But they have reacted no less vigorously to the social and political environment of their own country. Both of these aspects of their work have arisen from their preparedness to record the urgencies of contemporary life, both at home and abroad.[49]

Here Smith recognises the nationalist-internationalist conflict that was a feature of left cultural practice.

Film

The Waterside Workers Federation Film Unit (WWFFU) was, in the 1950s, the only film production unit in the world that was funded by a trade union.[50] The establishment of the Unit was possible through the industrial strength and the large membership of the communist-controlled Waterside Workers Federation (WWF), and the general vision of the leaders to accept that film could be a useful tool of propaganda. There were three members of the film unit: Jock Levy, Keith Gow, and Norma Disher, and the unit operated from 1953 to 1958. All three were members of the New Theatre, and up to 1956, were members of the CPA. Levy and Gow worked on the wharves as well as in film, whilst Disher was soon employed by the WWF as a filmmaker. In 1953 they produced their first film, *Pensions for Veterans*, to support the union's current campaign to achieve pensions for older members, many of whom had worked on the wharves for all their lives in terrible conditions. They produced seventeen films on subjects that other production units would never tackle, like housing shortages, industrial disputes from the union members' viewpoint, and issues concerning workers' rights and health and safety.

Inspiration for the Unit came from the New Theatre, as well as from the Party. Levy was certain that 'the Communist Party gave the impetus and the discipline that made it possible for us to work so effectively as a film unit';[51] what the WWFFU members gained from this affiliation was an impetus to articulate their perceptions of social justice and working-class solidarity. One of its explicit aims was to help trade unionists to 'consolidate the understanding of the use of film as a powerful propaganda weapon in their struggles for justice and social progress'.[52] The Unit's second production, *The Hungry Miles*, premiered in February 1955. Their best-known work, it presents a history of the Sydney waterfront, with an emphasis on unity and the need to fight for improved working conditions. They were commissioned to make films for other left-wing unions that perceived the value of film as a political and educational tool. *Hewers of Coal*, for example, was made in 1958 for the Miners' Federation; in the same year, *Think Twice*, on safety in the workplace, was produced for the Boilermakers' Union.

The Unit worked from a room at the top of the union's building. They produced animated sequences and cartoon films on a handmade animation bench housed in the basement. They travelled widely throughout the country to shoot their footage. Voices from the Waterside Workers' Choir and Cedric McLaughlin's Link Singers feature on some soundtracks. Known as the 'Voice of Australia', actor Leonard Teale recorded the narrations for eight of the Unit's films.

In the practices of the WWFFU a heightened sense of collaboration is evident in three areas: (i) the collective nature of their work; (ii) their inclusion of other workers in this process; and (iii) their conscious intention to investigate the community of their films' subjects. The Unit members had great respect for each other's contribution to the group process: they maintained that they worked collectively, not taking on strictly defined crew roles. As Levy recalled, 'the members of the Unit didn't want to specify who did what in terms of job descriptions; we were a Unit, we were interdependent'. Secondly, they involved wharfies and other workers, notably builders' labourers and miners, in their production practice as performers, extras or helpers. The filmmakers also seconded actors from the New Theatre.

In an important exercise of collectivism, the Unit members extended their energies to investigate the industries they documented. Levy commented on a difference he perceived between the Unit's worker-as-filmmaker circumstances, and other film production personnel who lacked direct experience in the industries they chronicled: 'we were workers on a job. We could see things that should be common knowledge to every member of the WWF ... I think the advantage was ... because we were working down on the waterfront, not some outside group ... but from our experience from underneath.'[53] The immediacy Levy describes – that of directly encountering working and living conditions in their political and social contexts – made for a particularly close examination of those circumstances.

One of the most fascinating aspects of this group's work is the low-cost, highly innovative and very personal methods the workers used to get their films seen by as many people as possible. The Unit bought a Kombi van, which they used as their production vehicle. The van was also used to screen films: they projected films from inside the van onto a screen on the door; in that way they could show films in daylight, a banner on the van boasting that 'We Film the Facts'. By travelling around and taking the films to the people, instead of the other way around, the

278 Lisa Milner

Unit was able to have direct contact with a surprisingly large audience. The wharfies' films were seen by non-union audiences as well. They were to be found on the programs of film society and festival screenings throughout the country.

The Realist Film Unit (RFU) predated the WWFFU and was the first organisation in Australia to produce labour films in any quantity. Based in Melbourne, the group came into existence in 1945 when Ken Coldicutt received his war-time accumulated pay from the RAAF of £300 and founded the unit.[54] He had been involved in screening Soviet films for the Labour Club at Melbourne University in the 1930s, and went on to become manager of Friends of the Soviet Union, and to vigorously support the Spanish Relief Committee from 1937.[55] He was joined by Bob Matthews, who had a long association with the New Theatre of Melbourne, along with Betty Lacey and Gerry Harant, who found that 'participating in such collectives is immensely satisfying'.[56] Like the WWFFU in Sydney, the RFU had strong connections with the Melbourne New Theatre.

Their films covered a variety of subjects. *In My Beginning* (1947) was made to emphasise the differences of progressive education. One lesson, for example, is on democracy: 'Democracy is not a lesson we can learn from books or teachers; it's a way of living together, using reason instead of force to settle the problems that arise – the beginning of a new and more reasonable order of things.' Deane Williams believes that the RFU's *Prices and the People* (1948), made to support the Yes vote in the 1948 Price Control Referendum, 'stands as the Unit's greatest film work'.[57]

The RFU produced fourteen films between 1945 and 1951, and a number of films in association with, or for, other organisations, such as Koornong Progressive School, and the Brotherhood of St Laurence. The Realist Film Association (RFA) was set up for the exhibition and distribution side of the business. Like the WWFFU, they screened films in venues that 'ranged from living rooms to large halls'.[58] RFA activities were wide and varied: Regular City Screenings, Classes and Other Services for Members, Films and Equipment for Hire, Film Goods and Equipment Bought and Sold, Reference Library, and Information Service.[59] Its influence was widespread, especially in the areas of the promulgation of information to film societies, the establishment of film festivals, the Victorian Government Cinematograph Film Bill in 1948, and on changing existing censorship laws.

Music

Along with these varied explorations in Australian pioneer traditions, the stature of folk music grew in the 1950s, largely due to the vigour of members of the CPA and the labour movement. This was the period of a championing of folk music and protest songs, bringing them to a newly appreciative audience. In Australia, 'it was a period when everyone seemed to be singing, far and wide', Len Fox remembers, and many local music and drama enthusiasts took up the call to promote an indigenous folk music celebration.[60] In 1952, the popularity of the music of the New Theatre's *Reedy River* (performed by the Bushwhacker's Band) was the crest of a wave of nationalist interest in folk and bush music. The CPA formed the People's Choir and the Unity Singers; New Theatre actor and vocalist Cedric McLaughlin co-ordinated the Link Singers for the WWFFU's later films; and there was a Sydney Bush Music Club to which many of these singers and musicians belonged. These were amongst the most lyrical manifestations of a radical nationalist movement.

The idea took hold that a specifically working-class music could have its own credibility, and such works were collected, published and recorded. Bushwhackers founder John Meredith formed the Australian Folklore Society in 1953. Brisbane CPA member, musician, and Realist writer John Manifold made an important contribution to the folk music genre and its rising popularity, culminating in his ABS publication *Who Wrote the Ballads? Notes on Australian Folk Song*. In 1955 Peter Hamilton and Edgar Waters founded Wattle Recordings with the aim of encouraging and preserving the folk and protest song tradition of Australia.[61] They believed that this type of music, 'with its specifically Australian character',[62] could be used for educational and historical purposes as well as entertainment. Wattle produced records alongside social, archival and biographical information, and formed a Folk Music Record Club. One reviewer noted, linking this interest in folk music to some intrinsically autochthonous Australian identity, that as 'a valuable addition to Australiana ... these first recordings have whetted the appetite of Australians for more of their musical heritage'.[63] After the demise of the WWFFU, Hamilton worked with the three Unit members to produce a number of short films based on folk songs. Like many concerns of the left cultural groups, there was some resistance from mainstream culture to the push to popularise folk music. Hamilton recalls some problems he faced: 'folk songs were seen [in] the McCarthy era as being subversive and that had an effect in Australia; and so the ABC, for example, who I was trying to encourage [to play them] wouldn't play folk songs because they were dangerous'.[64]

The Unity Singers groups were formed by members of the Melbourne and Sydney New Theatre around 1944. Bill Berry, New Theatre member and well-known folkie, friend of John Meredith, was a member of the Sydney group; as was Ross Thomas, a pianist for the New Theatre. Other members were Doreen Bridges (later Dee Jacobs), and Chris Kempster. The Unity Singers often performed alongside works by other organisations including the CPA, left-wing trade unions and the New Theatre; and they also performed internationally when the Sydney Unity Singers were chosen to attend the Fourth World Youth Festival for Peace in Bucharest in 1953.

One vibrant but short-lived group was the Sydney People's Choir, established by Hilda Lane. A poet, composer and teacher, Lane (niece of radical utopian William Lane) wrote numerous folk songs and composed an Australian folk opera. Monthly sing-songs at her home, a communal house in Clovelly, led to the establishment of the People's Choir, or Sydney People's Chorus as it was also known. Inspiration came from a People's Chorus in New York, which had around six hundred members in 1930. John Kane was the President; Hilda's great

280 Lisa Milner

friend, the musicologist John Meredith was a member; Willi Krasnik a conductor. Other members included Barbara Brooks, Joyce Hutchinson, Lili Kolos and John Cameron.

Joseph Flanagan, another Choir conductor, was also the Secretary and Treasurer of the NSW Guild of Choirs. Flanagan recommended choral participation. 'Group singing is a way to fuller living', he said. 'It is one of the best and most economical ways of sharing a wider community life with our fellows. It does not imply any intense hard study of music. All that is needed is a usable voice, enthusiasm, and ability to sing in tune.'[65] The Choir was a member of the NSW Guild of Choirs and took part in state choir concerts.[66] They won the Victory Eisteddfod in 1946. As well as rehearsals and performances, the Choir ran music theory classes. They performed at the Australian-Russian Society.[67] They also performed live on radio.[68]

Conclusion

The collectivist impulse in these groups was as strong as the political impulse in the CPA and the militant labour movement. The groups were often established and administered by comrades, but membership was by no means restricted. They extended the labour movement's aims to interest, entertain and educate a wide spectrum of society, including political party members and non-members, rank and file workers, intellectuals, and artists. Their functions included the constitution of social and political as well as cultural collectives, and in all these groups the solidarity and support of members were important. As artist-workers, the left cultural activists chose to stand up for their politics and resist conservative views. Their output was imbued with this sense of the collective strength of working-class solidarity. Colin Sparks argues that the most important aspects of such work were not necessarily the textual features of the works themselves, but the consequence that 'the organised, collective efforts of workers rather than the individualised efforts of the professional bourgeois artist' produce a certain type of work.[69] This is so in the case of these left cultural activist groups in post-war Australia, which prioritised working-class traditions of collective practices over the modernist individuality of the middle-class. Ian Burn notes that 'the political culture of mainstream art, including its intellectual supports, has strong middle-class attachments, social and economic dependencies on class institutions'.[70]

There were many forces involved in the work of the left cultural activists of the post-war era. They included the political and social training that came with membership of a political party or a workplace. The processes within these types of institutions were involved in the resistance of the dominant culture, in which, in Raymond Williams' term, 'development and advantage are not individually but commonly interpreted'.[71] The operation of informal and formal networks of groups helped to sustain the work of all of the artist-workers. These alliances may have been direct or indirect, through official channels, or word of mouth, or through personal friendships and acquaintances; however these occurred, they made for a rich cross-fertilisation of information, ideas and energies.

Notes

1 Norma Disher. Personal interview. 22 August 1996.
2 EP Thompson. 'The Moral Economy of the English Crowd in the Eighteenth Century'. *Past and Present* 50 (1971): 76–136.
3 Stuart Macintyre. *The Reds: The Communist Party of Australia from Origins to Illegality*. St Leonards: Allen and Unwin, 1998: 416.
4 Frank Farrell. *International Socialism and Australian Labour: The Left in Australia 1919–1939*. Sydney: Hale and Iremonger, 1981: 231.
5 Quoted in Patrick O'Brien. *The Saviours: An Intellectual History of the Left in Australia*. Richmond: Drummond, 1977: 36.
6 Eddie Allison. Personal interview. 4 September 1996.
7 Quoted in Edgar Ross. *Of Storm and Struggle: Pages from Labour History*. Sydney: Alternative Press, 1982: 123.
8 Quoted in Sergei Eisenstein. *Film Essays and a Lecture*. Ed. Jay Leda. Princeton: Princeton University Press, 1982: 23.
9 Ross, 127.
10 LH Gould. *Arts, Science and Communism: Communists in Congress No. 6. Report delivered at the Fourteenth Congress of the CPA, 10 Aug. 1945*. Sydney: Central Committee, CPA, 1945: 7.
11 Gould, 11.
12 John Shields believes that Ross is 'one of the most significant and controversial Australian labour movement intellectuals of the twentieth century'. 'Edgar Ross and Broken Hill'. *The Hummer* 3.8 (2002): 13.
13 Ross, 128.
14 Robin Gollan. *Revolutionaries and Reformists: Communism and the Australian Labour Movement 1920–1955*. Canberra: ANU, 1975: 288.
15 'Develop Our Culture'. *Australia's Path to Socialism*. Program of the Communist Party of Australia, Sixteenth Congress, August 1951. Sydney: Current, 1952: 24.
16 Evelyn Healy. *Artist of the Left: A Personal Experience, 1930s to 1990s*. Sydney: E Healy, 1993: 6.
17 John Douglas Pringle. *Australian Accent*. 1958. Adelaide: Seal/Rigby, 1978: 132.
18 Evelyn Healy, Interview by Shirley McLeod, 20 October 2002. http://fairfieldcity.ora lhistory.com.au/interviews/healy_evelyn/healye_fullstory.htm
19 John Docker. 'Culture, Society and the Communist Party'. *Australia's First Cold War 1953*. Vol 1. Eds. Ann Curthoys and John Merritt. Sydney: Allen and Unwin, 1986: 189.
20 Len Fox. *Australians on the Left*. Marrickville: Southwood, 1996: 179.
21 Gollan, 196.
22 The Sydney New Theatre began in 1932, with smaller branches following: Townsville in 1933, Melbourne in 1935, and Brisbane, Perth and Newcastle in 1936. Like the Unity Theatre family members, few of these branches survived longer than forty years. Sydney is the only remaining branch, with an unbroken record of performances from 1932 to 2016.
23 New Theatre, *New Theatre Constitution*, 1936.
24 See Cathy Brigden and Lisa Milner. 'Radical Theatre Mobility: Unity Theatre, UK, and the New Theatre, Australia', *New Theatre Quarterly*, vol. 31, no. 4 (2015): 328–342.
25 An estimated 450,000 Australians had seen *Reedy River*, on New Theatre stages, as well as other theatres, from 1953 to 2004.
26 See Lisa Milner, 'The Waterside Workers' Cultural Committee', *Radical Sydney: Places, Portraits and Unruly Episodes*. Eds. Terry Irving and Rowan Cahill. Sydney: UNSW Press, 2010: 273–278.
27 Rupert Lockwood, *War on the Waterfront: Menzies, Japan and the Pig-iron Dispute*. Marrickville: Hale and Iremonger, 1987: 180.
28 Norma Disher, personal interview, 22 August 1996.

29 Mona Brand, 'The MUA and New Theatre', *Spotlight* (1998), np.
30 Jock Levy, Address, Australian National Maritime Museum, 7 November 1993.
31 Ray Clarke, personal interview, 20 February 1998.
32 Clarke.
33 Ross, 120.
34 See Philip Deery and Lisa Milner. 'Political Theatre and the State, Melbourne and Sydney, 1936–1953', *History Australia*, vol. 12, no. 3, December (2015): 113–136.
35 Ian Syson, 'Out from the Shadows: The Realist Writers' Movement 1944–1970, and Communist Cultural Discourse', *Australian Literary Studies*, vol. 15, no. 4, 1992: 335.
36 Ian Syson, 'Fired from the Canon: The Sacking of Australian Working Class Literature'. *Southerly*, vol. 57, no. 3 (1997): 80.
37 *The Realist Writer*, Melbourne, vol. 1, no. 1, March 1952.
38 Frank Hardy, *The Hard Way*. London: Werner Laurie, 1961: 43.
39 Dorothy Hewett. *Wild Card: an Autobiography 1923–1958*. South Yarra: McPhee Gribble, 1990: 248.
40 Clarke.
41 'Frank Hardy on the New Book Society', *Tribune*, 9 July 1952: 7.
42 Albert Keesing. 'Some Comments on the ABS'. ABS ASIO file, NAA 12249135, p. 110.
43 Jack Beasley. *Red Letter Days: Notes from Inside an Era*. Sydney: Australasian Book Society, 1979: 142.
44 Beasley, 146.
45 Rod Shaw, interview with Barbara Blackman, February 1985, National Library of Australia, oh-vn712060.
46 Bernard Smith. 'The Studio of Realist Art'. *The Critic as Advocate: Selected Essays, 1941–1988*. Melbourne: Oxford University Press, 1989: 43.
47 Max Dimmack, 'Max Dimmack on Noel Counihan', *Overland*, no. 62, Spring 1975: 80.
48 'Men at Work – S.O.R.A. and the Trade Unions', *Progress*, January 1946: 10.
49 Bernard Smith. *Place, Taste and Tradition: A Study of Australian Art since 1788*. 2nd ed. Melbourne: Oxford University Press, 1979: 255–257.
50 See Lisa Milner, *Fighting Films: A History of the Waterside Workers' Federation Film Unit*. Sydney: Pluto Press, 2003.
51 *Film Work*. Dir. John Hughes. Exec. Prods. Jock Levy, Keith Gow, Norma Disher. 1981.
52 'Wharfie Film Unit Powerful Aid to Union Struggle'. *Maritime Worker*, 6 March 1956: 2.
53 Jock Levy, interviewed by John Hughes, Margot Oliver and John Witteron, 27 October 1979.
54 Ken Coldicutt, 'The Party, Films and I', *Sixty Years of Struggle: A Journal of Communist and Labour History*, vol. 2. 1980: 63.
55 Deane Williams, 'Making Waves: The Realist Film Unit and Association'. *Screening the Past: Aspects of Early Australian Film*. Ed. Ken Berryman. Acton: NFSA, 1995: 171.
56 Gerry Harant, 'We Laid 'em in the Aisles: Some Reminiscences of the Realist Film Unit'. *Overland*, 156 (1999): 39.
57 Williams, 173.
58 Harant, 36.
59 Realist Film Association. Untitled document, 18 October 1950.
60 Fox, 101.
61 Peter Hamilton, personal interview. 10 January 1998.
62 'Wattle Recordings: General Statement'. Unpublished publicity material, nd.
63 Percy Jones. 'Australian Traditional Singers and Musicians'. *Walkabout*, 1 May 1958: 10.
64 Peter Hamilton. Interview with Ian Bryson. 4 April 1995.
65 'People's Choir Planning Big Year', *Tribune*, 17 March 1948: 4.
66 'Choir Guild Gives Fine Concert', *Sydney Morning Herald*, 13 July 1948: 3.
67 'Australian Russian Musicale', *Sydney Morning Herald*, 30 July 1947: 2.

68 'Peoples Choir Planning Big Year', *Tribune*, 17 March 1948: 4.
69 Colin Sparks, 'The Debate on Art and Revolution'. *International Socialism*, 5 (1979): 78.
70 Ian Burn. Foreword. In Sandy Kirby, *Artists and Unions: A Report on the Art and Working Life Program*. Redfern: Australia Council, 1992: 4.
71 Raymond Williams, *Culture and Society: Coleridge to Orwell*. London: Hogarth, 1993: 326.

INDEX

Aarons, E. 6, 29–30, 31, 33, 60, 61, 63, 70, 71, 72
Aarons, L. 42, 43, 59, 61, 62, 63, 64, 65, 66, 67, 68, 71, 72, 145, 232,
aboriginal rights 3–4, 83, 99–117
Altman, D 249–266
anti-apartheid 4, 5, 7, 10, 137, 155, 171, 178, 181
anti-Discrimination: NSW Anti Discrimination Board 210, 211: steelworks survey 214: complaints 215: direct and indirect discrimination 215
anti-nuclear politics 118–132
Australian Black Panther Party 171–172, 176, 178–179, 181, 183
Australian independence 48, 51, 52, 54
Australian Labor Party 2, 3, 7, 9, 77, 82, 85, 90, 91, 92, 118, 119, 122, 123, 125, 126, 127
Australian Metal Workers Union 8, 14, 231–248
Australian Security Intelligence Organisation 3, 7, 25, 28, 29, 30, 32, 52, 66, 69, 89, 108, 125, 178, 183, 273
Australian Student Labor Federation 138, 141

Black Power 146, 171–186
Blake, J. 28, 30, 31, 33
Brown, W. (or Bill) 33, 60, 66, 67, 71
Builders Labourers Federation 8, 9, 4 9–50, 55, 192

Calwell, A. 86, 87, 137, 140
Campaign for Nuclear Disarmament 118–129, 139
celebrity 249, 258, 260
Charter of Democratic Rights 6, 63, 64, 65
Coalition of the Left 63
Chinese Seamen's Union 86-87
Communist Party of Australia 1–4, 23, 28–34, 42–45, 53, 59–72, 77, 80–92, 101, 104, 105–106, 107, 109, 110, 112–113, 118–119, 121, 122, 123, 124–126, 128, 145, 155, 157, 158, 161, 181, 191–198, 205, 212, 213, 217, 231–245, 261–280
Communist Party of Australia (Marxist-Leninist) 6, 8, 41–58, 192–193
Communist Party of China 3, 4, 86
Communist Party of Great Britain 2, 6, 8, 9, 26–28, 33
Communist Party of the USA 2, 23–26, 28, 29, 31, 34
conscription/national service 135, 137, 138, 139, 142

draft resistance 141, 142, 143
Draft Resistance Movement 134
Democratic Socialist Party 9, 10, 221–226

Federal Council for the Advancement of Aborigines and Torres Strait Islanders 172–178
Federated Ironworkers Association Port Kembla 213, 218, 225: Rank & File

Group 218, 219, 220, 221, 222: Union elections 1982 210, 220, 221
The Female Eunuch 157–158, 249–50, 252, 255–62
feminism (*see also* women's liberation) 249–52, 255, 257, 259, 261–2
feminist theology 256–8
Foley, G. 173,177–178, 185–186
folk music 278

Gay Pride week 192, 196, 197
gay rights/liberation 191–206, 249, 253–6, 258, 262
Greer, G. 157–158, 169
Gould, B. 6, 123–124, 126, 138, 222

Hardy, F. 62, 273–274
Hill, E. 4, 6, 28, 29, 32, 34, 42–44, 61
HIV/AIDS 199, 202, 205
Homosexual: Oppression and Liberation 249, 251–3, 256, 258, 260–2
Honi Soit 137, 184

Immigration Reform Group 88–90, 92, 136
Industrial Workers of the World 2, 78–79, 92, 200

Khrushchev, N. 4, 21–3, 28, 29, 32, 33, 41–42, 53, 62: Secret speech 22–7, 29, 60–61, 121

lesbianism/lesbian politics 159–160, 163, 165
Lockwood, R. 3, 273

Maoism/Maoists 4, 6, 7, 8, 10, 41–58, 64, 141, 145, 146, 181, 192, 200, 203
Mardi Gras 197, 201, 204
Matters, P. 221, 225, 226
McGuinness, B. 174, 177
Mejane 157, 160, 161
migrants 77–92, 210, 211:
   migrant women 212, 213
Monash Labor Club 141, 143
Mundey, J. 9, 49, 50, 66
Murphy, R. 214, 218, 219

National Homosexual Conferences 197, 201, 204
New Theatre 271

Percy, Jim 5, 219, 220, 221, 222, 223
Percy, John 5, 10, 200
Petrov, V. 3

Realist Film Unit 278
Realist Writers Association 273
Ross, E. 68, 69

Scarlet Woman 163, 165, 166, 170
Sendy, J. 30, 31, 69, 70
Sharkey, L. 3, 6, 28–30, 32, 42, 43, 61, 62
Sino-Soviet split 60, 62
socialist feminism 154, 155, 161, 163, 164, 165, 166, 167, 213
Socialist Party of Australia 6, 7, 8, 9, 10, 59, 192, 193, 213
Socialist Workers Party 7, 8, 9, 192, 193, 198–202, 210–228
Socialist Workers Action Group/ International Socialists 5, 7, 192, 202–205
Socialist Youth Alliance 5, 7, 192, 200
Spartacist League 8, 155, 162, 168
Stevens, J. 11, 17, 157, 158, 160, 166, 168
Studio of Realist Art 275
Students for a Democratic Society 140, 141, 142, 144
Summers, A. 90, 162, 251
Sykes, R. 177, 184

Taft, B. 30, 39, 43, 65, 69, 70
Turner, I. 30, 31, 32, 33, 274

Union of Australian Women 4, 90

Victorian Aborigines Advancement League 172–178
Vietnam War 5, 7, 12, 41, 45–46, 47, 48, 53, 55, 66, 77, 90–91, 119, 127, 129, 134, 137, 138, 139, 141, 143, 144, 145, 157, 181, 196, 200, 205, 222, 251,

Waterside Workers Federation Film Unit 276
Walker, D. 171, 176–177, 179–180, 182–184
Walker, K. 176, 177
Walker, P. 218, 219, 220, 221
Watt, A. 63, 66, 69
White Australia Policy 77–96, 137
Wollongong Jobs for Women Campaign 210, 213, 214, 215, 216, 225, 226, 217
women's liberation (*see also* feminism) 4, 6, 145, 146, 153–170
Workers' Arts Club 268
Worker Student Alliance 6, 47, 49, 51
Working Women's Charter Campaign 210

Youth Campaign Against Conscription 138, 141, 142